REVOLUTIONARY IRAN

Revolutionary Iran
Civil Society and State in the Modernization Process

MASOUD KAMALI

Ashgate
Aldershot • Brookfield USA • Singapore • Sydney

© Masoud Kamali 1998

All rights reserved. No part of this publication may be reproduced, stored in a retrieval system, or transmitted in any form or by any means, electronic, mechanical, photocopying, recording or otherwise without the prior permission of the publisher.

Published by
Ashgate Publishing Ltd
Gower House
Croft Road
Aldershot
Hants GU11 3HR
England

Ashgate Publishing Company
Old Post Road
Brookfield
Vermont 05036
USA

British Library Cataloguing in Publication Data
Kamali, Masoud
  Revolutionary Iran : civil society and state in the
  modernization process
  1. Iran - Politics and government - 1979- 2. Iran - History -
  1979-
  I. Title
  955'.0543

Library of Congress Cataloging-in-Publication Data
Kamali, Masoud
  Revolutionary Iran : civil society and state in the modernization
  process / Masoud Kamali.
    p.   cm.
  Includes bibliographical references and index.
  ISBN 1-84014-449-1 (hardcover)
  1. Civil society--Iran. 2. Iran--Politics and government--20th
century. 3. Islam and state--Iran. 4. Constitutional history-
-Iran. I. Title
JQ1785.K36   1998
320.955'09.04--dc21   98-17090
                                                            CIP

ISBN 1 84014 449 1

Printed in Great Britain by The Ipswich Book Company, Suffolk

Contents

List of Tables	viii
Preface	ix
Acknowledgments	x
List of Abbreviations	xi
Preface by Bryan S. Turner	xiii
Introduction	1

PART I: CIVIL SOCIETY IN IRAN, FOREIGN IMPACT, AND THE CONSTITUTIONAL REVOLUTION

1	The Construction of the Muslim Society of Iran	19
	State Authority	21
	Sunni versus Shi'ite Theory of State	21
	The Founding of the First Shi'ite State	25
	The Social Construction of Shi'ite Religious Authority	28
	The Realm of Economy	31
2	Civil Society in Iran	35
	Towards a Conceptualization of Iranian Civil Society	35
	Theological Basis of the Ulama's Social Authority	39
	The Bazaris and the Ulama in Iranian Urban Life	45
	The Relationship Between the State and the Religious Community	47
	The Ulama's Guardianship of the Divine Order of Society	51
3	Iran on the Eve of the Constitutional Revolution	63
	The Reconstruction of Theocratic Power	64
	The First Period of Reforms	66

	Abbas Mirza and the 'New Army'	67
	The Second Period of Reforms	69
	Opposition to the Reforms	75
	The Tobacco Movement	77
	The Main Social Groups on the Eve of the Constitutional Revolution	80
4	The Constitutional Revolution	87
	Modernization Efforts of the State	88
	Vitalization of the Alliance Between the Ulama and the Merchants	90
	The Bazaris' Protest and the Ulama's Support	92
	The Influence of the Intelligentsia	98
	Revolution and Counter-revolution	100
5	The Constitutionalism of the Ulama	105
	The Constitutionalism of the Leading Mujtahids	107
	The Ulama's Ideological Challenge on Constitutionalism	111
	Nuri, the Ideologist of the Anti-Constitutionalists	112
	The Theological Justification of the Ulama's Opposition	115
	The Victory of the Modern Civil Society	120

PART II: THE NEW MONARCHICAL REGIME, MODERNIZATION, AND THE ISLAMIC REVOLUTION

6	Iran Under the Pahlavis	127
	The Construction and Reconstruction of the 'New Iran'	127
	Reza Shah and the Ulama	134
	The Rise and Fall of Nationalism	138
7	Modernization and the Ulama	143
	The Ulama and the Shah's 'White Revolution'	144
	Vaqf, Sahm-e Imam and the Independence of the Ulama	146
	Religious Modernism	150
	The Theory of *Velayat-e faqih*	156
8	Iran on the Eve of the Islamic Revolution	161

	Transformation of the Traditional Civil Society of Iran	161
	The Main Occupational Groups	166
	Authoritative Modernization and the Creation of the 'Dispossessed'	172
	Political Opposition to the Shah	179
9	The Islamic Revolution	185
	The Alliance Between the Ulama and the Middle Occupational Groups	186
	The Effective Neutralization of the Army	189
	US Policy and the Threat of Communism	191
	The Process of the Revolution	192
	The 'Dispossessed' and Radicalization of the Movement	196
	Institutionalization of the Revolution	203
	The Victory of the Modern and the Traditional Civil Societies	207

PART III: DISCUSSION AND CONCLUSIONS

10	The Two Revolutions: Comparative Reflections	223
	Overview	223
	Early Modernization, Foreign Penetration, and Political Revolution	226
	Autocratic Societal Transformation and the Islamic Social Revolution	231
	Comparisons of the Two Modern Revolutions	236
11	Conceptual Reflections: Islamic Civil Society, Modernization, Revolution	247
	Civil Society and the Notion of *Umma*	247
	Modernization of Traditional Politics	252
	Religion and Revolution	256
	Revolution as Process	259
	Revolutionary Islam	274

Notes	*277*
Glossary	*299*
Bibliography	*303*
Index	*313*

List of Tables

2.1	The sources of power and legitimization of the state and the ulama in traditional Iran	60
8.1	The main occupational groups	167
8.2	Employment situation of the people residing in the 'outer zone'	177
10.1	The comparison of the Constitutional and the Islamic Revolutions	238

Preface

This work is a comparative study of two revolutionary changes in Iran during the twentieth century separated by an interval of more than seventy years. The focus of the work is on the interplay of the ulama, the bazaris (people engaged in trade and manufacturing in bazaars), and the state; three social actors who have gone through sociopolitical changes that led to the appearance of new ideological components and new frameworks of political power. Among other things, (1) the Islamic Revolution of Iran is shown to be a broad social movement combining modern ideas with more conventional, traditional concepts and practices–and therefore constituting a major innovation, ideological as well as practical, in the Muslim world; Khomeini was a major source of these innovations, contrary to what many would have expected on the basis of his background and earlier formulations; (2) the book articulates and applies the concept of Islamic civil society, a concept which is highly controversial (however, Islamic civil society is grounded in different cultural concepts and institutional arrangements than its Western counterparts); (3) the work stresses the role of movements arising or grounded in civil society opposing and countervailing state power, and helping to explain two major revolutions; (4) it emphasizes the crucial role of marginal/migrant groups (from the small towns and villages to the large cities) in providing a social base for radical Islamic movements; (5) finally, the book also shows how the Islamic Revolution was a dynamic and partially open process of interaction between different social movements in alliance, and there were outcomes and developments of the revolution which were never anticipated, or intended, by major participants. Although this work is focused on Iranian developments, it provides a basis to understand some features of Islamic movements in the contemporary Muslim world.

Acknowledgments

In the preparation of this work I am grateful to a number of people who have helped me in a variety of ways. Above all, I would like to thank Tom R Burns who provided guidance and intellectual input, but not only that. Pablo Suarez drew upon his considerable knowledge of political sociology to advise me. Among others I would like to single out for special thanks: Craig Calhoun who in the Spring, 1994, helped orient me theoretically at a very early stage of the work; Shmuel Eisenstadt who played a key role in the development of the concepts in the work of civil society and modernization; Said Arjomand and Bo Utas who provided important and constructive criticisms on one of the earliest drafts of the work; Bryan S. Turner for his support and encouragement; Rolf Nygren for his readings and suggestions with respect to the final version of the work. The Swedish Collegium for Advanced Study in the Social Sciences also played an important part by giving me an opportunity to participate in its workshop on 'Revolution', June 28-July 1, 1995. My Iranian friends who shared their knowledge and experiences with me and whose names I am not at liberty to mention must remain anonymous (they know who they are and I thank them for their assistance). Finally, I am thankful to the Iranian writer, Dariush Kargar, who obtained useful information about urban marginal groups prior to and during the Islamic Revolution.

List of Abbreviations

LMI   The Liberation Movement of Iran

NF   The National Front

SAVAK   Organization of Security and Intelligence

Preface
By Bryan S. Turner

Towards a Sociology of Shi'ite Civil Society

The concept of 'civil society' has a well-established tradition in Western political philosophy. It first emerged during the Scottish Enlightenment when Adam Fergusen deployed the notion in 1767 to contrast the barbarian state with civility and civilization. The historical background to this theoretical contrast was the traditional Highland culture of clannish warriors and the emerging sophisticated society of urban Edinburgh, whose elegant culture and complex social relations required new civil institutions in order to survive. The idea was then taken up by Hegel in 1837 to describe the dialectical growth of universal society in terms of a contrast between the state and such institutions as the family. The Hegelian legacy was embraced subsequently by Marx and Engels as a method of describing the relationship between the economic base and political forms, and from there the concept was transformed by Antonio Gramsci to analyse the nature of political leadership. For Gramsci, civil society lay between the coercive realm of politics and the dull compulsion of economic activity. Political hegemony was to be established by the exercise of decisive but morally persuasive action in civil society.

Its current revival in democratic theory, however, probably owes more to Alexis de Tocqueville (1805-1859) than to the Marxist tradition of Gramsci. Writing about the new democracy in colonial America in his *Democracy in America*, de Tocqueville observed that the main protection against the authoritarian exercise of power through electoral dictatorship in a mass democracy was the vitality of its voluntary associations which mediated between the state and the individual. In the New World, de Tocqueville feared that the negative consequences of a political revolution, whose central value was equality of opportunity, would be a tyranny of mass opinion, and hence he anticipated the manipulation of public opinion in a mass democracy, where the means of communication could be centrally organised by a party machine. The answer to this danger was to be found in voluntary associations, especially the churches and schools, which could foster local opinion and train individuals in democracy.

In Europe, de Tocqueville's ideas had a major impact on John Stuart Mill in the development of liberal theory and on Emile Durkheim in sociology. For Mill, democracy could destroy individual conscience and undermine individual opinion. A liberal democracy required a vibrant tradition of education if the individual was to resist the impact of mass opinion. Mill as a result resisted what he regarded as the premature spread of the franchise in a situation where the working class remained uneducated. For Durkheim, the growth of intermediary institutions was crucial to the development of a space between the individual and the state, in a social context where unfettered utilitarian individualism and uncontrolled economic growth were creating social anomie, that is a society without moral restraint. Durkheim's argument that these anomic conditions produced a rise in the suicide rate is well known, but less attention has been given to his views in *Professional Ethics and Civic Morals* on the role of occupational and professional groups in the regulation of modern society. The modern state had important moral functions in Durkheim's political sociology.

This concept of 'intermediary associations' has become influential in contemporary political analysis. Voluntary associations and intermediary groups in civil society are now thought to play an important role in 'associative democracy'. Devolution of power and the principle of subsidiarity in authority and decision-making are dynamic aspects of an effective democracy, because they permit individual representation and guard against the dead-hand of bureaucracy. Academic and public interest in citizenship and civil society were revived in Europe with the fall of centralized communist regimes at the end of the 1980s. It became clear that the Marxist-Leninist view of the role of the communist party in Stalinist Russia had resulted in a situation where intermediary groups had been absorbed into the party and hence pluralism had been negated or driven underground. The aspirations of individuals and local groups were often channeled into criminal associations through the black market or they were expressed illegally through unofficial church groups and religious sects. There was no informal vehicle for the legitimate expression of opposition, alternative views and minority cultures. With the fall of communism, there was the attempt to recreate the market by Western business interests, but it was equally clear that civil society had be rebuilt around the principles of active citizenship and associative democracy. There is the need therefore to foster and create a dense network of voluntary associations to cultivate civil society if societies like post-communist Russia are to avoid a return to authoritarian rule. Political philosophy is engaged with a renaissance of democratic theory in which questions of cultural identity, social difference and political membership have resulted in a revival of citizenship studies.

While Western societies have gone through a profound period of post-war reconstruction, it is also clear that the Islamic world has experienced an epoch of revolutionary activity and social transformation. From the end of the caliphate in Turkey in 1924, Islamic societies went through a long and bloody period of post-colonial revival and reconstruction which included the bloodbath of the Pakistan and Indian division in 1947, the end of French control over Algeria, the creation of modern Indonesia, the emergence of contemporary Afghanistan from external intervention and civil war, and more recently the catastrophe of Bosnia. This historical process of decolonization was undertaken under various ideological banners, including nationalism (in Egypt, Iraq, and Indonesia), secularism (in Turkey and Iran), puritanical 'new *jihad*ists' (in Nigeria), religious conservatism (in Saudi Arabia and the Gulf States) and religious fundamentalism (in Afghanistan). In many of these societies, independence and reconstruction were undertaken under the auspices of strong military regimes.

Within a larger perspective, many of the problems of post-colonial reconstruction were a legacy of colonial arrogance and mismanagement. The fate of the Indian subcontinent was in part a consequence of British cultural arrogance dating from Lord Macaulay's famous educational minute of 1835, which rejected the traditions of Hinduism, Islam and Sikhs as false religions and imposed on the educated middle strata of the civil service a diet of Anglicanism, afternoon tea and cricket. Lord Mountbatten's dislike of Jinnah, and fascination for Nehru, sealed the destiny of millions of Hindu and Muslim communities for the remainder of the century.

These revolutionary transformations of Islamic cultures have also revived a traditional Orientalist question, which is whether Islam and liberal democracy are compatible. However, these conventional questions have been given a contemporary urgency by the following new ingredients: the globalization of cultures through consumerism, transport and communication; the collapse of communism and the apparent triumph of Western liberal democracy; the decolonization of the non-Western world, which is combined with an increase in the wealth and power of multinational corporations; the dramatic growth of Asian economies (despite the financial instability of 1997), and the arrival of Islam as a revolutionary global force. This global context has given greater significance to the specific issue of the nature of Islamic civil society.

Western scepticism with respect to the internal capacity of Islam to foster democracy is well established. In sociology, Max Weber's *The Protestant Ethic and the Spirit of Capitalism* of 1904 confirmed the view that Christianity had a necessary relationship to civilization as such, and Talcott Parsons argued that modernization was the historical product of such seed-bed societies as Greece and that American values were simply a secularized version of Protestantism. Martin Heidegger had claimed in *What is Philosophy?* that the notion of 'Western-European philosophy' was a tautology, because philosophy is Greek in its nature and thus by implication philosophy (or rational *logos*) is not produced in Islamic cultures. In more recent scholarship, sociological understanding of Islamic social structures has been influenced significantly by the political anthropology of the late Ernest Gellner. Building on his anthropological research in the Atlas Mountains of central Morocco, Gellner borrowed and adopted ideas from Ibn Khaldun, David Hume, Robert Montagne and Edward Evans-Pritchard. On the basis of these ideas, Gellner created a controversial and frequently flawed view of Islam in his *Muslim Society*.

According to Gellner, tribal Islam, which was egalitarian and nomadic, was held together by an intense feeling of social solidarity (*asabiyya*), which was based on religious values. In the towns, there is a weak sense of social membership organized around the market, exchange and individualism. Periodically the nomadic tribesmen invade the city, impose a new social order in the name of Allah, and remove the existing corrupt elite. Although there is traditional hostility between town and desert, they also depend on each other. Tribal warriors require guns and grain, while merchants seek safe trading routes and luxury goods. In addition to this politico-economic division, there is also a religious division of labour. In the countryside, the Sufi saints practise a deviant, hierarchical and folk religiosity based on personal charisma (*baraka*); in the towns, the puritanical religious leaders (ulama) follow the ascetic religion of the book and the hadith. In the modern world, new systems of communication and trade have disestablished the old pattern of the circulation of elites, because urban, puritanical and fundamentalist Islam has become dominant. The dominant pattern of global Islam would not be compatible, in Gellner's view, with liberal and pluralistic patterns of democracy.

Gellner thus raised fundamental questions about the future of Islam as a global religious system after the fall of communism. Would Islam be the principal alternative to Western liberal democracy as a global ideology in a post-communist political environment? For Gellner, Islam is potentially an alternative route into modernity where urban scripturalist puritanism of the ulama works analogously to Weber's model of Protestantism and capitalism. While puritan Islam may foster economic growth, it is not compatible with democracy based on a pluralistic civil society. In this interpretation of Islam, Islamic fundamentalism provides a useful ideology for capitalist discipline, but the Islamic community (*umma*) is not a diverse and plural society which can function as the foundation of a robust and diversified civil society.

Gellner's analysis of Islam has been frequently challenged. Contemporary anthropological fieldwork, for example by Nadia Abu-Zahra, has shown that the gap between the urban puritans and the rural folk religion of the Sufi orders is exaggerated, and that in fact there is a strong interaction and interrelationship between these traditions. Other critics such as Sami Zabaida have questioned the historical relevance of Gellner's model in understanding contemporary politics. It is within this intellectual context that Masoud Kamali provides a vigorous and original sociological analysis of the role of civil society in Islam by concentrating on two major revolutions in twentieth-century Iran, namely the Constitutional Revolution (1905-1909) and the Islamic Revolution (1977-1979). He defines civil society as a social space where individuals and groups can interact and organize social life. It is the capacity of a society to organize itself without being organized by the state. He treats society as a dialectical and contradictory struggle between the state and civil associations. Civil society in Iran was constituted primarily by the Shi'ite ulama who enjoyed a traditional source of legitimacy and authority to challenge the state. In addition, the ulama's economic independence from the state resulted from religious endowments (*vaqf*) and religious taxes (*sahm-e Imam*), and it was also buttressed by the bazaar's economic support.

The bazaars formed the hub of the Iranian city, because they were the principal sites for guilds, workshops, banks and educational centres. There was a close social relationship, especially in terms of recruitment, between the bazaris and the ulama. Through religious interpretation and judgement (*ijtihad*), they also had independent religious and moral autonomy. The theory of *gheybat* (the Shi'ite doctrine of the Occultation of the Hidden Imam) deligitimized the claims of secular political authority to any ultimate religious authority. The only rightful political leadership, if it is to be just, has to be infallibile and only the Prophet and his family can be infallible. Secular political leadership is always temporary and imperfect. In short, traditional Iran had a vibrant civil society based on religious and economic associations and values, and this civil tradition was able to challenge the authority of the state and its elite.

In the Constitutional Revolution, there was an alliance of bazaris and clerics to challenge the state, which had introduced significant economic changes and which was increasingly dependent on foreign powers, especially the English and Russians. The reformist ideas of the constitutional ulama were influenced by the teaching of Sayyed Jamal al-Din Afghani (1838-1897). The ulama sought a constitution to limit the powers of the state, but their view of a constitution did not imply any endorsement of secular government, because the constitution had to be based on the sacred law (the Shari'a).

It is the contrast between the consequences of the Constitutional Revolution and the Islamic Revolution which is the core of Kamali's study of Iranian twentieth-century history as the history of its civil society. In the first revolution, the clergy failed in a traditional society to impose their political power, but in the second they were successful. The ulama participated in the Constitutional Revolution in order to influence Iranian politics and to secure their place in civil society, but in the Islamic Revolution they participated to gain complete political power and to reconstruct Iranian society, with the consequence that civil and political realms were conflated.

The Pahlavi Shahs were nationalists who sought to create an independent state and a strong economy; they supported the creation of a strong, secular state which would promote Iran as a society and economy which were independent of foreign powers. This version of authoritarian modernization of society and the economy by the state was characteristic of 'petrolic capitalism', which shaped many developing societies in the post-war period. In petrolic economies, there are three important and interrelated developments: oil production drags the society immediately into a global economy; oil revenues flow directly into national treasuries producing a centralized state and expanded bureaucracy; and oil revenues created huge and expanded opportunities for patronage and corruption. The social consequences of the OPEC price revolution of 1973-1982 were no less profound: the creation of a new middle class based on the service industry and a corresponding transformation of the old agrarian elite;

depopulation of the countryside, which experienced inflation and labour shortages; and the creation of a new urban lumpenproletariat of the dispossessed.

These social changes also involved a challenge to the traditional authority of the ulama as new educational institutions were established along Western models of utilitarian knowledge. The commodity boom and new consumerism offered the urban youth new lifestyles, identities and values. Secular educational institutions broke the traditional connections between the clergy, young people and social mobility. However, this consumerist society was inherently unstable, especially when the collapse of oil prices resulted in the 1980s and 1990s in IMF-imposed constraints, neo-liberalism and financial discipline. The crisis of the oil states produced a social environment where Islamic opposition against secularisation, bureaucratic corruption, police violence, rural depopulation and urban crime could flourish in societies like Egypt, Libya, Nigeria, and Iran.

As Masoud Kamali shows dramatically, the authoritarian programme of economic growth and political nationalization resulted in a decline of the social power of the traditional ulama as secular schools increased and expanded, but there was also a decline in the economic and social power of the bazaris as the state expanded its control over the market and the economy. The Shah employed oil revenues to push through five Seven-year Plans to modernize Iran starting in 1949. The unintended consequences of these Plans brought about severe social dislocation: rapidly rising rents, housing shortages, profound labour mobility, dislocation of rural populations, a rapid increase in the lumpenproletariat and the arrival of a large, unstable, disembedded mass. The dispossessed provided an ideal recruiting ground for the radical clergy, who were eventually organized behind Ayatollah Khomeini. Whereas the educated and secular middle class supported Marxist and nationalist opposition groups, the urban masses and traditional occupational groups supported the radical clergy. These religious forces grounded their political opposition to the state on the basis of the Shi'ite teaching with respect to the Hidden Imam; it proved to be a powerful anti-state doctrine. The clergy thus had a powerful vision of an alternative society, which drew its strength from traditional notions of justice.

Finally, in *Revolutionary Iran* Masoud Kamali provides a powerful criticism of Gellner's pessimistic analysis of the weakness of civil society in Islamic communities. Against Gellner's analysis, Kamali shows that in traditional Iranian social formations there was a coherent and powerful civil society which was able to offer significant resistance to the state. In modern Iran, while the old civil society was transformed by the Shah's modernization process, the new configuration of clergy, dispossessed, students, intellectuals and traditional occupational groups offered a solid basis for revolutionary change. Often the unintended consequences of these changes had profoundly negative effects, but the revolutionary nature of civil society of Iran cannot be denied or ignored. Kamali's political sociology of revolutionary change provides a model of social analysis: it is historical and comparative, it draws upon a wealth of empirical material, and it offers a sophisticated reflection on major philosophical questions concerning the nature and importance of sociological theory. More significantly, it points to the dynamic role of Islamic critical reflection in shaping the process of modernization in global politics.

Revolutionary Iran is the first comparative sociological analysis of the Constitutional Revolution and the Islamic Revolution, which takes civil society as its main conceptual tool. Although it is specifically concerned with the role of social classes in revolutionary politics, it does not analyse the revolution in exclusively economic terms. This study of Islam and politics demonstrates the crucial role of Islamic culture (such as the doctrine of the Hidden Imam) in revolutionary change. Masoud Kamali thus provides a model of historical sociology in explaining macro-political transformations.

Bryan S. Turner
Cambridge University

Introduction

Iran has gone through two major socio-political changes in the Twentieth Century: The Constitutional Revolution of 1905-1909 and the Islamic Revolution of 1977-1979. To explain these changes in purely economic or political terms usually leaves many questions unanswered or half-answered. Why, for example, did the clergy–who failed in the first revolution in a more traditional society–succeed in a more modern society in leading and winning the Islamic Revolution of 1977-79? Part of my analysis entails showing why Islamic-cultural beliefs played such a crucial role in the Islamic Revolution, and why the Shah's modernization program paradoxically strengthened religious groups and radical clergy in a rapidly developing society.[1]

In February 1979, a revolutionary group led by radical clergy seized political power in Iran. Two months later, through a referendum, the several thousand-year-old political system of monarchy was changed and replaced by an Islamic Republic, in which radical clergy had a leading position. Participation and leadership of religious agents in social movements have always been controversial. In the course of the twentieth century, the Shi'ite ulama of Iran have participated in – and led – two great revolutions of Iran, the Constitutional Revolution of 1905-1909 and the Islamic Revolution of 1977-79.

The Core Question and Method of Analysis

The main subject of this work is the two revolutions of Iran. My core question initially was: *why the clergy did not take the political power in the Constitutional Revolution (1905-09) when Iran was a traditional society, but succeeded in a modern Iran (1977-79)*. To analyze such social changes usually implies historical knowledge and comparisons. Besides studying other works on these two revolutions, in order to answer my core question, I felt the need to go back, as far as possible, to the sources and documents that were used by other researchers.

The process of the study can be divided into several parts. It was partly a contemplation of the works of other authors; partly investigation of the original sources, documents, pictures, videotapes, newspapers, religious texts, records, and statistics; and partly my own personal experiences as well as others who participated in the Islamic Revolution of 1977-79. I tried to avoid locking myself into a particular theoretical perspective or framework. But I used several theoreticians, among others Arjomand, Bourdieu, Burns, Skocpol, and Tilly, if and when I found them useful for increasing my understanding and deepening my analysis of revolutionary developments. The work is a historical and cultural analysis of a particular society. A historical and cultural analysis should avoid ahistorical conceptual biases, for instance, treating a social event 'A', taking place in a certain time and social context, as the same 'A' in other times and social contexts. Although the work is focused on the historical interplay of the three main social agents–the ulama, the bazaris, and the state–they are not considered the same agents in the Constitutional Revolution as in the Islamic Revolution. These social agents have changed, just as institutional arrangements have changed. Understanding the nature of continuity and changes of social agents and institutional arrangements is central to gaining knowledge about revolutionary events. Not only did the relationships between the ulama, the bazaris, and the state change crucially on the eve of the Islamic Revolution, but also the relationships, institutional arrangements, and ideological frameworks of these agents were replaced by more radical conceptions of change. State policies tended to eliminate the influence of the ulama and the bazaar,[2] but the ulama and the bazaris turned to eliminate the monarchy; this was a radicalism characterized by negation of the other.

The main focus of the study is on the socio-cultural changes that can help explain the social roots of the two modern revolutions of Iran during twentieth century. To avoid conventional assumptions about the revolution by which many theoreticians analyze a revolution in terms of its outcomes, I have tried to concentrate the study on the interaction-continuity as well as change-of the state and civil society. I avoided conventional models of analyzing 'large-scale social change', by which many analysts assume that social changes are coherent and general events appearing everywhere and every time. Tilly, in his book *Big Structures, Large Processes, Huge Comparisons* (1984), criticizes just such understanding of social changes as general phenomena involving the succession of standard stages in historical development. He also criticizes the idea that 'differentiation' is the inevitable logic of social change. To improve macro-sociological research, he suggests a return to historical analyses to avoid excessive abstraction and to include real times, places, and people (Tilly, 1984, p. 14). But the danger of overemphasizing 'a return to history' is the loss of a certain level of abstraction that is necessary for generating knowledge about the appearance of the new phenomenon and the disappearance of established phenomenon. It is not surprising that Parsa (1989), who is inspired by Tilly's theory of revolution in analyzing the Islamic Revolution of Iran, cannot accept the existence of new and 'historyless' social groups, the 'dispossessed'.

One often finds two extremes in the analysis of Iran's Islamic Revolution, namely the purely socio-economic approach and the purely cultural approach. The socio-economists–those Marxist inspired scholars such as Abrahamian (1982) as well as functionalist inspired ones such as Wilber (1981)–underestimate the importance of Persian-Islamic cultural factors. Although a number of well-informed political scientists, historians and sociologists have examined Iranian developments and the Revolution, most stressing economic explanations (Amuzegar and Fekrat, 1971; Lenczowski, 1978), there have also been a few culturally oriented studies dealing with that part of Iranian society referred to as 'traditional' (Binder, 1964). Also, Abrahamian (1982) tends to treat traditional culture as a historically separate phenomenon from Iranian developments as a whole. Traditional culture tends to be considered a specific property opposed to modern culture and limited to so-called traditional groups. Others are of the opinion that Islam, as a religion and system of jurisprudence, is a culture of the whole society. Purely cultural analysis, such as that of Bazargan (1984) and Hjärpe (1983), treats Islam as an abstract phenomenon that remains untouched by social, political and economic changes. Other broader approaches dealing with the Islamic Revolution are found in the writings of Arjomand (1988), Bakhash (1990), Parsa (1989), and Skocpol (1982) and are referred to and discussed in this work.

Islam is a part of Iranian culture that has been formed and reformed by social agents under a long historical process of concrete socio-economic and political developments. In analyzing the Islamic revolution of Iran, we must deal with Islam as a socio-cultural factor that has played, and still plays, a crucial role in the political life of Iran. But Islam is not just a culture in its common meaning, namely a set of beliefs, values, traditions, meanings and symbols that entail seeing and judging the world in a specific way. Rather, Islam is a complex of social rules and 'cultural capital' (Bourdieu, 1986) by which Muslims orient themselves socially and organize and regulate their activities. This cultural complex is the common quality of society. It constitutes channels and possibilities for social action by individuals in concrete social situations; it is crystallized in their lifestyles. According to this point of view, Islam can be recognized in individuals' everyday action, and it is an important basis of their habitual activities. Islamic life patterns are a well developed and widespread social reality in Muslim societies, even the most secular ones such as Turkey, Egypt, and Algeria. Although Islamic culture does not evoke the same intensity of feeling among all social groups, it nevertheless is a common denominator, to a significant extent, for the entire society.[3]

Islam in Iran, as a socio-cultural phenomena, has blended over fourteen centuries with the old Persian culture and shaped the everyday life of the people. It is concrete and familiar as well as normative, and is vibrant in the public as well as the private spheres of life. Islam is more than a religion of belief and ritual; it shapes and regulates people's orientations and attitudes. It is crystallized in the social interactions and practices of a wide variety of Islamic lifestyles. Islamic concepts, norms, and practices vary among Muslim communities. Even its socio-economic manifestations vary in different Islamic communities. The predominant socio-economic values and practices in different communities play a crucial role in the variation in and development of Islamic culture. For example, Persian elites adopted a specific branch of Islam, Shi'ite, which was appropriate to or consistent with their national interest to maintain their sovereignty against Arabs and Turks, who were in large part adherents of another branch of Islam, namely *Sunni* (see later discussion). Persians incorporated the new Islamic symbols and values into the old Persian culture, and thereby constituted a unique *pattern or style of life* (Bourdieu, 1986), appropriate for their history and cultural-institutional context.[4] This lifestyle has developed and changed over several centuries on the basis of a variety of socio-economic and political conditions.

Questions concerning Iran's Islamic Revolution cannot be properly answered without paying attention to specific historical and social actions and developments that conditioned the shaping and reshaping of social institutions, cultural patterns and lifestyles.

Traditional and Modern Features of the Islamic Revolution

The period after World War II was a period of optimistic assumptions that with growing modernization and industrialization the basic institutional and cultural aspects of modern societies would become very similar and that modernity as a model could be exported to less developed societies in other parts of the world. This assumed (1) that the very process of modernization or industrialization generates not only relatively similar institutional problems, but also (2) similar institutional solutions, and (3) that the dynamics of modern societies would therefore be shaped, above all, by the crystallization of such institutional solutions to these problems (Eisenstadt, 1995).[5] Even if Western scholars accepted some degree of diversity of transitional societies, many assumed that this Western project would spread throughout the world.[6] But, this strong convergence, which would be the result of a realization of a general blueprint of modernity, appeared neither in modern societies nor in transitional ones. The modernization of a society is a process of change rooted in distinctive socio-economic and cultural conditions. These differences in the institutional dynamics and in the discourse that has been continuously developing in different modern societies are above all rooted in distinct, cultural programs of modernity that emerged in these societies (Eisenstadt, 1995, p. 4). The institutional differences in political systems of modern societies such as France, Italy, England and Sweden, are proper examples of different cultural programs of modernity.

Modernization is a highly selective process. Different societies find their own ways of applying and adopting modern ideas and institutions. The modernization of transitional societies has also been highly selective–and this selectivity was reconfirmed and reinforced by authoritative political regimes. The Shah of Iran, for instance, used those parts of socio-economic and political components of modernity that were compatible with particular conditions of his regime. He created modern socio-economic institutions such as corporations, modern schools and universities, health care, a modern army, and so forth. The Pahlavi dynasty speeded the process of modernization of Iran and created a modern society in which the Revolution of 1977-79 took place. The Islamic Revolution was not only modern because it took place in the context of modern institutions, but also because it showed the influence of earlier revolutions of the twentieth century. As Arjomand (1995, p. 37) puts it: 'the earlier revolution becomes models of the later ones through the patterns of, and recipes for, action that they generate'.[7]

The Islamic Revolution of Iran has been referred to as 'traditional' or 'fundamentalist'. These labels refer not only to the Revolution's religious ideology and leadership, but also to religiously affected post-revolutionary political and social institutions.[8] 'Fundamentalist' movements, such as the Islamic movement of Iran, are often viewed as traditional and anti-modern because of their religious aspects, their opposition to some features of modern society. However, the 'fundamentalist' movements are, in a certain sense, highly modern. S. N. Eisenstadt pointed out several criteria by which one can interpret 'fundamentalist' movements as modern (1994):

1. Many of the fundamentalist movements share with the great modern revolutions the belief in *the primacy of politics*; and above all, the reconstruction of society through political means.
2. As with many revolutions, the fundamentalist movements tend also *to minimize the importance of primordial components of collective identity.*
3. The fundamentalist movements are among the *bearers and promulgators of modern Jacobean components and orientations.*
4. Fundamentalist utopias are also–as are 'progressive' ones *future-oriented*–aiming at a future reconstructed according to their vision.
5. Fundamentalist ideologies, like all Great Revolutions, emphasize *a total reconstitution of the social and political order, and espouse a strong universalistic, missionary zeal.*
6. These movements encourage the *active participation of women.*

Khomeini's religio-political declarations, which played an important role in the Islamic Revolution, cannot be labeled simply as 'traditional' or 'fundamentalist'. He formulated a new theory, *velayat-e faqih* (vicegerents of Islamic jurisprudents), which was an innovation in the traditional Shi'ite theory of community/state relationship. The Shi'ite ulama's traditional interpretations of the role of state in the Shi'ite community was based on acceptance of *temporary* political power during the time prior to the appearance of the true leader of Muslim community, the Hidden Imam. Prior to appearance of the radical clergy and Khomeini's theory *velayat-e faqih*, there was a consensus among the Shi'ite ulama not to claim the right to seize political power. Khomeini himself in his early book *Kashef al-asrar* accepted monarchies as a proper form of temporary political power. In his book, *velayat-e faqih*, Khomeini criticized the traditional interpretations of the role of ulama in the time of Great Occultation of the Hidden Imam and appealed for the active political function of the *fuqaha* (Islamic jurisprudents) as the leaders of the Muslim community until the appearance of the Hidden Imam. Accordingly, Khomeini did not propagate a return to the original texts, but a new revolutionary interpretation of religion.

Khomeini was an innovator of traditional Shi'ism in that he created a political ideology in which the ulama could participate in political struggle and seize political power. But the actual political struggles in the Islamic Revolution did not conform with Khomeini's theories. The modern economic reality, modern social groups, and modern politics came to play a crucial role in the making of revolution, taking political power, and establishing an Islamic state. To concretize his universalistic ideas–to use Hegel's term–Khomeini and other radical clergy used modern slogans, institutions, and strategies of compromise and mass medial politics. Modern institutions such as referendum and other electoral procedures, constitution, parliament, republic, and so forth, were to a great extent foreign to the traditional vision. 'The whole constitutional structure of the Islamic Republic was modeled less on the early caliphate than on de Gaulle's Fifth Republic'. (Abrahamian, 1993, p. 15). In this sense, the Islamic Revolution was a modern revolution that took place in a modern time. By the term 'modern' I mean socio-political and economic changes that followed the Renaissance and the Industrial Revolution in Western Europe and created certain types of political, economic, and social institutions. Some of these institutions are industry, market economy, parliamentarism, republicanism, and rituals such as May Day, among others.

Although radical clergy challenged and eliminated many of the possibilities created by the Revolution, the constitution of the Islamic Republic was not a traditional one. The regime of Iran was changed from a monarchy to a constitutional republic. As Abrahamian puts it:

> The text of the constitution, not to mention its pretext, subtext, and context, is highly non-fundamentalists. Its central structure was taken straight from the French Fifth Republic, with Montesquieu's separation of powers. It divides the government into the executive, headed by the president, supervising a highly centralized state; the judiciary, with powers to appoint district judges and review their verdicts; and the national Parliament, elected through universal adult suffrage (Abrahamian, 1993, p. 33).

Universal adult suffrage was implemented–even if for many years Khomeini and other radical clergy argued that women's suffrage is a means of prostitution and un-Islamic.

During the reign of Pahlavis, and as a result of their modernization programs, the traditional settings and boundaries of civil society of Iran changed. New social groups and relationships, together with the persistence of traditional ones, created a highly differentiated society in which the traditional division of civil society and political power was no longer viable. In the modernization of Iran under the Pahlavis, the ulama[9] lost their traditional role as the leaders of civil society and became somewhat marginalized. In order to regain their lost position they challenged modern ideas such as nationalism and socialism, which among other things were the ideologies of political leadership in the society. The theory of *velayat-e faqih* was the ideology of the Iranian radical clergy, by which they eliminated the traditional dualism between political and religious powers. According to this theory, the clergy were able to assume both political and social leadership. As Eisenstadt puts it:

> This strong totalitarian, Jacobean-like component or orientation is visible first in the attempts to effect the reconstruction of the centers of their respective societies; in the almost total conflation of center and periphery, negating the existence of intermediary institutions and association -- of what can sometimes be called civil society (Eisenstadt, 1994, p. 16).

In the ulama's participation in the Islamic Revolution, they did not simply want to regain their lost position in civil society but rather to 'totally conflate center and periphery'. In other words, the ulama, unable to maintain their prominent position in the modern civil society of Iran, wanted to eliminate the dualism between the political and social spheres of society. They wanted to seize political power in order to reconstruct the society in their own terms.

The main hypothesis of my work is that while the ulama participated in the Constitutional Revolution (1905-1909) in order *to influence the political system and reinforce their position in civil society of Iran*, in the Islamic Revolution (1977-79) they participated in order *to gain total political power and to reconstruct Iranian society so as to conflate the political and civil spheres of the society.*

In their struggle to gain power and reconstruct Iranian society, the ulama not only joined in alliance with their traditional allies, the bazaris, but also with new emerging urban groups. The new educated groups, such as bureaucrats, students, and teachers played a role, but most important were the 'dispossessed', the rural migrants to Iranian cities, marginalized, and unincorporated into the industrial and bureaucratic sectors. They became the 'social army' of the revolution led by the radical clergy. They formed the rank and file of the revolutionary guards, *basij-e pasdaran*,[10] Komitehs,[11] court guards, and so forth. In order to mobilize people and shape an effective movement, the clergy could not rely on traditional forms of religious civil society, although these were important ingredients. They also espoused and made use of modern concepts and forms, both to mobilize and to organize people in the Revolution. They continued after the seizure of political power, making use of modern institutions such as parliament, elections, republicanism, constitution, presidency, representation, ministries, army, modern bureaucracy, modern education, and so forth. They also utilize modern economic organizations such as banks and governmental steering of financial markets, as well as modern communication technologies, and modern propaganda techniques to reconstruct the socio-political system according to their ideology.

Revolution

There are different definitions of revolution. Some scholars use the concept of revolution in the sense of radical change in political structure through violent struggle, where one group replaces the political structure, and transforms the political order. Or it may mean simply the forcible transfer of power from one group to another where the latter has another model or institutional concept of political arrangements. Many leading scholars of socio-political revolution stress the aspects of structural transformation of society through revolution. Among these scholars are Marx, Skocpol, and Huntington. According to Marx, social revolutions are radical, qualitative changes of 'socio-economic formations' (slavery into feudalism, feudalism into capitalism, capitalism into socialism) (Sztompka, 1993, p. 32). Skocpol's definition of a revolution is rapid, basic transformations of a society's state authority and political institutions, class structures (ownership regime),[12] and its dominant ideology, accompanied and, in part, carried out by, class-based revolts from below. (Skocpol, 1979, pp. 4-5). According to Huntington, revolution is a rapid, fundamental, and violent domestic change in the dominant values and myths of a society, in its political institutions, social structure, leadership, and government activities and policies.

Burns and Dietz (1995) criticize 'structural transformation' theories for ignoring human agency in analyzing revolution. They stress, however, that a revolution entails the establishment or transplantation of a new order or regime – substantially or significantly different from the old – however this change or transformation is brought about: through collapse of the old order, gradual organic replacement, or violent struggle and overthrow. A new social equilibrium, that is a type of structural stability, is established through the institutionalization of new organizing principles and rule systems.

Collective action theorists such as Tilly take human agency into account. According to Tilly (1993, p. 8) revolution is a forcible transfer of power over a state in the course of which at least two distinct blocs of contenders make incompatible claims to control the state. Collective action of ordinary people in a revolution connects directly and solidly with the great political questions. By the actions that authorities call disorder, ordinary people fight injustice, challenge exploitation, and claim their own place in the structure of power (Tilly, 1986, p. 403). Others, such as Taylor (1988), define revolution as a rational choice. It is the 'collective choice' of people who decide to change a certain socio-political system into another.

The concept of revolution, which I use, is the transformation of the political system and the restructuring of authority and political order. Revolution is the result of a *process* of social mobilization of people by revolutionary elites that leads to immediate radical political changes. By 'people' I mean those social groups that aim to obtain socio-political, cultural, or economic advantages from revolutionary changes. My definition of revolution is close to the suggestion that 'revolution is the replacement of one political order by another. It is an event that transforms the constitution of the polity' (Arjomand, 1995, p. 1). Furthermore, I want to emphasize political mobilization of people against the state as an important component of revolution. In such a view, 'revolution through *coup d'état*' (Janos 1964, pp. 134-34)[13] cannot be considered as revolution, although it implies significant political transformations. In chapter ten I discuss, among other things, revolution as a process of social action of revolutionary agents.

Civil Society in Iran

A key concept in my work is that of civil society which is used in the analysis of the socio-political arrangements of Iranian society. I claim that Iran has had a civil society, but it differs significantly from that conceived of in Western societies. *It is a civil society of communities and institutions rather than individual citizens and their associations.* Civil society of Iran, up to the beginning of the twentieth century project of modernization/ Westernization of society, was an entity constructed by two main influential groups, bazaris and clerics. As opposed to the 'private sphere' of the courts, the ulama lived among the people in city quarters and bazaars. They were present in the 'public sphere' of people's life. Instead of the expression of the 'burgerlichen Gesellschaft' which initially took place in 'the coffee-houses', 'les salons', and 'die Tischgesellschaften' of the West (Habermas, 1984, pp. 42-78), the expression of socio-religious opposition of the ulama against the Iranian state took place in civil society's public arenas such as mosques, *madrasahs*, public baths, *manbars* (pulpits), and bazaars, and practised through religious ceremonies, theatrical rituals (*ta'ziyeh*), mournings of Imams and so forth. The two main influential groups in the traditional civil society of Iran, the ulama and the bazaris, through socio-economic and cultural bonds with each other and with other groups, enjoyed a social authority which played a crucial role in the two main revolutions of twentieth century Iran. The civil authority of these two groups rested on a traditional social structure which was divinely legitimized. Any attempt by the *de facto* accepted state to increase its power and sovereignty could ultimately be challenged by the civil authority as heretic intervention in the divine universalistic order of society and therefore illegitimate.

This work does not offer a systematic treatment of the concept of civil society. Nor is civil society of the West or Sunni Muslim of central concern. The main concern of my discussion is civil society of Iran and its strategic role in major political developments in modern history of Iran. The creation and development of a traditional civil society in Iran dates to the establishment of Shi'ite faith as the religion of Iran by Safavids in 1501, increasing the power of the Shi'ite ulama, and to the emergence of a historical alliance between the bazaris and the ulama. My broader concept of civil society can be a useful theoretical tool with which to analyze the socio-political history of Shi'ite Iran. The main argument is that the traditional civil society of Iran during several centuries operated periodically as an effective counterweight to the state, capable of mobilizing and countervailing the state. The period of the Tobacco Rebellion (1891) and the Constitutional Revolution (1905-1909) provide examples for this claim. Modernization programs of the Pahlavis shahs since the 1920s drastically changed the traditional settings of Iranian society and undermined partly the socio-economic power of the bazaris and the prominent position of the Shi'ite ulama. Modern developments created new social groups and ideologies which challenged the traditional segments of society and led to a modern civil society, which flowered especially during the first decade of the reign of last Shah of Iran, Muhammad Reza Shah Pahlavi. A major thesis of this work is that traditional and modern civil societies in Iran–as sources of authority and bases for social mobilization–played a major role in the Islamic Revolution of 1979.

The concept of Iranian, and more generally Islamic, civil society is controversial (however, see Arjomand (1988)). Among others, Gellner (1994) has rejected the idea of civil society in Islamic societies as incompatible with the notion of *umma*, or Muslim community. In chapter two and later in chapter ten I elaborate my concept of civil society and point out some of the limitations of arguments that Iran does not have, or has never had, a civil society. It is not only the existence of a traditional civil society which is discussed but also its weakness, marginalization, and change, and the appearance of a rival and modern civil society.

Sources of Information

As a sociological study of the modern history of Iran, my work has tried to comprehend the events which changed the traditional institutional setting of Iranian society and led to the creation of new concepts and relationships: a new social order. The main question of the work was actually influenced by a personal desire to understand the collective action of Iranian people. My point of departure was an aim not only to investigate the events of the two revolutions, but also to understand the pre-Revolutionary connections and interactions of social groups which made the 'revolutionary alliance'. And, moreover, to understand the complex causality of the revolutions.

There are a great numbers of books, articles, political announcements, programs, declarations, and observations, about the two major political changes in Iranian society of this century. Just after working for several months on this subject, which resulted in a paper, I realized that studying revolution is to deal with a moving target and requires a great deal of openness and flexibility. Old ideas and convictions had to be revised. Contradiction between my political convictions and the historical facts about the Iranian society could not be minimized or eliminated by 'properly grounded' political terms. I had to see the facts in new ways, risking seeing the facts in terms of the interpretations and understandings of others. Studying and using sources from contradictory perspectives and traditions served to minimize analytic bias. Two different kinds of materials were used in this work: recognized materials, such as books, newspapers, and journals; and materials which were used to complement the first ones, such as individual histories, interviews, photographs, even my own experiences.

I experienced the Islamic Revolution not as an observer who wanted to write a book about it. I was engaging in it as someone trying to bring about change. Therefore, in my preparations for this work, I had to 'rearrange' my experiences and to confront them with the experiences of other Iranians, both those who participated in the Islamic Revolution and those who only observed. Although individual knowledge may not be necessary for a proper understanding of collective actions, it is a useful means which provides many advantages in understanding specific socio-cultural settings of a collective process.

Since the time of the first mass demonstration and serious confrontations between the people and the police in Tabriz in 18 February 1978, a major question for many political intellectuals has been: who were the peoples on the street? At that time, I was a political prisoner in Tabriz where bloody confrontations took place.[14] On the evening of 18 February 1978 the iron door of the prison yard opened and about 800 wounded people rushed into the yard. We were surprised. We, who believed very much in revolution against the Shah, were not able to understand what was happening. While trying to provide the wounded medicine and warm clothes, we asked them who they were. The answers were not what we, the leftists, expected. They were shopkeepers, middle and low ranking bazaris, a few construction workers, and some students and intellectuals. The 'working class' was not there. As demonstrations and confrontations continued, the radical clergy became stronger. It could be felt even in the jail among the religious prisoners. The question was not any more why the 'working class' was absent, but rather why the engagement of traditional groups and the key leadership of Khomeini. From that moment, events and developments happened rapidly. The immediate overthrow of the regime of the Shah was more important than 'modifying' our ideological framework or changing our 'holy truths'. The Revolution freed us from jail and we participated in it. We came to witness our own failure and the triumph of the radical clergy. But one question particularly preoccupied me. Iran, at the time of the Revolution of 1977-79, was more modern than Iran in the beginning of the century. How could the clergy seize the political power in 1979. Why was the first Revolution 'constitutionalist' and this one Islamic. Indeed, I began the research on this work to find answers to my own questions. In doing so, I had to study other scholars who tried to analyze both the Constitutional and the Islamic Revolution from different perspective. The second stage of work was an attempt to 'depoliticize' books, studies, interviews, articles, and other sources of information including my own.

My experiences of the Revolution have, of course, the disadvantage of other participant observations, namely physical limitations. As Zelditch (1969) puts it, there are parts of social structure to which such an observer cannot have access. For example, my participation in the Islamic Revolution did not enable me to investigate the causes of the Revolution. But it did help me to understand some of the people who participated in the Revolution and also to distinguish different groups of 'people'. It also helped me to understand the process of the uprising and transformation of a movement into a revolutionary force. To offset the potential 'subjectivity' of my own experiences, and to reinforce the reliability of my materials, about the significant role of the marginals in the Revolution, my observations and hypotheses were checked with other Iranians. I tried to make contact with those who, during the final days of the Revolution, were in other parts of Tehran, or in other cities. The material gathered through participant observation was only a piece of the history and was not useful for other parts of the work. I had to find much of my materials through the work of other Iranians as well as other scholars studying Iranian history. These provided me with magazines, articles, films, and pictures that were enormously useful.

Another source of information were my interviews in Sweden of those who participated in or observed the Revolution (most of these are exiles). These were semi-structured interviews with persons who were accessible for face-to-face contact here in Sweden or via telephone. Of course, people participate in a movement for different reasons and with various intentions. Many of those who participated in the Islamic

Revolution and now live in exile have or had political attitudes toward the Islamic regime in Tehran which influenced their answers to some of my questions. I concentrated on those parts of their comments that were relevant for my study.[15] The material had to be 'depoliticized'. To overcome or counterbalance, as much as possible, the ideological bias of those I interviewed, I tried to interview and discuss with people from different social and political backgrounds. The same approach was used in my selection of books and reviews of other works about revolution, in general, and about the Islamic Revolution, in particular. I have tried to be open and eclectic in the face of a major historical transformation.

Part I
CIVIL SOCIETY IN IRAN, FOREIGN IMPACT, AND THE CONSTITUTIONAL REVOLUTION

1 The Construction of the Muslim Society of Iran

Questions concerning the Islamic Revolution of Iran call for an interpretation of the historical conditions of uprising, change, and the continuation of particular social institutions of Islamic, and in particular Shi'ite, Iran. After the Arab conquest and 'Islamicization' of Iran, Iranian socio-economic and cultural institutions went through crucial changes that led to reconstruction of the pre-Islamic society. The new Islamic society of Iran was reconstructed in part according to Islamic rules and norms. In this chapter 'Islamicization' of Iranian society will be discussed.

One of the most decisive historical changes in Iranian society was the conquest of Iran by Arabs in 637 AD and the introduction of the religion of Islam into Iran. The Arabs' tribal, and often unorganized, army defeated Sasanid's well equipped and professional army. They occupied the country and put an end to thousands of years of the old Persian Empire. In this way the Islamic vision of equality and brotherhood had a great impact on the Iranian people, who were subordinated to Sasanid's *Ständestaat* that was legitimated by the hierarchical religious authority of Zoroastorianism. Arabs cultural norms and social institutions, which were arranged by a tradition of more equality and kinder treatment combined with the Islamic vision of religious equality, brought about a social and cultural revolution (Wilber, 1981). Notwithstanding Arab invasion, Iranian people did not convert to Islam by force but as a reaction to the corrupted state of Sasanids and their despotic taxation system *Zimmis*. 'It is true, however, that there was no serious attempt at wholesale conversion to the Muslim religion. Much of the population of Iran converted to Islam in self interest' (Wilber, 1981, p. 37). The Arabs succeeded in conquering the entire plateau of Iran in 650, establishing the authority of the *Caliphate*. An interesting characteristic of the Islamic ruling system was its concentration in urban areas. Arabs established their socio-political and religious institutions either in the already existing cities or new ones that they built (Hourani, 1991, p. 24). They left the rural areas to the Sasanian landowners, *dihqans*. Much of Iran's high land plateaus were populated and controlled by tribesmen and therefore difficult for Arabs to conquer. Some of these tribes such as Afshars, Qezelbash, Zand, Qajars, and Bakhtiaris, came to play a crucial role in the post-Arab period of state formation.

The Islamic ruling system was based on a *Caliphate* system. The Caliph was the chief and leader of the whole Islamic empire. He ruled the conquered lands by a representative system, i.e., local rulers were the Caliph's representatives, directly subordinated to him. Caliphs who resided in Medina, Damascus (Umayyads), or Baghdad (Abbasids), were far away from the conquered lands and, naturally, could exert little control over them. Generally, local representatives possessed more authority than the Caliphs, and they resisted controls over distant Arab territories. This fact gave the local representatives an opportunity to adapt old socio-political institutions of conquered lands to enable governing and organizing the socio-economic life of their territories.

Iranian society after the Arab conquest has gone through crucial socio-economic and cultural changes that led to reconstruction of the pre-Islamic society of Iran according to new Islamic rules and norms. Social institutions such as marriage, family, inheritance, religious activities, ceremonial traditions, bazaars, and so forth, were changed and reconstructed on the basis of Islamic codes.[16] Perhaps the most important socio-political change was the creation of a new influential center in the society of Iran. Due to the appearance of new social duties and commitment to the new theocratic state, a group of religious leaders was gradually formed to exercise Islamic jurisprudence and act on behalf of the government, namely the ulama.

Questions concerning the socio-political life in Iran, and the ulama's role as a prominent social group who exert social hegemony and influence over the long duration of Iran's history, cannot be properly answered without paying attention to specific historical developments, in particular those concerning power balances and configurations. Iranian society since the early sixteenth century witnesses the appearance of two 'national' centers of power which in coexistence and conflict have played a crucial role in the social events and development of Iran: (1) *state authority,* and (2) *Religious authority.*

In the following chapter construction and continuation of these two institutions of power after the Arab conquest of Iran and the establishment of Islam up to the nineteenth century will be discussed. This period can be characterized by socio-historic processes that constituted and institutionalized socio-economic and political configurations of Iranian society.

State Authority

Islam initially appeared among Arabs who lived in a tribal society based on kinship and alien to the conception and institutions of the state (cf. Vatikiotis, 1987).[17] Islam's theory of leadership in Muslim community was clear: sovereignty is God's and 'so exalted be Allah the true king' (20:113); 'to Him belongs the majesty in the heavens and the earth;' (45:36).[18] Thus, all authority on earth comes from God and applies on earth by His deputy the Prophet, and, after him, by his successors. It explicitly means also that even the political authority of the Muslim community has to be divinely legitimized. Muhammad, as the only prophet of great religions who had both religious and political power, crystallized the theory of Islamic state.[19]

Sunni versus Shi'ite Theory of State

Differing perspectives and movements concerning the linkage between religion and politics, emerged in the decades following the death of Muhammad. The immediate issue concerned the question of the Prophet's successor, or Caliph. Sunnis believe that Mohammed died in 632 AD without choosing any successor. However, he left his *Sunna* (tradition), in which his *umma* could find guidance for their Islamic actions. Hence, through *shura* (consolidation), the most respectable men in the Muslim community, Abu Bakr, Umar, Uthman and Ali, were chosen to lead the Muslim community. After the Prophet's early death in 632, his four immediate successors, *Kholafa-ye rashedin* (the rightly guided Caliphs), tried to legitimize their religious and political authority through their family ties and personal connections to the Prophet. As discussed earlier, during the reign of the fourth Caliphs, Ali ibn-e Abu Taleb, the questions concerning the 'true succession' to the Prophet divided the Muslim community into two rival groups, *Sunnis* and *Shi'ites*. The later branch of the Muslim community was in the minority. They claimed that the true successor to the Prophet is one who had blood bonds with the Prophet, i.e. his *ahal-e beyt* (members of his family).[20] Under the Caliphate of Uthman, some of the respectable and influential men who were dissatisfied with Uthman began to preach in favor of Ali, Mohammed's nephew and son-in-law. They rejected any other Caliphate for the Muslims than Ali and his family. Some of these people believed that Muhammad, during his last pilgrim journey to Mecca in 631, had, in a place named Qadir-e Khom appointed Ali as his successor and Amir al-Mo'menin (the legitimized leader of believers). Such a belief was the basis for the founding of a religious group among the Muslims, called Shi'ite, or the Shi'ites of Ali. They believe that the members of the Prophet's home (*ahal-e beyt*) had the right to leadership of the Muslim community. Ali reigned a short time after the third Caliph, Uthman. He was assassinated, and the Umayyads took political and religious power in the Muslim community.

Shi'ism claims that succession to the prophet is a divine right inherited by his direct descendants. They recognize no immediate, legitimate leader other than Ali (d. 661), his cousin and son-in-law, and eleven of his descendants. In this view, no *Imam* (the legitimate and lawful leader of the Shi'ite community) aside from Ali ever occupied the position as head of the Islamic community. This belief was the motivation/justification for several Shi'ite revolts against the Umayyads dynasty that seized power after the Prophet's death. The Shi'ites did not accept the reign of Umayyads, they considered them illegitimate and continuously challenged the Umayyad Caliphs. In this challenge, the Umayyads succeeded in crushing Shi'ites resistance, and the third Shi'ite Imam, Husayn, was killed. The Shi'ites gradually took a quiet position in relation to the Sunni Caliphs.

The Sixth Shi'ite Imam in line, Ja'far al-Sadiq (d. 765), ordered his followers to give up armed struggle and to adopt instead an attitude of acquiescence towards the Sunni state. Historically, it was the first ideological shift towards the *temporary depoliticization of Shi'ism*. In 874 this process was completed when the son of the Eleventh Imam, Hasan al-Askari, disappeared from public life and was visible only to a group of four ulama who were his message bearers (*vakils*) to the Shi'ite community. This period of the Twelfth Imam's occultation and connection with the Shi'ite community continued for some seventy years and is called the 'Lesser Occultation', *gheybat-e soghra*. In 940, the death of the last *vakils*, Ali ibn-e Muhammad al-Samarri, put an end to this limited communication with the Hidden Imam and the community was led to the 'Greater Occultation', *gheybat-e kubra* (Algar 1969, p. 3). Hence, after the death of the fourth *vakil*, al-Samarri, the Shi'ite ulama declared the

Twelfth Imam, *Mahdi*, occulted (alive, even present in this world, yet invisible, the Hidden Imam). The Hidden Imam would not appear until 'the end of time'. Thus, Muslims who believe in the Imams as the only true and legitimized successor to the Prophet are called *Shi'i-ye Ali* (believer of the First Imam) or Shi'ite.[21]

The doctrine of *gheybat-e kubra* means implicitly that the time is not yet ripe for *Mahdi* to appear and help the 'true believers' to establish the reign of the 'just'. *The doctrine enabled Shi'ites to temporarily give up their immediate claim to political power.*[22] It also implies that temporal rulers are not legitimate as the 'true rulers' of the Muslim community. It does not, however, state or imply that the Shi'ites have no claim to power in such a society. While awaiting for the appearance of the 'Hidden Imam', Shi'ite religious leaders, such as *Imams, fuqaha* (Islamic jurisprudents) and Mujtahids (religious interpreters), have the freedom to practise their theology and jurisprudence. The immediate political consequences of the theory of *gheybat* was Shi'ites' *de facto* acceptance of Sunni states. This historical change of Shi'ites' attitude became apparent when the Buyids, a Shi'ite dynasty, took political power within the territory of Abbasid Caliphate (Algar, 1969). The Buyids defeated Abbasid's army and occupied their center, Baghdad, but they did not change the Caliphate and they accepted the sovereignty and symbolic authority of Abbasid Caliphs. The reign of some dynasties with Shi'ite sympathy in Iran under the Abbasids encouraged many Shi'ites, who were more or less persecuted in the Sunni territories, to move to Iran.

The Sunni theory of state, on the other hand, was based on the Caliphate until the second century after the Prophet (eighth AD), in which the political leader of a Muslim community gains social/pragmatist justification to reign. The attitude of the Sunnis was that it was important for all Muslims to live together in peace and unity, and this implied that they should accept what had happened. They came to accept all four of the first Caliphs as legitimate, and as virtuous or rightly guided (*Rashedin*); later caliphs, who ruled in Muslim community after the first four Caliphs, might not always have acted justly, but they should be accepted as legitimate so long as they did not go against the basic commandments of God (Hourani, 1991, pp. 60-61). After some two centuries of ideological and social conflict between Sunnis and Shi'ites, the latter seemed to have succeeded in gaining religious legitimacy for their theory of *Imamat*. The Shi'ites' theory of *Imamat*, as discussed earlier, is based on divine legitimization of the *ahal-e beyt*'s (the Prophet family's) right to lead the Muslim community. Shi'ite Imams' theological works, such as *Nahj al-balaghah* of the First Imam, Ali, *Sahifat al-Sajjadiah* of the Fourth Imam, Zein al-Abedin, the works of Muhammad al-Baqer the Fifth Imam, and Jafar al-Sadeq the Sixth Imam, and even the works of other Shi'ite theologians and philosophers such as al-Farabi, strengthened *the theological bases of Imamat as the only legitimate authority in Muslim community*. Even the Sunni caliphs, Abbasids, who were in conflict with other Sunni caliphs, Umayyads, attempted to gain legitimization for their rule in the Muslim community by cooperating with Shi'ites and choosing the Eighth Imam, Reza, as crown prince for Abbasid caliph, Ma'mun. The Sunnis Mujtahids who realized the critical situation of the Sunni theory of state and its legitimization crisis, attempted to form a theological framework for the Sunni state. One of the first theologian in this line was al-Baqillani, who wrote a book entitled *al-Tamhid fi'l-radd ala'l-mulhida al-mu'attala wa'l-khawariji wa'l-mu'tazila*,[23] which was a work of refutation and polemic against revival groups, Shi'ites, Kharijis, and Mu'tazilis (Lambton, 1981). Al-Baqillani adopted the theory of *Imamat* from Shi'ites' theological and political framework and tried to combine that with the theory of Caliphate. By this attempt he wanted to establish a divine legitimization for Sunni caliphs based on Islamic religious law, Shari'a.

The other Sunni theologian who tried to form a more sophisticated theory of *Imamat* was al-Baghdadi. In his book *Usul al-din*, he conducted a pragmatic polemic with the Shi'ites, trying to illegitimate their theory of *Imamat*. Al-Baghdadi, by discussing the historic necessity of leadership by one or more *Imam* in the Muslim community, rejected the Shi'ite theory of *gheybat*. He meant, in contrast to the Shi'ite theory of the Hidden Imam, that a visible imam, living in the Muslim community, is necessary (Al-Baghdadi (1928). The third Sunni theorist who more than others tried to create an ideological framework for the Islamic government, Caliphate, was al-Mawardi. Besides continuing in line with al-Baqillani and al-Baghdadi, he introduced the notions of *wizara* and *imara*, prepared the way for an historic innovation in the Sunni theory of state (Lambton, 1981, pp. 81-102). By adapting Islamic state authority to worldly authority of office, *wizara*, and divine authority of caliph, al-Mawardi unintentionally created ideological notions that were used by other Sunni theologians such as al-Juwayni and al-Ghazali to develop and formulate the theory of Sultanate, in which religious and political power gradually became separated. Al-Ghazali, who was Persian, adopted the Sasanid's (the last dynasty of Persian Empire) theory of state in which *din* (religion) was the base and *dawlat* (temporal power) was its guardian.[24] He meant that a coalition between the Sultan (the political leader), and *faqih* (jurisprudent) is a necessary condition to avoid *fitna* (civil war) and *fasad* (demoralization). Al-Ghazali reformulated the theory of *Imamat* and limited the imam as a symbol of the supremacy of the Shari'a (religious law), while the Sultan was acknowledged as the holder of coercive power (Lambton, 1981, pp. 114-15).[25] Al-Ghazali, like many other Islamic scholars, was aware of the importance of the ulama and their legitimate place in Muslim community. As Hourani pointed out:

> Not only the tradition of literate converts, but the essential nature of Islam itself–the revelation of words, and therefore of ideas and knowledge–made it imperative that those who wished to conform to the Will of God should seek knowledge and reflect upon it. The search for religious knowledge, 'ilm, began early in the history of Islam, and there gradually developed a body on informed and concerned Muslim scholars (Alim, pl. 'ulama) (Hourani, 1991, p. 60).

As we see, an important development in the Sunni theory of state helped Sunni Muslims to live harmoniously with different forms of states such as the Caliphate (Umayyads and Abbasids), the Sultanate (Ottoman Sultans), and the Mamluks (in Egypt).

The Founding of the First Shi'ite State

In 1501, a Shi'ite dynasty, the Safavids, came to power in Iran through Isma'il, who declared Shi'ism as the state religion of Iran. The declaration of Shi'ism as state religion could not be legitimized since Shi'ism was, historically, an oppositional religion to the state and ideologically incompatible with any form of state led by a person other than the Hidden Imam. To legitimize their state as a Shi'ite state and to solve the paradox of the combination of state and Shi'ism, the Safavid shahs laid claim to the Hidden Imam's vicegerency (*niyabat*). The theory of *niyabat* meant that the Safavids ruled the Shi'ites' land in the manner of purely Islamic justice until the appearance of the Hidden Imam. The Safavids' reign (1501-1722) meant a turning point in Iranian history after the introduction of Islam. They regained and reconstructed some social organizations and institutions that were decisive for the sovereignty of Iran. The most important social changes can be categorized in three points:

1. *The creation of a powerful and centralized government.*
2. *The socio-cultural construction of an Iranian/Shi'ite identity.*
3. *The creation of a powerful religious group by superiority of the ulama.*

(1) After more than 800 years of occupation by Arabs and some weaker Iranian tribal groups, the Safavids, especially during the reign of their two charismatic leaders Shah Isma'il I (1501-1524), and Shah Abbas the Great (1588 -1629), created a highly powerful and centralized state in the plateau of Iran. They used the term *dawlat* which means 'bliss', 'felicity' (Savory, 1980), or 'dynasty' (Hjärpe , 1993). This term began to be used later in the Ottoman Empire and Arab lands to characterize 'state'. The Safavids' ruling hierarchy was based on a well developed bureaucracy controlled by *vazir* (minister) one of the most important authorities in the Safavid state. The Shah, who had been actively supported by ulama and consequently possessed a high degree of divine legitimacy, had the absolute power in the ruling hierarchy.[26] The Safavids' sovereign and powerful Shi'ite state was, however, the first necessary condition for the creation of a powerful Iranian society in the neighborhood of the expansive Ottoman Empire.

(2) One of the most important crises that violated the old 'Persian identity' was the lack of a powerful and sovereign Persian state. Before the Safavids, Iran was ruled by powerful dynasties such as Buyids; but they could not gain legitimacy because of the lack of a religion separate from other Sunni countries–and in particular the Ottoman Empire–surrounding Iran. It is commonly believed that Islam, an Arabic religion, successfully gained foothold among the people of Iran, while the old religion of Persia, Zoroastrianism, retreated from a hegemonial position in society–and limited to a very small area in southeastern Iran–and caused an identity crisis for non-Arab political authority in Iran. As Calhoun (1990) points out, national identity is a political project by which a group of people are differentiated or separated from another group by political means. Following the Arab conquest of Iran up to the Safavids era, other dynasties, even the Shi'ite dynasty such as the Buyids, who revolted against the Arab conquerors and tried to create an Iranian state, failed to separate from the Sunni Caliph residing in Baghdad. This happened partly because the Sunni theory of state in which the Caliph is divinely legitimated, implied the lack of an ideological framework for a political project intended to create an

alternative national identity against the Sunni Arabs. By declaring Shi'ism the state religion of Iran in 1501, the Safavids succeeded in making the Shi'ite faith into an ideological framework in a political project for the creation of an Iranian identity. In addition to Shi'ism as a nationwide religion, the Safavids used the old Persian forms of state, kingdom, and crowned themselves *shahs* (kings).

The first shah of Safavids, Isma'il I (1501-1524), began the project of creation an Iranian identity. After crowning himself shah in the city of Tabriz, he announced the Shi'ite *Ithna Ashari* (Twelve Imami, which believe in Twelve Imams after the Prophet as his successors), as the official religion of Iran. With the help of a radical Shi'ite group known as *tabarra'iyan* (those who have pledged themselves body and soul to the shah), he began to seize every socio-cultural foothold of the Sunni branch in Iran. This group walked through the streets and bazaars cursing all enemies of Ali (the First Imam of Shi'ites), and Sunnis in general (Savory, 1980). Those who rejected the Shi'ite faith, in particular the Sunni ulama, were put to death (Savory, 1970). Some Sunni ulama who refused to convert to Shi'ism escaped to the Sunni states of the Ottomans and Timurids. The Safavids' Shi'isation of state and society began by proclaiming themselves *nayeb-e Imam* (vicegerent of the Hidden Imam), and sharing with the Shi'ite ulama political power. They introduced and maintained particular socio-cultural changes, such as the reparation of Shi'ite shrines, the construction of many new mosques, *Sufi Khanqahs*,[27] *Takyehs*,[28] *Jame' mosques*,[29] and so forth, to create and reinforce their cultural sovereignty.

(3) As mentioned earlier, shah Isma'il I invited the Shi'ite ulama, residents of southern Iraq, Damascus, and the Persian Gulf area to settle in the new Shi'ite country of Iran. To legitimate his political power based on claiming vicegerency of the Hidden Imam, and to end the religious domination of the Sunni ulama, shah Isma'il needed the Shi'ite ulama and Mujtahids to reside in Iran. The Shi'ite ulama who had been persecuted and badly treated by Sunni leaders, came to Iran with the help of the Shah, who treated them well. The ulama accepted Isma'il's *niyabat* (vicegerency) to the Hidden Imam and guaranteed his domination over political and religious affairs.[30] The Safavids created a religious administrative power named *sadr* whose duty included the propagation of Shi'ism. The *sadr* can be called the ministry of religion. Another important duty of the *sadr* was the administration of *auqaf* (pious foundations) which was an important institution that made it possible for the ulama to be

separated from the state. Under the Safavids, Shi'ite's influence and the Shi'ite ulama's social power in the society drastically increased (Savory, 1980), and they gradually became a sovereign power in the society. Even if the construction of *sadr* was an attempt by the shahs to exert control over the ulama, it paradoxically helped them create their institutions and reinforce their hegemony in civil society. 'Even the strongest rulers were constrained to treat them with respect and could not flout their opinions with impunity. The Shaykh al-Islam Husayn b. Abd al-Ali al-Karaki exercised great influence over Shah Tahmasb while Shah Sultan Husayn (1694-1722), the last of the Safavids, came under the domination of Muhammad Baqir Majlisi' (Lambton, 1981, p. 268).

The Social Construction of Shi'ite Religious Authority

Through cooperation with the Safavids, the Shi'ite ulama gained the lawful right to arrange marriage, divorce and funeral ceremonies, to act as religious jurists *(fuqaha)* and religious landowners *(muttovalli-ye auqaf)*, to obtain a share of the farmers' harvest, to collect religious taxes and alms, and to exercise monopoly over 'the true religion'. These social practices were organized by the most learned of ulama, the Mujtahids. The Mujtahids had generally exercized leadership and guidance among the Shi'ite community. The institutionalization of religious authority could not be successful without creating a proper hierarchy for religious groups. Shi'ite educational centers in Isfahan (under the Safavids), Qum and Najaf (under the Qajars and Pahlavis), and in *'atabat*, are examples of legitimizing and institutionalizing the Shi'ite hierarchy. And because of the social nature of each hierarchy, which, as Weber says, is a matter of dominance, the theocratic dominance among Mujtahids was solved by creating the position of *Marja'-e taqlid*. This is the most qualified and competent among all Mujtahids whose example and guidance in matters of practice is binding for *muqalleds*, i.e. believers who follow him. In the nineteenth century another supreme position was proposed among the Shi'ite ulama, namely that of *marja'iyat-e taqlid-e tamm* (complete authority of one Mujtahid over other Mujtahids and the whole community).[31] Even *fuqaha* (Islamic jurisprudents) had to follow the decrees of *Marja'-e taqlid* because of his authority and hierarchical dominance in the Shi'ite community. Although no adequate way of selecting *Marja'-e taqlid* was established (Algar, 1969, pp. 16-17) and in many cases there was more than one *Marja'-e taqlid*, it was a very important position in Shi'ite that reinforced clerical hierarchy and power, even if, as Amanat (1988) says, there were no institutional authorities, such as the church or the state, to verify and designate their possessors (Amanat, 1988).

One of the most important positions of the ulama, one which helped them to establish and reinforce their authority in Shi'ite community since the Safavids, was their participation in the administration of justice and their function as *qadi* (religious judge). *Fuqaha* as legitimated jurisprudents became an important partner for the state. Iranian history from the Safavids until the late reign of Qajars exhibits an arena of dual authority divided between the state and the Shi'ite ulama.[32] Also, jurisprudence was the privilege of the ulama because of the nature of the code of laws, i.e. their religious sources. Jurisprudence is an inheritance from the Prophet to the Imams, during the Occultation of the Hidden Imam to the *fuqaha*. The conclusion of the Safavids' reign and the establishment of Shi'ism as state religion has meant that, since the sixteenth century, the political authority of dynasties and states emerged and disappeared in Iran, but the authority of the ulama remained and even increased over time. But this reality has depended on historical and decisive changes in the ulama's social position in Iran.

The Safavid's socio-political construction of a theocratic state led to a division of traditional state authority into: (1) a religious or more social authority having to do with the reconstruction of society according to Shari'a (religious laws), and (2) a political authority which was to protect the Shi'ite community against foreign enemies. In the early Safavid period, the ulama were dependent on the financial and political support of the shahs (Keddi, 1981, p. 16), due to disestablishment of the ulama and other Shi'ite groups and the lack of independent income sources. The Safavid shahs, who claimed patrilineal descent from the Seventh Imam, Musa' al-Kazem (Lambton, 1981, p. 264), introduced the Shi'ite as state religion, and engaged in a longterm war with the Sunni Ottomans, needed the ulama's support for legitimacy. But this relationship between ulama and the Safavid state underwent some significant changes. During the reign of Shah Abbas the Great (1588-1629), some separation of the state's and the ulama's power took place (Savory, 1980). Shah Abbas' cautious secularization policy, which was intended to create a strong central power, forced the ulama to reorganize their economic position and use the incomes of *auqaf* (religious endowment), and religious taxes such as *khoms* and *zakat* to constitute their independent identity. To compensate for the lack of political authority and reinforce their social authority, the ulama had to deal with two main problems:

1. Legitimizing the clerical hierarchy.
2. Guaranteeing their economic independence and social support.

For the first purpose, as mentioned earlier, the ulama introduced some notions such as *Mujtahids, Marja'-e taqlid, Marja'-e taqlid-e tam* and *Marja'-e taqlid-e kamel*, in the Shi'ite theory of authority in the community. But it is important to mention that these notions cannot be discussed only through theological interpretations. The Shi'ite clerical community has to be considered as a social group with ties to the whole society. To be *Marja'-e taqlid* (sources of emulation), for instance, is neither merely a personal nor a theological matter, but is directly connected with the Shi'ite community which is supposed to be *muqalleds* (emulators of *Marja'-e- taqlid*). *Marja'-e taqlid* have to be accepted and followed by *muqalleds*, in order to be regarded as *Marja'-e taqlid*. It was therefore a status based on practicalities of leadership rather than on doctrinal grounds (Amanat, 1988). After the Safavids era, and for the purpose of creating their own authority, the Shi'ite ulama used their prominent position as *muttovalli-ye auqaf*,[33] Mujtahids,[34] and collector of *sahm-e Imam*,[35] to establish personal and functional connections with the poles of socio-economic power that gathered in the bazaar.

The appearance of some ideological and theological Shi'ite schools was also important for legitimizing and further increasing of the ulama's power and right to authority in the society of Iran. In the late eighteenth century, the Shi'ite community faced a theoretical struggle between two Shi'ite schools, namely Akhbaris and Usulis. Akhbaris believed that each Shi'ite individual can, by religious ability, and without help from any other person interpret and incorporate the sayings and doings (*akhbar*) of the Prophet and Imams. According to their theology, there are no religious ground for special groups who are learned in religious matters–Mujtahids for instance–to function as a link to the Prophet and Imams. A rival school, called Usulis, argued for the necessity of a religious body that could facilitate understanding of the foundation (*usul*) of Islam. This religious body had to be the most learned of clergy, namely Mujtahids. Usulis believed in and propagated the principle that each Shi'ite believer must choose a Mujtahid to follow as 'source of emulation', and must always be guided by a Mujtahid

(Keddie, 1981). According to Usulis the Shi'ite community is divided into two main groups: believers who follow Mujtahids and their decrees (*muqalleds*), and the supreme group of Mujtahids who are 'the source of emulation' (*Marja'-e taqlid*) that the first group follows. Mujtahids, in Usulis doctrine, which, in time, won over Akhbaris, were presented as those who alone could understand Islam and the will of the Hidden Imam. This legitimized their position against any political power in Shi'ite community and provided a basis for the concentration of 'the legitimate power' in the hands of Mujtahids.

The Realm of Economy

Since the foundation of the first cities in Iran, the main economic activities take part in bazaars. The establishment and development of cities have been connected with the history of bazaars. The traditional major cities of Iran such as Isfahan, Shiraz, Tabriz, Qazvin, and others were located along the old trade routes. The formation of such cities began with a house that served as a resting place for trade caravans (*karavansarays*). *Karavansarays* became trade centers over time. They attracted traders and artisans from neighboring areas. Growth in economic activities led to the appearance of new public buildings such as religious places, shops, restaurants, and new *karavansarays*. They were built near each other along the main trade route, and, thereby, shaped a linear trade center that gradually became known as the bazaar. To protect the bazaars from the hot sun in the summers and rain in the winters, they were covered by roofs. The bazaar became the major center of socio-economic and cultural life of traditional cities of Iran. A settlement without a bazaar is not considered a city (Falamaki, 1977; Kheirabadi, 1991). Bazaars were the palace of both industry and commerce. After the Arab conquest of Iran in the seventh century, and particularly during the reign of Safavids, many religious buildings, such as mosques, *madrasahs* (religious schools), and other clerical centers, were constructed within the bazaars. Islam had direct economic and cultural consequences–in part redistributive, in part shaping and reshaping social conditions and developments. For example, during the last period of Safavids, the bazari traders paid Islamic taxes (*khoms* and *zakat*) to the ulama; economic support for the ulama enabled them to grow in numbers in the cities; rich bazaris also often built their own mosques in connection with bazaars (Kheirabadi, 1991, p. 67). Through the payment of religious taxes, Muslim traders 'permitted' (*halal*) their income and established and maintained a favorable reputation in the Muslim community. Such a reputation has not only a religious meaning–namely, becoming a 'clean' Muslim trader or shopkeeper–but it also has a practical economic side crucial for the bazaris' position and prestige within the bazaar.

In the pre-Shi'ite period of the Islamic history of the bazaar, i.e., Sunni Iran, there was a strong socio-economic connection between the bazaars and the state bureaucracy. The large merchants were strongly connected to the notables, and some of them rose to the level of *vazirate* (chief state official) and others to the office of *vakil-i dar* (Lambton, 1981, p. 328). Bazaris were engaged both in business in goods and business in money. The merchant was often a moneylender as well. They served not only private individuals but also the government, which suffered from a perennial shortage of funds and was frequently in need of money to finance its operations (Lambton, 1981, p. 29). Loan-giving bazaris, to protect themselves against borrowers who held positions of political influence, i.e., statesmen and bureaucrats, and to secure repayment of the loans, had to gain support from the ulama. Repayment of loans from private individuals–and even for security of trade roads–depended on state support. But the bazaar's linkages with the state were through merchants who were a small group within the bazaar community. Temporary changes such as state crises and shift of international trade could always marginalize this connection. For example, by the end of the Saljuq period, the merchant communities, with the shift of international trade away from Iraq to Egypt, had declined in importance (Lambton, 1981, p. 331). And the state crisis in the pre-Safavid period loosened the linkages between the bazaar and the state.

The reign of the Safavids and the Shi'itization of Iran led to the construction of a powerful Shi'ite religious authority and an increase in the ulama's power in bazaar. The bazaar's traditional economic activity, which was dependent on trade, not only inside the country but also with other countries, was more compatible with the Islamic idea of non-national communities.[36] The Safavids' political project to create a national state, coupled with wars with the Ottomans, did not work in favor of the bazaris. They were interested in keeping the trade roads open and secure. Under the reign of Shah Abbas the Great, when the Safavids Empire increased, and through the large market created by great treaties with European countries, the bazaris enjoyed a period of economic flourishing. In the second half of the reign of the Safavids, who Shi'itized the community of Iran, paradoxical religio-social and economic connections between state and bazaris decreased, in favor of a tremendous increase of the ulama's influence in the bazaar.

This great alliance between the ulama and bazaar community was due, among other factors, to the ulama's position of *mutovalli-ye auqaf*, which helped some of them to become big landowners (Savory, 1980). In addition to this religious support, some even became economic partners of bazari traders, craftsmen, artisans and *dukkan dars* (small shopkeepers). Other factors such as the ulama's position as Mujtahids, which provide them monopoly over interpretation of religious law, and *Shaykh al-Islam*,[37] were not less important for their alliance with the bazaris. This historically important alliance was even reinforced by inter-marriage between the ulama and merchant families.[38]

2 Civil Society in Iran

Towards a Conceptualization of Iranian Civil Society

The idea of civil society has a long intellectual history. The concept has been presented in different theoretical frameworks, including Locke, Hobbes, Hegel, Marx and Durkheim, as well as Habermas, Alexander, Eisenstadt, Calhoun, and Gellner, among many others. Durkheim considers the realm of civil society a *shared community based on 'universal individualism'*. Civility based on 'pre-contractual' elements is a result of socialization. He means that individual contracts are not the sources of the modern social order but the social order is prior to the contracts and based on the division of labor (Durkheim, 1984, pp. 101-23). The process of socialization creates a social ethic that provides the proper means of negotiation and contract making. According to Durkheim the very existence of societies is based on *solidarity*. In more traditional societies it is a form of mechanical solidarity, and in modern societies an organic solidarity. In both cases, solidarity is not dependent on the intervention of the state but on collective consciousness and reciprocity. (Durkheim, 1984).[39] Habermas, in order to define the sovereignty of the civil *vis-à-vis* the state, stresses ethical aspects in the definition of civility. He consider civil society as a realm of democratic action of 'will formation' based on 'communicative interaction' (Habermas, 1990). Habermas' civil society consists of a sphere of communicative action where new social movements, such as environmentalism, form. Habermas' concept of civil society is related to that of a group of social scientists whose perspective is labeled as 'New Social Movements-Civil Society'.[40] They consider civil society as a basis for new social movements. Others define civil society as a civil realm that is to some degree separated not only from the state but also from the other 'non-civil' spheres of religion, science, economy, and primordial communities; a sphere where individual interaction is protected (Alexander, 1995, p. 8).[41]

While there are various conceptions and interpretations of the notion of civil society, one can say generally that civil society is a social sphere where non-political individuals and groups interact and organize their social life. In other words, it is the capacity of a society to organize itself without being organized by a state (Calhoun, 1993). This interpretation of civil society leads us to consider the society as divided between civil society and state. The dialectical relationship between these two spheres is constituted by the state and civil individuals and their associations as they struggle for sovereignty. Many studies of the emergence of 'civil society' and its development presume that civil society is based on the autonomy of its individual members.[42] Indeed, the notion of civil society is often conceived of as synonymous with individual freedom and democracy. The appearance of a civil type society is, in my view, not necessarily connected to individualism or democratic associations. The simplified linkage of state/ people, which is an outcome of a socio-cultural development in Western history, is not reliable in the case of Iran and even other Muslim communities.[43] A more general concept is required, one stressing not so much individuals (citizens) and their associations but groups or communities and their institutions.

Drawing on Eisenstadt (1993, 1995a),[44] one can consider three social structural conditions for a civil society, stressing the relatively autonomous position of societal spheres *vis-à-vis* the state and the capacity of civil society agents or representatives to take initiatives toward, and to influence, the state. The three conditions are:

1. *Relative autonomy of a societal sphere from the state.*
2. *Relative autonomous access to the state or its elite.*
3. *Existence of a relatively independent public sphere.*
4. *Legal protection.*

Civil society in Iran is not directly conditioned by the existence of 'sovereign' and 'free' individuals, but by groups or communities and their institutions enjoying a significant degree of autonomy from the state. The autonomy of these civic society groups is based on social authority and legitimacy as well as socio-economic institutions. The Shi'ite ulama enjoy a particular religious and legitimate basis to challenge the state, as will be discussed in detail later in this chapter. The ulama's economic independence from the state, which depended on the economic institutions of *vaqf* and *sahm-e Imam*, and the bazaar's economic support, created a basis for the ulama's autonomy from the state. *Ijtihad* has been another important source of the ulama's position and authority. *Ijtihad* is the quality of

Mujtahids who possess proper knowledge and can provide Muslim individuals guidance in matters of religion. The other main group of Iranian traditional civil society, namely the bazaris, were also independent from the state in organizing their economic activities and making and pursuing their social commitments. It is worth mentioning that, in many cases, even the security of the people in urban areas was maintained by *lutis* (chivalrous) under the ulama's influence in local communities.

Autonomous access to the state, as a second condition for civil society, means that autonomous civil groups can institutionally influence the state. As discussed later, the ulama, as representatives of civil society, have exercised influence over state authority. They possessed a basis of authority independent of the state. They also enjoyed a certain autonomous jurisprudence, and, in many cases, had access to their own executive means. In addition, the bazaris could influence state authority, partly through giving loans to the state and partly through their close connections with the ulama.

According to Eisenstadt, the third condition of civil society is a relatively independent public sphere. Socio-political institutions in which public debate takes place and influences political decision-making constitute the public sphere of civil society. This public sphere should be relatively independent of the state, the family, and tribal bonds. In Iran, this independent public sphere has existed over centuries. The most important institution in this independent public sphere was the *manbar* (pulpit). The importance of *manbar* in propagating political ideas goes back to the very beginning of Islam. For example, during the period of conflict between the First Shi'ite Imam, Ali, and Ma'aviyeh, over succession of the third Caliph, Othman, both sides used the *manbar* to illegitimate the other and to gain support (Fathi, 1993). Control of the *manbars* was a crucial means to mobilize people and influence the state. The ulama could influence the state directly, through their connections with the state, and indirectly, through preaching in the *manbars*. Critical sermons against the state had in many cases serious consequences for the state. Both the Constitutional and the Islamic revolutions showed the importance of the *manbars* in influencing and mobilizing people. It was not only the revolutionaries who used the *manbars* for propagating their ideas, but also the state used it against the opposition (Fathi, 1993). In general, *va'z* (preaching in the *manbars*) was a very effective means in mobilizing people and influencing state policy. In Iran, during the Constitutional Revolution, the public sphere of society, namely *masjids* (mosques), *takyehs* (the places for the performance of religious dramas), *bazarchehs* (small bazaars), *coffee-houses*, *ta'ziyeh-khanehs* (the place for dramatic performances of the martyrdom of the Third Imam), etc. increased in importance and became the real political sphere of society. The charismatic preaching ulama, such as Seyyed Jamal-e Va'ez and Malek al-Mutokallemin, used the *manbars* to discuss politics. The state's foreign policy, economic development, social injustices, the political order, and even technological development were some of the topics of the ulama's sermons. The people who gathered around the *manbars* and listened to the political discussions of the ulama were not only religious people, but consisted of all urban groups who were interested in politics. Several state spies who reported on the public gathering around the *manbar* of Seyyed Jamal-e Va'ez reported to authorities: 'A little group of people participated in the pre-va'z prayer, which was held by Seyyed Jamal, but after the prayer, when Seyyed Jamal climbed the *manbar*, the number of the people–both women and men–were considerably more than those participating in the prayer (Yaghmai, 1978).

The fourth condition is the normative, including legal protection of the institutional relationships which make up civil society. The ulama's monopoly over Islamic jurisprudence, Shari'a, provided them the opportunity to protect the traditional civil society and legitimize and protect it against the state's intervention. Free economic activities are protected by norms of poverty rights as well as Quranic verses, *hadiths* (the sayings of the Prophet), and Sunna (the deeds of the Prophet). The Prophet Muhammad was himself a trader and faithful to the moral imperatives of business. He left a tradition of business and guidance for how to engage in economic activities. This tradition which was supported by Quranic verses came to provide a frame for economic activities in many Muslim countries. The bazaars received a sovereign position in such countries. The ulama's monopoly over the jurisprudence provided the bazaris some legal protection against the state. The close connection between the bazaris and the ulama was the basis for a powerful civil sphere which made any attempts to substantial change in the structural properties of the Muslim societies difficult and risky for the state. The interventions of the state for changing the traditional structure of society had to be legitimized by the ulama's *fatvas*. For instance, when Abbas Mirza (d. 1833) heir apparent of Fath Ali Shah tried to create a new army system in Iran he had to ask the ulama to accept the reforms. As will be discussed later, he used the Quranic verses and *hadiths* for legitimizing this reform.

The ulama's *fatvas*, which were based on interpretation of the Islamic law, Shari'a, worked as decrees, in many cases more important than those of the state. They, as Mujtahids, had a monopoly over interpretation of Islamic law by which they legitimized their own position in society and could illegitimize the position of state–as they did in the two Perso-Russian wars of nineteenth century and during the Tobacco Movement (1898) and the Constitutional Revolution (1905-1909).

In sum, one of my main theses is that, Iran has had a civil society even on the eve of its two modern Revolutions.[45] Civil society in which the ulama and the bazaris were two powerful groups could influence the state and its decision-making. The legitimization of civil autonomy and authority was, in part, religious and, therefore, external to society.

Theological Basis of the Ulama's Social Authority

In Iranian Muslim society–as well as in the pre-Islamic era–the political order was always an axial order, and, in a certain sense, *external* to the society. Namely, the position of leaders, as representatives of God, was religiously legitimized. This externality of social order had to do with the hierarchical ruling system legitimized as divine order. Ideas of secular or rational order of society, as emerged in the West, were heretical and unacceptable to the clergy for legitimizing socio-political order. The pre-Islamic notion of shahs as the 'Shadow of God on the Earth'[46] and the sacred Shi'ite notion of 'vicegerency of the Hidden Imam' were readily adopted and even reinforced by Muslim rulers such as Safavids and Qajars. They sought to maintain and legitimize the social order–and their political rule–as divinely ordained. Safavids, as already explained, called themselves both shah and the vicegerent of the Hidden Imam. In this sense, they sought to combine two models of divine legitimization for their ruling system. Qajars, on the other side, tried to gain legitimacy by adapting only the notion of 'The shadow of God' (Arjomand, 1984).

From the time of the Arab conquest of Iran until the early nineteenth century, the political community of Iran legitimized their ruling system as a divine order, and as such, *external* to the society. To keep this externality alive and secure their political power, the ruling dynasties of Iran were dependent on religious support of the ulama who had a monopoly over religious matters. According to the Shi'ite theory of State, the ulama, as vicegerents of the Hidden Imam and even descendants of the Shi'ite Imams, were the most legitimate social group for dealing with matters of Muslim community. The state was accepted only if it respected the social authority of the ulama and protected the Muslim community against non-Muslims. Organizing society and maintaining social institutions such as marriage, divorce, funerals, education, tax collecting, pilgrimage, endowment, jurisprudence, and so forth, were the responsibilities and the duties of the ulama. Practically speaking, there was a state of coexistence between the political authority of the state and the social authority of the ulama, side by side. These two competing authorities needed each other for securing their positions and for continuation of a beneficial social order. The ulama needed the state to protect them both against non-Muslims and against Sunni rulers surrounding Iran; the state needed the ulama to legitimate the political order and to secure their positions. A state, thus, could not become a sovereign organ that could be legitimized on the basis of a profane 'natural law' or the triumph of reason. There were attempts by some Muslim philosophers, such as Ibn-e Sina,[47] Tusi, and founders and inheritors of Akhbari school,[48] Mulla Muhammad Ali and Muhammad Amin Astarabadi, to bring about compromises between the divinely external order of society and the profane innerworldly one. They were unsuccessful because of the uprising of powerful religious and philosophic schools–supported by the social authority of the ulama–such as Usulis and *Sheykhis*, which propagated the divine right of the ulama to social power.

After the Safavids (1501-1722) gained state power and launched their political project for the creation of a Shi'ite state against the Sunni Ottomans[49] the power of the Shi'ite ulama substantially increased in civil society of Iran. Naming themselves as *nayeb-e Imam* (vicegerents of the Hidden Imam), Safavid shahs intended to create a powerful central state on the basis of an extremely coherent legitimization with the help of the Shi'ite religious term of *niyabat* (vicegerency). During more than two centuries of their caesaro-papist reign, the Safavids incorporated religious institutions into the state (Arjomand, 1984, p. 211). But paradoxically, they created a submissive group of the Shi'ite ulama whose domination over religious, judicial, and social matters was exclusively institutionalized. In the last four decades of the seventeenth century, this group of religious professionals consolidated their position and emerged as a Shi'ite hierocracy (Arjomand, 1984, p. 211). One important change brought about by religious ascendance during the Safavids was popularization of Shi'ism. Some prominent Mujtahids, such as Mulla Muhammad Baqer Majlesi, through extremely detailed interpretation of religious practices, introduced religiously grounded models for the daily actions of people. The process by which the social practices were combined with and adjusted to extremely detailed religious patterns was not only applied to the public sphere of social actions such as marketing, bathing, marriage and so forth, but was also extended to private individual practices such as sex, toileting, dressing, sleeping, and eating. This form of *socialization* of religion created a close connection between the ulama and the civilians, and increased their influence and role in organizing the social life of people.

According to Islamic theology, the typical Western dualism between individual/society and private/public do not exist. The original notion of an Islamic community is *dar al-Islam* which means the home of Islam. This is not a single country, but a very homogeneous community constituted of Muslims, and non-Muslims who are *ahl al-kitab*, i.e. believers in almighty God.[50] Dar al-Islam stands in opposition to *dar al-harb,* which is the community of infidels, i.e. unbelievers. The leadership of *dar al-Islam* had, after the death of Mohammed, been a subject of theoretical challenge between rival Muslim theological schools.[51] As discussed earlier, the first distinction between Muslims was a matter of succession to the Prophet as leader of the Muslim community, which divided the community into two rival groups, namely Shi'ite and Sunni. But for both of these groups the Muslim community was constructed of three groups, *umma* (the Muslim people who do not rule but are ruled), *Imam/Caliph* (the leader and the head of *umma*), and legitimate non-Muslim religious groups. In the face of the appearance of opposing groups who succeeded in gaining political power in the community, Muslim philosophers such as al-Baghdadi were compelled to put forward a theory of acceptance of two authorities or rulers in the community. It was, however, not accepted by other Muslim theologians such as al-Mawardi and Ibn Taymiyya.[52]

The existence of different political authorities and the Islamic notion of the unity of leadership in the community posed a dilemma for Muslim philosophers. In order to solve this dilemma, al-Mawardi attempted to 'lay down that the office of imam was necessary to guarantee the existence of the community, thus making the imam the symbol of legitimate authority' (Lambton, 1981, p. 308). When the first form of leadership in *dar al-Islam*, the caliphate, as the leader of the community, declined, Sultan, the leader of the Turkish structure of leadership, Sultanate, became the real leader of the Muslim community. The Muslim philosopher al-Ghazali provided theological legitimization for the Sultan's legal, worldly, and religious leadership and appeared to solve the dilemma of dual leadership. The

Sunni state of caliphate and Sultanate became a Godly state that represents God and executes His law, Shari'a. Such a Godly state naturally calls for complete obedience from individuals. As a result of such a divinely legitimized state, 'the doctrine of civic responsibility did not arise. Any affirmation of the value of the human person and human rights rested on the inscrutable will of God' (Lambton, 1981, p. 310). The Western separation between church and state that emerged in the seventeenth century had its theological roots in the pagan Rome, where Caesar was God. Later Christians were taught to differentiate between that which is due to Caesar and that which is due to God' (Lewis, 1993, p. 181). In Sunni Islam, where the state was the vicegerent of God, there was no problem of dualism between state and religious authority, and therefore no solution through the triumph of secularism emerged. Because of the unity between state and religious leaders, no existing sovereign and autonomous religious institution had to be separated from secular institutions.

The ideological Shi'ite term that made the continuity of opposition to the state possible was the theory of *velayat*, total loyalty to the Hidden Imam. According to Shi'ites, the Hidden Imam is the only true and legal ruler of the Muslim community and since his return and guidance of the community is not yet actual, the community requires other sources of guidance. Shi'ite ulama, in particular the Mujtahids (learned in practising religious law), are a type of substitute for the Hidden Imam who provide immediate guidance in matters of practice. Consequently, Shi'ites theoretically divide society into two groups, *muqalled*, and *Marja'-e taqlid*. *Moqalleds* are those who are not supposed to be able to exercise independent judgment in matters of their religious practices and have to follow a religious *marja'*, i.e. a most learned Mujtahid who can exercise independent judgment in religious law and must be emulated by *moqalleds*. In this sense, all individuals who are not qualified as *marja'* are dependent on the religious community led by *Marja'-e taqlid*. According to the Shi'ites' theory of society, the state is not legitimized as the leader of Muslims, but only, and in the best case, as the defender of the community against the threat of non-Muslims (Khomeini, 1943).

A crucial change of relationship between the Shi'ite ulama and the state took place in 1501 when the Shi'ite dynasty Safavids seized political power in Iran and declared Shi'ism the state religion of Iran. They laid claim to *niyabat-e Imam*, vicegerency of the Hidden Imam. The Safavids' political project to establish a powerful Shi'ite state against the Sunni Ottomans favored the Shi'ite ulama becoming a very powerful group even to the extent of competing with the state. Consequently, these ulama refused to accept the Safavids claim to the vicegerency of the Hidden Imam and declared, through Shaykh Ahmad Ardabili, that the monarch was ruling over a 'borrowed kingdom' (*mulk-i ariya'*), (Algar, 1969, p. 22). But the Shi'ite ulama avoided openly criticizing the state, because of the threat from the Sunni Ottomans and from the rival Sufists. The last thirty years of the Safavids' reign witnessed a great increase of the ulama's influence in the state machinery of Iran. The last Safavid, Shah Sultan Husayn, was strongly controlled by the main Mujtahid of that time, Muhammad Baqir Majlisi, and by his grandson Mir Muhammad Husayn Majlisi after him. The Shi'ite idea of the state resulted in a weakening of the state, and, 'ironically, contributed to the fall of the Shi'ite-Iranian state in 1722' (Algar, 1969, p. 29). The Safavids created a powerful social group, the ulama, who through state support established and institutionalized their authority in Iranian society. Using their socio-political position in the Shi'ite Iran during the reign of Safavids and Qajars, they created and secured their leadership position in Iranian civil society.

Civil society of Iran is thus not constituted of individual citizens contra state and church–as was the case in the West–but as a civic sphere of local communities, the bazaris, *Muslim* individuals, and the ulama, where the ulama have had a leading position. Exploiting the illegitimacy or limited legitimacy of the state because of the religious illegality of state influence in the Shi'ite community and their legality as a temporary bearer of *niyabat-e Imam* (vicegerency of the Hidden Imam), the Shi'ite ulama succeeded in gaining a crucial social position in Iranian society. They used this position in relation to rich as well as poor people. The Shi'ite ulama's competitive opposition to the state on the basis of the theory of *velayat* placed them in closer contact with the people than with state machinery. As already mentioned, they established a permanent connection with the bazaar, which constituted a social authority, in some instances, stronger than that of the state. They exercised powerful influence over everyday life through ritual and religious activities such as: *raudakhani*, which is the public recitation of the tragic story of martyrdom of the Third Imam, Husayn, in the Karbala and normally takes place in mosques; *pishnamazi*, which is leading the religious prayers; and *feqahat*, which is Islamic jurisprudence by which the Shi'ite ulama acted as *qadi*, religious judges, and practised the Shari'a, Islamic law. Thus, they 'socialized' their religious legitimacy, institutionalized their social role among the people, and, as a result of this, created a powerful basis for social support in civil society of Iran.

According to Shi'ite *fiqh*, Muslim individuals are *moqalleds* who are to act in accordance with Shari'a, Islamic law interpreted by Mujtahids.[53] In Iran, the notion of individuals as subjects of a divine order was articulated and reinforced by the spread of Sufism during the reign of Safavids. Sufis believed that knowledge of the supernatural becomes possible only through individuals' identification with it. This is to say, a possible union between humanity and divinity. According to Sufism, there is no individual identity because individuals are a part of God. I is Him, and He is I. An individual does not exist by himself. He has been forced away from his origin, i.e. the soul of God, and is to find the way back to this godly origin. As Jalal-al-Din Rumi (*Movlavi*), one of the most famous models of Sufism, puts it:

Anyone who remained away from his origin,
the day of his rejoining he re-search [54]

Thus, according to Sufis monistic philosophy, the project of an individual's life is not to create a personal identity in relation to other individuals, but to surrender the realm of selfishness and fuse together with man's origin, God. Sufism represented an uncompromising mystic monism, the total elimination of any distinction between the 'I' and the rest of the physical and metaphysical world (Rosenthal, 1977, p. 51). The impact of Sufism on Shi'ism was not, however, of great significance, and Shi'ism adopted only that part of Sufism that was compatible with–and reinforced–the Shi'ite term, *taqlid* (emulation). The interaction of *Marja'-e taqlid* and *muqalled* individuals provided a proper theoretical framework for the existence of an individual who was subject to divine order.[55]

According to Shi'ism, secularization, in its literal meaning, had happened at the very beginning of the construction of the Sunni state after the death of the First Shi'ite Imam, Ali. The Sunni state of Umayyads was considered illegitimate by Shi'ites, because of its loss of divine legality. By Occultation of the Twelfth Imam in 874 and the emergence of the theory of *gheybat*, Shi'ites absolutized any transcendental basis for legitimization of any state except for the just reign of *Mahdi*[56] –until the reign of the Shi'ite Safavids. As a result of this position, a historic separation occurred between the state and the Shi'ite's religious authority. In addition, the Shi'ite term *taqiyya*, dissimulation of belief in times of danger, which usually appeared as a survival strategy against the Sunni state, and was practised even after the

Safavids, is an indication of this separation. Muslim individuals are members of the community and *muqalleds* of Mujtahids and not citizens of state. *As a result the entire realm of legitimacy of power–both social and political–is divinely defined and supports the position of the ulama.*[57]

The Bazaris and the Ulama in Iranian Urban Life

Another social phenomenon that reinforced the importance of the social role of the ulama is their connection with the socio-economic and cultural center of social life, namely the bazaars. The bazaris are a very important social group in civil society of Iran. The group consist of shopkeepers, guilds, craftsmen, traders and workers gathered in the bazaar. Bazaars were crucially important even in the pre-Islamic society of Iran. Almost all urban life in Iran depends on existing and active bazaars. Bazaars are usually located in the center of Iranian cities and constitute the heart of urban economic and cultural activities. As Falamaki (1977) suggests, without a bazaar a settlement is not considered a city. In the traditional bazaars, guilds headquarters, workshops, banks, storehouses, the commercial hubs, bathhouses, educational centers (*maktabs* and *madrasahs*) and religious centers were established. There was a close connection between bazaris (people who worked in bazaar) and the ulama, because many ulama came from the ranks of the bazaris. There were many small cities in Iran, and even as late as 1956 just 29 percent of the population was settled in the cities (Wilber, 1981). The main social groups of inhabitants in cities were occupations producing marketable goods, both for local communities and for export. Those tradesmen, manufacturers, merchants, and workers who had the same occupation gathered in the same productions area in the bazaars called *Rasteh bazaar*. Other urban groups were farmers who had their farms around the cities, small shopkeepers and people in the transport sector that had strong linkages with the bazaars, and the ulama. The latter were composed of *modarresin* (prominent teachers of religious schools), *fuqaha (Islamic* jurisprudents), Imam juma'a (religious leader for Friday prayer), Mujtahids (interpreters of Shari'a), *tullab* (students in Islamic theology), and some other *hojjat al-Islam's* and *mullahs* or *akhonds* (the religious groups who are ranked lower in religious hierarchy). One can find many indications of the impact of religious beliefs on economic activities of the bazaris. For instance, bazaris who wanted to enjoy the benefits of their economic activities had to gain two socio-religious statuses in the Muslim community. First, they had to make their income *halal,* i.e. 'permitted' or 'religiously legal'. To legalize their activities, they paid religious taxes, such as *khoms* and *zakat*,[58] and thereby received legitimization from the ulama. Second, through more visible socio-religious activities such as constructing mosques and *madrasahs,* and making pilgrimages to Mecca, they socially constructed and established their purified character.[59] The social construction of bazaris' purified character was a conscious project that aimed to turn the religiously subjective legitimization to a socially recognized one.

The social authority of the ulama and the bazaris was mainly concentrated in urban communities. But this does not mean that these groups did not influence and even control rural areas. The ulama, through the system of *auqaf,*[60] took control over a considerable part of arable land, and, consequently, some of them 'entered the ranks of the landowning classes' (Savory, 1980) and controlled many of the villages. Religious leaders received their endowments partly from the state, which depended on their support, and partly from rich urban families usually connected to the bazaar. Bazaris were an influential group in rural areas too. Bazaris were the main economic partner for both peasants and tribal groups. Bazaars were the main purchaser of peasants' agricultural products and tribal carpets and rugs. Bazaars also provided urban commodities. In addition, inter-marriage between the bazaris and the ulama–and among their relatives–also the bazari origin of many ulama reinforced and increased the influence of bazaris in the rural area. Indicating the role of religious landowners is not the same as saying that the religious leaders became landowners and thereby shared economic power with the bazaris and other landowners.[61] In the nineteenth century, the majority of the ulama remained dependent on bazaris' economic power in the urban areas. The interdependent relationships between these two main urban groups constituted Iranian civil society up to modern times.

While the bazaar's economic activity (*kasb-o-kar*) was legitimated by the ulama, the ulama's economic needs were satisfied by the bazaris. These socio-economic interconnections and family ties, which create a very significant interdependency, was the basis of a historic alliance that generated a center of social authority countervailing state authority. The dialectical interconnection of the private sphere of family life and the public sphere of economic life, divinely legitimized, created a secure basis for the continuation and reinforcement of the social authority of the ulama and the bazaris in Iranian civil society.

The Relationship Between the State and the Religious Community

The process of secularization in the West suggests a division of authority between church and state. These two centers of authority presume two realms of conflict, competition, and even cooperation throughout the history of Western Christian countries. Max Weber states that the history of world religions bears witness to compromises between political and religious power:

> It is very rare that the antagonism between political and hierocratic power claims finds a simple solution in the full victory of one side or the other. The history of all churches demonstrates that even the most powerful hierocracy is continuously forced to compromise with the economic and political realities (Weber, 1968, p. 1174).

Pure religious power, according to Weber, is institutionalized in the hierarchical body of a church, which was constructed of cardinals, popes, bishops, priests, and so on. He considers the church a necessary organization for the realization of the religious power of priests. It was also important to separate charisma from the *person* and linkages to the *office*. The church is a bureaucratic organization that defines the roles and places of its members according to their religious competence. Weber tries, unsuccessfully in my view, to generalize the case of the Christian church to Islam. He also claims that there is such a bureaucratic organization even in Islam.[62] This Western duality of centers of distinct authority—in its common understanding—is missing in Islam for two reasons:

1. The lack of a general theological legitimization of the dualism of authority.
2. The lack of a bureaucratic organization such as the European Catholic church.

Many factors such as specific historical events, independent economic properties, and the cultural and religious characteristics of some Western communities led to the appearance of the powerful Christian church as the main organization competing with the state. The church became the realm of the power of God on earth, and the state became the realm of secular affairs. This dualism of authority existed until the beginning of the modern era. But this proposition does not deny the cooperation between the church and state. Hierocracy had to cooperate with the state to secure and reinforce the boundaries of interdependency between church and state.[63] But in contrast, in the main doctrine of the Islamic theory of leadership in Muslim communities, Sunnism, there is no differentiation of authority between sacred religious authority and the mundane state. Leaders of the Muslim communities, *umma*, are caliphs who are both religious and political leaders. Two Islamic systems of state after the Prophet up to the modern era, the Caliphate and the Sultanate, crystallize religio-political leadership in Islam. That is one of the most decisive causes of the lack of a religious bureaucratic body like the Western church which claims legitimate authority. Even according to the Shi'ite theory of state–which *de facto* accepted the political authority of state–there is actually little difference between the political and religious leadership in the Muslim community. The temporary power of states can be accepted as temporary during the great Occultation of the Hidden Imam who is the true political and religious leader in the community. The main difference between the Shi'ite theory of state and the medieval Christian theory was the legitimacy of state power. The Church accepted and cooperated with the state, even in the form of divine authority, while the Shi'ites denied the divine legitimacy of political power and rejected any cooperation with it until 1501. Of course, compromises between the church and state took place based on mutual recognition of each other's interests. The state recognized the power of the church and its activity in society. But here too, the Sunni states of the Muslim world, during a long period of time, refused to recognize the Shi'ites community as a religious group; and therefore Shi'ite ulama could not advance any institution of power. As Weber puts it:

> The church advances its demands toward the political power on the basis of its claims on office charisma. This charisma is used for a radical elevation of its bearer's dignity. For its officials the church secures immunity from secular jurisdiction, exemption from taxation and all other public duties, and protection, through heavy penalties, against any show of disrespect (Weber, 1968, pp. 1164-65).

Because of the lack of a legitimized and recognized office, office charisma could not be advanced. This resulted in institutional demands to political power in medieval Islam. But at the beginning of sixteenth century an epoch-making change was brought about by a Shi'ite dynasty, that of the Safavids, who facilitated the formation of a powerful Shi'ite community in Iran and thereby changed the socio-religious position of the Shi'ite ulama. The Safavids were surrounded by Sunni Ottomans who did not recognize any other political power in the Muslim community other than Sultanate. To create an absolute state in Iran, the Safavids were thus forced to religiously legitimize their political power through claiming adherence to the Shi'ite Imams, and incorporating the Shi'ite ulama in the state machinery. By establishing the office of *sadr*, which was practically the ministry of religion, they attempted to control the ulama and other religious groups and sects. But paradoxically, as a result of the Shi'itization of society and economic independence of the ulama from the state, the power of the ulama increased enormously and during the last decades of the Safavids reign, the last Safavid shah, Shah Sultan Husayn, was completely in the hands of the ulama (Savory, 1980). The post of *mullabashi* (chief mulla) created by Shah Sultan Husayn, superseded in importance that of *sadr* (Algar, 1969, p. 29), and marked the increasing power of ulama and a sign of the ulama's influence on the shah. Hence, the Safavids attempt to create a caesaro-papist state, where 'government treats ecclesiastic affairs simply as a branch of political administration' (Weber, 1968, p. 1162) failed. But the failure to establish a caesaro-papist state did not result in the triumph of its counterpart, the *hierocracy*, because of the lack of a bureaucratic organization such as the European church, with its stable hierarchy and vast economic resources.[64] The lack of 'office charisma' is the main factor underlying the historic dependency of the ulama on either political or economic power. In the Sunni states, the Caliphate and the Sultanate, the ulama were 'natural' allies with the Caliph and Sultan. In Shi'ite Iran, after the reign of the Safavids–which resulted in creation of a powerful body of the Shi'ite ulama and other religious groups–the ulama created a historic alliance with the socio-economic authority, i.e., the bazaar. The social construction of this historic alliance was dependent on several factors of which the most important are:

1. *The theory of gheybat.*
2. *Political instability.*
3. *The lack of sufficient sources of income for the ulama.*

The doctrine of *gheybat* was incompatible with the existence of any sovereign political power other than the reign of the Hidden Imam. During the reign of Safavids, the Shi'ite ulama had to deal with the dilemma of cooperation with the political power. Even if Safavid shahs called themselves vicegerents of the Hidden Imam, it was theologically not permitted for the vicegerent of the Imam to reign on behalf of the Imam, because political reign in the Muslim community was supposed to be the just reign of the Imam himself and not anyone else.

After a long period of political stability under the Safavids the seizure of power by Sunni Nader and confiscation of the ulama's religious endowments, *vaqf*, by the state, they were forced to reinforce their connections with the economic realm of society, i.e. the bazaar, and even to create some kind of office charisma. The ulama, who, under Nader Shah's pressure moved to the *'atabat*[65] and those who stayed in Isfahan, the capital of Safavids Empire, attempted to create Shi'ite regular education and religious centers. The main aim of these religious centers was to create a legitimized and well-defined hierarchical discipline for the ranking of the Shi'ite ulama. The theory of *ijtihad*[66] and *Marja'-e taqlid*[67] were the proper theological instruments used by the Shi'ite ulama for such purposes. The theory of *ijtihad* provided the ulama monopoly over the interpretation of religious laws and legitimized legal norms. In reality the theological term *ijtihad* was transferred to the status of *riyasat*, which was a term used by the Shi'ite ulama to transfer the function of Mujtahids from mere teachers of the *madrasah* (religious school) to powerful figures in the life of urban centers (Amanat, 1988, p. 102). Practising Mujtahids' role as *Marja'-e taqlid* guaranteed, to some extent, a publicly accepted hierarchy among the ulama. But this vague form of hierarchy was never developed as far as office charisma in Weber's sense. Weber says that:

> In one world, the church is bearer and trustee of an office charisma, not a community of personally charismatic individuals, like the sect. In the full sense of the term, churches have arisen only in Islam and Lamaist Buddhism, apart from Christianity; in a more restricted sense - because of the national delimitation (Weber, 1968, p. 1164).

The Shi'ite centers at *'atabat* and within Iran lost a well-defined organization such as a bureaucratic hierarchy. These centers were normally dependent on 'charismatic individuals', the most respectable Mujtahid of such centers who possessed key sources of income as *mutavalli-ye auqaf* (conductors of religious endowments). The ulama's role as *mutavalli-ye auqaf* could not develop into an independent office of religious supremacy because *vaqf* properties were dependent on, and guaranteed by, the state. For instance, many religious endowments that were confiscated by Nader Shah, called *ruqabat-e Naderi*, were returned by Qajars (Amanat, 1988). Other semi-official roles of the ulama such as the office of Imam jom'a (leader of Friday prayer) and jurists were also dependent on state authority. One other important source of the ulama's income, as discussed earlier, was the bazaar. In this case the ulama were dependent on the bazaar's economic power. The ulama's dependency on the state and the bazaar prevented the full development of a sovereign religious authority and the construction of a system of office charisma.[68]

The other theological term used by the ulama to reinforce their influence in society and to create a system of office charisma was *Marja'-e taqlid*. *Marja'-e taqlid* was supposed to be the most learned and respectable Mujtahid whose supremacy was accepted by other Mujtahids and by the Shi'ite community. Such a marja', who was fully accepted by other Mujtahids, was exceptional. Only under certain socio-historical conditions could such charismatic individuals as Shaykh Murtaza Ansari (d.1864), who was considered *Marja'-e taqlid-e kull* (supreme sources of emulation), emerge and gain widespread legitimacy and acceptance as leader of the Shi'ite religious hierarchy. As mentioned earlier, even a powerful religious school, Usulis, in the eighteenth century tried to reinforce the supremacy and social position of the ulama through the creation of a more organized clerical body.[69] But even after the eclipse of the rival Akhbaris, who challenged the authority of Mujtahids, they could hardly overcome the traditional Shi'ite resistance to institutionalization (Amanat, 1988). The ulama did not construct an independent institution of power but, through compromises with the economic center of power, the bazaar, they gained prominent social sources of influence and authority as a counterpart to that of the state. It should be mentioned that since the Safavids establishment and construction of Iranian society in accordance with Shi'ite legal codes and norms, the state had to take into consideration the influence of ulama in civil society and to seek compromises with them. During the final decades of the Safavids, and the long reign of Qajars, the state tried to cooperate with the ulama.

The Ulama's Guardianship of the Divine Order of Society

In the traditional society of Iran, the ulama, using their influential position in civil society, established a system of guardianship of the divine order of society. It was possible partly because of traditional and religious beliefs and values of community, and partly because of institutionalization and popularization of such beliefs. The ulama's position in civil society, which equipped them with a unique social authority, was a decisive factor in the continuation of the traditional order of Iranian society. There were of course several factors that reinforced the traditional institutions of society and prohibited social, political, and economic differentiation of such institutions. But in analyzing a society, cultural and ideological factors that are incorporated in institutions and traditions are of crucial importance, and cannot be reduced to abstract entities distinct from their social contexts. The ulama were a social group participating in reproducing and leading many important institutions that bore the traditional order of society. In the following section, some factors underlying the ulama's role in institutionalization of the divine order of society, particularly the marginalization of political power through creation of an alternative power center resulting from their active participation in the social and economic spheres of society, will be discussed. The discussion that deals with the socio-cultural shaping of social institutions is organized according to the following main features:

1. Doctrinal and ideological factors.
2. Institutional factors.
3. Strong interconnection between the ulama and the bazaar.
4. The historical ambivalence between the religious community and the state until the modern period.
5. State's dependence on the ulama.

1. Since its appearance Islam has been a political religion and has made theologically legitimized claims on the political leadership of Muslim communities. The matter of political power in the Muslim community has always been of great importance and problematic because of the fundamental Islamic doctrine of the unification of religious and political leadership. The development of two main religious branches of Islam, Sunni and Shi'ite, exhibits two different characteristics of political leadership. In the Sunni world, through the political system of the Caliphate and the Sultanate, a strong center of political and religious power was embodied in the political leadership of Caliph and Sultan. The strong power of the Caliph and Sultan depended on their claim to legitimacy based on succession to the Prophet. That is why a sovereign 'office charisma', as a counterpart to the political power, could not be developed. In Shi'ite Iran, Safavids in sixteenth century tried to create a strong state by centralizing political and religious power, and combining these two sources of authority in one, i.e. a theocratic state. Such a state, as the Sunni state, needed a religiously accepted and legitimized theological framework. By claiming adherence to the Shi'ite Imams and vicegerency of the Hidden Imam, a theoretical framework necessary for the creation of a strong state in Shi'ite community was temporarily constructed. Paradoxically, by increasing the power of the Shi'ite ulama, such a legitimation system became untenable. The only true and just political leadership in the Muslim community was the Hidden Imam's, who is the true successor to the Prophet and, as such, infallible. Since the end of the seventeenth century a 'conditional state', dependent on religious authority for its legitimacy, was created. But the relationship between the state and the ulama was not a simple one of state dependency, but based on the mutual dependency of the civil authority of the ulama and the political authority of state. Since 1501 and until the reign of Pahlavis (1925-1979) in Iran, with the exception of the relatively short reign of Nader (1736-1747), there was no sovereign state independent of the civil authority of the ulama.

2. The position of vicegerents of the Hidden Imam and the theological victory of Usulis over the traditional Akhbaris led to the establishment and reinforcement of the ulama's power and the creation of a strong religious network. The ulama were vicegerents of the Hidden Imam and, as such, had the rightful position in leading the community in matters of religion. This enabled them to act as *fuqaha* (Islamic jurisprudents), *mutovalli-ye auqaf* (conductors of religious endowments), *Marja'-e taqlid* (sources of emulation), *aghed* (those who arrange marriage), religious tax collectors, and so forth. The importance of the social duties of the ulama increased their material income and social status. These developments led, to some extent, to the institutional autonomy of the ulama. The increase in the social importance of the ulama also depended on their theological and practical struggle against the traditional school of Akhbaris, who propagated the doctrine that Muslim individuals have the capability to understand matters of religion without needing the ulama as interpreters of God's word. The Usuli movement believed in the necessity of the role of the ulama as *fuqaha* (Islamic jurisprudents). 'The Usuli movement reestablished and greatly enhanced the juridical authority of the Shi'ite hierocracy' (Arjomand, 1984, p. 231). The ulama's institutionalized social duties did not mean that they became religiously institutionalized as an independent and autonomous group with their own institutions. Rather, social and ideological movements increased their role and influence in social institutions instead of purely religious ones.

The lack of a central religious organization led to the individual leadership of socio-religious organizations such as *auqaf*. Religious endowments were divided between various charismatic Mujtahids, who were known as pious and influential in their local communities.[70] Although the income of *auqaf* was used by the ulama to increase their 'autonomy' *vis-à-vis* the state (Arjomand, 1984, p. 231), and some of them even became large landowners in the eighteenth century (Momeni, 1990), the Shi'ite ulama traditionally resisted institutionalization (Amanat, 1988). Institutionalization would, in the case of the Shi'ite ulama, mean a theoretical separation between political and religious authority; i.e. recognition of the state's political supremacy over the whole community. Some theologians, such as Al-Karaki, for instance, who was positively inclined towards political authority, was criticized by others, such as Ibrahim al-Qatifi and by Ahmad Ardabili, both of whom upheld the idea of pious antipathy to political power (Arjomand, 1984, p. 206). The differentiation of attitudes and theological doctrines among the Shi'ite ulama depended, to a great extent, on the lack of a Shi'ite organization that could homogenize Shi'ite theological principles and establish regular pragmatic basis for their relationship to the state.

The religious community of the Shi'ite ulama was divided among different 'charismatic Mujtahids' residing in religious centers of Qum, Isfahan, and *'atabat*. The ulama residing in *'atabat*, which was the territory of Sunni Ottomans, showed a more world-rejecting tendency than their counterparts in the religious centers of Iran (Arjomand, 1984, pp. 202-207). The majority of the ulama residing in Iran had to participate more actively in matters of politics and economy. But, in purely theoretical aspects, the ulama of *'atabat* held a prominent position. For example, the triumph of the Usuli school was, to a certain extent, dependent on theoretical activities of the Shi'ite ulama of *'atabat*, such as Aqa Muhammad Baqir Behbahani (d.1790) and his colleagues because of their effective control over the teaching circles of Najaf, Karbala, and Kazimayn. The interdependency among the Shi'ite ulama led to creation of a theological basis for some kind of consensus to avoid dangerous conflicts among them. The proper theoretical term for this was *niyabat-e 'amm*, general deputy-ship of the Hidden Imam. Shaykh Ja'far Najafi (d.1813) was a prominent Mujtahid who originated the term *niyabat-e 'amm* (general deputy-ship of the Imam) as the collective function of the ulama (Amanat, 1988, p. 103). This was a factor that helped the ulama to create an effective network that could serve them in time of need for collective action. But the individual basis of religious authority in Iran not only led to domination of local communities by the charismatic Mujtahids, but also gave charismatic families a prominent role. For example, for more than half a century, close family ties, often with remote but vital genealogical links to the Majlisis of Isfahan, guaranteed the domination of three families–Behbahanis, Tabatabais, and Najafis–over the clerical establishment (Amanat, 1988, p. 104). Thus, the lack of 'office charisma' was connected to the appearance of charismatic individuals who, through interconnections and family ties, could establish a type of consensus and leadership hierarchy among the Shi'ite ulama.

The Shi'ite ulama's resistance to institutionalization as a Western church organization did not mean that they were against all forms of institutionalization. They compensated for the lack of a central organization by establishing and institutionalizing their position of leadership in civil society. The ulama's connection to the bazaar was institutionalized by a system of religious tax collecting, by the establishment and control of Islamic economic rules and features, through intermarriage and family ties between the ulama and the bazaris, through holding religious mournings, ceremonies, and religious rites in bazaars and in *takyehs* (places for theatrical playing of tragedy of martyrdom of the Third Imam, Husayn, in Karbala), which were located close to bazaars. The ulama's connection to the non-wealthy urban people was institutionalized in Friday prayers, religious institutions of marriage and divorce, jurisprudence, private and public *roudakhani* (the recitation of martyrdom of the Imams, particularly that of the Third Imam, Husayn), funeral rites and ceremonies, by helping the poor through religious taxes, and so forth.

3. The theory of gheybat and political instability forced the ulama to seek alliance with other parts of civil society and, in particular, with the bazaar. The theory of *gheybat* illegitimated any political authority in the Muslim community as 'just'. The only just and rightful political leaders for the community are those who are infallible. Infallibility is not everyone's quality but that of the Prophet's and his family, *ahl-e beyt*, who are twelve Shi'ite Imams in rank. According to Shi'ite political theory, discussed earlier, the Imams, after Ali, were eleven of his descendants, the true successors to the Prophet and leaders of the community. Consequently, the Twelfth Imam who is occulted is the true leader of the community. The Occultation of the Imam means, in a certain sense, the disappearance of the true political leadership. The political authority, in the most favorable interpretation of the Occultation of the Imam, can be accepted as temporary protector of a community awaiting its true political leader. Hence, the most prominent ulama are vicegerents of the Hidden Imam in the matter of religious commitments of Muslims. Consequently, the ulama were supposed to avoid dealing with the 'dirty affairs of politics'. But this did not mean that they were to avoid the affairs of community leadership.

Both religiously and practically, the ulama constructed and institutionalized a system of civil leadership that equipped them with a countervailing power against the state. Their close connections to the bazaar and urban people were the main basis of their civil authority, which made them the 'natural leaders' of the people. The ulama's connection to the bazaar also reinforced certain changes in the traditional political system of Shi'ite Iran. Nader Shah's almost secular and pragmatist political system, and the Qajars Westernization policy were other parameters in reinforcing the ulama's 'civil policy'.

4. The core of Iranian civil society was based on the strong interconnection between the ulama and the bazaar. Even in pre-Islamic Iran there existed a close connection between religious foundations and bazaar (Kheirabadi, 1991). After the *Islamicization* of Iranian society, some pre-Islamic religious institutions such as *Atashkadehs* (Zoroastrian religious places), which were located close to the bazaars, were transformed into congregational mosques. The bazaar was the heart of all socio-economic activities in the main cities of Iran. In medieval Persia, industry and commerce were not rigidly separated from each other and the bazaris who were called 'men of affairs, included those engaged in both industry and commerce (Lambton, 1988, p. 328). Relationships and connections between the 'men of affairs' and two other centers of authority, namely the ulama and the state, changed during the Shi'ite period of Iran after 1501. In medieval Persia, the ulama were generally Sunnis and they had strong bonds with both the state and the bazaar. The differentiation of the centers of religious and political authority in Iran took place in the last decades of the Safavids' period. Merchants in the medieval Persia played a more active and direct role in the political and socio-economic life of the people. For example, Abu Mansur b. Yusuf (d. 1067), a rich Hanbali merchant of Baghdad, played a prominent part in commercial affairs and in the life of the city. He was close to the caliph and acted as a mediator between him and Toghril Beg in the negotiations for the marriage of the latter to the caliph's daughter (Lambton, 1981, p. 329). The relationship between patrimonial state bureaucracy and large-scale traders is also important to mention. In some cases the merchants could rise to the *vazirate* (ministry). For example, Nizam al-Din Muhammad b. Sulaiman Kashghari, who became *vazir* to Sanjar in 1122, belonged to a rich merchant family of Turkistan (Lambton, 1988, p. 304).

The pre-Shi'ite period of the relationship between the ulama and the bazaar can be categorized in two groups. The first group consisted of family ties and traditional interconnections between wealthy merchants and high-ranking ulama. This group also had close connections with the state. The second group consisted of craftsmen and artisans, who were not as wealthy as the merchants, and who had relations with the low ranking ulama. At the end of the pre-Shi'ite period of Iran, wealthy merchants lost their socio-economic importance, because of the change and insecurity of traditional trade roads and the decline of trade overall.

During the reign of the Safavids and the Shi'itization of Iranian society, many high-ranking ulama who were Sunnis left Iran for the territory of the Ottomans. Through the conversion of many low ranking-and even some high-ranking-ulama to Shi'ism, and through the movement of many Shi'ite ulama from the territory of the Ottomans to Iran, a powerful Shi'ite group of ulama was established. As mentioned earlier, the Safavids tried to incorporate the Shi'ite ulama into the state bureaucracy through creation of the religious offices of *sadr* and *Shaykh al-Islam*. But, using state support, the ulama established and reinforced influential interconnections with the bazaar and other urban groups. Interconnections between the ulama and the bazaris were not only based on socio-religious supports of the ulama, but also on the strong family ties between these two groups, since many ulama came from bazari families. Family ties through intermarriage reinforced the interconnections. The major cause behind the mutual interest of such interconnection were the bazaris' need of legitimization in Muslim community and the ulama's need of economic and social support from the bazaris. This very strong and stable interconnection led to the weakening of the connections between the state and the bazaar and resulted in the appearance of the ulama as intermediator between state and the bazaris. The socio-cultural alliance between the ulama and the bazaris made up the core of civil society in Iran and manifested its stability and continuity during the two main revolutions of the twentieth century.

5. *The state never freed itself from the religious boundaries of the ulama and their institutions and did not develop a sovereign bureaucracy.* The ulama's cooperation with the state was intended to employ political means for exerting some control over the political authority of the monarch and state on one side, and influence and control over civil society on the other. But the ulama resisted being incorporated into state machinery. The ulama and other religious groups, atavistic in outlook, refused to participate in the embryonic bureaucratic institutions (Sheikholeslami, 1978). Their

general acceptance of the worldly rulers, however, was dependent on the three main factors:

1. *The ulama's pragmatic need for security and protection against rival groups and Sunni states.*
2. *The lack of organizational unity among the ulama.*
3. *The lack of theological legitimization of and justification for an independent Shi'ite state.*

The ulama considered themselves both religious and political leaders of the community awaiting its real leader, the Hidden Imam. One of the most important aspects of the ulama's socio-political power is their limited right to proclaim *jihad* intended to mobilize the people of Iran against foreign intervention. During the first Perso-Russian War (1810-1813), the ulama expressed their ideas about the true leadership in the Muslim community of Iran. The most eminent Mujtahid of the time, Shaykh Ja'far Kashif al-Ghita' (d.1812) exhibited the source of authority in the Muslim community through declaring a war against Russians incumbents. Kashfi's declaration shows clearly the Shi'ite ulama's attitude to the state. He wrote: 'if I be a man of *ijtihad* and worthy of the vicegerency of the Imam, peace be upon Him, I give permission to the ruler', Fath Ali Shah, to conduct the *jihad* against the Russians (Arjomand, 1984, pp. 224-25). As we see, the sources of divine authority of the Shaykh, which is uttered in the phrase 'I give permission to the ruler', characterize the ulama's authority in society and their attitudes to political power. Political actions of kings and states were to be legitimized and should take into consideration the authority of the ulama. The ulama's authority in relation to the state was based on institutionalization of their traditional relationships with the bazaar and with urban social groups, more than on 'office charisma' only.

Almost all the states of Iran had tribal roots with local boundaries that made them known and accepted in local communities. The state's lack of state-wide support, in particular in the urban areas, forced them to seek support from the ulama. The ulama were a country-wide group with strong support among the bazaris, urban people, peasants, and even some rival tribes. They provided the state with some legitimization among the people. But the ulama did not support the state without compensation. They received, in return, economic support through religious taxes, endowments and so forth, and used the state's power against rival groups such as the Akhbaris and *Sufis*.

Thus, the state/ulama relationship and power balance in Iran was based on socio-cultural and economic conditions grounded in institutionalized social practices different, in many aspects, from those in the West. As mentioned earlier, the powerful and independent organization of the church was absent in Iran, and the ulama had developed other modes of institutions and authority. Max Weber presents four features that characterize the emergence of the powerful and independent Church as follows:

> 1) the rise of a professional priesthood removed from the 'world' with salaries, promotions, professional duties, and a distinctive way of life; 2) claims to universal domination; that means, hierocracy must at least have overcome household, sib and tribal ties, /.../; 3) dogma and rites (Kultus) must have been rationalized, into objects of a systematic education, as distinct from mere training in technical skills; 4) all of these features must occur in some kind of compulsory organization. /.../ In one word, the church is the bearer and trustee of an office charisma, not a community of personally charismatic individuals, like the sect. (Weber, 1968, p. 1167)

The Church is the realm of 'the state of God' which is imbedded in a professional organization. In contrast to the Shi'ite theory of state, the independent organization of the Church, which is accepted by the state, means also accepting the 'state of the Empire'. It means consequently recognition of the state by the Church. But, as discussed earlier, Weber's reasoning about hierocracy and the organization of the Church resulted in the conclusion that: 'In the full sense of the term, churches have arisen only in Islam and Lamaist Buddhism, apart from Christianity' (Weber, 1968, p. 1167). This is not historically correct, at least in the case of Iran. This is in large part because of the ulama's resistance to institutionalization as an independent organization,[71] in a certain sense limiting their sphere of influence, in another sense expanding its scope and the potential for all-encompassing claims. In Islam, there is no organization comparable to the Christian church. Religio-professional education does not take place in 'church seminaries' (the mosques), but *hozehs* which were dominated by a few well known Mujtahids. A well-defined Islamic hierarchical priesthood, a single independent organization separate from the state, never existed and is actually incompatible with the theory of leadership in the community. The most important characteristic of the state in traditional Western society was its 'inner worldly' sources of its power based on the feudal division of property among kings, lords, and vassals. Consequently, in contrast to the

Shi'ite Iran, the state could organize its own army with the help of lords and vassals and without the Church. The State was religiously legitimated as an independent organization without many direct religious commitments.

In the following table, the sources of authority and legitimacy of the ulama and the state in Iran are characterized:

Table 2.1 The sources of power and legitimization of the state and the ulama in traditional Iran

INSTITUTION	POWER	LEGITIMACY
ULAMA *Niyabat-e Imam auqaf*, jurisprudence, *Imamat-e jom'a*, *raudahkhani*, taxation, religious mournings.	Mainly based on their alliance with the bazaar and urban people.	Shi'ite theory of state in the Muslim community; *Imamat, ijtihad,* and the theory of *gheybat*.
STATE patrimonial bureaucracy, police, taxation, foreign policy.	Based on tribal, communal and religious boundaries.	Based on the doctrine of protector of 'dar al-Islam'; and pre-Islamic notion of the Shadow of God.

As mentioned earlier, the authority of the ulama was based mainly on their alliances with the economic sphere of society, the bazaar, and their relationship to the urban populations. Because of the lack of a monolithic, hierarchical, Shi'ite organization with institutionalized division of roles and duties, the ulama had to make alliances with the two other sources of authority, the bazaar and the state. The bazaar provided much of the economic support, and the state provided military aid against rival religious groups and sects. In return the ulama gave the bazaris religious legitimacy and status, and they supported the state as 'temporarily legitimate' and necessary. But the real right of leadership in the community was preserved for the Hidden Imam and his vicegerents, the ulama. This was always a basis for potential challenge. Recognition of the political powers–if such recognition existed–by the Shi'ite ulama was always *temporary* and due to the pragmatic demands of their situation. When Shaykh Ahmad Ardabili (d. 1585) reminded the Great King of Safavids, Shah Abbas (1581-1629), that he was ruling over a 'borrowed kingdom' (*mulk-i ariya*) (Algar, 1969, p. 22), he, as the most accepted Mujtahid of the time, expressed the Shi'ite ulama's attitude toward the state.[72] The theory of *gheybat* (Occultation of the Hidden Imam) and the worldly vicegerency of the Imam created a powerful group of the Shi'ite ulama who claimed actual leadership in the community.

The power of states in Iran was typically based on tribal groups. Almost all the states before Pahlavis (1925-1979) had tribal roots and came to power through the support of tribal warriors.[73] The ulama's statewide network provided a means of control over the whole country. The tribal roots of the dynasties who ruled Iran since the Safavids made the arena of competition for political power a field of tribal struggles for seizing political power. This remarkable situation, and the lack of feudal division of property and authority, forced the Iranian states to seek cooperation with the social and urban authority of the ulama. The state's dependence on the ulama was based on three important functions of the ulama that, in turn, facilitated the ulama's influence over the state:

1. *Granting of legitimacy.*
2. *Mobilization of people for wars.*
3. *Iinfluence in the bazaar.*

The states had to be recognized by religious leaders as legitimate through reading the king's name in the prayer *khutbas*.[74] This was the sign of that religious groups accepted political leader. Again, it was difficult for Iranian states to war against other countries because of the lack of a tradition of vassals providing soldiers to the kings. The ulama was the main group who could, through the religious tradition of *jihad,* declare holy war against other countries, mobilize the community, and build up an army.[75] The third pillar of state dependence on the ulama was the economic dependence of the state on the bazaar.[76] In order to borrow money, pursue economic interests, and even conduct their own economic activities, the state's authorities were dependent on the bazaar. And, as mentioned earlier, the ulama and the bazaris made up the most stable alliance in Iran. Therefore, the state had to maintain a good relationship with the ulama to make the connection to the bazaar possible. Thus, the ulama was a very important group in the traditional civil society of Iran, and, together with the socio-economic power of the bazaars, made up the core of the traditional order of society.

In sum, civil society in Iran, up to the beginning of the twentieth century modernization/Westernization project, was an entity consisting of two main influential groups, bazaris and clerics. As opposed to the 'private sphere' of the courts, the ulama lived among the people in city quarters and bazaars. They were present in the 'public sphere' of people's life. Instead of the expression of the 'burgerlichen Gesellschaft' which initially took place in 'the coffee-houses', 'les salons', and 'die Tischgesellschaften' of the West (Habermas, 1984, p. 42-78), the expression of socio-religious opposition of the ulama against the Iranian state took place in civil society's public arenas such as mosques, *madrasahs*, public baths, *manbars* (pulpits), and bazaars, it was practised through religious ceremonies, theatrical rituals (*ta'ziyeh*), mournings of Imams, and so forth. The two main groups in the traditional civil society of Iran, the ulama and the bazaris, through socio-economic and cultural bonds with each other and with other groups, enjoyed a social authority that came to play a crucial role in the two main revolutions of twentieth century Iran. The civil authority of these two groups rested on a traditional social structure which was divinely legitimized. Any attempt by the *de facto* accepted state to increase its power and sovereignty could ultimately be challenged by the civil authority as a heretic intervention in the divine universalistic order of society and therefore illegitimate. In the next chapter the first confrontation of these two authorities, which leads to the Constitutional Revolution of Iran 1905-1909, will be discussed.

3 Iran on the Eve of the Constitutional Revolution

After the fall of the Safavids in 1722, and the seizure of power by the Qajars in 1796, two main dynasties ruled in Iran: Afshars (1726-1747), who were Sunnis, and Zands (1750-1779) who were Shi'ites. The founder of the Zands reign, Karim Khan, never called himself Shah (king), but *vakil* (regent), as demonstration of his Shi'ite belief and connection to the Safavids.[77] The reign of Nader Shah over a Sunni state in Iran is of some interest. Nader Shah began a serious struggle with the Shi'ite ulama through confiscating *vaqf* properties, changing the Safavid state apparatus, and abolishing many Shi'ites posts such as *sadr* and *sheik al-Islam*. He also introduced many restrictions on the ulama's jurisprudent and religious foundations. Many ulama moved to the Shi'ite territory of Iraq, which was controlled by the Ottomans. Ironically, Nader Shah's political plans to create a powerful state without any Shi'ite influence, helped the ulama solve the dilemma of participation in the illegitimate state apparatus and reinforced their position in civil society. In addition, using economic and administrative independence from the state, the Shi'ite ulama could develop their theology and political theory. All in all, Nader Shah did not succeed in eliminating the influence of Shi'ism in society and, on the contrary, tried gradually to incorporate and to adapt Shi'ism into the main body of Islam. He failed in his attempts, and was assassinated in 1747. Nader Shah lost his 'secular' state and in 1779, Agha Muhammad Khan, who belonged to the Turkish tribe Qajar, founded the Qajar dynasty in Iran.

The Constitutional Revolution of Iran took place more than one hundred years after the establishment of the reign of the Qajar dynasty. The reign of the Qajars can theoretically be divided in two periods, namely the attempt to reconstruct theocratic power, and the attempts at modernization. In the following chapter, these two socio-political characteristics of the Qajars will be presented.

The Reconstruction of Theocratic Power

The Qajars were one of the seven Turkish tribes that had helped and supported the rise of Shah Ismai'il I, the first Safavid ruler (Wilber, 1981). The Qajars, using the cultural capital created by helping the Safavids to power, tried to legitimate themselves as the faithful Shi'ite dynasty and the 'shadow of God on the earth'. They tried, through social and symbolic actions, to restore the status of the Shi'ite ulama to the state–which was damaged by the reign of Sunni Afshars. Agha Muhammad Khan, who crowned himself shah in 1785 as a symbolic action and green light to the Shi'ite ulama, changed the crown of Nader Shah, with its four plumes, symbolic of Afghanistan, India, Turkistan, and Iran. He used other Shi'ite symbols, such as girding the Safavids sword, reducing court etiquette, refusing to wear the jeweled crown, strictly prohibiting wine-drinking, constructing new mosques, and reparation of the Shi'ite holy shrines, both in Iran and Iraq. Although the tribal basis of Agha Muhammad Khan was an obstacle to the ulama's greater political influence, they were pleased with Agha Muhammad Khan's attempt to create a religious basis for his political legitimization. Many of the ulama who resided in the Shi'ite cities of Najaf and Kazemeyn in Iraq began to return to Iran, 'and the religious classes in the country had, however, again become numerous'.[78]

The main political project for the creation of a religiously legitimate state began with the reign of the second of the Qajars, Fath Ali Shah (1797-1834). His first and main political project was to legitimize his state by bridging the chasm between state and the ulama. He ordered the building of new mosques and other religious places, and the embellishment of shrines. The Shi'ite ulama were encouraged to settle in Tehran, the capital, to be near the Shah, so that he could visit frequently (Algar, 1969, p. 44). The shrine of the Eighth Shi'ite Imam, Reza, in Mashad, and Fatimah, in Qum, were repaired and decorated with gold. Fatimah's tomb received a new golden grill, and the tomb of Imam Reza a golden door. Two of the most important works of Fath Ali Shah, were exempting the inhabitants of the holy city Qum from taxation, and building a large religious center, *Madrasah-ye Faydiya*, which came to play a crucial role as one of the most influential centers of the ulama's power. 'Another method whereby the Shah might hope to gain the sympathy of the ulama, or even to influence them, was the regular allotting of sums of money among them and granting other material signs of goodwill' (Arjomand, 1984, p. 49). *Auqaf*'s property of the ulama drastically increased, and, thereby, the ulama regained their lost prominent place behind the state. Some influential ulama such as Mirza Abu'l-Qasim Qumi (d.1817), set forth the principal of legitimacy of temporal rule of Qajar shahs, in response to the state's favoritism. As a new theological legitimization of shah's power, he announced that God has made the shah his lieutenant on earth for the preservation of order and the ulama for the protection of religion (Arjomand, 1984, p. 223). Finally, some other Shi'ite theologian and prominent ulama such as Shaykh Ja'far, the Kashif al-Ghita' (d.1812) and Sayyed Ja'far Kashfi (d.1850) legitimated the mutual authority of the ulama and the Qajar rulers through a division of the Hidden Imam's political and religious leadership of the community between state and ulama (Arjomand, 1984, p. 229). Fath Ali Shah, who through this political project reinforced the ulama's influence, could not act independently of the ulama and had to consider their will and attitudes in the affairs of state. He accepted the leadership of the ulama in religious matters and took their social authority into account. For instance, one of the prominent ulama, Mirza-ye Qumi, was addressed by the monarch as 'the refuge (marja') of the East and the West, and the Mujtahid of the age' (Amanat, 1988, p. 105). Using the economic and political support of the state, the ulama succeeded in reinforcing their influence in civil society of Iran. They became a link between the bazaar and the state, they organized and exercised jurisprudence, they regained and organized religious endowment; and–not less important–they built religious theaters, *takyehs*, for passion plays on the martyrdom of Husayn,[79] *ta'ziyeh*, and the tragedy of Karbala. Even their connections with some tribes that had military importance improved.[80] In many cases, their *fatvas* were more important than the shahs' decrees. The social power of the ulama was so strong that, during the reign of Fath Ali Shah, they could organize the urban population and, against the Shah's will, revolt against the governors. Therefore, in many conflicts between the ulama and local governors, the Shah was forced to take the side of the ulama and punish or depose the governors. In many of these conflicts, the ulama stayed behind the people and supported them against the oppressive governors. The social power and popularity of the ulama forced the Shah to show more public respect for them. He used to receive prominent ulama at the royal court and visit them in Isfahan, which, since the time of the Safavids, was the most important religious center of Iran.

    The reign of Fath Ali Shah is mainly known for his efforts to restore state power with the help of the ulama. But that is not the whole truth. During his reign, the first attempts at modernizing Iran were initiated. The introduction of modernization projects did not initially result from socio-cultural and economic changes, but from connections with the West. The state itself was the initiating agent of some modern changes in the traditional machinery of the state. But modernization of the state without attendant socio-cultural and economic changes that could eliminate traditional groups' resistance to change–especially the court and the ulama–was destined to fall.

The First Period of Reforms

As already mentioned, during the reign of the second Qajar king, Fath Ali Shah, religious legitimacy of the temporal rule of the shah was reconstructed. The Safavid's legitimized power as vicegerent of the Hidden Imam was changed by the Shi'ite ulama, such as Mirza Abal-Qasim Qumi, to 'the shadow of God upon earth'. Qajars' legitimacy based on the theory of 'shadow of God' instead of vicegerency of the Hidden Imam, released them from the dilemma of being infallible which was claimed by Safavids vicegerents and kings. Through this theory, they could secure political authority and accept the social authority of the ulama as a complementary part of state authority. This means that the social authority of the ulama was legitimized by the term vicegerency of the Hidden Imam, and by the political power of Qajars as shadow of God. Mirza Abal-Qasim Qumi, in his interpretation of the term 'shadow of God', states that the actions of the king are not necessitated by divine decree. He is not absolved from performing his ethical duties by virtue of kingship, and will be punished by God for all evildoing. Finally, he stresses the interdependence of kingship and religion; kings were needed for the preservation of order, the ulama for the protection of religion (Arjomand, 1984, p. 223). This interpretation of the role of the state freed the state from some religious boundaries and made it possible for the state to introduce some 'non-religious' actions intended to reinforce its authority and modernize its traditional apparatus. One of the most important factors in the relationship between the state and the ulama was the balance of power. Even if cooperation between the political and religious power was the main characteristic of the Qajars period, the balance of power was crucial for such cooperation. As Weber puts it: 'As a rule, a compromise is concluded between the other-worldly and the this-worldly powers; this is indeed in their mutual interest' (Weber, 1968, p. 1175). But this cooperation is conditioned by the arrangement of power relationships between the state and the ulama. Weber emphasized this reality by saying:

Whether an individual compromise between political and hierocratic power tends more toward caesaro-papism or hierocracy depends of course upon the power constellation of the status groups concerned (Weber, 1968, p. 1174).

The constellation of power between the state and the ulama began to change through some reforms initiated by the state with an intent to reinforce its power. These reforms were inspired by Western or Ottoman models of state apparatus, and, therefore, used to be called Westernization/modernization efforts. The main characteristic of the reforms is that they were normally brought about by the state but, paradoxically, did not include the state itself. The traditional apparatus of state–including its primitive bureaucracy– remained untouched during the long reign of Qajars.

Abbas Mirza and the 'New Army'

The first of such reforms was initiated by Abbas Mirza (d.1833), heir apparent of Fath Ali Shah and governor of Tabriz. Abbas Mirza discovered during the first Perso-Russian war that traditional tribal strategies were not efficacious against the mobile artillery. He was influenced by a model of 'New Order' introduced in the Ottoman Empire by Sultan Selim III. As governor of Tabriz, he began to recruit a number of permanent troops who received fixed and regular pay and wore uniforms. They were trained according to contemporary European models and equipped with modern weapons such as rifle and canon. By regular training and hard discipline, he tried to create a professional armed force that could be a model for the Iranian army. This new model of armed forces, which had a core of six thousand men, was called *Nezam-e jadid*, the 'New Army'.[81] 'To supply the new army, Abbas Mirza established in Tabriz a cannon factory, a musket plant, and a translation office for military and engineering manuals' (Abrahamian, 1982, p. 52). He sent some students to London, workers to Russia, and established the first printing press in Tabriz (Eqbal, 1951, p. 292). He also initiated some bureaucratic reforms such as cutting court salaries and pensions, and reforming the payment tradition of bureaucrats' salary. To support national manufacturers, merchants, and other bazaris, Abbas Mirza raised protective tariffs and placed restrictions on foreign commodities.

Abbas Mirza's reforms influenced three main components of Iranian society: trade, the court, and the army. The protective policy of trade limited the important English and Russian trade with Iran and prompted their hostility and protests. Ellis, the commercial attaché from England, in his report to his colleague Palmerston, called the reforms 'dogma' and against the principle of free trade (Issawi, 1971, p. 78). To force the Persians to change their protective policy and renew negotiations on a Commercial Treaty with England, he suggested threatening the Persian government: 'I have little doubt that a serious demonstration of displeasure on the part of the British government will force the shah to abandon his commercial dogma' (Issawi, 1971, p. 7 9). The enmity of Russians was obvious in 1817, when through their ambassador Yermelov, they proposed Muhammad Ali Mirza as a more pliable candidate than Abbas Mirza for the succession of the Shah (Hazhir, 1935). The other powerful opposition to Abbas Mirza's reforms was the court. Restrictions against their economic advantages evoked the hostility of princes and many courtiers against the reforms, and prepared a suitable opportunity for both foreign and domestic rival groups to block the reforms.

Abbas Mirza's reform policy, as long as it was intended to reinforce the state's power in his theologically accepted policy, i.e. as protector of the Shi'ite community of Iran against foreigners, caused no clerical opposition. He had full clerical support for his reforms. Opposition to the reform of the army initiated in the hostility of the brother of Abbas Mirza, Muhammad Ali Mirza (Algar, 1969, p. 76). He, who was a rival to Mirza as heir apparent of the Shah, used the ulama's traditional opposition to any reform that could influence the balance of power between the state and the ulama to illegitimate the reform of army. Abbas Mirza, on the other side, would legitimate *Nezam-e jadid* through religious support gained by returning to *Qur'an* and *Hadith*. He used some Our'anic verses, among them that recorded by Reza Quli Khan in his discussion of the *Nezam-e jadid*, to defend his reforms and himself against accusations of unbelief. He presented the *Nezam-e jadid* as being not merely compatible with the Shari'a, but deriving in fact from the forgotten and neglected practice of the Prophet himself (Algar, 1969, p. 5 3).

Thus, the ulama had no objections to Abbas Mirza's reform policy. The conflict between Abbas Mirza and the ulama was about the ulama's role in the two Perso-Russian wars. Although Abbas Mirza wanted clerical support for his reforms, he was supportive of the ulama's engagement in matters of government. In the First Perso-Russian war, it was Fath Ali Shah who wanted to gain the ulama's support for declaration of *jihad* against Russians and not Abbas Mirza. After the surrender of Tabriz to the Russians, he ordered Qaim Maqam to cease all association with the ulama to 'shake himself free of their dust', and instead to cultivate the company of capable men of affairs (Algar, 1969, p. 80). But even in the Second Perso-Russian war he had to accept the social leadership of the ulama, and in accordance with their declaration of *jihad*, he participated in a catastrophic war which ended disastrously with the humiliating Treaty of Turkamanchay. Defeat in the second war meant a reverse for Abbas Mirza'a reform policy, and it began to decline due to declining importance and increasing opposition. Although the ulama had not always succeeded in declaring *jihad*, for instance the declaration of *jihad* in 1850s failed but by declaring successful *jihad* in the two wars against the Russians, the ulama reinforced their authority as 'civil leaders' and even increased it to the level of leaders of the whole nation. This first period of serious reforms showed that, as long as the reforms did not influence the traditional structure of civil society of Iran–and the civil leadership of the ulama–the ulama accepted them.

The Second Period of Reforms

The Ministry of Mirza Taqi Khan 'Amir Kabir' (1848-1851)

After the death of Abbas Mirza, the reforms faced a period of quiescence under the ministry of a Sufi follower, Haj Mirza Aqasi (1836-1848). During the ministry of Aqasi under the reign of Muhammad Shah, the traditional socio-cultural structure of the society was unchanged. Haj Mirza Aqasi, in accordance with his Sufi faith, was satisfied with the traditional institutions of society and did not attempt any reform. After the death of Muhammad Shah in 1848, Aqasi, too, lost his influence and was finally forced to take secret refuge from other rival groups in the shrine of Abd al-Azim in Tehran. The death of Muhammad Shah and the passivity of Mirza Aqasi resulted in rebellions in the major cities of Iran such as Shiraz, Mashad, Isfahan, and Tabriz. In many of these rebellions, the ulama had a leading position against the local governors. Elsewhere, the ulama participated enthusiastically in the promotion of disorder (Algar, 1969, p. 125). The social power of the ulama was a factor Amir Kabir tried to reduce in favor of asserting the power of the state wherever possible. In the spring of 1848 the heir apparent of Muhammad Shah, Nasir al-Din, with the great help of Mirza Taqi Khan, known as Amir Kabir, seized political power and appointed Amir Kabir as the chief of ministry of Iran. When Amir Kabir began his ministry the state was very weakened because of the reign of Aqasi and Muhammad Shah.

Rebellions in the major cities, the revolt of Husayn Khan Salar in Khorasan and, in northern Iran, the movement of Babiyeh, rivalry groups claiming kingship and ministry, dissolution of state bureaucracy and army, and finally economic bankruptcy: these were the main problems Amir had to solve.

The immediate effort of Amir was devoted to creating a strong state that could bring order to the entire territory of Iran and create the first prerequisite for other social and economic reforms. He succeeded in defeating the rebellions in the cities and among the tribes and began to introduce some crucial reforms. Amir's reforms can be characterized in three categories: 1) political reforms; 2) economic reforms; and 3) social reforms.

Political Reforms

One of Amir's first actions towards the concentration of the appropriate means for reinforcing state authority was the reorganization of the army. When Amir Kabir became chief minister of Nasir al-Din Shah and moved from Tabriz to Tehran, the military forces, who officially should be 4000, were not more than 300 (Eqbal, 1951, p. 309). Amir Kabir, who was the chief of the army and during the reign of Abbas Mirza in Tabriz had been trained in military skills, revitalized the military reforms of Abbas Mirza. With the help of several European countries, the regular army with regular salaries was reconstructed and increased. The revitalized army was a decisive means to defeat rebellions and reinforce state authority. To make the army independent of the West, Amir Kabir sent some skilled Iranian workers to Europe to learn the new technology of weapons production. He established some weapons industries that produced rifles and canons for the army. Amir Kabir had no pressure to religiously legitimize the reforms of the army because of existing tradition of Abbas Mirza.

Other political reforms were intended to reorganize the bureaucratic apparatus. The main characteristic of the political system of Persia was based on family ties. Power was concentrated in the hands of the royal family and some other close-connected families who stayed loyal to the monarch. The governance of the provinces belonged to the royal or connected families. Such governance was by no means a kind of decentralization of power, rather an extension of the monarch's power. Amir's intentions to reform the patrimonial bureaucratic apparatus was equivalent to changing the traditional boundaries between the monarch, his family, and other loyalist families. The bureaucratic system was to serve the monarch and his family. The Qajar bureaucracy during Nasir al-Sin Shah's reign fulfilled the most important criteria in the Weberian model of a primitive bureaucracy (Sheikholeslami, 1978, p. 200). To change the patrimonial characteristic of Persian bureaucracy 'where the bureaucrats operate as household servants whose duties and responsibilities change according to their master's desires' (Sheikholeslami, 1978, p. 201-02), Amir had to change several tyrannical governors who were directly connected to the royal and loyal families. Amir changed several provincial governors, such as the governors of Natanz, Yazd, Isfahan, and Tabriz. He then ordered the elimination of all 'useless' and 'meaningless' words used by bureaucrats in their correspondence with the state and the royal families. In addresses to himself, he ordered the use of the word 'sir' (Eqbal; 1951, p. 308). The lack of a regular and secure system of income for the bureaucrats increased the incidence of robbery. He stopped the illegal income of bureaucrats and robbery through reforming the salary system for all state officials and introducing the regular bureaucratic salaries related to different duties. To finance his bureaucratic reforms, he cut some of the high income of the members of the royal family and some ulama who were paid from the state budget. He regulated the taxes and created a new taxation system intended to increase the income of the state and decrease the role of the ulama in collecting taxes.

Amir Kabir's main intention of the reforms was to reinforce state authority and promote its position of effective control over the political, economic, and social activities of domestic and foreign centers of power. One of the most important areas of the challenge of power for the state was the judiciary. The judicial system was a central arena of conflict between the state's intention to monopolize power and the ulama's control of jurisprudence through their socio-religious power. Aware of the importance of jurisprudence for increasing the power of state and reducing the influence of the ulama, Amir began to challenge the extension of the *shar'* courts, which were controlled by the ulama, in favor of *u'rf* (custom) courts, which were controlled by the state organ *Divankhaneh*. There can be little doubt that this was intended to break clerical power, or at least to reduce it to a point where it was no longer able to challenge the state (Algar, 1969, p. 129). He directly challenged the power of the ulama in the matter of jurisprudence. He exerted some control over the *shar'* courts and the *qadis*. For example, the Imam jom'a of Tehran was deprived of his judicial functions for suspected dishonesty, and Mirza Ali Asghar was expelled from Tabriz because Amir did not trust his judgment (Algar, 1969, p. 132). For a time he even sought to supersede the *shar'* courts of the capital by sitting in judgment himself on

72 *Revolutionary Iran*

cases brought before him (Algar, 1969, p. 131). In order to limit the influence of the ulama, he ordered that cases involving religious minorities be brought to the *Divankhaneh* in Tehran (Algar, 1969, p. 131). During the short reign of Amir Kabir (three years and three months), *Divankhaneh* became more important than the *shar'* courts. All judicial cases were to be brought in the first instance to the *Divankhaneh*. If some cases were considered purely religious, then they could be passed on to the *shar'* courts.

Economic Reforms

Amir believed that the policy of free trade would help only the European companies and in the long run destroy the domestic economy. He thus supported a protective policy in trade. In addition to introducing an effective *tariff* system for supporting Persian merchants, he encouraged the establishment and development of national industries. At the time of the reign of Amir, Iran had three main trading partners: the Ottomans, Russians and the English. An economic balance existed in the trade with the Ottoman Empire and Russia but not with England. Iran imported increasing quantities of industrial commodities from England, but exported only a small amount of wool to it. To protect national products, Amir introduced taxes and tariffs on foreign imported commodities in order to reduce imports. Such a policy supported increasing domestic production. Amir was well aware of the importance of new technology for the development and wellbeing of Iran. Many industries were imported and established through the direct support of Amir. Such industries, which helped to begin a new era in Iran, were:

- *Two sugar factories in the Ark square of Sari.*
- *Glass factories in Tehran, Qum, and Isfahan; and china factories in Tehran and Qum.*
- *Paper factory in Tehran which produced high quality papers known as Amir papers.*
- *Textile factories in Tehran and Kashan* (Adamiyyat, 1944, pp. 246-47).

In order to learn the use of the new technology of the West, Amir sent skilled Iranian workers to Europe. On returning to Iran, they founded many factories and even industries such as steel.

Amir, who wanted to increase the income of the state for the implementation of state projects, reformed the taxation system of Iran. There were two main taxes collected from merchants engaged in trade between Iranian cities, namely 'rahdari' (road tax) and 'darvazebani' (gate tax). To encourage exports, the merchants engaging in foreign trade were exempted from paying *rahdari* and *darvazebani* and had to pay only a one time tariff of 4 percent at the borders.

> /.../ this had opened the way of abusing the situation by foreign merchants; in particular Russian merchants who bought the commodities in the name of export and because of paying the tariff, did not pay any rahdari and darvazebani taxes; and instead of export they sold the commodities in other Iranian cities (Adamiyyat, 1944, p. 271).

When Amir Kabir learned about the new situation, he reformed the taxation system in favor of the Iranian merchants. Aware of the importance of the bazaris for the economic growth and social stability of the country, Amir supported the economic activities of the bazaris. He created a high degree of security on the Iranian trade roads and constructed new roads which led to better and faster communication between different bazaars. One of these efforts was the construction of a bridge known as Dallak on the Qarachaj river between Tehran and Qum, because this river disturbed the caravans engaging in trade between these two rivers (Adamiyyat, 1944, p. 2 61).

The economic policy of Amir resulted in increasing exports and GNP. Iran's income from exports at this time was counted at about 1,000,000 English pounds (Adamiyyat, 1944, p. 270). During the ministry of Amir, Iranian imports from Europe which in 1850 was about 11,825,000 thalers reduced to 9,642,000 in 1852 (Issawi, 1971, p. 132).

Social Reforms

Amir Kabir founded the first secular high school in Iran where education was provided according to European style. The school was called *Dar al-Fonun* and was located in Tehran. It included technical, medical and military instruction. Courses were taught mainly by European teachers with the aid of local translators (Keddie, 1981, p. 53). He founded also the first gazette of Iran, called *Vaqayeh-e etefaqiyye,* to create a central source of information that could help the state to implement reforms. The gazette was devoted to teaching farmers about growing new agricultural products such as American cotton (Adamiyyat, 1944, p. 263). The social power of the ulama was still one of the most important challenges facing Amir. In addition to the limitation of the ulama's judicial influence, he tried to expel the sources of the ulama's popular influence, such as the ritual activities of *ta'ziyeh* and the institution of *bast,* which provided refuge in the shrines for people in distress. The shrines and mosques were used as a secure place by individuals who were persecuted. Amir Kabir, in his attempts to reduce the popularity and influence of the ulama through abolition of *ta'ziyeh, raudakhani,* and restricting *bast*, used some ulama's opposition to some of these traditions. For example, several ulama not only realized such rituals' incompatibility with the Shari'a, but saw in the *raudakhans* competitors in the excitement and control of religious emotion (Zarrinkub, 1958, p. 314). Amir succeeded in some of his reforms because of his successful struggle against the followers of the rival religious sect *Bahaism*, in favor of Shi'ism, before becoming chief minister. He sent a well-trained army to defeat the Bahais, and at last he destroyed them in Mazandaran and Zanjan, where he faced the Bahais' strong defense (Eqbal, 1951, p. 306). Amir, through persistent struggle against the Bahais, gained many Shi'ite ulama's respect. The support of some prominent ulama, such as that of Shaykh Abd al-Husayn, Imam jom'a of Tehran, not only provided Amir a necessary and proper means for legitimizing his political and economic reforms, but also helped him in diminishing the juridical function of the ulama. But it must be mentioned that though Amir had limited success in reducing the ulama's influence in some peripheral parts of society, he failed to eliminate their strong connection with the bazaar and urban peoples. The role and place of ulama in the traditional socio-cultural institutions such as marriage, *roudakhani, auqaf,* and *ta'ziyeh*, was deeply rooted and not easy to be changed by political means. As Algar pointed out:

> The deep and widespread attachment to *ta'ziya*, however, as a means of expressing loyalty to Shi'ism was too strong to be broken by the Amir, even with the sanction of some of the ulama; and in the face of strong opposition, particularly from Isfahan and Azerbayjan, he was obliged to relent (Algar, 1969, pp. 135-6).

Amir Kabir's success in gaining legitimization for his reform policy was not only dependent on his direct connection with some ulama, but also on the improvement of the socio-economic position of bazaris. To a great extent, Amir's economic and political reforms were of use for merchants and other groups of the bazaar. Through the protective economic policy, Amir not only intended to reduce the import of foreign commodities, but also made many efforts to improve the quality of Iranian commodities to satisfy foreign markets (Adamiyyat, 1944, p. 270).

> It was owing to this policy of Amir that Persian handicrafts developed greatly; Kirman woolen textiles were as choice as those from Kashmir, so that even experts were unable to differentiate between the Kirman woolen textile, which was and still is known as Amiri cashmere, and that made in Kashmir.[82]

In addition, Amir supported actively the bazari producers in their efforts to reach a competitive level with their foreign counterparts. For example, when Amir learned of the difficulties facing the weavers of Isfahan in selling their products, he gave them financial assistance, stimulated their market, and arranged for them to sew 50,000 military uniforms delivered to state officials annually (Adamiyyat, 1944, p. 252). The Iranian artisans and craftsmen, who enjoyed the serious support of Amir, were encouraged and made further innovations. For example, Haji Muhammad Husayn Kashani in Kashan produced a high quality textile from cotton and silk and showed it to Amir. Amir liked it as an army overcoat and gave him 900 tumans for producing 2000 military overcoats of the same textile to be delivered to the state (Adamiyyat, 1944, pp. 252-3). Increasing domestic production not only increased the income of the bazaris but also gave rise to the trade activity of merchants. Accordingly, the bazaars of Iran received considerable benefits during the reign of Amir Kabir and, consequently, were positively inclined towards his premiership. For example, in March 1849, when a revolt of Azerbayjani troops garrisoned in Tehran forced Amir to temporarily resign, the bazaris closed the bazaars and, together with some ulama such as Mirza Abul Qasem and the Imam jom'a of Tehran Shaykh Abu al-Husayn, protested against the resignation of Amir (Eqbal, 1961, p. 374).

Opposition to the Reforms

Although the reign was short and there were problems of traditional resistance, Amir Kabir's reforms influenced–although not drastically or for long enough–different parts of the political, economic, and to a lesser extent, social spheres of Iranian society. Consequently, Amir could not realize his programs without facing strong opposition in the three above-mentioned arenas of society. The political reforms of Amir were generally intended to rationalize the patrimonial bureaucracy and reduce the involvement of the shah in political matters. In particular, Amir reduced the cost of the court and changed the patrimonial system of choosing provincial governors and other state authorities from a basis of personal bonds to that of bureaucratic and political ability. These reforms evoked strong opposition, mainly from former governors, traditional state officials, and the majority of the royal family including Mahd U'lya, the mother of the king.

In addition, the reign of Amir Kabir coincided with the imperialistic expansion of the influence of England and Russia. Amir's economic reforms limited the interest of many English and Russian traders in favor of their Iranian counterparts. This tendency of the reign of Amir was reinforced by changing the 'Russophile' and 'Anglophile' governors and state officials. Russian provocation through the occupation of several islands in the Caspian sea in order to control the northern Iranian trade, and England's political (the affair of 'slave trade in Persian Gulf') and economic pressures (such as military control of the trade in the Persian Gulf) exemplify the negative standing Amir had with respect to these nations.[83]

The third source of opposition to Amir came from the ulama. The position of the ulama during the reign of Amir and their reaction to his reforms is of great importance for understanding the conditions and events that led to the ulama's participation in the Constitutional Revolution of 1905-9. In dealing with the modernization of Iran, the reign of Amir Kabir is usually considered the most important period in the process of modernization of Iran and reinforcing the authority of the state.[84] As mentioned earlier, Amir stood in good favor with the ulama because of his challenge to and defeat of the rival religious sect, Bahaism. As Weber pointed out, in the history of the West, the Christian church always reinforced its bonds with the state because of the fear of losing control and power in favor of other secular centers of power, and consequently of monopolization of power in the hands of the state (Weber, 1968, pp. 1173-76). In Iran too, the Shi'ite ulama had to reinforce their bonds with the state, but for other reasons. The prominent position of the Shi'ite ulama of Iran was partly threatened by the surrounding Sunni state of the Ottomans, partly by the impact of the West; and partly by internal rivalry with religious groups such as Sufism, Shaykhism, and Bahaism. Accordingly, the Shi'ite ulama needed the state to protect their position in Iran. Therefore, as long as the reforms would reinforce the state authority against the external threats of the West and the Sunni states, the ulama were not negative to them. Such was the case with Abbas Mirza's 'Nezam-e jadid', and with Amir Kabir's political reforms. But, if the reforms were intended to reduce the authority of the ulama in favor of the state, they did not accept them and actively reacted against them. This was the case when Amir intended to reduce the influence of the ulama by abolishing the institution of *bast* and *ta'ziyeh*. Amir's retreat from his claims to abolish such institutions neutralized the opposition of the ulama.

Accordingly, Russia and England in alliance with the royal families and their traditional allies made up the core of the opposition to Amir. This reactionary alliance continued to hinder the attempts at political and economic modernization initiated by other governmental officials such as grand *vazirs* Mirza Husayn Khan Sepahsalar and Amin al-Sultan. The opposition of the ulama to the changes that intervened and influenced the traditional economic hegemony of bazaar and the social authority of the ulama continued during the nineteenth century and appeared in the organization of social movements against the state. One of the most typical examples of the ulama's reaction to the intervention of the West and the state in civil society of Iran is *junbesh-e tanbako* (the Tobacco Movement), which is of great importance in understanding the coherence of the socio-political leadership of ulama.

The Tobacco Movement

The Qajars' foreign policy was based on continued concessions to foreign companies. The limited income of such concessions used to pay Nasir al-Din Shah's journeys to Europe. In one of the Shah's visits to England in 1889, preliminary negotiations about the 'tobacco concession' to an English company, Imperial Tobacco Corporation, were completed (Mustaufi, 1942, p. 420).

According to the concession, all rights concerning the sale and distribution of Iranian tobacco inside Iran and in export were given to the English company, which, in return, was to pay the Iranian government: £ 15,000 a year (Kasravi, 1951, p. 15). From the spring of 1891 on, the employees of the company arrived in Iran and began to work. Many governors were paid by the company to make its establishment and success possible (Malekzadeh, 1949, p. 127). The bazaris and, in particular, the merchants of the bazaars, whose economic activities were influenced directly from the monopoly of the English company over the sale and trade of tobacco, were the first to react against the concession. In Ramadan 1308/April-May 1891, one of the chief tobacco merchants of Fars, Haji Abbas Urdubadi, caused the bazaars of Shiraz to be closed in protest against the monopoly (Algar, 1969, p. 207). As mentioned earlier, both the bazaris and the ulama cooperated with each other when one or the other suffered state or foreign intervention that could change the economic position of bazaar or the social position of the ulama. During the 'Tobacco Movement' too, the bazaris whose immediate economic interest was violated by the concession, used the ulama to mobilize the urban people against the concession. In Shiraz, where, at first, the bazaris took the initiative in the protest and closed the bazaars, the ulama backed the bazaris. One of the ulama, Aqa Sayyed Ali Akbar Fale' Asiri, mounted the pulpit in Shiraz flourished a sword, and said that today the *jihad* is obligation of Muslims (Malekzadeh, 1949, p. 127). In other cities too, it was the bazaris who began the protest and asked the ulama for support. In Tehran Malek al-Tojjar, the chief of merchants, raised and caused the ulama's engagement (Ansari, 1942, p. 314). The bazaris' reaction to the monopoly over tobacco continued in other cities and gained the support of the ulama. In Tabriz, for instance, bazaris closed the bazaars and together with about 20,000 urban dwellers participated in mass demonstrations (Malekzadeh, 1949, p. 128).

The role of the ulama was a very important feature in the Tobacco Movement. As mentioned earlier, the ulama were natural allies of the bazaris; in this movement, too, the ulama actively supported the bazaris in their claim for canceling the concession. The ulama, by participating in the movement–first spontaneously, then locally, and then organized through a network of connections–and by mobilizing urban people, reinforced their traditional alliance with the bazaris. Perhaps more important, the ulama established themselves as the single and real leaders of the city dwellers. Everywhere, the ulama were the leaders. In Tabriz, Hajji Mirza Djavad, in Isfahan Ahga Najafi, and in Tehran Muhammad Hasan Ashtiani (Kasravi, 1951, p. 16). In Mashad, demonstrations against the monopoly were led by Taqi Burujirdi and Shafti.[85] A very important event at that time was the participation of the more conservative theologians of the *'atabat*. From Samara, the great Mujtahid Mirza Muhammad Hasan Shirazi sent a telegraph to the Shah, explaining the harms of the concession and asking him to cancel it (Algar, 1969, p. 209). The Shah, who, for the first time, faced such a great and widespread movement, was confused. He decided to first modify the concession and then take back the sale of tobacco inside the country, but the bazaris and the ulama did not accept that and then continued to protest.

An interesting tactic introduced by the ulama during the movement was declaring *fatva*, forbidding the people from using tobacco. Some of the ulama, such as Aqa Najafi in Isfahan prevented the sale of tobacco even before the issue of the celebrated *fatva* (Algar, 1969, p. 209). But the first *fatva*, which simultaneously declared the absolute political leadership of the ulama, came from Samara and from the prominent Mujtahid Mirza Hasan Shirazi, who was known as the *Marja'-e taqlid*. There are different ideas about the sources of influence that caused him to participate in the Tobacco Movement through declaring the *fatva*. Some researchers such as Keddie (1966), and Malekzadeh (1949), emphasize the influence of Sayyed Jamal Afghani on Shirazi's attitudes toward the concession. But they do not consider the well-organized connection between a network of the ulama residing in Iran with the ulama resided in *'atabat*. For example, the connections between the ulama of Isfahan through Aqa Munir al-Din whom the ulama had deputized to obtain a ruling from Mirza Hasan on the question of the concession (Teymuri, 1949, p. 79). After the demonstrations and conflicts inside Iran and the forging of connections between the ulama residing in Iran and the ulama of the *'atabat*, early in December 1891, Mirza Hasan Shirazi declared a *fatva* by which 'the use of tobacco in any form was considered as the war against the Hidden Imam and forbidden' (Malekzadeh, 1949 p. 129; Kasravi, 1951 p. 16; Algar, 1969, p. 211). Since the *fatva* reached the Iranian cities by telegraph, people everywhere, women and men, young and older, rich and poor accepted that, closed the tobacco shops, and put the *qalians* and *chopuqs*[86] aside (Kasravi, 1951, pp. 16-17). The people gathered the *qalians* in the squares and burned them up (Malekzadeh, 1949, p. 129). The Shah tried to use the Qajar's traditional weapon, namely 'divide and rule', through exerting pressures on the chief ulama of Tehran, Mirza Hasan Ashtiani, to either declare the use of tobacco permissible or leave Tehran. He rightly chose the second alternative and succeeded in keeping the ranks of the ulama together. Some of the ulama went to his house and said that they, too, wanted to leave Tehran with him. When the people became aware of this, they closed the bazaars and a crowd massed around the citadel and surrounded the royal palace. Aqa Bala Khan, who became a high government official and was killed in the events of the Constitutional Revolution, ordered troops to fire. Seven were killed and more than twenty injured (Kasravi, 1951, p. 17). The demonstrations and protests continued for days and the Shah was forced to send Adud al-Mulk to meet Mirza Hasan Ashtiani, present him with a ring and promise to annul the concession.[87]

After more than six months of rebellion, a telegram sent by Mirza Hasan Shirazi, who declared the *fatva*, put an end to the boycott on tobacco. Consequently, the first state-wide rebellion led by the ulama in the Qajar period came to an end. It is noteworthy that the ulama's protest against the concession was also partly due to their position as guardians of the religion. During the movement, they railed against the anti-religious effects of the concession (Keddie, 1966, p. 66).[88] But what is of great importance in the events of the tobacco concession is not the nature and causes of the ulama's participation in the movement, but rather the mere process of movement which led to construction of a political network of the ulama, and to the vitalization and institutionalization of their political leadership that comes to play a decisive role in the Constitutional Revolution. The ulama, through their close connections with the people and the use of *manbars* (pulpits) as one of their most effective means of propagating their message, established themselves as unquestionable leaders of the movement. The Tobacco Movement also showed that the bazaris, who began the protests against the state and the concession, could not, as has been the case during the Islamic history of Iran, create and lead a political movement. In other words, the ulama played their traditional role as the true leaders of civil society of Iran and forced the state to accept them as its civil counterpart.

The Main Social Groups on the Eve of the Constitutional Revolution

The main social groups at the end of nineteenth and the beginning of the twentieth centuries were:

1. *the aristocrats*
2. *the ulama*
3. *the landlords*
4. *the bazaris*
5. *the modern urban groups*
6. *peasants*
7. *tribes*

In the late nineteenth and early twentieth centuries, Iran was a land of great social complexity and regional diversity. Geographic factors had made many Iranian towns and villages isolated and economically self-contained. It was a country lacking navigable rivers and lakes, a marked shortage of rainfall–half of the country's present 636,000 square miles receive less than ten inches of rain per year, and vast central desert surrounded by four formidable mountain ranges-the Zagros, the Elborz, the Mekan, and the Uplands. This physical ecology served to fragment the population into secluded villages, isolated towns, and nomadic tribes (Abrahamian, 1982, p. 11).

Such a fragmentation and social mosaic makes the classification of the people into groups and classes difficult. The classification presented above is an attempt to present a model which hopefully would include most of the Iranian population relevant for our purposes.

The first group consisted of Qajars and families related to them. They possessed a prominent economic position which was supported and reinforced by a patrimonial bureaucracy. The Qajar dynasty had, as many previous Iranian states, tribal origin. They established a tribal form of government based on the distribution of provincial governance among the Qajar families. 'Delegation of authority on the bases of personal and family ties did not stop at the royal level and pervaded all central and provincial administration, creating monopoly over the political power. The prime minister also appointed sons, relatives, kinsmen, and stewards to the most important offices' (Arjomand, 1988, p. 25). During a long period of reign (1796-1924), through owning substantial amount of lands and villages, collecting taxes, and so forth, they became the most wealthy groups of Iranian society. In spite of the economic backwardness of the country, through guaranteeing economic successions to foreign companies and receiving loans, Qajar kings and princes spent huge amounts to retain their wealth and aristocratic position in society.

The second key group in Iranian society was the ulama. As mentioned earlier, since the time of the Safavids the Shi'ite ulama had become one of the most important and influential groups of society through the position as Mujtahid and *nayeb-e Imam*, their monopoly over education and jurisprudence, and ownership of *vaqf* properties. But the ulama did not consist of a homogenous group in Iranian society undergoing socio-economic changes at the late nineteenth and early twentieth centuries. During the Constitutional movement, for instance, the Shi'ite ulama were divided into three groups:

1. The clergy who owned huge properties of land and had close ties with the rural areas and other landlords. This group of clergy were very traditional and against any form of change which could influence their prominent economic position. They were against any attempts at reform, even through government. For example, when Naser al-Din Shah tried to support the tradesmen through establishing 'Parliaments of deputy for tradesmen', the clergy of this group protested and succeeded in eliminating it. Among others, Mulla Ali Kani (1871), landowner and a famous religious leader (*alem*), Seyed Kazem-e Yazdi, and Seyed Hosein-e Mosavi can be named.

2. The second group were those with close ties with bazaars, guilds, and poor people. These ulama had control over *madrasahs* and *vaqf* properties devoted to the *madrasahs* and shrines. Some of them had the position of *marj'aiyyat* among the urban people. Among others, Ayatollah Tabatabai and Ayatollah Behbahani, can be mentioned as members of this group of ulama.

3. The third group of ulama were those prominent and more traditional ulama residing in the cities with close connection to the government. Among others, Imam jom'a of Tehran and Sheykh Fazl Allah Nuri can be mentioned.[89] These ulama either received direct compensation from the state, or managed *vaqf* properties.

Statistical figures presented by Charles Issawi (1971) shows that in 1891, about 4.5 million of a total population of 9 million Iranians lived in the rural areas. They were twice as many as the 2.25 million people living in the towns. There is unfortunately no statistics about the numbers of the land lords on the eve of Constitutional Revolution. But the statistics which became available in a later period shows that as late as in 1963, half of the cultivable land of the country was in the hands of the *khans* (landowners) and great land proprietors, held absolutely as private property, *melk* (Denman, 1978, p. 256). The landowners maintained their lands and villages free from the state and had no obligation to it. The domains of these landowners could be vast, extending to twenty, thirty, or forty villages. Only 20 percent of the cultivable land was owned by the small farmers, called *khordemalekin* (Denman, 1978, p. 256). This social group was traditionally conservative and against social change.

The role of the bazaris and other urban middle occupational groups is more complicated. An economic relationship between towns, on the one hand, and villages located near the towns, on the other, has existed for a long time. This relationship was based on trade activities between bazaars in the towns and producers in the villages, such as weavers and farmers of cotton and rice. But the connections were fragmented in terms of linkages to many small locally bounded communities. This economic order was complicated through the integration of the bazaars into a network of world trade. Concessions, given by the government to foreigners, paved the way for foreign economic penetration and changed much of the traditional Iranian economy. The importation of manufactured products into Iranian markets (the bazaars), and foreign interest in Iran's agricultural goods, such as cotton, rice and tobacco, commercialized agriculture and intensified contacts between town and country. Paradoxically, it also increased the economic and social importance of some branches in the bazaar dealing with the export of agricultural goods. But uncontrolled importation of mass-manufactured products undermined the traditional handicrafts, such as textiles, and threatened many native manufactures which either belonged to the bazaar, or depended on it. The lack of protective tariffs for native production and the government's generous 'concession policy' to foreign merchants deepened the already difficult relations between the traditionally religious bazaar and the shahs of the Qajar (1794-1921).

Arthur de Gobineau, who served as first secretary of the French legation in Tehran in 1854-58 and again as minister in 1862-64, described the position of merchants and craftsmen in Iran before the beginning of significant foreign impact:

> The Persian merchant does not pay a penny in taxes. He sells all sorts of things: silks, cotton fabrics, porcelain, crystal ware, spices, goods from Europe and Asia. He carries out banking and brokerage, and no taxes or duties are levied on such operations. He is regarded as a capitalist. What he has to pay is rent on his shop to the bazaar owner; nothing else (Issawi, 1971, p. 36).

Of course what de Gobineau meant by taxes are only those taxes collected by the state, and not the religious taxes which merchants paid to the ulama. But it is evident that the position of the ulama in the mid-nineteenth century, before the initial impact of foreign companies, was much better than their economic position at the end and in the beginning of the twentieth century (as discussed in the next chapter).

The engagement of the bazaars in modern trade with Western countries increased the flows of market-oriented products, such as silk, cotton, rice, and opium. Many of the merchants received advantages from the new flourishing trade, and even the banking activities of the bazaris increased. Rich merchants from the ranks of bazaris and state officials appeared in the social arena of the cities. For example, the governor of Kerman, Bahjat al-Mulk, engaged in advanced economic ventures through buying profitable agricultural products and keeping them in storehouses to be sold in winter. Also, among the merchants who enjoyed a major increase in their capital were Haj Muhammad Hasan Amin al-Zarb, Hajji Agha Muhammad Muin Tujjar, and Hajji Muhammad Taqi Shahrudi. In 1896, for example, the fortune of Amin al-Zarb's family was put at 25 million tumans.[90] Rapid accumulation of capital in the hand of some merchants led to increasing banking activities by *sarrafs* (money lenders), who represented a traditional banking institution in the bazaar. But the rapid increase in their capital changed the local characteristics of their activities to state-wide banking. As a result of the economic activities of these groups, banking activities increased and some of their capital was spent on the creation of new industries.

The other new occupational group which was being formed were the industrial workers. New industries and manufactures attracted poor peasants and nomads who lived near cities. One of the most important sectors of the Iranian economy was the English-owned oil industry, which attracted many poor people seeking jobs. Increases in trade led to growing laborcraft in the harbors. But it must be mentioned that the new monied merchants and industrial workers were just beginning to form and it would take more than half a century for these two modern groups to be fully shaped.

On the eve of Constitutional Revolution, peasants constituted 75 to 80 percent of the whole population of Iran (Issawi, 1971, p. 49). The peasants of Iran were rarely an autonomous occupational group. The unique agrarian structure of Iran divided the peasants into four main groups: landowners, landless poor, small landowners, and independent peasants. The first group I have already discussed. The second group, the landless peasants, constituted the majority of Iranian peasants. They had neither land nor cultivation rights. They could only work for landlords. The third group of peasants were middle peasantry which owned just enough property to be independent of the large landlords but not enough to require the hired labor of poor peasantry (Kazemi & Abrahamian, 1978). The fourth group of peasants were sharecroppers, *Zare'* or *barzegar*, who held no property but enjoyed the right to cultivate *nasaq* (the landlords property) (Kazemi & Abrahamian, 1978). As Kazemi and Abrahamian stress, the lack of a powerful and independent peasantry was one of the most important reasons for the non-revolutionary peasantry of modern Iran. In the Constitutional and the Islamic Revolutions of Iran, the peasants remained non-revolutionary and in some cases counter-revolutionary.

The last major social group on the eve of the Constitutional Revolution were the tribes. In 1891, the nomadic population of Iran was as large as the population settled in towns. They constituted 2.5 million of the whole population of 9 million (Issawi, 1971, p. 33). The history of tribes in Iran is an old one, and they had often played a crucial role in the political life of the country. Almost all the states of the Shi'ite history of Iran had tribal roots. Safavids, Afshars, Zands, and Qajars had been tribal dynasties. The main tribes of the nineteenth century Iran were Bakhtiaris, Baluchis, Lors, Kurds and Turkish tribes such as the Qajars. In the periods of military weakness of the state which occurred after the decline and fall of dynasties the country became a scene of tribal competition and struggle for seizing power, providing a free zone of influence of the tribes, and, in general, increasing their importance in the country's power struggles. Even in the time of dry weather and hot summers, the tribes attacked villages and towns and plundered them. The traditional architecture of many villages which were situated in tribal areas exhibits the defensive features of the houses. They are, for example, built very close to each other, the doors of the houses are very short to hinder the tribesmen, who used to come riding their horses, from entering into the houses, and the villages were situated in the front of mountains to make the defense easier (Torabi, 1973). The tribal way of life made them very skillful and capable of using horses and weapons. The military significance of the tribes in times of weak states, which normally occurred after the fall of each dynasty, gave them an important and decisive role in the transformation of political power in traditional Iran. Even in the Constitutional Revolution one of these tribes, Bakhtiaris, played a decisive role in defeating Muhammad Shah's forces and forcing him to resign.

4 The Constitutional Revolution

The Constitutional Revolution (1905-1909) was among those historical events that forced the ulama to play not only their traditional role as the leaders of the Shi'ite community of Iran, as in the case of the Tobacco Movement, but also to modify their traditional views on the state in the Shi'ite community awaiting its true leader, the Hidden Imam. The importation and elaboration of some features of modernization, such as new schools, secular law institutions, reinforcement of secular administration, bazaars' new economic connections with the West, and the spread of liberal ideas in Iran, made the ulama's traditional position in society unstable. The new socio-economic and political situation needed new theological interpretations and the role of the ulama had to be justified in the new Iranian society. The economic and ideological impact of the West changed the traditional setting of Iranian society, creating a more differentiated society. In the new storm of changes, the ulama were not excluded. The events and tensions leading to the Constitutional Revolution changed the traditional basis of the ulama's more or less ideological unity concerning the role of the state in the Shi'ite community of Iran. In this chapter some social events which led to engagement of the ulama in the Constitutional Revolution will be discussed. Participation in the Revolution led to the appearance of the 'constitutionalist ulama' whose ideas about the role of state were decisive for the continuation and outcomes of power constellations after the political triumph of the Constitutional Revolution. Therefore, the constitutionalism of the ulama is of great importance for understanding their leadership in the Revolution, and their participation in the power challenge after the political victory in 1906.

The Constitutional Revolution of Iran, as a process of social movement for political change, began in 1905, won a formal victory in the summer of 1906, and continued to protect constitutionalism until 1909. But the Constitutional Revolution was actually the result of a process that began long before the mass movements of 1905. The traditional society of Iran had, during a few decades, gone through several structural changes, such as successively increasing the state's dependency on the foreign

88 *Revolutionary Iran*

powers of England and Russia, at a cost of decreasing their connections with the ulama, and increasing economic intervention of Western companies which was to undermine the traditional economic and social position of the bazaars. The bazaris and the ulama were the two main groups of civil society of Iran who suffered through these structural changes. The Tobacco Movement was the beginning of a long process of the traditional civil society's reaction to the structural changes. The years following the victory of the Tobacco Movement witnessed the same patterns of change in the balance of power between the ulama and the state. Meanwhile, the state continued to seek closer relations with the West, mainly through loans and concessions, and the ulama continued to reinforce their connections with the bazaars. Accordingly, many of the ulama began to successively cut their bonds with the state and restructure their connections with the bazaar and some other urban groups in order to reinforce their position in a society undergoing socio-structural and even ideological changes. The state, too, increased efforts at modernization, by which the power of the ulama could be reduced and the sphere of their influence limited to religious groups. The state's efforts to decrease the power of ulama aroused and intensified their hostility to the state. At the same time, paradoxically, economic pressure on the bazaris, as a result of the intervention of Westerners and their companies, increased the sphere of the ulama's influence among the bazaris and other urban groups connected to them.

Modernization Efforts of the State

One of the state officials who believed in reinforcing the secular power of the state was Amin al-Daula, who became prime minister (Sadr Azam) of Muzaffar al-Din Shah.[91] Amin al-Daula was one of those statesmen who believed in the separation of state and religion. He opposed the intervention of the ulama in matters of state. He considered the ulama the greatest obstacle to reforms (Algar, 1969, p. 223). One of the most controversial reforms of Amin al-Daula was his active support of the establishment of the new schools. There were, in Iran at that time, already two known schools, i.e. *madrasahs* and *maktabs*. There were many *madrasahs* in Iran, which were used by the ulama for teaching *fiqh* and other religious matters to *talabahs* (religious students). *Maktabs* were the other kind of school, in which students, who came mainly from the rank of merchants, learned writing and reading (Kasravi, 1951, p. 19). Both of these schools were controlled by the ulama.

In 1888, Haj Mirza Hasan Rushdiya, who was inspired by the new European schools, founded the first modern school, *madrasah-ye Rushdiya*, in Tabriz. But the clergy could not accept the challenge the new schools represented to their traditional monopoly over education, and they finally attacked the *Rushdiya* school and destroyed its modern facilities, including benches and blackboards. Haj Mirza Hasan, who was afraid of the clergy and did not see any progress in the new schools in Iran, left Iran for Egypt. When Amin al-Daula became the *vazir* of the governor of Tabriz, he sent a telegraph to Haj Mirza Hasan asking him to come to Tabriz and restart his secular school (Algar, 1969, p. 221). Despite the protest of some Tabrizian clergy, the *Rushdiya* school was restored. When Amin al-Daula became Sadr Azam of Iran, he brought Haj Hasan to Tehran to start other schools in the capital (Algar, 1969, p. 221). To encourage improvement of the new education, he established Anjuman-e ma'arif (Council of Education) to coordinate the establishment of the new education. One of other hostile reforms of Amin al-Daula against the ulama was the extension of *u'rf* jurisdiction. By increasing the domain of influence of *u'rf* jurisdiction, the judicial power of the ulama was restricted, reinforcing their hostility to Amin al-Daula (Algar, 1969, p. 224). To improve the state treasury, the prime minister (Sadr-e Azam), like his predecessor, Amir Kabir, reduced the budget of the court. By doing so Amin al-Daula encountered opposition from the royal families and clerics. In order to reorganize Iranian customs according to European model, Amin al-Daula assigned the task to three Belgian merchants. This was an important factor in the bazaar's dissatisfaction which drew them into the Constitutional movement.

The ulama, whose position in civil society was threatened by the reforms of Amin al-Daula, began a range of protests located mainly in Tehran and supported by the ulama of *'atabat*. Amin al-Daula did not listen to the demands of the ulama for banishing and modifying the reforms. The leaders of the protests, Abdullah Behbahani, and Mirza Hasan and Mirza Mustafa Ashtiani, in response threatened to leave Iran and immigrate to *'atabat* intending to reinforce the urban masses' protests. As a result of the ulama's protest (Algar, 1969, p. 225), and pressure from some royal family members and officials who had lost their income and influence by prime minister's reforms (Kasravi, 1951, p. 23), Amin al-

Daula was forced to resign from office on 4 June 1898. For the second time, Amin al-Sultan became prime minister (Sadr-e Azam).

Vitalization of the Alliance Between the Ulama and the Merchants

During the second period of the reign of Amin al-Sultan, the problem of loans from Russia began to cause problems which resulted in a major reaction from civil society, in particular the ulama and bazaris. The story began with Muzaffar al-Din Shah's decision to travel to Europe. The Shah, on the recommendation of his physician, decided to travel to Europe to use the warm mineral waters. To finance the journey, Amin al-Sultan negotiated and received a 22.5 million ruble loan from Russia, with an interest rate of 5 percent over seventy five years. In exchange, the Russians received the monopoly over the trade of the Northern Iran (Kasravi, 1951, p. 25). In the summer of 1900, the Shah and the Sadr-e Azam began their journey to Europe, spent the loan, and returned to Iran. In the summer of 1903, Amin al-Sultan received a second loan, this time of ten million rubles from Russia, and, together with the Shah went to Europe. He gave the Russians the concession to construct a road from the border at Julfa to Tabriz. The state's loans and commitments caused immediate opposition from the ulama. In Gilan, Hajji Muhammad Rafi' Shari'atmadar, the chief Mujtahid of Gilan, came from Rasht to Tehran to coordinate opposition to the loan. The ulama of Tabriz also opposed the loan and the concession (Algar, 1969, pp. 230-31). The ulama's opposition to the loans was based on two main grounds: 1) they considered the loans as a mean of increasing the state's dependency on foreign and non-Muslim powers; and 2) the loans would extend Russian sphere of influence in Iran. Both these consequences of the loans were against the position of ulama in society. This not only influenced the boundaries between the ulama and the state, but also harmed the traditional allies of the ulama, the bazaris.

To ensure repayment of their loans by the Iranian state, the Russians and the English agreed that Iranian customs be reorganized by Europeans (Malekzadeh, 1949, p. 279). As mentioned earlier, the administration of customs had been given to three Belgians, under the leadership of Nauz. Merchants and other groups in the bazaars considered the appointment of the Belgians and their treatment of Iranian Muslim traders unacceptable. Nauz and his colleagues discriminated against Iranian Muslim merchants in favor of Iranian Christian merchants (Malekzadeh, 1949, p. 29). In addition, the Belgians established a customs tariff that favored Russian traders and suppressed the activities of Iranian traders whose trade was mostly with non-Russian territory of Europe. This reinforced dissatisfaction the Belgians felt towards the merchants. In Bushehr, Yazd, Shiraz, and Isfahan, traders and the ulama demonstrated their opposition to the appointment of Belgians (Kasravi, 1930, p. 29). Amin al-Sultan did not listen to the opposition of the ulama and the bazaris. The dissatisfaction with the governance of Amin al-Sultan led gradually to revolts in other provinces. An event in Tabriz gave the ulama the impetus they needed to mobilize people against the state. In June 1903, a certain clergyman, Mulla Mirza Ali Akbar, while passing by a liquor store in Tabriz, was invited to drink wine by a drunken man. Mirza became angry, went to his *madrasah,* and told the story to the *tullab* (religious students). They revolted and went to the house of Haj Mirza Hasan Mujtahid, and with him went to the Masjid-e Shah. The merchants of Tabriz, who, as merchants of other cities, were angered at the conduct of a Belgian customs officer, Priem, they closed the bazaar and came to the Masjid (mosque). The alliance of the ulama and the bazaris expressed itself in their statements of protest. As Kasravi writes, they claimed that 'monsieur Priem must go, and the liquor store, hotels, and the new schools must be closed' (Kasravi, 1930, p. 31). After two days of protests and revolts, Muhammad Ali Mirza, the governor of Tabriz, was forced to write to the merchants and the ulama gathered in the Masjid-e Shah and accept their demands. Hearing the decree, *tullab* rushed out from the Masjid and destroyed liquor stores, hotels, and the new schools (Kasravi, 1930, p. 31). Priem himself was obliged to flee from the town.[92]

The incident is of great importance for understanding the conditions of cooperation and alliance between the ulama and the merchants. It illustrates the traditional role of the ulama as the leaders of civil society, as well as the interdependency of these two groups. Meanwhile, the bazaris' main goal in the revolt was to remove the Belgian control of trade, the ulama wanted to prohibit non-Islamic patterns of life and revitalize their leadership in the community. The hotels and liquor stores of Tabriz were owned by Armenians in which alcoholic drinks were served. The liquor store were non-Islamic places and the immediate target of the opposition of the ulama. The new schools were also not yet accepted by the ulama.

The mass protests against the Sadr-e Azam made it very difficult for him to remain in power. In such a situation, a *fatva* signed by the ulama of *'atabat* was published that declared the Sadr-e Azam *kafar* (infidel).[93] In

August of 1903, the Sadr-e Azam was forced to resign and Ayn al-Daula took the position of Sadr-e Azam. This retreat of the Shah was considered another triumph of the ulama in leading the just struggle of the people against the state. From then on, the movement for changes–not necessarily for a Constitutional Revolution–began, and the ulama made up its leadership. Before further discussing the process of the Revolution, it must be mentioned that the ulama–as a group–did not participate in the Revolution. The process of the events which led to the Constitutional Revolution did not begin with the demands of participants and their leadership for a Constitutional government. Rather, the ulama, who were leading the movement aimed to limit the power of the state, cut its bonds with the West, and reinforce their own position in the community. The bazaris wanted to restrict the role of foreigners in Iranian customs. But events forced the ulama to abandon the traditional justification of their role in the society and reformulate the nature of their leadership according to modern codes, such as constitutionalism. In the second part of the discussion about this course of events, the constitutionalism of the ulama as a theological point of view which emerged out of the process of the Revolution will be discussed. But now, a few words about another event that reinforced the interconnections of the ulama and the bazaris.

The Bazaris' Protest and the Ulama's Support

As mentioned earlier, the Belgian management of Iranian customs was a result of an agreement between the Iranian government and Russia and England, intended to establish a secure source of income that could be used in repayment of the Iranian loans. But as many researchers and historians have mentioned, neither Russia nor England really wanted their loans to be paid by the Iranians.[94] The loans were a pressure factor used by the Russians and the English to force the Iranian government to accept their policy in Iran. The chain of events after the appointment of Belgians as managers of Iranian customs demonstrated that the conduct of the Belgians, in particular Nauz, did not help the Iranians increase their income from trade with the West and pay back their loans. On the contrary, it reduced exports and increased foreign economic and political influence. In 1903, Nauz introduced a trade treaty with Russia. The new treaty was completely against the interests of Iranian bazaars. The treaty reduced tariffs on commodities imported from Russia and increased tariffs on exports from Iran. This tariff arrangement motivated the English to force the Iranian government to accept a new treaty, which guaranteed the same advantages for English traders too (Kasravi, 1951, p. 37). Iranian merchants who suffered from the treaty began to protest and ask the ulama for support. The ulama both within Iran and from *'atabat* wrote protest letters to Ayn al-Daula and the Shah complaining about Nauz's actions on the Iranian trade, his treatment of Iranian merchants, and the increasing foreign influence. The state did not pay attention to the protests, continued to support Nauz, and even gave him greater power. He was even appointed Minister of Post and Telegraphs. The ulama needed a religious pretext for mobilizing the protest against both Nauz and the state. This was provided by Muhammad Taqi Khan, one of the Amin al-Sultan, ex-Sadr-e Azam and rival to Ayn al-Daula (Algar, 1969, p. 242). In March 1905, the ulama received a picture of Nauz, in which he was dressed in the religious clothes of the ulama participating in a fancy-dress ball. This picture was actually taken two years earlier (Kasravi, 1951, p. 37), but in the new situation when the bazaris were angry with the new tariff, and the ulama, in particular Behbahani, with the Sadr-e Azam, it provided a pretext for influencing the religious feeling of the people and encouraging them to participate in the protests. The ulama's protests against the picture was based on the notion that Nauz scorned Islam and the ulama. Behbahani mounted the pulpit and preached about Nauz's harmful treatment of the traders and other Muslims and, at the end, said that we must demand that Muzaffar al-Din Shah remove Nauz from office.

The agitation against Nauz coincided with the holy month of Shi'ites, i.e. Muharram[95] and it helped the ulama to reach a wider public. Finally, in July 1905, the merchants of Tehran, who did not receive any serious attention for their protests against Nauz, closed the bazaars and took refuge in the holy shrine of Shah Abdul Azim, near Tehran. The leaders of the merchants in the *bast* (refuge) were Haj Muhammad Isma'il Maghazei and Haj Ali Shalforosh, who were in contact with the two Mujtahids, Muhammed Tabatai and Abdullah Behbahani (Kasravi, 1951, p. 51). Although the mediation and promises of the crown prince Abbas Mirza about the removal of Nauz, and the Shah's third journey to Europe, temporarily solved this first real crisis, it must be considered a first step in the process of the Revolution. The mass movement against the local governors of Shiraz, Sabzevar, Qazvin, and Kirman would further this process.

The Russians, unaffected by the movements, continued to establish and reinforce their position in Iran. They wanted to establish their hated bank, the Russian Bank, in the center of Tehran. They bought the ground of an old cemetery and an old damaged school, and began to construct the bank. Many of the ulama of Tehran, under the leadership of Tabatabai, protested and warned the bank against continuing the construction. He announced that the construction was taking place in the *vaqf* property and is against *shar'* (Kasravi, 1951, p. 55). When the ulama did not receive any response from the authorities in hindering the construction, they mobilized people against the bank and destroyed the half-completed building of the bank. Under the leadership of Behbahani and Tabatabai construction of the bank was hindered. This was another step in reinforcing the role of these two Mujtahids as the leaders of the movement.

Another event in the process of movement brought the bazaris and the ulama closer to each other. The story began with the rise of the price of sugar. Sugar was imported from Russia, and, because of the war between Japan and Russia, imports were reduced and prices raised. To reduce the price of sugar, the governor of Tehran, Ala al-Daula, summoned several merchants to his palace and ordered them to be whipped in his presence (Kasravi, 1951, p. 58). In the evening, when the bazaris heard about the whipping of the merchants, they closed the bazaar, and together with the ulama, marched toward the Masjid-e Shah, gathered there, and protested against Ala al-Daula and Sadr-e Azam (Prime Minister). The protest continued the following day and resulted in an open conflict between the bazaris, the ulama, and others on one side, and the governor-appointed Imam jom'a, Mirza Abul Qasem, and the state agents, on the other. The meeting in the Masjid-e Shah dissolved in chaos. The following day the people, led by the two Mujtahids, Tabatabai and Behbahani, marched to the shrine of Shah Abdul Azim and took refuge. In addition to the two Mujtahids, the other ulama who left Tehran in protest were Haj Shaykh Murteza, Sadr al-Ulama, Sayyed Jamal al-Din Afja'i, Mirza Mustafa, Shaykh Muhammad Sadeq Kashani, and Shaykh Muhammad Reza Qumi.[96] During the march to Shah Abdul Azim, soldiers attacked the participants, and some were injured and arrested.

The *bast* in Shah Abdul Azim was the beginning of the radicalization of the movement through the creation of a network of reformist ulama, bazaris, and some intellectuals. The symbolic action of the *bast* was a sign of absolute destruction of the bonds between the state and the ulama. The ulama became now both the social and the political leaders of the community. But this does not mean that they wanted to seize state power; rather, they intended to limit the power of the state and increase their own power and sources of influence in society. The important point is that they could not increase their influence without taking into consideration the reforms and changes claimed by the people of civil society, in general, and the bazaris, in particular. In other words, not only did they have to compromise with the bazaris–as they always did–but they also had to take into consideration the claims of the new groups appearing in civil society as a result of Westernization/modernization. The traditional role of the ulama, as the leaders of civil society, was not changed, but the content changed radically through their participation in the constitutional movement. The movement until–and a few months after–the *bast* in the Shah Abdul Azim was known as a movement against the arbitrary rule of the government, not the Shah or the traditional structure of the kingship. The demands of the *bast* in Shah Abdul Azim shows the aims of the movement against the government of Ayn al-Daula. The nature of the demands shows also the alliances of the ulama and the bazaris. The ulama who did not accept any more direct negotiation or contact with the government sent their demands through the Shams al-Din Bey, the Ottoman's ambassador, directly to Muzaffar al-Din Shah. They demanded:

1. The banishment of Asgar the cart driver from the road between Tehran and Qum. (That man received the concession of the transport between Tehran and Qum and treated the passengers harmfully, therefore the tullab (religious students) and the ulama traveling that road complained to the ulama of Tehran).
2. The return of Haj Mirza Muhammad Reza to Kerman.[97]
3. The return of the management of Marvi madrasah to Haj Shaykh Murteza.[98]
4. The foundation of adalatkhaneh, 'house of justice', in all the country.
5. The establishment of the Islamic law in the whole country.
6. The removal of Nauz from the management of customs and finance of the country.
7. The removal of Ala al-Daula from the governance of Tehran.
8. No reduction in the salaries of the officials (Kasravi, 1951, p. 67).

The demands mainly address the nature of the claims of the two main groups of Iranian civil society, namely the ulama and the bazaris. But something new was introduced by the ulama: the notion of *adalatkhaneh*.

Through the foundation of *adalatkhaneh* (the house of justice), the ulama did not intend to establish a center for exerting secular law, but they wanted to re-establish their traditional monopoly on jurisprudence. The foundation of *adalatkhaneh* would limit the influence of the state in civil society. As Kasravi pointed out, at that time the people did not need a 'house of justice', because their conflicts were solved by the ulama and the elders of the community. He explains that sometimes the arbitrary governments invaded the private properties of the people, and that, in such a situation, a court, which did not exist in Iran, was needed (Kasravi, 1951, p. 72). But the foundation of *adalatkhaneh* did not mean that the ulama wanted a secular center of jurisprudence. 'Yet there was no name of the *mashruteh* (constitutionalism)' (Kasravi, 1951, p. 68).

At last, after many days of conflict and negotiation between the ulama and the state, the Shah accepted the demands, and the ulama were welcomed by a celebrating crowd on their return to Tehran. In spite of the promises from both the Shah and the Sadr-e Azam, the state did nothing about the foundation of *adalatkhaneh*. Simultaneously, in some of the main cities of Iran, the people rose up against the local governors and openly demonstrated their dissatisfaction. The most important uprising was the revolt of Mashad, in which 40 people were killed and many injured (Kasravi, 1951, p. 84). In Shiraz, too, people demonstrated against the arbitrary governor, Shu'a al-Saltana, and forced the state to remove him from Shiraz. The unrest of the provinces, in particular the revolt of Mashad, and the state's failure to fulfill its promises, forced the ulama to take a more radical position against the state. Meanwhile, Tabatabai, wrote a letter to Ayn al-Daula criticizing him and mentioning for the first time, the establishment of a Majlis (consultative assembly). The chronological connections between the events. in which the people became more and more engaged in the direct conflicts with the state, and the appearance of the demand for the foundation of a consultative assembly, *majlis-e mashvarat*, influenced the radicalization of the movement on the attitude of the ulama. For example, the bloody conflict between the people of Mashad took place at the beginning of March 1906 and the letter written by Tabatabai to Ayn al-Daula, in which he claimed the foundation of Majlis, was written in April.[99] Tabatabai wrote in his letter to Ayn al-Daula:

> What happened with those mass of promises and commitments? Certainly, you are aware from the damage of the country, the disasters of the people,

and the dangers which surrounded this country; it is obvious, and you know, that the management of the problems is dependent on the foundation of the Majlis, the unity of the state and the nation, and the unity of the statesman and the ulama.[100]

Here Tabatabai is taking about Majlis instead of *adalatkhaneh,* on the one side, and the unity of the statesman and the ulama on the other. In the following part, the ulama's understanding of constitutionalism will be discussed, but it is noteworthy to say here that the ulama did not have a clear definition of the notion of Majlis. For Tabatabai the Majlis was not a surrogate for *adalatkhaneh,* but another institution, behind the *adalatkhaneh.* The terms 'constitution' and 'parliament' were developed later as a result of the revolutionary process. In his propaganda against Ayn al-Daula at the end of May, he again talked about both the Majlis and the *adalatkhaneh.*[101] He said:

If it takes one year or ten years, we want justice and *adalatkhaneh,* we want the applying of the Islamic laws, we want a Majlis in which the king and the poor are equals according to laws. We do not say constitutionalism and republicanism, we say the parliament of Islamic justice (*majlis-e mashro'e-ye adalatkhaneh*) (Kermani, 1983, p. 453).

Here, too, we do not see the definition of the Majlis referred to by Tabatabai. Sometimes the notion of Majlis was synonymous with *adalatkhaneh.*

The struggles among the people which consisted mainly of the bazaris, urban poor, and the *tullab*, continued. The movement became more and more radicalized by events such as the killing of Sayyed Abdul Hamid, and the massacre in the Masjid-e Jom'a. The ulama found it difficult to control events. One example of the confrontation of the radicalized people with the ulama was the former's refusal to leave the Masjid-e Jom'a when the leaders Behbahani and Tabatabai wanted them to leave. At last, Behbahani managed, through the symbolic action of taking the Qur'an in hand and swearing, asked the people to leave the Masjid (Kasravi, 1951, p. 103). Kasravi mentioned, too, that some of the people wanted to struggle against the state with the limited instruments they had, but the ulama hindered them from doing so (Kasravi, 1951, p. 101).

After several weeks of riots in Tehran, and the *bast* of ulama in Masjid-e Jom'a, the brutality of the state forced the ulama to leave Tehran

98 *Revolutionary Iran*

for the holy city of Qum saying that, until their demands were fulfilled they would remain in Qum. Two days after the departure of the ulama, the bazaris and the *tullab*, who could no longer take refuge in the mosques, went to the British embassy in Tehran and took refuge. At the beginning of the *bast* in 19 June, this group numbered about forty/fifty bazaris and *tullab*; on the 30 June, it went up to twelve thousand, and, in 2 July, to fourteen thousand.[102] The people refused to negotiate with the deputies sent by the Shah and then agreed to negotiate with him only through the British ambassador, Grant Daff (Wright, 1986, pp. 380-81). The people, who, at the beginning of their *bast* in the British embassy, presented a list of 'moderate demands', radicalized their demands after a few days and claimed among others things, the foundation of 'Dar al-Shura', a consultative Majlis. They now explicitly wanted a constitutional government.[103] The *bast* of the bazaris, which led to the closing of the bazaars, the collapse of the economic life of the city, and the departure of the ulama from Tehran, which violated the social and religious life of people,[104] forced the Shah to accept the claims of the refugees. On 29 July 1906, after more than two years of struggle, Ayn al-Daula saw himself obliged to resign, and after a week, the Shah issued a decree calling for a Majlis. On August 18, the ulama welcomed by the thousands of celebrating people, returned to Tehran in triumph.

The Influence of the Intelligentsia

There are several writers who discussed the role of the intelligentsia in the Constitutional Revolution. Some of them eagerly over-emphasized the influence of the intelligentsia as one of the most important factors in the mass uprising and the victory of the Constitutional Revolution.[105] Others have tried to lessen the importance of the role of the ulama in the Constitutional Revolution and reduce it to a state of passive following of the movement and its 'real leaders', the intelligentsia and the bazari merchants.[106] The reality is that the Iranian intelligentsia at the end of the nineteenth century consisted largely of young students who were sent to Europe to study. They usually came from well-to-do families with direct connections to the court and the government. They had, of course, tried to influence both clerical and non-clerical groups such as merchants and traders. Their most effective means in the ideological challenge to the government was *shabnamahs* (leaflets). As Malekzadeh (1949) and

Kasravi (1951) pointed out, they wanted the ulama to assume their responsibility and lead the movement.

The traditional characteristics of the Iranian civil society limited the Western-inspired and non-clerical intellectuals in their contact with the masses. Because of the traditional connections between the ulama and the urban people, the non-clerical intellectuals could not propagate their ideas directly to the people, as their European counterparts did during their pre-revolution periods. The lack of educated people who could read the newspapers and the lack of newspapers printed inside the country made the connections between the intelligentsia and the urban people difficult in general. There were, of course, a few newspapers printed outside Iran such as *Qanun*, printed in London; *Habl al-matin*, printed in India; and *Parvaresh*, printed in Egypt. But as Malekzadeh pointed out, because of the 'arbitrary wall of sensor' in Iran, it was very rare to receive such newspapers (Malekzadeh, 1949, pp. 240-44). Accordingly, because of the structural setting of Iranian society, the intellectuals had been forced to take into consideration the important role of the ulama for agitation of new ideas. Besides their direct connection with the people by living among them and participating in their religious and social activities, the ulama had the best means of agitating the people, namely the *manbars* (pulpits). During the constitutional movement many of the ulama used the *manbars* to speak out against the government and mobilize the people. The two most famous clergy who successfully used the *manbars* in propagating constitutional ideas and mobilizing the people were Malek al-Motokalemin and Sayyed Jamal al-Din Va'ez, whose sermons were of great importance for the mobilization of the urban people.

Aware of the decisive function of the ulama in civil society and the reality of their monopoly on the using of *manbars*, the intelligentsia found it more effective for the succession of their ideas to influence the ulama and through them the urban masses. One example of such influence of the non-clerical intellectuals on the ulama, and, through them, on the people, is the influence of the ideas of Mirza Malkom Khan the editor of the *Qanun* newspaper printed in London, and other non-clerical intellectuals on the Sayyed Jamal al-Din Va'ez.

> When we are looking at the subjects of the sermons of Sayyed Jamal on his pulpit, we find out strong similarities between them and the social and political issues of the intellectuals such as Mirza Malkom Khan, Mirza Fath Ali Akhondzadeh, Mirza Aqa Khan Kermani, Talbof, and the others. In the

constitutional riots Mirza Malkom Khan was more known than the others and perhaps because the liberals had more access to his issues than others. I think that Mirza Malkom Khan had more influence on the Sayyed Jamal than others (Fathi, 1993, p. 521).

Sayyed Jamal's ideas about the constitutionalism and the form of the state were very close to Mirza Malkom Khan's. He even cited Malkom Khan from the pulpit (Fathi, 1993, p. 521). Accordingly, the intellectuals' ideas, which, in reality, were known among a little group of educated people from the urban middle and upper occupational groups, reached the urban people through the sermons of the ulama.

Revolution and Counter-revolution

> In the morning, I was informed that they occupied the port of Majlis. I wore my uniform and when I wanted to pick up my gun I realized that it was missing. I shouted where is my gun? My wife bearing Qur'an together with my girls came to me and said: My dear, I know that nobody would join you, you go alone to Majlis and they will kill you /.../ suddenly the cannon shot was heard. I went to the roof, sitting toward Majlis and cried.[107]

On 22 and 23 June, the Shah, by military aid from Cossack brigades, began the final attack on the Revolution. Tuesday 22 June, military forces gathered around Majlis, occupied Masjid Sepah Salar, and surrounded Majlis. On Wednesday 23 June, the army fired on the Majlis and after several hours of war with the defenders of the Majlis, put an end to the first phase of the victory of constitutionalism in Iran. Many revolutionaries were killed or arrested and executed.

The Constitutional Revolution arrived at a new phase. The traditional structure of power changed and the state became 'an organization which controlled the principal concentrated means of coercion within the population' (Tilly, 1978, p. 52). As in any other post *coup d'état* situation, the old political coalitions came under hard attack. To challenge the counter-revolutionary forces, the revolutionaries had to reorganize themselves and make a new alliance for the mobilization of the people in civil society. Although, the state succeeded in destroying the military power of the constitutionalists, it was more difficult in other provinces. In Tabriz the revolutionaries made a brave defense against the military forces and continued to fight for the Revolution. Some intellectuals, who had already been in Europe or fled after the *coup d'état*, established new political groups and defended the internal struggle against the Shah. In Istanbul *Anjoman-e sa'adat-e Iran* (The society of success and development of Iran) was established presenting itself as the representative of Azarbayjan movement. This *Anjoman* distributed reports of the struggles in Tabriz to important centers of Europe and *'atabat*.

The ideological sphere of overall challenge between the revolutionaries and counter-revolutionaries reached *'atabat*, one of the main centers granting legitimacy to the contenders within Iran. Before the *coup d'état*, Muhammad Ali Shah tried to gain some legitimacy for his counter-revolutionary action by seeking the support of the ulama in *'atabat*. The ulama called his intentions and struggle with the constitutionalists unacceptable and un-Islamic. After the coup, the ulama declared a *fatva* by which they forbade the army to cooperate with the Shah. They declared that 'Cooperation with anti-constitutionalists and obeying them against constitutionalists is like obeying Yazid ibn-e Ma'aviyah' [the Sunni Caliph, who gave the order to kill the Third Shi'ite Imam, Husayn] (Kasravi, 1951, p. 729). As mentioned earlier, the residence of the ulama in *'atabat* protected them from the direct attack and impact of the state and provided them with a very effective means to propagandize and express their opinions. To reinforce the constitutionalists' alliances against the state, the ulama of *'atabat* supported the brave struggle of the revolutionaries of Tabriz against the state and declared a *fatva* saying that war with the people of Tabriz is 'like war against the Hidden Imam' and cutting off the water of the city is 'like cutting the water of *Forat* to Sayyed al-Shohada' [the Third Imam] (Kasravi, 1951, p. 729). Kasravi also pointed out that the support of the ulama of *'atabat* in the ideological challenge between the constitutionalists and anti-constitutionalists was of great importance for continuation of the struggle against the Shah (Kasravi, 1951, pp. 729-30).

Tabriz became one of the most important centers of internal challenge against the counter-revolutionary forces. Though under great pressure from the army, the revolutionaries continued to keep the fire of the revolution and constitutionalism alive. Further, they established a substitute for the closed Majlis. 'Anjoman-e iyalati-ye Tabriz' (The Provincial Association of Tabriz) became recognized as a substitute for Majlis. As Tilly pointed out about the revolutionary conditions:

Population find themselves confronted with strictly incompatible demands from the government and from an alternative body claiming control over the government-and obey the alternative body. They pay taxes to it, provide men for its armies, feed its functionaries, honor its symbols, give time to its service, or yield other resources, despite the prohibition of the still-existing government that they formerly obeyed. Multiple sovereignty has begun (Tilly, 1975, p. 521).

With the establishment of Tabriz as the free arena of constitutionalism the 'multiple sovereignty' began. In the beginning of 1909, the Mujtahids of Najaf issued an injunction forbidding believers to pay any taxes to the state (Arjomand, 1988, p. 55). But, as Tilly says too, multiple sovereignty is a necessary, but not sufficient, factor for the victory of a revolution. The formation of coalitions between the revolutionary groups is of great importance for providing and advancing alternative model of governance (Tilly, 1978, p. 213). Meanwhile, although constitutionalists had a modern vision of governance, that was legitimized and adopted by different groups of civil society, the counter-revolutionary groups failed even to gain legitimacy for the traditional role of the state. The Shah, by his *coup d'état* not only violated the traditional role of the state, but also the very basis of the traditional Perso-Islamic legitimacy of the state. The Shah's attempt to regain the ulama's support for his reign failed and the anti-constitutionalist ulama were not powerful enough–especially in a revolutionary process which put pressure on many groups to clarify their position and choose sides–to provide him legitimacy. Besides receiving support from the Russians, the Shah tried to include tribes in his counter-revolutionary coalition. The governor of Tabriz, prince Ayn al-Daulah, for instance, used Shahsavan, Qarah Dagh, and some Kurdish tribes, Shakkak and Jalali, against the constitutionalists of Tabriz.

As mentioned earlier, the basis of many dynasties that ruled Iran had been tribal. The tribes' skillful use of weapon and horses provided them an important role in the power struggles in the country. In the events of the civil war of 1908-9 between revolutionary and counter-revolutionary forces, the tribes played a significant role. The tribes not only participated in a counter-revolutionary alliance, but also in the revolutionary one. The Bakhtiyari tribe, one of the largest tribes in central Iran, participated actively in the last period of the civil war and helped the constitutionalists in their struggle against the Shah. Of course, the participation of tribes in revolutionary or counter-revolutionary alliances depended mainly on their leadership. The tribes with traditional chiefs, such as Rahim Khan the chief of the Shahsavan tribe, supported the Shah, and the Bakhtiyaris, who had an educated and constitutionalist chief, Ali-quli Khan, Sardar As'ad, supported the revolutionaries. The Bakhtiyaris, by defeating the government's forces and occupying Tehran in July 1909, played a very crucial role in the restoration of constitutionalism.

5 The Constitutionalism of the Ulama

The theoretical and theological framework for the ulama's participation in the Constitutional Revolution is of great importance for understanding the motivation and justification of their participation in the Revolution, and why they did not succeed in seizing political power.

As mentioned earlier, the movement against the arbitrary concession policy of the state began with the bazaris, who were directly affected by such policies. From the beginning, the movement was not aimed at establishing a constitutional government, but rather at initiating reforms for the limitation of state authority and foreign influence. Constitutionalism was the fruit of the dialectical process of events taking place during the spring and summer of 1906. The dialectical action and counter-action of the movement *vis-à-vis* the state led to the growth and adoption of the idea of constitutionalism by the ulama and the bazaris. But the adoption and elaboration of the idea of constitutionalism by the ulama needed some kind of formalization, rationalization, for the Shi'ite community awaiting its just and true leader, the Hidden Imam. A temporary political system religiously legitimized in a Shi'ite community, as mentioned in the first chapter, had always been controversial for the Shi'ite ulama. Here, too, the ulama were not united in their conceptions of an appropriate model for the political system in the community. The movement against the state faced many of them, who were dependent on a civil society in revolt, to the difficult choice between participating in, and supporting the movement, or rejecting it and joining the state. The majority of the ulama either participated in the movement or supported it with *fatvas* and decrees. To remain as leaders of Iranian civil society and as advocates for people, the ulama had to participate in the movement. Even Shaykh Fazl Allah Nuri who, as a result of the secularization efforts of the constitutionalists, became the ideological enemy of constitutionalism participated in the constitutional movement against the state until the temporary victory of the Revolution in August 1906. But the real social and ideological struggle about constitutionalism began after the temporary victory of the Revolution in the ranks of the ulama.

Many scholars of Constitutional Revolution agree that the ulama who participated in the Revolution, and even the leaders, did not know much about constitutionalism.[108] First, after Muhammad Ali Shah gained power and re-established an absolutist government with help from Russian brigades in Tehran, the constitutionalism of the ulama and their ideological position were seriously discussed. Before discussing the ideological justification for the ulama's participation in the Constitutional Revolution, it is important to point out the social motives for such participation. It seems that two main motives were decisive for the ulama's participation in the movement:

1. Reinforcing their traditional leadership in civil society.
2. Limiting the absolute power of the state.

Before the initial victory of the Revolution in 1906, there was not much discussion by the constitutionalist ulama about the meaning of the constitution. One of the first ulama who advocated the reforms and encouraged the ulama to unify and revolt against the tyranny was Sayyed Jamal al-Din Afghani (1838-1897). There is consensus about the influence of his reformist ideas on the constitutionalist ulama. Many of the ulama who were the leaders of the movement were highly influenced by the ideas of Jamal al-Din.[109] One of the most important agitators in the Constitutional Movement, Malek al-Mutakallemin, was influenced by him. Malek al-Mutakallemin lived with him during Sayyed Jamal's first journey to Iran and corresponded with him until his death in exile in Turkey (Malekzadeh, 1949, p. 191). He also influenced the leader of the Tobacco Movement, Haj Mirza Hasan Shirazi, before beginning to agitate against the Tobacco concession (Malekzadeh, 1949, p. 191). Although Sayyed Jamal is considered by some writers as a constitutionalist, he actually did not believe in a constitutional form of government for the East because the 'East was not yet ripe for parliamentarism'. He was most concerned about uniting and strengthening the Islamic people through religious ties against Western influence (Hairi, 1977, p. 54). Consistent with the ideals of the Shi'ite ulama, Sayyed Jamal opposed the absolute power, i.e. the despotism, of government, much more than any concern with the form of government. Even if Sayyed Jamal did not concern himself with the configuration of alternative governments to the tyrannical governments, his radical ideas against tyrannical rulers highly influenced the religious opposition to the dictators in Muslim countries from Iran to Egypt. The Iranian ulama participating in and leading the Constitutional Revolution were influenced by him and his liberal ideas.

During the constitutional movement between 1905-09 many of the ulama participated in the struggle for establishing a constitutional government. It is not possible to discuss the ideas and understanding of all of the ulama who participated in the movement, and because of the main issue of this book, a limited presentation of the ulama's ideas is necessary. Therefore, in the following part, a short survey of the constitutionalism of a few ulama who were the most influential in religious justification of constitutionalism will be discussed.

The Constitutionalism of the Leading Mujtahids

Some of the Iranian ulama resided in *'atabat* (holy cities of Iraq) and supported the people's movement against the despotic state of Iran. Their opposition to the regime and their support of the movements, such as the Tobacco Movement and Constitutional Movement, were issued by the *fatvas*. Their support of the Revolution in Iran was of great importance for legitimizing the movement and illegitimating the state, which was continually trying to gain support against the ulama who were participating in and leading the Revolution within Iran. During the process of the revolt begun in 1905 until the certain victory of the Constitutional Revolution in 1909, three high-ranking Mujtahids from *'atabat*, Tehrani, Mazandarani, and Khurasani, actively supported the Revolution.

As mentioned earlier, the ulama reacted negatively to the Qajars' policy to reinforce their powers through connections with the West. The Qajars' concession policy illegitimated their position as the protectors of the Shi'ite country of Iran and changed the balance of power in society. Accordingly, the ulama's intentions for participation in the Constitutional Revolution were not directed at the creation of a democratic society, but rather for a parliamentarian government which could limit the power of the state in favor of civil society. The ulama were mainly against the absolute power of the state that was formulated in their letters and *fatvas* as despotism and tyranny against the Muslims.

One of the three constitutionalist Mujtahids of *'atabat*, Khurasani pointed out his intention of participating in the Revolution:

> Our aim in taking such trouble is to bring a comfortable life for the people, to remove oppression, to help the oppressed, and to give aid to troubled persons, and to carry out God's laws and to protect the Islamic land from infidels' attacks. We intend to practice the Islamic concept of *amr-e bi ma'ruf va nahy-e as munkar* (to enjoin right conduct and forbid evil) and Islamic laws which are in the interest of the people (Kermani, 1983, pp. 195-96).

As we see, the aim of the ulama, according to Khurasani was to fight against 'oppression', and 'to carry out God's laws'. Such intentions obviously had very little to do with the establishment of a constitutional government based on parliamantarism as its only body of constituting laws. In a letter that Mazandarani wrote to a merchant, he said:

> We participated in the movement to protect the territory of Islam and to remove aggression and tyranny, and to apply religious laws (Hairi, 1977, p. 267).

Here too, the main two reasons for the ulama's participation in the movement are expressed as the government's 'aggression and tyranny', and 'applying of religious laws'. In a letter sent from *'atabat* to the Muhammad Ali Shah, the ulama explained their motives for participation in the Revolution. They wrote that they aimed to 'protect the religion', 'the progress and comfort of the people', and 'the protection of life and honor of the Muslims' (Kasravi, 1951, p. 617). Accordingly, for these ulama constitutionalism was a way of limiting state power and eliminating foreign influence through applying (religious) laws. Even if, as Kasravi pointed out, the ulama did not know the meaning of the *mashruteh* (constitutionalism), they knew the way through which they were able to limit state power and reinforce their influence in civil society.

The ideas of the leaders of the constitutionalist movement did not differ much from the ideas of the ulama who resided in *'atabat*. For example, in a letter to Ayn al-Daula, one of the leaders of the Revolution stated that: 'Improvement of all the problems depends on the establishment of the Majlis, the unity of the government and the people, and the unity of the authorities with the ulama' (Kasravi, 1951, p. 81). Apparently, Tabatabai believed that constitutionalism is a means by which a unified country would be constructed in which the ulama and the state could share power. There was no question about secularism, i.e., the division of political and religious power. On the contrary, the idea of unity between political and religious authority aimed to eliminate Western influence was introduced by Sayyed Jamal Afghani.

One of the two leaders of the Constitutional Revolution was Tabatabai, who may be the only one of the constitutionalist ulama who was aware of the consequences of the establishment of a constitutional regime for the prestige of the ulama. In a meeting with the Sadr-e Azam, he said:

> The *adalatkhaneh*, which we [the ulama] want established, harms us more than you; the safety and freedom of the people would be ensured. It would make them independent from us, and nobody would knock on the doors of our houses anymore (Kasravi, 1951, p. 76).

But, he continued, the only way out of the crises of the society is the establishment of a constitutionalist regime. There is a doubt about whether Tabatabai knew the real meaning of constitutionalism. Meanwhile, Algar believes that Tabatabai was confused about the meaning of constitutionalism and like other ulama saw in the constitution a means of applying the Shari'a (Algar, 1969, pp. 253-54). Even if Tabatabai was not established 'as a fully fledged secularist', he was not confused about the meaning of constitutionalism and did not see it as a means of applying the Shari'a (Hairi, 1977, pp. 86-87).

What is evident is that Tabatabai engaged, as did other ulama, in events that began as protests against the tyrannical government and demanding *adalatkhaneh* (the House of Justice). The events passed through a Revolutionary process claiming constitutionalism, and ended with the establishment of a constitutional regime. During this relatively long process, not only the urban groups in the movement, but also the ulama who were leaders in the movement had gone through ideological changes. Many theological legitimations of and justifications for the movement appeared during the period between the issuance of 'the order of the establishment of *mashruteh*' in August 1906 and the social victory of the Revolution in July 15, 1909.

One of the first demands of Tabatabai and other refugees in the *bast* of Abdul Azim was 'applying of the Islamic laws' (Kasravi, 1951, p. 67). In an other letter, he pointed out that 'We want justice, the execution of Islamic law' (Kermani, 1953, p. 381). But, during the following years of the Constitutional Revolution, he showed that he was perhaps one of the most constitutionalist, of the ulama in the modern sense. Tabatabai advocated modern education, nationalist ideas, dismissed the old Persian tradition legitimizing the king as 'the shadow of God', and even introduced the ideas about 'election of the king' (Hairi, 1977, p. 86). But the constitutionalism of Tabatabai was not against his and other ulama's position in civil society of Iran. The continuation and growth of the Constitutional Revolution greatly influenced urban social groups, in particular bazaris, whose desire for national capitalism was expressed in the foundation of the 'National Bank of Iran' during the First Majlis.[110] The urban masses who participated in the Revolution were, through close connection with the leaders' and intellectuals' ideas, influenced by the modern ideas of parliamentarism. Constitutionalism, as the aim of the movement, claimed theological justification for the ulama's participation if they wanted to remain as the leaders of civil society. The ulama who participated in the Revolution and were aware of the reality of social changes within the traditional setting of civil society[111] adjusted their desire for the limitation of the power of the state in the modern ideas of constitutionalism. Tabatabai claimed that:

> It is necessary to study modern sciences. We should study international law, mathematics and foreign languages. Why should not even one of the ulama know any foreign languages? If we had any connection with modern sciences and if we knew history and the science of law, we would have understood the real meaning of monarchy.[112]

In all Tabatabai's issues concerning the meaning and configurations of a constitutional form of conduct, he did not even mention the separation of religion and the political power. For Tabatabai and other constitutionalist ulama, *mashruteh* did not mean a constitutionalism in Western manners. In his definition of constitutionalism, the laws, in almost all cases, are identified with the Islamic laws. As mentioned earlier, Tabatabai and other constitutionalist ulama developed their initial ideas about constitutionalism and adjusted them to the necessity of the time. This evolution paralleled the process of the Revolution. Kasravi pointed out that:

> A larger group was the *mullahs*, who were the leaders. They consisted of two groups: One group was Behbahani, Tabatabai and their companions, and *akhond* Khurasani, Haji Tehrani, and Haj Shaykh Mazandarani and their companions. Because of their concern for the country and at seeing its destruction by arbitrary Qajars, in order to hinder this, they saw the

establishment of constitutionalism and the Majlis, as necessary. And at the same time, they did not know the meaning of constitutionalism, as they did later, and did not want a constitutionalism of the European type, and they were very far away from the ideas of administrating and leading a country and seeing to the progress of the people (Kasravi, 1951, p. 2 59).

Even if Tabatabai was the most radical ulama in terms of the interpretation of the notion of constitutionalism, the constitutionalist ulama never had a fully modern or Western definition of constitutionalism.

The Ulama's Ideological Challenge on Constitutionalism

After about two years of political freedom and constitutionalism in Iran, the successor of Mozaffar al-Din Shah, Muhammad Ali Shah, with the help of a Russian brigade bombarded the Majlis in June 23, 1908, and re-established the old dictatorship of the Qajars. During this period of his reign, 23 June, 1908-15 July, 1909, which is called *estebdad-e saghir* (minor autocracy), many constitutionalists were arrested and executed. Some of the constitutionalist ulama who were crucially important in protesting against anti-constitutionalists such as Malek al-Motokallemin and Sayyed Jamal Va'ez, were killed by the regime. Anti-constitutionalists, on the other side, began to protest against constitutionalism, saying that it was not Islamic. The most famous of the anti-constitutionalists was Shaykh Fazl Allah Nuri, reputedly a pious and knowledgeable Mujtahid who introduced the notion of *mashruteh-ye mashru'a* (Islamic constitutionalism). In such a situation, where anti-constitutionalism was supported by the regime and ideologically reinforced by the notion of *mashruteh-ye mashru'a*, and the lack of a famous propagator on the side of the constitutionalists, the ideological defense of constitutionalism was of great importance for the continuity of the struggle against the new/old regime and the anti-constitutionalists.

The center of the movement moved to Tabriz, in the province of Azarbayjan. As Kasravi pointed out, 'Tehran began the constitutional movement, and Tabriz continued it' (Kasravi, 1951, p. 137). But the movement needed ideological and theological legitimation to justify its continuation. The ideological, or theological, crisis of the *mashruteh* depended partly on the diffuse understanding of constitutionalism by the ulama. As mentioned earlier, *the ulama's participation in the Constitution-*

al Revolution was not because of the Constitution, but because of the Revolution. Their participation intended to re-establish and reinforce their supreme position in civil society. 'If we want to know the truth, the ulama of Najaf [Tehrani, Mazandarani, and Khurasani], and the two Sayyed [Tabatabai and Behbahani], and other ulama who were active in the constitutional movement, did not know the true meaning of constitutionalism and the application of the European laws. They also did not truly know about the obvious contradiction between the constitutionalism and Shi'ism' (Kasravi, 1951, p. 287).

Before Muhammad Ali Shah's *coup d'état* against constitutional government, some theological actions, such as Nuri's *mashruteh-ye mashru'a* (Islamic constitutionalism), had questioned the pragmatic pre-constitutional legitimation of the ulama's participation in the movement. Shaykh Fazl Allah Nuri was a prominent Mujtahid in Tehran, and, like other ulama, in order to reinforce his popular position participated in the movement. He was the first one who began to illegitimate the *unconditional mashruteh* and propagate for a *conditional* one, *mashruteh-ye mashru'a*.

Nuri, the Ideologist of the Anti-Constitutionalists

Shaykh Fazl Allah Nuri, the main knowledgeable Mujtahid in the ranks of the anti-constitutionalist ulama who participated in the constitutional movement, wanted to reinforce the social power of the ulama and limit state power. But they did not want any change in their position in the community, and they saw constitutional changes in the society as a change toward secular conditions.[113] They began to change their attitudes toward the movement after the establishment of the First Majlis, and to religiously illegitimate the constitutionalism. Nuri, who was by no means the only one of the ulama who participated in the movement, left it during the establishment of the First Majlis. The first anti-constitutional protest of the ulama was organized in Tehran by seventy eight ulama, including Shaykh Zayn al-Abedin, Sayyed Muhammad Tafreshi, Sayyed Akbar Shah, Sadr al-Muhaqeqin, and their *tullab* (religious students) who, unsuccessfully, tried to repeat the history of the *bast* (refuge) in Shah Abdul Azim by the constitutionalist ulama and to abolish the Majlis.[114] Sayyed Ahmad Tabatabai, who together with his brother and the leader of the movement, Sayyed Muhammad Tabatabai, participated in the new movement, turned away from the establishment of constitutionalism because it contributed to the spread of non-Islamic 'naturalism' and 'bahaism' (Kasravi, 1951, pp. 288-89). Even one of *Marja'-e taqlid* form *'atabat*, Sayyed Kazem Yazdi, turned against the non-Islamic nature of unconditioned constitutionalism and joined Shaykh Fazl Allah's theory of *mashruteh-ye mashru'a* (Kasravi, 1951, p. 294). During the heated discussions about the Supplement to the Fundamental Law in 1906 and the spring of 1907, ideological conflicts among the anti-constitutionalist ulama, the constitutionalist ulama, and other urban groups inside and outside the Majlis, clarified many of the positions and attitudes towards constitutionalism. The conflict was mainly over the nature of the Fundamental Law, whether it was Our'an or other sources. Some deputies of the Majlis had said that 'the Our'an is our Fundamental Law. Other deputies corrected that by saying that the Our'an is the foundation of religion, whereas the Fundamental Law determines the principles of the state and the limits of government and the rights of the nation' (Adamiyyat, 1976, p. 413). The theoretical challenge between the radical intellectuals–mainly the deputies from Tabriz–who wanted a secular constitutionalism and the ulama who believed in the Shari'a as the Fundamental Law led the constitutionalist ulama to seek compromise. Sayyed Abdullah Behbahani, one of the leaders of the Constitutional Revolution, stated his attitudes towards a compromise with the opposite group in Majlis who did not want a religious constitution. He said:

> I do not want to say do not name the country. Name it and mention it, but explore the matter so that it becomes clear that what they have done has been based on wisdom and drove from our Sacred Laws (Adamiyyat, 1977, p. 412).

Finally, a compromise was reached and a solution was found. The ulama oversaw all laws passed in Majlis to determine that they did not oppose or contradict any of the sacred laws of Islam. Also, Majlis could enact customary laws as long as they were not in contradiction with the Our'anic laws.

As mentioned earlier, the most important of the ulama in the camp of the anti-constitutionalists was Shaykh Fazl Allah Nuri, and even the idea of giving the ulama supervision of all laws passed in Majlis was his. He did not want compromises, but rather an 'Islamic consultative assembly'. His religious knowledge, prominent position in the religious schools in Tehran, and the lack of a well-developed theological justification of constitutionalism, made him an important ideologist in discrediting un-conditioned constitutionalism. To limit constitutionalism, he introduced an article to the Supplement to Fundamental Law, which was approved as the second article.

> Art. 2. At no time must any legal enactment of the holy National Consultative Assembly, /.../, be in contradiction with the holy sacred principles of Islam or the laws of His Holiness, the best of mankind, on whom and his family be the blessing and the peace of God; and it is evident that the determining of the contradiction between the legal enactment and the principles of Islam has been, and is, the duty of high-ranking ulama (Kasravi, 1951, p. 372).

Even if the approval of Article 2 was considered a victory for Shaykh Fazl Allah, he was not satisfied. On the contrary, he was determined to eliminate constitutionalism which he considered 'anti-Islamic'. The Shi'ite ulama of Iran were apparently divided into two groups, the constitutionalists under the leadership of Tabatabai and Behbahani, and the anti-constitutionalists, led by Shaykh Fazl Allah Nuri. When, on 23 June 1908, Muhammad Ali Shah with the help of Russian Brigades bombarded the Majlis and abolished the constitutional government, the struggle between the constitutionalists and anti-constitutionalists intensified. Besides the government's active support of the anti-constitutionalists, Shaykh Fazl Allah's theological challenge to constitutionalism was of great importance for mobilizing the anti-constitutionalist and conservative ulama, both inside Iran and in *'atabat*. Aiming at the theological mobilization of the anti-constitutionalists, he wrote a book which discussed the incompatibility of constitutionalism with Islam. He pointed out that:

> It is evident to all believers that the best of laws are the sacred laws and for a Muslim there is no necessity for proofs, and, Thanks to God, we the *emamiyyeh* people [Shi'ites] have the best and the most complete sacred laws, because these are God's commandments to His best and last messenger. /.../ If there is somebody who thinks that the changes of the time bring about the change in some of the principles of these sacred laws, he is not a believer Muslim. /.../ because our prophet is the last messenger and his laws are the last ones (Nuri, 1993, pp. 532-36).

After a discussion about the contradictions between the sacred laws of Islam and the Fundamental Law, Nuri attacked the constitutionalists and accused them of not being Muslims. He then discussed the position of political power in the Muslim community. He wrote that in the Muslim community the 'consultation of the deputies' is against sacred laws, because the 'representation' is a matter of the *velayat* (leadership) of Hidden Imam and his deputies and does not concern anybody else (Nuri, 1993). He then supported Muhammad Ali Shah and challenged the constitutionalists, asking that, 'if they wanted to reinforce the power of Islam, why did they weaken the Islam supporter Shah' (Nuri, 1993). He then attacked the idea of establishment of the Majlis and supported the bombing: 'Muslims destroyed that house of sin [the Majlis] which was made the sources of harm to Islam and Muslims' (Nuri, 1993, p. 536). He was against the establishment of new schools and the modern education propounded and applied by the constitutionalists. Satisfied with the execution and arrest of the intellectuals and founders of such schools, he wrote:

> Where are those non-believers who wanted, according to the need of time, to introduce the natural laws, according to their damaged brain, in Iran, and educate the children to naturalists? Where are those who have said and have written that the obligatory education of the Iranian children in the modern schools was necessary? /.../ You committed such ugly mistakes that God destroyed your houses (Nuri, 1993).

However, Nuri's theological attacks on constitutionalism did not remain unanswered. The constitutionalist ulama began to provide theological arguments for establishment of a constitutional assembly in the country.

The Theological Justification of the Ulama's Opposition

In such a situation in which the constitutionalists were pushed back from their social positions and were ideologically unstable, some ulama provided reasons for their participation in the Revolution. One of the constitutionalist ulama, Shaykh Isma'il Mahallati, presented what may be the clearest theological motives for the ulama's participation in the Revolution against the 'Islam supporter shah'. He pointed out that:

> There can be considered to be three kinds of governments: 1) the rule of the infallible Imam; 2) an absolute tyrannical monarchy; 3) a limited

> and constitutional form of government. The first type is presently impossible. The choice, therefore, would be between the other two and, of course, every person of intelligence would choose the third type of government system.[115]

As seen here, the constitutional ulama's justification for the Revolution is the other side of the practical reason for their participation in the movement. As mentioned earlier, they participated in the movement to protect and reinforce their leading position in civil society of Iran. Consequently, they worked to limit the absolute power of the state. As Mahallati suggested, the constitutional form of government is the appropriate form in which the Majlis construct a suitable means for limiting the power of the state. The constitutionalist ulama's participation in the movement was not aimed at introducing or establishing a Western constitutional regime instead of the 'Islam supporter shah' in Iran. Rather they wanted to adjust constitutionalism to the Islamic principles and the structure of the Iranian society in which they had a leading position. Mahallati clearly stated the ulama's intentions in participating in the Revolution:

> If the ulama do not participate in the constitutional movement, the politics of this Islamic country will follow the European model. Therefore it is compulsory for them to lend a hand to the politicians to establish laws which are in accordance with Islam (Hairi, 1977, p. 101).

In other words, if the Constitutional Revolution succeeded without the participation of the ulama, it would have changed the structure of Iranian society, and the ulama would lose their exclusive position in civil society. Accordingly, they wanted the establishment of a Majlis by which they would increase their influence and limit state power. To justify the Constitutional Revolution and to face the 'evil thoughts' of Shaykh Fazl Allah Nuri about constitutionalism, Mahallati felt that 'Any opposition to the establishment of the National Consultative Assembly would be like fighting a war against the Hidden Imam' (Hairi, 1977, p. 101).

Among the constitutionalist ulama, Mirza Muhammad Husayn Na'ini (1860-1936) was, ideologically at least, the most important supporter of the Constitutional Revolution. His theological justification for the ulama's participation in the mass movements of 1908-09 that defeated Muhammad Ali Shah's dictatorship and regained constitutionalism was of great importance for the ideological mobilization of the constitutionalist ulama against anti-constitutionalist ones. Na'ini offered evidence for the justification of the constitutional form of government from Qur'an and *hadith* (the sayings of the Prophet). He used several Qur'anic verses to condemn the tyranny. He, for example, pointed out the Qur'anic verses:

> And they said: Shall we put faith in two mortals like ourselves, and whose folk are servile unto us? (23:47).
> The chiefs of Pharaoh's people said: (O King), wilt thou suffer Moses and his people to make mischief in the land, and flout thee and the gods? He said: We will slay their sons and spare their women, for lo! we are in power over them (7:127).
> They ascribe no thing as partner unto Me. Those who disbelieve henceforth, they are the miscreants (24:55) (Hairi, 1977, pp. 173-74).

He equated living under tyranny with slavery. To justify his political declarations, he used several hadith, speeches, and sayings of Shi'ite Imams. Like Mahallati, Na'ini offered the Shi'ite explanations for the establishment of the constitutional regime. He wrote that: 'The best means to preserve such privileges as a constitutional regime and to avoid tyranny is immunity to sin, or infallibility (*'ismat*) on which rulership in the religion of us Twelver Shi'ah depends' (Hairi, 1977, p. 191). But, he continued, because 'such a qualified man, namely the Imam, is not presently available', we have to choose a constitutional form of government (Hairi, 1977).

The major dispute anti-constitutionalists had with constitutionalism was that it violated the absolute right of the Hidden Imam for *velayat* in the Muslim community. Even if Na'ini accepted that such a regime would be a usurpation of the Imam's authority, he meant that it is permissible according to Islam (Hairi, 1977). To neutralize the usurpation of the Hidden Imam's authority, which was the main weapon against the constitutionalist ulama, he argued that:

> There are three points of which one should not lose sight: first, if one commits several evils at the same time, it is compulsory to prevent the person from performing each one of them. Every single evil creates a separate responsibility for a Muslim to prevent it (*nahy-i az munkar*). Bad deeds should be prevented as far and in as many cases as possible. If, for instance, one is able to make another person to abandon only one of several evils he has committed, it is necessary to prevent him without taking into

consideration his other bad deeds. Second, whatever action that may be against Islamic law should be handled by the administration of the *hisbah*; the latter office is unquestionably under the authority of the *fughaha* during the Greater Occultation of the Twelfth Imam. It is true that the ulama's responsibility as General Agents of the Imam in all other offices, i.e., rulership, is not unquestionably recognized, but we know that Islam does not allow disorder and the loss of the Islamic territory. We also know that establishing order in Islamic countries is more important than every other duty, *hisbah* or otherwise. Therefore, it also becomes a definite right and a religious duty of the ulama to possess the ruling power. Third, it is generally recognized by all the ulama that if someone establishes illegal power over a certain thing which is in the sphere of *vilayat* (supervisorship), i.e., *auqaf*, and his complete removal from that position is not possible, it is still compulsory to limit his unlawful hold as far as possible. Every learned man, whether Muslim or materialist, can have no doubt about this matter (Hairi, 1977, p. 193).

Here Na'ini provides three reasons for legitimating a constitutional regime. The first is about the compulsory duty of every Muslim, namely *amr-e be ma'ruf va nahy-e az munkar* (to enjoin right conduct and forbid evil). He means that, even if we, as Muslims, can only forbid one evil (oppression) of the government by the establishment of a constitutional regime, we have to do that. Second, he argues that, even if in a constitutional regime, the authority of the ulama over the legislative system is not 'unquestionably recognized', because of the necessity of order in Muslim society and for the defense of the Islamic territory we have to accept a constitutional regime in the community. Third, he said that if we, during the Occultation of the Imam, cannot remove an unlawful holder of an office, it is still compulsory to limit it. Therefore, the limitation of the state power is of great importance in his argument for the establishment of a constitutional regime. Na'ini argued that the tyrannical regime of the shah consisted of three usurpations and oppressions:

1) It is usurpation of the authority of God and injustice to Him; 2) it is usurpation of the Imam's authority and oppression of the Imam; 3) it also involves oppression of the people. By contrast, a constitutional system is only oppression of the Imam, because his authority is usurped. Thus, a constitutional regime limits three sets of oppression to one; consequently it is necessary to adopt it (Hairi, 1977, pp. 193-94).

Na'ini considered the tyrannical power *sherk* (usurpation to God), and the ulama who supported the tyrannical regime by using the religion, infidels (Momeni, 1993, pp. 259-60). But his discussions and interpretations about constitutionalism were not intended to justify a separation between the political and religious power of the ulama. Rather, he sought to find a solution for preservation of the ulama's position in the society and limitation of the power of the tyrannical state.

Shaykh Fazl Allah Nuri attacked constitutionalism as an innovation (*bid'at*) against Islamic laws Shari'a. In order to neutralize the opposition of Nuri, Na'ini pointed out that:

> Legislation would be a *bid'at* (innovation) and consequently against Islam only if one declares a non-Islamic provision to be a provision of Shari'a and apply that; but if one does not address the non-Islamic provision to Shari'a, then there would not be any *bid'at* (Na'ini, 1955, p. 7 4).

Even in the necessity for writing a constitution, he expressed the Shi'ite ulama's historical and structural need to limit the power of the state. He saw the establishment of a constitution as the only way for limiting the power of the state in modern times. But it does not mean with the term constitutional law Na'ini meant secular laws completely separated from Shari'a. On the contrary, he pointed out that constitutional law must be drafted according to religious law; and the laws must be religiously legitimized under the supervision of the ulama (Na'ini, 1955, p. 15).

Another burning matter of theological contradiction between the constitutionalist and anti-constitutionalist ulama was the matter of establishing a legislative parliament. The ideologist of the anti-constitutionalists, Shaykh Fazl Allah Nuri, challenged the idea of parliament on the following grounds:

1. Dealing with the affairs of the people is a responsibility of the qualified Mujtahids, not of any individual from among the people, such as a grocer or a draper (*baqqal va bazzaz*).

2. The idea of the majority, whose agreement makes the law, is an innovation that is against Islam.

3. In the *fiqh*, the problem of *vekala*, or representation, has been discussed in the sense that one person appoints another as his lawyer to perform certain actions on his behalf. This arrangement involves individual matters; for instance, one person may appoint another to buy a house for him and sign necessary papers on his behalf. The lawyer is called *vakil* and

his action *vekala*, However, when a problem belongs to the public and a *vekala* is required, no one but the Mujtahids are capable of handling the matter' (Hairi, 1977, p. 205).

To face this religiously justified opposition to constitutionalism, Na'ini again used the notion of *hisbah*. The institution of *hisbah* implies the ulama's administration of social institutions such as justice and *auqaf*. According to the Shi'ite *fiqh*, during the Greater Occultation of the Hidden Imam, the ulama are responsible for the administration of such institutions. 'According to the Shi'ite ulama, any action which opposes the teachings of the Shari'a must be prevented by the institution of *hisbah*, which is unquestionably under the authority of the ulama' (Na'ini, 1955, p. 101). Na'ini, through making the prevention of disorder in the Muslim country the main duty of both the state and the ulama felt that 'Order in Muslim countries is more important than all matters of *hisbah*' (Na'ini, 1955, p. 46).

Na'ini, like other constitutionalist ulama, tried to justify the ulama's participation in the movement and the acceptance of a constitutional form of government by adjusting constitutional demands to the Islamic laws and *hadith*. For him, as for other constitutionalist ulama, the main motive for objection to the shah was his tyrannical reign, which influenced the position of the ulama and their 'natural' allies, the bazaris.

The Victory of the Modern Civil Society

Revolutions have, of course, much more wide-ranging consequences than the destruction of the old regime. The immediate victory of the Constitutional Revolution in August 1906 resulted in the establishment of a parliament (Majlis). The establishment of the Majlis was initially the aim of intellectuals and, during the process of the Revolution, was adopted also by the bazaris and the ulama. But there was no clear, common definition of constitutionalism: different groups had different conceptions or understandings. For the ulama and the bazaris constitutionalism was a means by which they could limit the power of shah and the foreign impact. In other words, constitutionalism could protect the basis of traditional civil society. For intellectuals constitutionalism not only would limit the power of the shah and eliminate dictatorship, but would also create a democratic system of government in which the ultimate sources of power would come from the people. A division of power between Majlis and state was created–even if not fully developed–after the victory of the Constitutional Revolution. This was primarily a great victory for the emerging groups which were to make up the modern civil society of Iran. The division of power between Majlis and state was the beginning of a violation of the traditional socio-political order of society. On the one hand, the Majlis was a constitutive organ which could make up new laws and challenge the Islamic laws Shari'a. On the other hand, concentration of executive power in the state organs challenged the absolute power of the shah. Such controversies made up a sphere of contestation and challenge between the groups who defended the traditional and religiously legitimized order of society and the intellectuals and other modern groups who were interested in a new order which was legitimized according to modern ideas.

The death of Mozaffaredin Shah just ten days after signing 'the command of constitutionalism' sharpened the challenge between the democratic movement and anti-democratic and traditional groups. The anti-constitutionalists were headed by the crown prince Muhammad Ali Shah who became the king and began immediately his challenge against other centers of power and influence than his own. His enmity against the Majlis and the constitutional government, which were the fruits of the Constitutional Revolution, became apparent from the very beginning of his reign by his questioning of his father's decree. He tried to pressure his father's physician to proclaim that Mozaffaredin Shah had been very sick when he signed 'the command of constitutionalism' and did not really know what he had done (Adamiyyat, 1987, pp. 30-2). When Mozaffaredin Shah's physician did not accept the new Shah's order, the Shah ordered Mokhtar al-Dula from the police to obtain the physician's proclamation:

> We ordered A'lam al-dula to prove our father's sickness and that because of sickness, he could not understand the content of the letters in his last days. I ordered Kamran Mirza to obtain the proclamation (Adamiyyat, 1987, p. 31).

As Adamiyyat (1987, pp. 33-4) pointed out, according to constitutionalism the power of the shah was not divinely legitimized, and the Majlis in one of its first proclamations in March 1907 stated: 'When the country was highly corrupted and dissolute, the people of Iran saw the way towards civilization and the development of the country by changing the regime to a constitutional one'.

The Majlis and the new order was not only challenging the power of the Shah, but also the traditional power of the ulama. One of the most important means of ulama's influence in civil society was their monopoly over the judicial system. When, according to the new constitutional order, the judicial system was to be modified and subordinated to the Majlis, a sphere of contestation between the ulama and the Majlis was created. The matter of controversy was the extent of influence of *shar'* and *u'rf* courts and the role of the ulama. A compromise was reached and presented to the Majlis in a parliamentary commission, in which the ulama were represented by Haj Mirza Yahya Khoi and Saqat al-Eslam Shirazi. According to the new law (§ 71) 'the supreme court and *adliyyeh* (justice) courts are the official instances of treating people's disputes, and judgments in religious matters are the task of the qualified Mujtahids' (Adamiyyat, 1987, p. 46). *In a word, separation of judicial matters.*

For the first time in Iranian history, the Constitutional Revolution constructed a compromise between the traditional civil society of Iran and the modern liberal groups who came to make up the basis of the modern society of Iran during the twentieth century. But, this cooperation, which made the Constitutional Revolution possible, was also a conflictive one. As mentioned earlier, the ulama participated and led the Constitutional Revolution not for the sake of constitutionalism and freedom, but rather for the maintenance of their position in civil society and reinforcement of their relationship with the bazaris. They adopted the idea of constitutionalism as a means for realizing their intentions. But, the outcome of the Constitutional Revolution did not fit their expectations. The new groups and associations came to play a central role in the political arena and to complicate the traditional relationship between state and civil society.

One of the new means in propagating against the dictatorship of the Shah and supporting the democratic groups and institutions was newspapers. Although, the newspapers played a role before the political victory of the Revolution in 1906 by propagating against the regime, the victory of the Revolution led to the increased importance of newspapers for modern intellectual and literate groups. The liberals and intellectuals who depended on the role of the *manbars,* that were completely controlled by the ulama, in political propaganda, tried to establish their own means of broadcasting and making political propaganda. Shortly after the victory of the Revolution many newspapers were being published. The most important ones were *Majlis, Hebl al-matin, Sobh-e sadeq, Mosavat,* and *Sor-e esrafil*. The latter was published in twenty four thousands copies and played a central role (Mustaufi, 1942, p. 249). The newspapers were effectively used by new groups as a modern alternative to the traditional *manbars*. In the conflict between the anti-constitutionalists and the revolutionary forces, the newspapers played an effective role in isolating and illegitimating the former. One of the most important religious leaders of the anti-constitutionalist groups, Shaykh Fazlallah Nuri, was continually under the attack of liberal newspapers.[116] Even after the Shah's *coup d'état* against the constitutionalists in 1908, the newspapers played a crucial role in the struggle against the Shah. Newspapers which could not be published in Iran moved abroad. 'Everywhere they were publishing in Arabic, the liberals came together and published the newspaper and conveyed the news back to Iran of the resistance in Tabriz and other Iranian cities and even the commands of the ulama of *'atabat*[117] to Iran' (Mustaufi, 1942, p. 264).

Accordingly, the mass media came to provide the modern civil society with a crucial means in their ideological struggle against both the dictatorship and the old balance of power between the ulama and the state. The Constitutional Revolution put an end to the traditional monopoly of ulama in civil society and created a potentially powerful rival for domination in the political arena of Iranian society. By leading and participating in the Constitutional Revolution, the ulama succeeded to a certain degree in reinforcing their position in the traditional civil society, in part by helping the bazaris in their struggle against the regime. But, simultaneously, they helped to establish and legitimize modern political games in which emerging groups apparently had greater capabilities to participate and to compete effectively.

PART II
THE NEW MONARCHICAL REGIME, MODERNIZATION, AND THE ISLAMIC REVOLUTION

6 Iran Under the Pahlavis

The last monarchical regime in Iran was founded in 1925 by Reza Shah. He and his son Muhammad Reza Shah held power until the victory of the Islamic Revolution in February 1979. During more than fifty years of reign, the Pahlavis created a very powerful central government separated from religious authority. They created a powerful military force, fifth in size in the world, statewide modern middle occupational groups, new industrial sectors, new educational and health care systems, modern transportation and communication sectors, modern cities, and so forth. Briefly, Iran under the reign of Pahlavis, changed from a state on the edge of chaos to a country with considerable socio-economic and military power. In this chapter, the reconstruction of Iran according to the Pahlavis' model of modernization, its effect on the social groups, in particular the urban occupational groups, the ulama, and the intellectuals will be discussed.

The Construction and Reconstruction of the 'New Iran'

After the Constitutional Revolution, Iran became embroiled in civil war (June 1908-July 1909) followed by a period of disintegration (1909-1921). This took place in the context of the loose compromise among the main social groups that constituted the deputies of the parliament. These groups could not be expected to sit in the same Majlis (parliament) and discuss or negotiate such important matters as the economic or social policies in a time when foreign powers had such a strong presence in Iran.

The years after the end of World War I were a period of disintegration and turmoil in Iran as a result of the weakness of the central government. Most of Iran was divided among local landowners, tribes, and *khans*. In some provinces such as Gilan in the north, a republic was constituted by Kuchik Khan, who was supported by Russian troops staying in that province. The foreign powers of Russia and England, which, shortly before the beginning of the War had actually occupied the country and highly influenced its policy, were still in Iran, although the balance of power favored England because of the revolutionary conditions in Russia. Almost all social groups suffered disintegration and instability due to the lack of a powerful central government. During the Constitutional Revolution, constitutionalism had been legitimated as the only way of rescuing the country from the hands of foreigners and dictators.[118] But in the period after the establishment of constitutionalism in Iran, the 1907 treaty between Russia and England by which Iran was divided between these two colonial powers, World War I, the Ottoman invasion, the continuing weakness of the central government, economic decline, and the internal rival groups, illegitimated, to a large extent, the ideas of democracy and constitutionalism. As Kasravi pointed out:

> The existence of many autonomous power centers, which led to a complete lack of security and the almost disintegration of the country, was the main reason that the people of Iran supported the establishment of a dictatorship (Kasravi, 1942, pp. 36-7).

The political sphere, too, was a scene of fractional rivalry that divided and weakened the political parties such as the Democrats and Moderates (Bahar, 1944). After the revolution of 1917 and the civil war in Russia, England attempted capitalize on the opportunity by imposing the Anglo-Persian Treaty of 1919, which would virtually have turned Iran into a British protectorate (Milani, 1994, p. 31).

This was the atmosphere, under which Reza Khan, then an army officer of the Cossack Brigade, successfully unified the military forces. These were divided into two main groups, the Cossacks and the gendarmery led by the Swedish general Westdahl. Reza Khan brought both groups under his personal command and created a powerful alternative to the government–and the young but weak Shah. Reza Khan successfully defeated several local powers and the most important one, the Republic of Gilan. Reza Khan's military capability had before the *coup d'état* impressed the local commander of British forces in Iran, Ironside. These factors played a role in him becoming established as the chief commander of the Persian armed forces.

On 21 February 1921, Reza Khan, together with an Anglophile politician, Seyyed Zia, initiated a *coup d'état*. Reza Khan's troops gathered in Qazvin, occupied Tehran, and imposed martial law. Ahmad Shah, impressed by the rapid events, appointed Zia prime minister and Reza Khan the commander of the Army, *Sardar-e Sepah*. In the Zia's cabinet, Reza Khan became the minister of Army. Reza Khan was a nationalist who believed deeply in a strong and independent army as a guarantee for the country's independence from foreign powers. In a declaration he made shortly after the *coup d'état*, he stated his goals quite clearly:

> Our aim is to establish a /.../ strong government, which will create a powerful and respected army, because a strong army is the only means of saving the country from the miserable state of its affairs. We want to establish a government that will not discriminate among Gilanis, Tabrizis, and Kermanis. We want to establish a government that will not be an instrument of foreign politics.[119]

After a short reign as prime minister, Zia lost his office to other political leaders. But Reza Khan maintained control of the Army and received support from almost all political groups who saw him as the one who could save the country and even the constitution.[120] Reza Khan continued to struggle against the different power centers in the country, such as the revolt of Colonel Pesian in Khurasan, Sheykh Khaz'al in Khuzestan and Simko in Kurdistan. Reza Khan's military victories increased his popularity and charisma over the entire country. During the period of the Fifth Majlis, events in Turkey[121] inspired Reza Khan to advocate the elimination of the Iranian monarchy and the creation of a republic. He probably knew that his popularity would guarantee him the presidency of an eventual Iranian republic.[122]

The ulama who largely supported Reza Khan, opposed the idea of republic without gods, like the one they had recently seen take hold in Turkey (cf. Ghods, 1989, p. 96). Prominent ulama outside the Majlis, such as Ayatollah Abdol Karim Ha'eri, declared republicanism contrary to Islam. Inside the Majlis, Modarres, who forced Reza Khan to temporarily resign, also forced him to retreat from republicanism in favor of the crown of the Shah. Enjoying the popularity he received from his military victories, Reza Khan convinced the Fifth Majlis to dethrone Ahmad Shah and the reign of the Qajars. At the end of 1925 the Constitutional Assembly voted to support the creation of the new Pahlavi dynasty in Iran. The new dynasty was recognized by both Britain and the Soviet Union, who were both interested in establishing a powerful government in Iran–but for different motives. England saw Reza Shah as a leader who could construct a major obstacle against the communists, and the Soviet Union recognized him as a nationalist who could put an end to the influence of its rival, England, in Iran (Ghods, 1989, pp. 98-9).

Crowned as Shah, Reza Khan began an unique modernization program. Ideologically, he and his administration used the pre-Islamic legitimation of the kingdom. Choosing the name Pahlavi, which was the pre-Islamic language of Persia, and changing the name of country from Persia to Iran as an emphasis on Iranian people's Aryan heritage, were among those changes intended to release the political leadership from the religious authority. Reza Shah is considered as the founder of modern Iran and the promoter of national integration. His reform programs 'turned the regionally and tribally segmented Qajar society into a reasonably homogenous nation' (Arjomand, 1984, p. 71). Reza Shah's modernization programs can be divided into three categories: (1) economic reforms, (2) administrative reforms, and (3) social reforms.

Economic Reforms

Thousands of miles of new roads, railways, and bridges were constructed. The most famous of these was the Trans-Iranian Railway, which linked the northern port of Bandar Shah with the port of Bandar Shahpur in the south, a distance of 1,394 kilometers. The army provided security on the roads, which substantially increased the commerce between cities and foreign countries. 'Reza Shah established state controlled monopolies in sugar and tea (1925), opium (1928), tobacco (1929), and many other commodities' (Ghods, 1989, p. 101). Private industry was encouraged by exemptions from customs duties and certain other taxes, by rebates and preferences, by credit supplied by the Agricultural and Industrial Bank founded in 1933, and by protective measures including tariffs, quotas, and exchange controls. In addition, the government set up and ran several plants in textiles, sugar refining, cement, and other industries, and a steel mill and iron foundry were under construction in 1941. By then, the cement, textile, food, drink, and tobacco industries met a large part of domestic consumption.[123] State monopoly over some industries made effective controls over imports possible. New tariffs on foreign commodities were introduced in order to support the native production. These, in turn, increased both internal production and state income. State expenditures were effectively controlled by the government as a result of modernizing the fiscal system. The banking system was improved and the new national bank, Bank-e Melli, was founded in 1927.

Reza Shah's economic policy was mainly aimed at moving Iran from a position of near collapse to one of security and strength. During his relatively short time as Shah, he arranged the investment of about $260 million in railways and another $260 million in industry. These figures, as Issawi pointed out, represent a very high investment ratio for an economy of the size and level of Iran (Issawi, 1978, p. 132). Reza Shah's nationalist intentions led him to oppose foreign loans, even for modernizing the country. All the projects were financed by taxes and the meager income from oil. The social consequences of Reza Shah's economic reforms were more important, in some sense, for the future socio-political development of the country than the economic one. For example, Iran's industrial workforce tripled between 1931 and 1941. By the end of Reza Shah's reign, there were about 700,000 workers in the country, including those in older industries such as carpet weaving and fisheries as well as the recently created factories and construction projects (Ghods, 1989, p. 111).

Administrative Reforms

As the commander of the army, Reza Shah believed deeply in the strong army for a powerful state. He introduced conscription in 1925 to create a disciplined army independent of foreign and religious influence. A third of the budget was devoted to it (Ghods, 1989, p. 103). He used the army to curtail almost all the centrifugal power of landowners and tribal *khans*. Through a modern taxation system, he reformed the state financial institutions and created thousands of new state employees. The income from taxes and oil revenue secured a basis for the development of an enormous state bureaucracy during the reign of Reza Shah. State officials increasingly made up a major part of the new modern middle occupational groups. Reza Shah was determined to secularize Iranian politics and release the state from the influence of religious authority. Consequently, he would have to challenge the power of the ulama. To suppress their judicial power, a new law was passed by which all judges were required to have a formal judicial degree. Gradually European civil and penal laws replaced Islamic laws (Milani, 1994, p. 33).

Social Reforms

The educational system was reformed along a modern model. Hundreds of new schools were built. The university of Tehran, also Iran's first modern university, was founded in 1934, and the government sent many students to Europe for higher education.[124] Many ulama who, in accordance with the tradition of religious education were trained in Islamic jurisprudence, were forced out of the courts. Furthermore, no cases were to be referred to Shari'a courts 'without authorization from state courts and the Attorney General' (Ghods, 1989, p. 105). The establishment of the new schools crowded out the majority of the traditional religious *maktabs* and *madrasahs*. Intending to modernize the social institutions and challenge the very basis of the religious authority of the ulama, he wanted to bring women into the new public life of the cities. In 1927, he established a school to educate women as teachers, and he later made it possible for women to participate in higher education at Tehran university. One of Reza Shah's most controversial 'reforms' was outlawing the veil, especially the traditional *chador* for women. Veiled women were forbidden to appear in the public places, and the police and soldiers were ordered to unveil women by force. Western clothing became obligatory for governmental employees, and bearing religious clothes in public places by non-clergy was forbidden. Even the clergy who wanted to bear religious clothes had to get permission from the Ministry of Education.[125] Uprisings against Reza Shah's intentions to secularize the country from above, such as the revolt of Shiraz and Mashad, were suppressed in bloody confrontations. Reza Shah had this to say about his new reforms concerning the status of women:

> I am exceedingly pleased to observe that, as a result of knowledge and learning, women have come alive to their condition, rights and privileges /.../. We should not forget that up to this time one-half of the population of the country was not taken into account. No statistics of the female population were taken /.../. I am not trying to point out contrasts between today and the old days but you ladies should consider this as a great day. You should avail yourselves of the opportunities which you now have to improve your country.[126]

In connection with authoritarian modernization programs, Reza Shah established a very centralized and powerful regime in order to promote national unity, independence, and economic development, in line with Western industrialized societies. He centralized power and established a strong army and bureaucracy. He limited the economic freedom of the new middle occupational groups and destroyed non-governmental political institutions. He began a bloody struggle against the intelligentsia and the clergy. 'The merchants lost freedom of enterprise as they were drawn into the governmental system of monopolies and of control over industry, commerce, and trade' (Willer, 1981). Reza Shah's modernization programs were partly directed against the ulama, who had a tight grip on many aspects of public life.

Some of Reza Shah's major reforms especially challenged the ulama: the outlawing of the veil, the establishment of a modern educational system in the entire country (earlier, the clergy had a monopoly over education through *maktabs* and *madrasahs*), and establishment of the modern legal system. Although Reza Shah intended to industrialize the entire country, his reforms were limited to the towns. In the beginning of his reign, he mentioned the necessity of land reform, but peasants remained under the domination of landowners. Gradually, Reza Shah himself became a landowner, through marriage with the traditional Qajar families, and through taking land by force. By abolishing heavy taxes on 200 guilds, putting other restrictions on merchants, and by establishing state-financed enterprises and government monopolies, he created a few favored import-exporters and court-connected industries. Reza Shah's socio-economic reforms led to the creation of two main social groups that came to play a decisive role in the socio-political history of Iran. One of these groups was the modern urban middle occupational groups which, paradoxically, came to make up the main base of modern political ideas. The middle occupational groups provided considerable support for the nationalistic ideas of National Front (NF), and participated in the movement for the nationalization of the oil industries after Reza Shah's abdication. Intellectuals from the modern middle occupational groups founded Iran's first communist party, Tudeh Party (Ghods, 1989, pp. 113-16).

All in all, Rezah Shah succeeded in creating modern middle occupational groups, 'centralizing the state, pacifying the tribes, disciplining the clergy, unveiling women, eliminating aristocratic titles, introducing mass conscription, undermining "feudal" authorities, integrating population, and establishing modern schools' (Kasravi, 1942). He changed the relationship between the state and the ulama. Under his regime, the clergy were restricted and pushed back into the religious schools and mosques. At the same time, he established a regime of state terrorism with the physical elimination of intelligentsia, through torture and jails. In 1941, when the allies occupied Iran, Reza Shah was accused of supporting Germany in the War and shipped off to the island of Mauritius.

Reza Shah and the Ulama

From the beginning of his career, Reza Shah was aware of the power of the ulama and Shi'ism in Iran. In his first years in power, he continuously tried to demonstrate his Shi'ite faith and respect for prominent ulama. He participated in mournings held in the memory of the Imams. The ulama chose days, such as Muharram 9th and 10th, called *tasu'a* and *ashura*, when the Third Imam, Husayn, and many of his family were killed by Ummayyids in Karbala in 680, to express their dissatisfaction with the tyrannical regime. These particular days are the most important days in Shi'ite communities, involving the participation of the people. Both in the Constitutional and the Islamic Revolution, the ulama effectively used these days to propagandize and mobilize the people. Well aware of this, Reza Khan participated in the religious ceremonies, in particular in the mourning of *tasu'a* and *ashura*.

> Muharram 10th, 'the day of martyrdom', the Cossacks division, in a very disciplined character, playing mourning march, with horses and other military facilities, came in the bazaar and *Sardar-e Sepah* [Reza Khan] himself, meanwhile have naked his head and strewing hay on his head and face, was observed in the front of the division, other Cossack's officers were mourning behind him/.../. Even in the night of Muharram 11th Cossack division come to the bazaar and participated in the ritual of *Sham-e ghariban*, and *Sardar-e Sepah* himself with naked head and feet bearing candles, arrived Masjid Jame'a Tehran and Masjid Sheykh Abdul Hossayn, which was the most important mourning place of that days (Bahar, 1944, p. 183).

After the settlement of the semi-government of Sheykh Khaz'al in the south, Reza Khan made a pilgrimage of thanksgiving to the holy shrines of Najaf and Karbala.[127]

The years between Reza Khan's coup of 1921 and his total seizure of political power in 1925 coincided with the beginning of the revolution in Iraq. Some of the Shi'ite ulama who supported the revolution, such as Shaykh Muhammad Khalisi and Sayyed Muhammad Sadr were exiled to Iran. Later in June 1923, a prominent Mujtahid, Mahdi Khalisi, was deported to Hijaz. Na'ini, Isfahani, and several other leading ulama of Karbala and Najaf protested against Khalisi's deportation by leaving Iraq for Persia (Hairi, 1977, pp. 131-32). The Iranian government welcomed the exiled ulama. They settled down in Qum, the religious center of Iran. The clerical center of Qum was under leadership of the grand Mujtahid, Sheykh Abd al-Karim Ha'iri's. Highly apolitical, Ha'iri had left Iran during the events of the Constitutional Revolution, he moved to Karbala from Najaf because of the Najaf ulama's participation in the uprising of the people. But his attitudes toward political activism did not preclude him from undertaking other social activities, such as establishing a library, hospital, public cemetery, and housing for the poor (Hairi, 1977, p. 136). Isfahani and Na'ini presented a challenge to Ha'iri's apolitical attitude. Reza Khan needed the support of the ulama in order to change the regime of Iran. After Ahmad Shah's last trip to Europe in November 1923, Reza Khan, in order to put an end to the reign of the Qajar dynasty, began his propaganda for the establishment of a republic. The ulama, both inside the Majlis, such as *Modarres*, and outside–in particular in Qum–opposed the idea of republicanism, pointing out the secularization process in Turkey that had resulted. Ha'iri who was an apolitical person became also engaged in this 'non-Islamic' idea of republicanism. The ulama organized several meetings in the major religious cities, such as Mashad and Qum, in protest against Reza Khan's republican ideas. Reza Khan who wanted a good relationship with the ulama in order to seize political power and overthrow the Shah, began to listen to the ulama's protests, he went to Qum in the name of bidding farewell to the expelled ulama who wanted to move to Iraq. The visit resulted in an agreement between Reza Khan and the ulama which put an end to the idea of republicanism. In a letter sent by Isfahani, Na'ini, and Ha'iri to the ulama of Tehran, they announced the agreement:

> There have been expressed certain ideas concerning a republican form of government that do not please the public and do not suit this country. We, therefore, asked the Prime Minister to put an end to this issue, while he came to Qum to bid farewell to the ulama, by announcing the matter all

over the country. He accepted our request. All the people should be grateful and should appreciate this solicitude (Hairi, 1977, pp. 142-43).

Reza Shah, intending to demonstrate his good relationship with the ulama, which was essential if he were to become the new king of Iran, issued a manifesto in which he gave up the idea of republicanism.

> The will of the people, public opinion, and respect for religion and the religious feelings of my fellow-citizens, are of primary importance for me in running the government. To these ends I have given a favorable response to the request of the religious leaders in Qum. From now on, accordingly, the abandonment of the idea of a republic is highly recommended.[128]

The ulama's protest against Reza Khan's ideas about the establishment of a republic provided a suitable basis for him to claim the throne of Iran. Reza Khan, like many other political leaders in Iran, was aware of the power and influence of the ulama in civil society of Iran. Therefore, he sought a good relationship with the leading ulama, at least until securing his position as the Shah. To do so, he was ready to compromise with the ulama and accept the most controversial problem of the Iranian Constitution, namely the supervision of the ulama over the decisions of the Majlis. As mentioned earlier, after putting an end to the rebellion of Shaykh Khaz'al in the southern provinces, Reza Khan made a pilgrimage to Najaf and met the leading ulama.

> According to an eye-witness quoted by Na'ini's bio-grapher, Hirza al-Din, the theme of the conversation between the Sardar-e Sepah [Reza Khan] and the Najaf ulama was that the former would soon become the Shah of Iran and that he earnestly promised to the ulama to enforce the Second Article of the Persian Constitution by placing the Parliament under the control of five high-ranking ulama (Hairi, 1977, p. 147).

The good relationships between Reza Khan, later Reza Shah, and the ulama was already established through kindly treatment of them during their stay in Qum and during their return journey to Iraq. In a telegram sent by the ulama, in particular Na'ini and Isfahani, they expressed their 'deepest gratitude' to Reza Khan, and 'to protect that most honorable personage and to enjoy the perfect form of auspiciousness, a sacred portrait [of the First Shi'ite Imam, Ali] which was taken from the holy shrine is now presented to Your Highness. Thanks to God that the solicitude of

Your Highness (Hazrat-i Ashraf) has been continuous in our journey and during our stay in Qum' (Hairi, 1977, p. 145).

The support of the leading ulama, in particular Na'ini who enjoyed a high degree of respect and acceptance among the people of Iran through his participation in the Constitutional Revolution, depended on the actual position of Iran as the only Shi'ite state. Na'ini, in his book *Tanbih al-ummah va tanzih al-mellah,* which was written during the turmoil of the Constitutional Revolution, offered two main reasons for the necessity of having a strong state in the Shi'ite community awaiting the Hidden Imam:

> 1. The establishment of internal order in the country, the education of all the subjects, the consideration of everyone's rights, the prevention of all individuals from assault and aggression against one another, and other duties which are related to the internal interest of the country and the people.
> 2. Preventing any foreign intervention, avoiding the tricks which are usually exercised [by foreigners], preparing a defensive force and war ammunitions, and the like. [129]

Here Na'ini presents these two main reasons for having an order created by the reign of Reza Shah. Hence, the support of the Najaf ulama is not contrary to the reign of Reza Shah. But, as already mentioned, the ulama were also against tyranny and dictatorship, and Na'ini himself provided reasons such as *Sherk*, to illegitimate the tyrannical rule of the Qajars. To accept the authoritarian regime of Reza Shah, some events played a decisive role for the ulama. These events, which seriously threatened the existence of the Shi'ite country of Iran, were:

1. The occupation of Iran by allied forces after 1912, and during World War I.
2. The Perso-English treaty of 1919, which would change Iran into a colony of England.
3. The maltreatment of the Shi'ite ulama in Iraq by the English, and their exile to Iran as their 'native home'.

These events influenced the ulama, in particular Isfahani and Na'ini, in their attitudes toward Reza Shah as the only capable person who could create the 'internal order' and 'prevent any foreign intervention'. It must be taken into consideration that before the Constitutional Revolution, foreign interventions were mainly economic; before the reign of Reza Shah, however, Iran was near political collapse and dissolution.

Another important factor for the position of the ulama towards Reza Shah, were the attitudes of their social allies, the bazaris. To understand the position of the ulama towards Reza Shah, we have to consider the attitudes of ulama's allies, bazaris, to his reign.

> When Iran's disintegration and governmental collapse had reached such a level that the administration and army existed in name only, and we had become a laughing-stock to the foreigners, /.../ the strong leadership of our Lord General, the commander of our armed forces, Reza Khan, created a strong, unified national army, which restored the independence of Iran, reasserted the authority of the government by suppressing provincial and tribal revolts, and reformed the government apparatus. Under Reza Khan's leadership, our country will enjoy internal security, progress, and prosperity.[130]

Hence, the ulama had to share—or pretend to share—the bazaris optimism toward the reign of Reza Shah. The positive position of the bazaris and the ulama's support of Reza Shah as the proper temporary ruler provided a very suitable basis from which Reza Shah could launch radical secular changes. But, both the bazaris and the ulama were subject to great restrictions and humiliation during the reign of Reza Shah. His protective economic policy and support for production and large industries favored the high-ranking bazaris and harmed many middle and low ranking ones. Reza Shah also destroyed much of the basis of the power of the ulama through an authoritative secularization of the judiciary and education system.

The Rise and Fall of Nationalism

Reza Shah was a nationalist who wanted Iran to be independent from the great powers and become a strong and secular state. But his nationalism was based on a dictatorial rulership. In other words, he wanted to create a strong and unified country without social and political diversity. He forbade ethnic identities such as languages to be used officially. All Iranians were citizens of Iran without any consideration of their social, ethnic, and religious backgrounds.

After Reza Shah's abdication in 1941, a period of about ten years of political democracy began in Iran. During these years, two main political fronts became the main agents of the political arena, namely the communist Tudeh Party and the National Front. The Tudeh Party used the new political freedom and established and developed its connections with the new industrial workers and the modern middle occupational groups. They had even been elected for the Majlis. In January 1948, the Tudeh Party split, and in February 1949 it was banned by the Majlis on the charge of complicity in the attempted assassination of the Shah at Tehran University (Katouzian, 1988, p. 23).

During the election-rigging activities for the Sixteenth Majlis, some of the leaders of the opposition group in the Fourteenth Majlis founded the National Front as a leadership umbrella for nationalist opposition. Some parties such as Hezb-e Zahmatkeshan led by Baqa'i, the Iran Party led by Sanjabi, and popular nationalists, such as Fatemi, Shayegan, Nariman, and most important Musaddeq himself, constructed the National Front. 'The Front's constitution contained, *inter alia*, the following points: (a) The Front is made up of its founding members, and democratic parties and groups which desire social justice and the protection of the constitution; (b) The Front's council will comprise its founding members plus the representatives of democratic parties; (c) The aim of the Front is the establishment of democracy (Hukumat-i Melli)' (Katouzian, 1988, p. 26).[131]

A new phenomenon at that time was the appearance of young religious fanatical groups mainly associated with a relatively small organization called Fadaiyan-e Islam. They were influenced by the Egyptian Ikhvan al-Muslemin (the Islamic Brotherhood). One of their main tactics was to assassinate principal persons of political and social influence whom they considered enemies of Islam. Some famous political, military, and cultural figures, such as Abdulhusayn Hazhir, and Ahmad Kasravi, were assassinated by this group. One of the members of this group, Khalil Tahmasebi, was accused of the assassination of the prime minister Razmara in 7 March, 1951. In May 1951, Muhammad Mosaddeq, one of the most influential politicians and a highly respected nationalist, and leader of the National Front, was elected prime minister of Iran. At this time, religious leaders who were actively participating in the opposition against the Shah, such as Ayatollah Kashani, were unwilling or unable to act as an alternative to the Shah, and were acting on behalf of the nationalists. The members of the National Front 'came from both the traditional, religious bazari and the modern, secular middle occupational groups. This diversity of origins gave the groups in the National Front differences in political socialization that extended through all aspects of life' (Ghods, 1989, p. 182). More than two centuries of the Iranian people's bitter experience of the impact of the West culminated in the great support for the National Front. It is evident, too, that because of the structural setting of the society, Ayatollah Kashani's participation in the Front was important in providing a means to influence the traditional middle groups and mobilize them to support the Front (cf. Safari, 1992). The diversity of the social backgrounds of the members made the National Front an inappropriate means at a time when a powerful and stable political front against the Shah would have been decisive. One of the most important reforms pushed by the National Front was the nationalization of Iranian oil on 20 March, 1951.

Whereas Mosaddeq's nationalization of oil production and distribution in Iran created many foreign enemies, it increased his popularity and reinforced his position as prime minister. Nevertheless, under the short period of his government (May, 1951-August, 1953), he managed to provoke opposition from the Tudeh Party, military generals and royalists, and from foreign powers, such as British oil companies. In spring 1953, Mosaddeq asked the Shah to leave the country for a time. With the intention of introducing economic reforms, Mosaddeq joined in close collaboration with the secular wing of the National Front. This led to a conflict between the traditional and religious wing of the National Front, on the one hand, and the modern wing on the other. Mosaddeq lost two groups in the National Front who represented the bazaar merchants: The Society of Muslim Warriors and The Toilers party. In this circumstance, military generals, certain security forces, and the US Central Intelligence Agency planned and executed a *coup d'état* against Mosaddeq. The Shah returned to power in August 1953. He consolidated his power and placed military officers in key government positions.

During the years between 1941-1953, Iran enjoyed a period of considerable political democracy. Foreign occupation and the weakness of the new central government facilitated this democratic period in which new political parties and alliances were founded. But some institutional shortcomings and weaknesses hindered the development and establishment of strong and stable relationships between different political institutions. Fakhreddin Azimi (1989), who studied this period, believed that some factors such as the unlimited power of Majlis, the great power of the monarch, and the weakness of the democratic governments hindered the establishment and institutionalization of a powerful democracy in Iran. The events during the reign of Mosaddeq witnessed some changes in the position of the bazaar towards the ulama. Although the most influential member of the ulama, Ayatollah Kashani, opposed Mosaddeq in 1952, the bazaris did not support Kashani in his opposition. For example, when Mosaddeq presented a bill to the Majlis concerning increasing the legal authority of the prime minister, and the opposition in Majlis managed to stop him, the bazaar of Tehran arranged large demonstrations supporting Mosaddeq (Azimi, 1989, p. 182). People were aware of the conflicts between Mosaddeq and Kashani, and this certainly influenced the unified support of the national government of Mosaddeq. Although Kashani was a prominent Mujtahid of the time, other grand Mujtahids, in particular Ayatollah Borujerdi who was the *Marja'-e taqlid* for many of Shi'ites, did not want to deal with the 'dirty matters of politics'. Social differentiation, which mainly had taken place during the reign of Reza Shah, led also to changes in the position of the ulama. After the Constitutional Revolution, foreign occupation, the events of the Iraqi revolution, and a period of social disintegration, leading ulama such as Na'ini and Isfahani, chose to support Reza Shah in his attempts to create a strong and independent state. Meanwhile, others such as Ha'iri, took a position of acquiescence.

The bazaris' initially positive position *vis-à-vis* the nationalistic ideas and reforms of Reza Shah, and after his abdication of Mosaddeq, greatly influenced the position of the ulama toward the state. Accordingly, the traditional theological justification for the role of the state in the Muslim community became unsuitable in modern and democratic Iran (1941-53), where the state was divided among three main centers of authority, namely (1) the government, (2) the Shah, and (3) the Majlis. Hence, the complexity of the new socio-political reality and the lack of a new theological justification for the role of the ulama in the new society left the political sphere mainly to the new political groups such as the nationalists and communists. But it did not mean that the clergy left the political arena. As mentioned earlier, some of them participated in political challenges to restore the Constitution. Some of the out-of-parliamentary religious groups, such as Fadaiyan-e Islam, took a radical position against the political elite. And finally, some of them, such as Mahmoud Taleqani, enjoined the National Front. The new socio-political mosaic of Iran could not be simplified by the traditional categories used by the ulama to justify their traditional authority in the modern society.

7 Modernization and the Ulama

The focus of this chapter is on the changing role and orientation of the clergy, above all their use of and commitment to several key features of modernization, especially to the reconstruction of society through political processes.

The state elite and the clergy coexisted harmoniously until the end of the nineteenth century.[132] Government modernization plans, which were influenced by the socio-economic changes in the secular West, were judged negatively by the clergy. And, as pointed out earlier, the modernization during the time of Reza Shah (1925-41) entailed considerable marginalization of the clergy. As a result of the Shah's policies, the clergy were excluded from politics, their activities limited to religious schools and mosques. At the same time, there was substantial state support for and development of secular schooling.

The Shah's government secularized and codified laws, adopted European-style legal codes, and established a system of secular courts that greatly reduced the judicial functions of the ulama. Judges were required to hold a law degree from the newly established Tehran University, effectively preventing graduates of religious seminaries from becoming judges (Bakhash, 1990, p. 21). This took place in a society with a long history of religious legal studies, discourse, and courts–of course, linked to sacred laws and regulations as opposed to technical or secular.[133]

Bakhash (1990, pp. 21-22) stresses the challenge the Shah's program made to the ulama: 'The network of schools and colleges Reza Shah established broke the near monopoly the ulama had exercised over education'.[134] By establishing a rival center of Islamic studies at Tehran University, he challenged the ulama even on their home ground of religious education. Under his direction, the government began to interfere in the certification of seminary students and graduates, and in the curriculum of the religious schools, ostensibly in an effort to 'modernize' them. Bakhash (1990) points out that 'the government went far in extending its jurisdiction over the administration of religious endowments, a step which the ulama could only regard as an attempt to tamper with the financial independence of the ulama and to make religion subject to the direction of the state. Clerics were harassed in a multitude of petty ways: the government interfered in matters of religious dress; restrictions were placed on the holding of religious mourning services and prayer meetings; and religious students (*tullab*) were in certain instances made subject to military service'.

The Ulama and the Shah's 'White Revolution'

In 1962, as a result of pressures from the Kennedy administration, the Shah was forced to appoint Ali Amini as Prime Minister. Amini introduced democratic reforms and exiled General Bakhtiar, who had headed SAVAK (Organization of Security and Intelligence). Intending to launch land reform, Amini appointed as minister of agriculture Hassan Arsenjani, a former member of the Tudeh (communist) Party. Arsenjani who was a well-known advocate of land reform launched a serious Land Reform intending to reduce the power of landlords and to create small landowners. Landlords had to sell excessive holdings to the state. Although the Amini administration brought about Iran's first serious effort to reform the traditional land ownership, it failed to liberalize the political system and came into conflict with liberal groups, such as the National Front. Some ulama who were among the rank of landowners also protested against the Land Reform. After fourteen months of reign, Amini was forced to resign and was replaced by Alam. Shortly after, the Shah adopted Arsenjani's radical Land Reform, modified it in favor of landowners, and presented it, together with five other reform points as the White Revolution. The Shah's White Revolution consisted then of six points: land distribution, nationalization of forests, sale of state factories to the private sector, profit sharing of industrial workers, extension of the vote to women, and establishment of a rural literacy corps.

The Shah's 'new land distribution' not only allowed the landowners to keep more of their lands than Amini's reform program, but also permitted religious foundations to lease their lands. Some of the ulama opposed the reforms, in particular the land reform and extending the vote to women. The Shah, disregarding this, organized a referendum to legitimize the reforms. One of the radical clergy, Ayatollah Ruhullah Khomeini, in Muharram 1963, using the traditional means of public voice and challenge, the *manbar*, opposed the Shah's political system and accused him of despotism. Khomeini, as a very skillful politician, did not talk directly against the reforms, but rather expressed the dissatisfaction of civil society against the Shah. 'Although many clerics opposed the regime because of land reform and women's rights, Khomeini, revealing a masterful grasp of mass politics, scrupulously avoided the former issue and instead hammered away on a host of other concerns that aroused greater indignation among the general population' (Abrahamian, 1982, p. 425).[135] Many of the issues used by Khomeini in propagating against the Shah witnessed his concern about a new civil society with democratic demands. For example, he denounced the regime for rigging elections, violating the constitutional laws, stifling the press and the political parties, and destroying the independence of the university (Abrahamian, 1984, p. 425). In June 1963, Khomeini succeeded in gaining leadership of the riots against the regime. The Shah put down the uprising, arrested many leaders of the opposition, including the leaders of the National Front (NF) and Khomeini himself. The latter was exiled to Turkey, from where he moved to Iraq, living there fifteen years before returning to Iran in 1979.

Although Khomeini, in June 1963, used popular slogans to gain support in the modern society of Iran, he did not propagate against the entire monarchy. He advised the Shah to 'respect the religious authority, not to cooperate with the USA, and not to aid Israel'. The uprising of June 1963 was the emerging radical clergy's attempt to restore their prominent position in civil society and to force the state to 'respect religious authority'.

All in all, the Shah crossed and threatened a group that was not simply an interest group, but a moral community of clerical leaders and radical seminarians who became increasingly indignant at the injustice, the disruption of valuable and even sacred patterns, the spread of immorality, libertinism, and alien culture. The clergy was capable of exercising authority and organizing and mobilizing support, *particularly in the context of a lack of institutional arrangements for expressing opposition and negotiating changes in policies and programs.* They had the institutional settings (mosques, seminaries, religious schools) and times (religious events and ceremonies) to carry on and build up opposition, even in the face of a formidable state apparatus (including secret police). Previous political activities of the clergy in this century had never had a *compelling political framework*. Their association with political power was always a major subject of discussion and controversy among the clergy.

Vaqf, Sahm-e Imam and the Independence of the Ulama

In medieval Persia, the tradition of charitable *auqaf* was very strong. Considerable land properties were made into *vaqf* intending to be used by *madrasahs*. That was a common tradition among the governors who established religious *madrasahs* and gave them *vaqf* properties (Lambton, 1988, pp. 150-51). This tradition continued and was reinforced by the Safavids. After the Safavids, and during the reign of Nader Shah, many *vaqf* properties, which were controlled by the ulama, were confiscated and religious endowments declined. During the reign of the first Qajar shahs, the *vaqf* properties increased and the ulama regained the control over the administration of the *auqaf*. The position of the ulama in Iranian society was reinforced by Usuli victory over the traditionalist Akhbaris, who intended to illegitimate the prominent position of Mujtahids in the Shi'ite community. They did not believe in *ijtihad* (interpretation of religious sources), and they conceived the Mujtahids as interpreters unnecessary. The victory of Usulis under the leadership of the prominent Mujtahid, Muhammad Baqir Behbahani (d. 1803), who strongly believed in the necessity of Mujtahids for the Shi'ite community, theologically legitimized the position of the ulama. From the beginning of the nineteenth century, the improvement in the economic condition of the ulama depended on an improvement in the state of *auqaf* (Akhavi, 1980, p. 57). The medieval tradition of the connection of the *vaqf* endowments to the *madrasahs* continued even into modern times. For example, during the Constitutional movement, as an attack on the Constitutionalist ulama, the state confiscated two famous *madrasahs* of Tehran, *madrasah-ye Khazan al-Mulk* and *madrasah-ye Marvi*, which had large *vaqf* endowments.

During the reign of Reza Shah, the state began to restrict religious endowments under the Civil Code of 1928 in order to weaken the role of the *madrahahs* and reinforce the new educational system. The intervention of the state, intended to control *auqaf* (the plural of *vaqf*)–the main sources of income for the *madrasahs* and a very important factor in the ulama's independence from the state–continued during the whole reign of the Pahlavis. The law of 1934 put another administrative restriction on religious endowments. According to this law, all public endowments that lacked an administrator or had an unknown administrator, were to be administered directly by the Endowments Department of the Ministry of Education. In addition, the Department was empowered to exercise '*nizarat-e kamel* (full supervision) over all public endowments, irrespective of the status of their administration (Akhavi, 1980, pp. 56-7). Hence, through an effective centralized control over religious endowments, many clergy became dependent on the state bureaucracy. But it must be stressed that, in spite of state control of many *vaqf* properties, many of the prominent ulama retained their *auqaf*. For example, Ayatollah Shahrestani one of the Mujtahids who played an important role in keeping the relations between the ulama and the Shah peaceful during the short period after the *coup d'état*, had a large amount of *vaqf* properties. His family possessed extensive land holdings in Karbala (Iraq) and the Isfahan region, as well as in Najaf, Kazemeyn (both in Iraq), Kirmanshah and Hamadan (two cities in Western Iran) (Akhavi, 1980, p. 75).

The government's land reform bill of 1959 faced strong opposition from the ulama. Ayatollah Borujerdi and Ayatollah Behbahani declared the land reform anti-Islamic. Borujerdi wrote to the Shah requesting him to prevent its passing in Majlis. Borujerdi's prominent position in the country and the ulama's opposition to the land reform made it difficult for the state to begin the reform, although the bill was ratified on 17 May 1960. One of the most important reasons for the ulama's opposition to the land reform was the impact the reform had on lands held by the clergy as *vaqf*.

> Only a week after dispatching his letter attacking the December 1959 draft law to Ja'far Behbahani, Ayatollah Borujerdi received the Director-General of the Endowment Department at his home on 20 February 1960. At this meeting, Borujerdi was reported to have issued instructions on 'the maintenance and safeguarding of income from endowments;' the Director-General of the Endowments Department submitted to him a report on the measures taken by the Department in implementing the wishes of those individuals who had made the bequest (Akhavi, 1980, p. 95).

Although the ulama's opposition to the Shah's reforms was not directly connected to the threats the reform had for their economic position, the impact of the reform on the *vaqf* properties was an important factor. The reason is clear. Many of the ulama's public activities, such as religious education in the *madrasahs* and *hovzahs*, mosques, ceremonials, and salary to the *tullabs*, were financed by the income of *vaqf* properties. During the first phase of the land reform, the public endowments, *vaqf-e 'amm*, were excluded (Denman, 1978, p. 265).

In 1964, in accordance with the Shah's reform policy, *Sazeman-e auqaf* (The Endowment Organization) was constituted. The *vaqf* properties were still significant for the independence of the clergy from the state. The statistics of that time (Akhavi, 1980) show that the *vaqf* properties numbered about 73,694, with a total income of 275,458,342 Rials. The Iranian journal, *Mihr*, counts the ulama as a landholding class at the level of the aristocracy, merchants, and professionals. Gradually, through the intervention of the state, the ulama lost their control over some of the religious endowments and several *madrasahs*. The large scale *vaqf* and shrine endowments in Qum and Mashad came under the control of the Endowments Organization, and their *mutavalli-ye auqaf* (the administrator of the *auqaf*) became government deputies. During the 1970s, the most important *madrasahs* came under state control. In 1971, for instance, three of the most important *madrasahs* in Mashad came under the control of the Mashad Department of Endowment, and even Ayatollah Ashtiyani, whose family had administered the Marvi madrasah ever since the Constitutional Revolution, assented to an arrangement whereby the Tehran Department of Endowment 'has a say' in that school's administration (Akhavi, 1980, pp. 130-1).

Unfortunately, there are insufficient data to study the changes in the *vaqf* properties. But it is evident that a rapid decline in *vaqf* properties occurred since the establishment of Endowments Organization. For instance, during the administration of Manuchehr Azemun, the director of the Organization in the seventies, many of the *vaqf* properties were divided among high-ranking army officers, singers, court-connected families, the state-appointed *mutavallis*, and others (Akhavi, 1980, pp. 133-4). Although the importance of the traditional sources of the ulama's income declined in the 1960s and 1970s, it did not disappear totally and retained its significance. That significance depended on the reality that the decline in the sources of income entailed a decline in the number of the *tullab* and teachers of the *madrasahs* and by a decrease in the number of Mujtahids. Hence, the ulama did not need as much economic support as they had received before the reforms.

Another source of income of the ulama that contributed to their autonomy from the state was *sahm-e Imam* (the share of Imam). Every good Muslim should pay 10 percent of his annual income to the ulama to be used for religious institutions. The Usuli movement of late eighteenth century 'assured a large measure of financial autonomy for the hierocracy through the authorization of the collection of religious taxes on behalf of the Hidden Imam' (Arjomand, 1988, p. 14). *Sahm-e Imam* as a considerable source of the ulama's income was reinforced during the time that one of the most important Usuli scholars, Shaykh Ja'far Najafi (d. 1813), was the deputy. Najafi possessed a prominent position within Iran and in *'atabat*. Najafi is often considered as the first to contemplate the *niyabat 'amm* (general deputy) of the Imam mostly as the collective function of the ulama body (Amanat, 1988, p. 103). During the time that Najafi was deputy, the function of the ulama as the deputies of the Hidden Imam was reinforced. Paying *sahm-e Imam* to the ulama was reinforced and their income increased. This led to a flourishing of religious schools and seminaries. It strengthened the ulama's autonomy from the state and strengthened their bonds in civil society. *Sahm-e Imam* was used by the ulama to increase their influence in society. They paid pensions of the *tullabs* (religious students), *Sayyeds* (clergy who claimed to have blood ties with the Prophet), and *lutis* (the urban brigands). The latter group functioned as an army of the ulama. During the reign of Qajars, the prominent ulama of each period, such as Najafi, Shafti, and Ansari, collected considerable amounts as *sahm-e Imam*. For instance, 'at one stage in the late 1850s, the figure of two hundred thousand *tumans* has been given for the lawful funds (*vujuhat.i shar'iya*) annually received by Ansari, a substantial figure, taking into account government's total revenue of about three million tumans for the same period' (Amanat, 1988, p. 112).

Although *sahm-e Imam* was an important source of income of the ulama, there is no reliable figures on the extent of the ulama's income from this source. The economic growth of in the 1960s and the 1970s favoring the bazaris seems to have led to an increase in the revenue of the ulama from *sahm-e Imam*. Akhavi (1980, p. 141) points out the role of the *sahm-e Imam* for religious students:

> In 1973, the average monthly stipend to students from the state was 228 rials. A decade earlier (1963), the monthly student stipend in Qumm had been between 300-400 rials on average (and in some cases as high as 1,000 rials), as distributed by the clergy from the *sahm-i imam*. In 1975, funds distributed by six *marji'-yi taqlid* to Qumm students from the *sahm-e Imam* averaged 1467 rials.

The decrease in the income of the ulama as a result of the state's expropriation of some *vaqf* properties appears to have been compensated through increase in the *sahm-e Imam*. It is evident that *sahm-e Imam*, particularly during the 1960s and the 1970s, did not came from poor people, but from wealthy bazaris many of whom performed their duty *vis-*

à-vis religious institutions and at the same time supported the ulama as an important counterweight to the state. Another factor in the continuation of the independence of the ulama was the appearance of the radical clergy, who reinforced bonds–including economic ones–with the bazaar.

Religious Modernism

The relationship between the ulama and the state improved somewhat after the re-establishment of the Shah in 1953. The fear of communism evoked by the Tudeh Party and the increase in the influence of the Baha'is forced the ulama to take a more positive stance towards the Shah. Ayatollah Borujerdi, Ayatollah Behbahani, and Ayatollah Shahrestani were the most important Mujtahids of the time, and their positive attitudes to the Shah as the enemy of their enemies reinforced the peaceful relationship between the ulama and the state. But the land reform and the other reform programs of the Shah known as the 'White Revolution' transformed these peaceful relations into a period of tension and conflict. Ayatollah Borujerdi and Behbahani declared the land reform anti-Islamic (Akhavi, 1980). Some other ulama such as Khomeini actively challenged the state and wanted the Shah to stop the plans. Although the ulama's position in civil society of Iran was still important, their political issues seemed old-fashioned and out of step with a society undergoing rapid change. Their political monopoly in civil society was already challenged by modern ideas and political groups such as the communist Tudeh Party and the National Front.

The modernization programs did, however, change the traditional social groups and boundaries in Iranian society. The ulama were gradually losing their leading position in the society, not only through the reduction of their power, but also because of the appearance of new social groups and social institutions. The expansion of modern education weakened the traditional importance of the *madrasahs*. In the years between 1962/63 and 1967/68, for example, the number of *madrasahs* was reduced by 40 percent and, in the same period, the number of *tullab* was reduced by 45.8 percent (Akhavi, 1980, p. 189). Other religious groups whose influence extended gradually in accordance with the implementation of the modernization programs came to provide alternatives to the ulama's traditional role as the leader of Iranian civil society.

The nationalist movements led by Mosaddeq in the 1940s and the beginning of 1950s, created a new political tradition in Iran. Nationalism, as an anti-imperialist ideology, could be accepted and institutionalized in the political sphere of Iran. The main representatives of this relatively new ideology crystallized in the body of the National Front. The Front's anti-dictatorship and pro-nationalist ideology attracted the bazaris in their resistance to the Shah's modernization plans. Some bazaris, such as Abolhasa Lebaschi, actively participated in the revival of the NF during the political liberalization of the early 1940s. For example, 'among the National Front's High Council, there were two representatives from the bazaar, Mahmud Manian and Hasan Qasemieh' (Chehabi, 1990, p. 146). Although Mosaddeq himself was a religious man, the National Front lost– in some cases intentionally–the religious face of the organization. Therefore, in March 1961, some of the radical and religious members of the National Front, such as Bazargan, Sahabi, and Taleqani founded the *Nehzat-e azadi-ye Iran*, the Liberation Movement of Iran (LMI). Bazargan pointed out the reasons for the foundation of such organization:

> The National Front was, as its name indicated, a Front. That is a union of social philosophies and prominent personalities which had a common goal, namely the independence of the country and the freedom of the people. But having a common goal is not tantamount to having common motivations. One cannot expect that. Some may be motivated by nationalism, others by humanitarian feelings, race consciousness, or socialism/.../.
> However, for us, for many of our friends, and perhaps for a majority of the Iranian population, there could be no motivation other than the principles and religious tenets of Islam.
> I am not saying the others were not Muslims or that they were opposed to Islam. Only, for them Islam did not constitute a social and political ideology. But for us it was the basic motivation for our social and political activism (Chehabi, 1990, p. 153).

The LMI was one of several modern Islamic organizations such as the Muslim Student Associations, Islamic associations of engineers, physicians, and teachers, Muhammad Taqi Shari'ati's Mashad-based Center for the Propagation of Islamic Truth, and several other groups (thirteen total) (Chehabi, 1990, p. 155), that arose simultaneously and created new non-cleric religio-political spheres in Iran's politics. The Shah's land reforms, which led some of the ulama to take a conservative position against them, engaged other ulama and clergy in serious discussion of the necessity of the reforms and the weaknesses in the Shah's reform programs. This position led to the creation of an anti-regime discussion group called 'The

Monthly Talks Society'. Some of members of this group later became the leaders of the Islamic Revolution. The group includes, Seyyed Mahmud Taleqani, Morteza Motahhari, Ahmad Aliabadi, among others. The subjects of the Society's talks were very modern in the sense that they dealt with modern socio-economic problems and the role of Islam in the new differentiated society.[136] This novel and yet appropriate forum attracted the bazaris. It is not surprising that 'the main movers for the Monthly Talks Society were Alibabai and Ja'far Khazzazi, a prominent and trusted bazaar leader, whose spacious house could accommodate up to 1,000 listeners' (Chehabi, 1990, p. 171). At the same time Western ideas such as liberalism and Marxism were challenged by religious intellectuals. Jalal Al-e Ahmad was one of the most important of these. His book, *Gharbzadegi* contributed to the ideological framework of the religious students and intellectuals in their challenge to the liberals and leftists.

Among the new religious intellectuals who contributed to the creation of a revolutionary Shi'ism, before the publication of Khomeini's *velayat-e faqih*, was Ali Shari'ati. Shari'ati, who came from a deeply religious family, was one of the most influential constructors of revolutionary ideas among the youths and religious groups in Iran. Ali Shari'ati (1933-1977) had studied sociology at Sorbonne university in the 1960s. He was influenced by the student revolts and liberation movement of Algeria, on the one hand, and the theories and ideas of Jean-Paul Sartre and Frantz Fanon, on the other. Through his intellectual activities, he certainly modernized and reconstructed many Shi'ite beliefs and social theories. Shari'ati's revolutionary ideas had a crucial impact on high school and university students and also became an influential ideological weapon against socialistic ideologies. Many students and religious groups associated his ideas with radical ideas of Khomeini. Shari'ati was a sociologist educated in France and aware of the challenge of the modern Western ideas to Islam. He was a well-known intellectual, who, during his short life (he died at forty-four), produced several books and articles that highly influenced and ideologically equipped the religious intellectuals. To devalue Western materialism he wrote the book *Marxism and Other Western Fallacies*. After a critical review of such ideologies, he pointed out:

> Today, in philosophy, Heidegger does not speak in the terms of Hegel or Feuerbach. In science, Max Planck, the outstanding exponent of the new physics, opposes the ideas of Claude Bernard. Heidegger is searching for

Christ in humanity, and Planck is searching for God in the world of physics. Modern literature and art, expressing alarm at the futility of modern life, review the deformation of modern man and the dark and deadly loneliness that has enveloped him. Eliot, Strindberg, Guenon, Pasternak, Toynbee, Erich Fromm, Senghor, Uzghan, Omar Mawlud-all are in some way searching for light /.../.

Today, in contrast to Marx, who felt human liberation depended upon the denial of God, and Nietzsche, who boasted, 'God is dead', even an atheistic philosopher like Sartre speaks of God's absence from the universe 'with painful regret', seeing in this a source of the futility of man and existence, the loss of values (Shari'ati, 1980, pp. 94-95).

Shari'ati then made his theoretic understanding of Islam clear. His ideas went against many of the current theological issues of the separation of the political and religious affairs. The emphasis on the theory of *gheybat* was changed, by Shari'ati, to the emphasis on the theory of *tauhid* (unity of God). Shari'ati wrote:

> It [Islam] strives to realize the world-view of *tauhid* and of human primacy within real life. Unlike the subjectivist philosophies and mystical religions, it does not accept in human existence the dichotomies of sacred and profane, belief and behavior, idea and actuality. Thus Louis Gardet says, 'Islam is both a religion and a nation'. This future, which begins with the discarding of capitalism and Marxism, is neither predestined nor pre-fabricated. Instead, it remains to be built. There is no doubt that Islam will have an appropriate role in its construction, when it has freed itself from the effects of centuries of stagnation, superstition, and contamination, and is put forth as a living ideology (Shari'ati, 1980, pp. 95-6).

In contrast to Khomeini, who put this agentic Islamic duty on the *fuqaha*, Shari'ati turned to the 'intellectuals'.

> That is the task of the true intellectuals of Islam. Only in this way will Islam-after a renaissance of belief and an emergence from isolation and reaction-be able to take part in the current war of beliefs and, in particular, to command the center and serve as an example to contemporary thought, where the new human spirit is seeking the means to begin a new world and a new humanity (Shari'ati, 1980, p. 96).

Shari'ati had a major impact on intellectuals, in particular on university students who were one of the most active groups in opposition to the Shah.

The roots of Shari'ati's political influence goes back to the foundation of Huseynieh Ershad in Tehran in 1965. 'Huseynieh' refers to a place where the mourning of the martyrdom of the Third Shi'ite Imam, Imam Husayn, is held. The title 'Huseynieh Ershad' refers to the 'guidance of the action of the Husayn'. Imam Husayn and 72 of his family and believers were killed in Karbala during the reign of the Sunni caliph Yazid in the year 680. According to Shi'ite theology, the tragedy of Karbala is recorded as the rise of the just against the unjust and tyrannical caliphs. Hence, the name Huseynieh Ershad refers to the heroic action of the Imam against unjust rulers, and 'was to be a place where Iranians were to be guided toward fundamental change in the affairs of society' (Chehabi, 1990, p. 202). The founder of the Huseynieh Ershad institute was Muhammad Humayun who had been a philanthropist inspired by the Monthly Talks Society. The bazaar of Tehran participated in building, establishing, and continuing the institute. Muhammad Humayun (d. 1978) was himself a prominent wealthy merchant. 'While he remained the main financial benefactor of the institute, other merchants also made commitments to pay 5,000 Rials ($70) per month to help meet expenses' (Chehabi, 1990, p. 203). The original members of the institute were Ayatollah Mutaharri, Seyyed Hossein Nasr (the Dean of the Faculty of Literature of Tehran University), Ezatollah Sahabi, Ali Shari'ati, and Huseyn Mazini (Akhavi, 1980, p. 144). Besides Mutaharri, who was very close to Khomeini, other figures who came to play crucial roles in the Islamic Revolution and the establishment of the Islamic Republic were included. These were Ayatollah Beheshti (the founder of Islamic Republican party), Hojjatoleslam Refsenjani (the president of the Islamic Republic 1989-97), Hojjatoleslam Javad Bahonar (the third prime minister of the Islamic Republic). Other religious intellectuals such as Kazem Sami and Habibollah Peyman (among the founder of the LMI) and Hojjatoleslam Sadr Balaghei (Mosaddeqist) participated in the activities of the institute. The location of Huseynieh Ershad in the modern area of Qolhak in northern Tehran may symbolize the differences between the religious– and political as well–subjects and issues discussed in this modern institute and the traditional religious sermons presented in the mosques, situated in the traditional part of the city. Ironically, the regime was unaware of the revolutionary changes of traditional Shi'ism, and accepted the activities of the institute, in the hopes that it would weaken the traditional power of the ulama.

Among the activists of the institute, Shari'ati was the most radical. He believed that the activities of the institution could not be limited to traditional religious discussions, but rather, should bring 'pressure to bear on the political aspects' (Akhavi, 1990, p. 144). He was constantly hostile to the traditionalist ulama. To him, they were 'the timeless ones', *bi zaman*, as he called them. He saw them operating in a vacuum, as it were, oblivious to social reality in any meaningfully temporal sense. 'In a simile he frequently employed, he likened these unreconstructed ulama to zombies mindlessly regurgitating *fiqh* lessons (Akhavi, 1990, p. 146). Shari'ati's radicalism and anti-clerical lectures, which were well formulated in his book *Mazhab alayh-e mazhab* (Religion against religion) evoked opposition from the clergy. Even the clerical members of the institution opposed him. Ayatollah Motahhari sent a message to Khomeini in Najaf, requesting him to condemn Shari'ati, which Khomeini did not. Khomeini's rejection of Motahhari's request partly depended on Shari'ati's popularity among the young religious groups–who were also Khomeini's supporters–and partly depended on the acceptance of the Shah by many of the ulama. Khomeini himself was, to some extent, influenced by Shari'ati's radical ideas. Similarities exist, as well, in their mutual treatment of certain basic themes, such as the theory of the Hidden Imam. To those who argued for a passive waiting for the appearance of the Imam, Shari'ati, like Khomeini, argued that the Hidden Imam has not, like Christ, gone to live in another world. The *Mahdi* (messiah) indeed lives in the real world, and he has his 'feet on the ground', is among us, and the Muslim must be ready for him when he comes (Akhavi, 1990, pp. 150-51). Shari'ati was a religious modernist who conceived of religion as a political ideology for social revolution. He wrote:

> I, at this part of the world and at this moment of history, am expecting, in a future that might be tomorrow or any other time, a sudden world Revolution in favor of Truth and Justice and of oppressed masses; a Revolution in which I must play a part; a Revolution which does not come about with prayers/.../but with a banner and a sword, with a holy war involving all responsible believers. I believe that this movement shall naturally triumph (Shari'ati, 1982).

Finally, the increasing popularity of Shari'ati and Huseynieh Ershad forced the Shah to shut down the institute and arrest its ideologue, Shari'ati. After his release from prison in 1975, he was permitted to leave Iran for

156 *Revolutionary Iran*

England, where he was found dead in his room on 19 June 1977. Many believe that he was assassinated by the Iranian security forces, SAVAK. The death of Shari'ati in 1977, on the eve of the revolution, allowed Khomeini's theory of *velayat-e faqih*–which already dominated the clerical revolutionary groups–to influence the young religious and non-clerical intellectuals, who were attracted by Shari'ati's revolutionary ideas.

The Theory of *Velayat-e faqih*

A New Framework for Religio-political Action

Previous political activities of clergy had never had a compelling political framework. Their association with political power was always a major subject of discussion and controversy. In 1971, Khomeini's lectures for theology students were published in a very important book named *Velayat-e faqih, hukumat-e eslami* (The guardianship of Islamic jurisprudents, the Islamic governance) which was to play a crucial role in the Islamic Revolution of Iran. In his book, Khomeini rejected his own and many other clergy's theory of state.[137] In his book of 1943, *Kashf al-asrar* (Secrets revealed), Khomeini had legitimized the necessity of a state, even a non-religious one. But in *Velayat-e faqih* he formulated the theory of an Islamic state as the only legitimate government in Muslim communities.

To reject some of the ulama's traditional ideas about the control of jurisprudence as the only legitimate way to hold authority during the Great Occultation, he lectured:

> A body of laws alone is not sufficient for a society to be reformed. In order for law to ensure the reform and happiness of man, there must be an executive power and an executor. For this reason, God Almighty, in addition to revealing a body of law (i.e., the ordinances of the Shari'a), has laid down a particular form of government together with executive and administrative institutions (Khomeini, 1981, p. 40).

For the first time Khomeini, in contrast to his predecessor ulama, emphasized the role of the executive body for applying the Islamic law, Shari'a. He also stressed the interdependency of the implementation of Shari'a and the executive power:

> The Sunna and path of the Prophet constitute a proof of the necessity for establishing government. First, he himself established a government, as history testifies. He engaged in the implementation of laws, the establishment of the ordinances of Islam, and the administration of society. He sent out governors to different regions; both sat in judgment himself and appointed judges; dispatched emissaries to foreign states, tribal chieftains, and kings; concluded treaties and pacts; and took command in battle. In short, he fulfilled all the functions of government. Second, he designated a ruler to succeed him, in accordance with divine command. If God Almighty, through the Prophet, designated a man who was to rule over Muslim society after him, this is in itself an indication that government remains a necessity after the departure of the Prophet from this world (Khomeini, 1981, p.41).

Khomeini, through theological sources such as Sunna and Qur'an, tried to justify the necessity of an Islamic government in Iran. He changed the traditional religious justification of the ulama, including himself in 1943 (see above) about the necessity of a government in the Muslim community. As mentioned earlier, the Shi'ite ulama's main reason for justification of a state in Muslim community was the necessity of protecting the community against foreign invasions, and the need for order in the community.[138] In addition to these two reasons, Khomeini added one more, which made the existence of a secular and non-religious government impossible, namely for protection against the social and moral corruption of society. He said that:

> Without the formation of a government and the establishment of such organs to ensure that through enactment of the law, all activities of the individual take place in the framework of a just system, chaos and anarchy will prevail and social, intellectual, and moral corruption will arise. The only way to prevent the emergence of anarchy and disorder and to protect society from corruption is to form a government and thus impart order to all the affairs of the country (Khomeini, 1981, p. 42).

Khomeini, thus, rejected the idea of separation between the juridical and political arrangements of Muslim society. Against the traditional Shi'ite theology, by which the only lawful and just political leader of the Muslim community is the Hidden Imam, he argued:

> Is it proper that the laws of Islam be cast aside and remain unexecuted, so that everyone acts as he pleases and anarchy prevails? Were the laws that the prophet of Islam labored so hard for twenty-three years to set forth, promulgate, and execute valid only for a limited period of time? Did God limit the validity of His laws to two hundred years? Was everything pertaining to Islam meant to be abandoned after the Lesser Occultation? Anyone who believes so, or voices such a belief, is worse situated than the person who believes and proclaims that Islam has been superseded or abrogated by another supposed revelation (Khomeini, 1981, p. 42).

He, then, felt that an Islamic government must be established to apply the law of God, Shari'a, for the purpose of creating a state and administering the political, economic, and cultural affairs of society (Khomeini, 1981, p. 43). Accordingly, Khomeini, rejected the *de facto* acceptance of the political ruler based on the theological argument of the dualism between the political and judicial authority, which existed since the Great Occultation of the Twelfth Imam. He meant that the application of Shari'a is not independent from the state and the supervision of the Islamic ruler (Khomeini, 1981, p. 47). He said that from the time of the Lesser Occultation until the present, all forms of government in Muslim societies have been non-Islamic. He also introduced for the first time, the 'Islamic political order' as an alternative to other forms of government in Muslim society:

> Both law and reason require that we not permit governments to retain this non-Islamic character. The proofs are clear. First, the existence of a non-Islamic political order necessarily results in the non-implementation of the Islamic political order. Then, all non-Islamic systems of government are the systems of *kufr*[139] Since the ruler in each case is an instance of *taghut*,[140] it is our duty to remove from the life of Muslim society all traces of *kufr* and destroy them (Khomeini, 1981, p. 48).

Khomeini clearly declared the model of government he wanted to replace the *taghut* regimes of the Muslim societies. He said that: 'Islamic government is a government of law. In this form of government, sovereignty belongs to God alone and law is His decree and command' (Khomeini, 1981, p. 56). He pointed out in detail the differences between an Islamic government and other forms of governments.

Islamic government does not correspond to any of the existing forms of government. For example, it is not a tyranny, where the head of state can deal arbitrarily with the property and lives of the people, making use of them as he wills, putting to death any one he wishes, and enriching anyone he wishes, /.../. It is not constitutional in the current sense of the word, i.e. based on the approval of laws in accordance with the opinion of the majority. It is constitutional in the sense that the rulers are subject to a certain set of conditions in governing and administering the country, conditions that are set forth in the Nobel Qur'an and the Sunna of the Most Noble Messenger /.../. The fundamental difference between Islamic government, on the one hand, and constitutional monarchies and republics, on the other, is this: whereas the representatives of the people or the monarch in such regimes engage in legislation, in Islam the legislative power and competence to establish laws belongs exclusively to God Almighty. The Sacred Legislator of Islam is the sole legislative power (Khomeini, 1981, p. 58).

In Khomeini's theory of Islamic government, the legislative assembly has no place. The laws, Shari'a, already exist. To become a just ruler necessitates proper knowledge in Islamic jurisprudence and laws, *fiqh*. 'Since Islamic government is a government of law, knowledge of the law is necessary for the ruler, as has been laid down in tradition' (Khomeini, 1981, p. 59). Hence, the Islamic government is the reign of the *fuqaha*.[141] He, then, concluded that:

> The two qualities of knowledge of the law and justice are presented in countless *fuqaha* of the present age. If they would come together, they could establish a government of universal justice in the world (Khomeini, 1981, p. 62).

Accordingly, Khomeini formulated the concept of the Islamic state, based on the Qur'an and pointed out that this ideal is not achievable only in some distant future, but is a practical form of government realizable in the lifetime of the present generation. He also advanced the claim of the clergy, as heirs to the mantle of the Prophet and as authoritative interpreters of the Sacred Law, to the leadership of the community. While the ulama may exercise leadership over the community collectively, in consultation with one another, ultimate leadership and authority may be vested in a single, outstanding religious figure, whom all Muslims should obey (Bakhash, 1990, pp. 38-39). Khomeini's theory of *velayat-e faqih* was a bold innovation in the history of

Shi'ite philosophy, in large part eliminating the duality of religious and temporal authority (Arjomand, 1988, p. 98).

He rejected any withdrawal from this holy duty on the part of the clergy. He even charged all Iranians, such as bazaris, teachers, and university professors, to work for establishing the Islamic state. In Iran, *velayat-e faqih* became the political theory for a group of clergy, the 'radical clergy' which made up the 'Khomeini network'. This group consisted mainly of Ayatollah Beheshti, Ayatollah Motahhari, Hojat al-Islam Rafsenjani, Hojat al-Islam Bahonar and Hojat al-Islam Khamenei, Ayatollah Montazeri, and Ayotollah Ardabili. Khomeini's religious work and the theory of *velayat-e faqih* provided an intellectual framework for an Islamic government as the only legitimate government in Muslim communities.[142] The main difference between the 'radical group' and other secular and religious groups in the opposition was that their political activities were intended not to re-establish the constitutional monarchy, but to overthrow the Shah and to construct an Islamic government.[143] Especially noteworthy in the story above is not only the historical engagement of the clergy in political processes, but the variation in their level of engagement and orientation. They played a significant role in the 1905-1909 constitutional process of alliance with the traditional middle occupational groups (which prepared the soil for later coalition formation). Khomeini's religious work (1971) provided an intellectual or cognitive framework for an Islamic government as the only legitimate government in Muslim communities. He rejected any withdrawal from this sacred duty on the part of the clergy, and this became the guiding theory for the group referred to as the 'radical clergy'. The main difference between this group and other secular and religious groups in the opposition was their *unambiguous objective to reconstruct society as an Islamic republic*, that is to overthrow the Shah and to establish a new system of government and a new social order.

8 Iran on the Eve of the Islamic Revolution

In this chapter several aspects of Iranian society on the eve of the Islamic Revolution, such as the main urban social groups and political opposition to the Shah, will be discussed. I focus particularly on several key groups, among others the urban marginals, who played a decisive role in the Islamic Revolution. The urban marginals, referred to by Khomeini as the 'dispossessed', were the most important social army of the radical clergy. Without the support of the 'dispossessed', and without organizing them through mosques–and by the active role of *tullabs* and bazaris–the radical clergy were not able to establish their monopoly over the movement and seize political power. Another important issue of this chapter is the discussion about the transformation of the traditional civil society of Iran.

Transformation of the Traditional Civil Society of Iran

For more than half a century Iranian society had gone through major socio-economic changes as a result of an autocratic modernization. New social groups and modern institutions were created which destroyed the traditional socio-political stability of society based on the balance of power between state and the ulama. The new socio-economic reality, in which the ulama lost their dominant influence and power in favor of the state, drastically changed the characteristics and structures of civil society. Civil society of Iran on the eve of the Islamic Revolution was a mosaic of new and traditional social groups and political agents. The influential role of the ulama as the only legitimated agent in the leadership of civil society was challenged by new political groups. New social groups, modern institutions, and political groups violated the traditional settings of civil society and marginalized its core alliance, i.e., the ulama and the bazaris. The traditional Shi'ite socio-political view of division of power to a temporal political one and a more permanent social one of the ulama, awaiting the real leader, the Hidden Imam, who would appear and unify these two sources of authority could not challenge the new dominating political ideologies. New ideologies, such as socialism and nationalism, which believed in seizure of–or sharing–political power as the only means for reconstructing society, dominated the political arena of Iranian society and had great influence not only on the modern social groups but also on the traditional ones. The traditional Shi'ite view could not remain as influential as in earlier centuries since it did not represent the new social groups and modern institutions, and had no ideological framework for legitimation of the new social order.

During the reign of Reza Shah (1925-1941) through an autocratic central power, attacks on traditional groups, mainly the ulama and the bazaris, and very intensive authoritative modern reforms, the traditional civil society of Iran was drastically marginalized. The ulama went back to their seminaries and mosques and the bazaris were forced to accept some undesirable features of modern economic order. Consequently, the traditional civil society of Iran, which mainly consisted of the relatively stable relationship between the ulama and the bazaris, weakened. This depended on three main factors:

1. *Emergence of new urban social groups.*
2. *Emergence of modern concepts and ideologies.*
3. *Decrease in the urban power of the bazaris and the ulama.*

Reza Shah's reforms created powerful and modern occupational groups which were not politically responsive to the traditional groups of civil society. Many of these groups became politically interested in modern ideas of nationalism and socialism and made up the core support of national-liberal movement during the democratic period of 1941-53. The main body of the communist Tudeh Party consisted of people from modern middle occupational groups. 'The modern middle class played an important role in this party' (Abrahamian, 1982, p. 328). Modern political ideas not only influenced these groups, but also the bazaar and other urban groups such as workers. The traditional Shi'ite theory exhibited its weakness in challenging the new ideologies and changes. Some ulama, such as Ayatollah Kashani and Taleqani, engaged in the new political arenas, while the major part of the ulama stayed out of modern politics. This small group of clergy participated in the democratic movement of the 1940s and early 1950s as allies with the nationalists. The other important group of the traditional civil society of Iran, i.e. the bazaris, had drastically changed their political position in the emerging new civil society.

As early as 1944, in the fourteenth parliamentary elections, the bazaar supported Mosaddeq, giving him the largest number of votes for any representative. Mosaddeq's nationalist economic policies in turn helped promote certain local industries and expanded the export of local products. At the same time, the nationalist-liberal discourse provided the ideological context for the formation of the Society of Merchants and Guilds (*Jaami'ih-ye Bazarganan va Pishevaran-i Bazaar*), which was in turn used as a vehicle for the mobilization of the bazaris against the Shah and for the nationalist causes (Moaddel, 1993, p. 116). Even one of the most important groups in traditional civil society allied with the modern national-liberals.

This period exhibited appearance of powerful ideologies and groups in civil society of Iran. The emergence of a modern civil society during the last years of the reign of Reza Shah witnessed the weakness and incompatibility of the traditional religious ideas with the modern changes. In the modern civil society of Iran–which dominated the democratic period of 1941-53–the alliance of the ulama and the bazaris was marginalized and new social groups constructed a modern political sphere based on modern political parties, ideologies, mass media, and so forth. The new political parties and associations, such as the Tudeh Party and NF, became more representative for a modern civil society in rapid change and more successful in speaking for and mobilizing new as well as old social groups against the state.

However, the *coup d'état* of 1953 put an end to the democratic power challenge of 1941-53. The shortcomings and weaknesses of the National Front and Tudeh Party in confronting the Shah's power–and the latter's concentration on blocking the influence of nationalists and communists–provided suitable circumstances for political activities of the radical clergy. The new group of clergy, the radical clergy with Khomeini, became engaged in popular politics of early 1960s. The radical clergy attempted to restore their prominent position in society and mobilize people against the state. Notwithstanding the leading position of the radical clergy in the uprising of June 1963, and even if the national liberals of the NF and some leftist fractions participating in the uprising accepted its religious leadership, the uprising showed the power of the new modern middle occupational groups and organizations.

Although the radical clergy failed in gaining statewide support, its leading position in this uprising provided the ulama a new political role in modern Iran. The uprising legitimated radical religious ideas as appropriate against the Shah and in a modern society which for more than two decades had been dominated by nationalist and socialist ideologies. After the bloody crash of the uprising, the Shah reinforced his dictatorship and continued to tighten his grip on the modern civil society. He continued his father's economic policy in 'destroying the social power of the ulama' which were the traditional sectors of society. Many of the ulama's sources of income, i.e. *vaqf* properties, came under state control. The traditional allies of the ulama, i.e. the bazaris, also remained under state's pressures for destroying its socio-economic power. The Shah explicitly pointed out his intentions in some of his economic plans for reducing the position of bazaars in the society:

> The bazaris are a fanatic lot, highly resistant to change because their locations afford a lucrative monopoly. I could not stop building supermarkets, I wanted a modern country. Moving against the bazaars was typical of the political and social risks I had to take in my drive for modernization (Milani, 1994, p. 63).

It should be pointed out that the traditional bonds between the ulama and the bazaris was also influenced by the modern changes of the Pahlavis. The bazaris were no longer required to send their children to the traditional schools. Modern society needed educated people who could handle the new and complicated matters of business affairs and market dynamics. They utilized the new education system and even sent their sons to Western countries for receiving modern education. Among the Iranian students who were sent to the West, there were even students from the ranks of the ulama. Many of these students later became the core intellectuals of the modern Islamic movement of Iran, such as Ali Shari'ati. Even the rate of the intermarriage between the bazaris and the ulama was reduced. These changes influenced the intensity of the bonds and relations between these two important groups. Another important change was the appearance of a new religious group, religious modernists–including Shari'ati and Bazargan[144]–who challenged the ideological monopoly of the ulama in civil society of Iran.

The ulama, as many other traditional groups of Iranian society, faced a decrease in their number and importance. During the period 1960 to

1968, the number of *madrasahs* (religious schools) was reduced from 252 to 138; and the number of *tullab* (religious students) was reduced, in the same period, from 14,419 to 7,482 (Akhavi, 1980, p. 187). Akhavi also presents data according to which the ulama's control not only over *madrasahs*, but also over religious endowments, declined. The clergy in general felt that they were slowly losing their influence in one of the only spheres in public life in which the regime had permitted them to continue to be active: religious education (Akhavi, 1980, p. 129). Abrahamian (1982) estimates that on the eve of the Revolution the number of clergy was 10,000 theology students, and an unknown number of low-ranking *mullahs, maktab* teachers, *madrasah* lecturers, prayer leaders, and procession organizers. (Abrahamian, 1982, p. 433). What is suggested is that the Shah's reforms and political attacks on the social basis of the ulama succeeded in undermining their social position.[145] Akhavi (1980, p. 132) refers to the Pahlavi dynasty's policies having succeeded in converting the ulama into a déclassé stratum.

The creation of the LMI, which had a more religious ideology than the NF, modern religio-political institutions such as 'The Monthly Talks Society' and Huseynieh Ershad, and appearance of radical modern religious ideas such as those of Shari'ati and Mojahedin-e khalq, witnessed a turn in orientation toward the traditional Shi'ite ideology. Khomeini's theory of *velayat-e faqih* was a great innovation in the traditional Shi'ite theology and came to create a new ideological framework for the ulama, and legitimate their participation in modern politics. 'Khomeinism' became an alternative to nationalism and socialism. *Velayat-e faqih* also eliminated any theological obstacles for the ulama's seizure of political power and provided the most important means in regaining the leading position in Iranian civil society. Through innovation of traditional orientation and beliefs the radical clergy could reorient themselves in a modern society and reconfirm their connections with the traditional part of society and, more importantly, find new social allies. The new social groups, among them the ulama, had to find their allies countervailing state authority.

In sum, the following developments led to a decrease in the power and authority of the ulama and bazaris in Iran:

1. *Establishment of new educational and juridical system.*
2. *Emergence of new social groups.*
3. *Emergence of a modern political public sphere.*

4. *Integration of bazaar in international and modern trade.*
5. *Marginalization of the economic power of bazaar.*
6. *Decreasing of vaqf properties.*

Consequently, traditional civil society of Iran, as a result of authoritative modernization and creation of new social groups and ideologies was increasingly weakened and marginalized. According to the second component of our model for existence of a civil society, namely *relatively autonomous access to the state or its elite*, discussed in chapter two, the ulama and bazaris were less and less able to gain access to state power and to influence it. At the same time, the modern civil society was also attacked and greatly weakened after the *coup d'état* 1953.

The Main Occupational Groups

Here it is important to identify several of the relevant occupational groups of Iranian society on the eve of the Revolution, since some of the groups or parts of them played key roles in the Revolution. Because rural sectors did not participate to any great extent in the Revolution, I do not discuss all rural occupational groups. The only rural occupational group discussed is the peasants because of their importance for the formation of marginal urban groups, the 'dispossessed'. The occupational groups of Iranian society are distinguished here in urban and rural areas. Further, they are divided into three categories: a) upper, b) middle, and c) lower (see table 8.1).

Modern Sectors

Modern urban upper occupational groups. The first category consisted of the Shah's family and court relatives, aristocrats, high-ranking military officers, and owners of modern enterprises and industries who had close connections with the court. The latter controlled almost the entire Iranian industry, mines, enterprises, and financial markets, and so forth. In pursuing their interests, the modern industrial and financial groups maintained 'good connections' with the Shah and other aristocrat families connected to the court. High-ranking military officers also received many economic advantages during the reign of the Shah. They became governors, heads of companies, etc.

The modern urban middle occupational groups. Reza Shah's administrative and economic reforms led to the creation of modern occupational groups, changing the traditional setting of Iranian society. Muhammad

Table 8.1 The main occupational groups

	URBAN		RURAL	
	Traditional	Modern	Traditional	Modern
Upper	Bazari merchants, money lenders (*sarrafs*)	Governmental and industrial groups	Landowners	Modern agricultural companies (*sherkat-ha-ye kesht va san'at*)
Middle	Bazari guilds, artisans, small shopkeepers related to bazaar	Bureaucrats, bankers, teachers, professors, white collar industrial employees, communication employees, modern shopkeepers, etc.	Small independent farmers (*dihqans*)	Some farmers engaging in modern farming (*kesht-e mekanizeh*)
Lower	Workers of bazaars such as porters, *shagerds*,[146] workers of public baths, slaughter houses, carpet weavers, etc.	Industrial workers	Peasants	Workers of modern agricultural companies

Reza Shah continued Reza Shah's reforms intending to modernize the traditional society–but not the political system–of Iran. The Shah's deterministic conviction that economic modernization implied social and cultural modernization, constituted the ideological basis for his economic plans and reforms.

One of these modern groups, which had their roots in the educational reforms at the time of the Constitutional Revolution and are usually referred to as the intelligentsia, increased in number and influence through the reforms of the Pahlavis. During the democratic period of 1941-53, they played a crucial role. During the sixteen years of the reign of Reza Shah, the size of the modern occupational groups–including women–tripled. Paradoxically, these groups, which were created by Reza Shah to help him in his modernization programs, made up the main basis for anti-regime propaganda and political activities. These groups made up the main body of the communist Tudeh Party, and the national-liberal National Front (NF). The Shah's negative experience of the modern middle occupational groups' engagement in political actions against him followed him during the entire period of his reign. He never trusted the modern middle occupational groups and their liberal representatives, the NF and the LMI. His fear of strong political opposition made it impossible for him to see the heterogeneity of the opposition.[147]

The modern middle occupational groups were constituted of teachers, professors, authors, modern shopkeepers, some middle ranking governmental employees, bank employees, white-collar employees in the new private economic activities etc. The statistics presented by the National Census of Population and Housing describing Iran's labor force showed that, in 1976, a third of Iran's Employed Population, 2,694,778 individuals, worked within the service sector (Milani, 1994, p. 61). To be sure, the figure does not include all groups that normally can be considered among these groups, such as many students of higher educational centers. For example, in 1976, 437,089 students were studying in institutions of higher education (Milani, 1994, p. 62). In 1977, about 650,000 students participated in the *Konkur* (university test), to be accepted into universities and high schools (*Keyhan*, 1977).

The modern urban lower occupational groups, industrial workers. There is no reliable statistics showing the number and size of the Iranian industrial workers on the eve of the Islamic Revolution. Abrahamian (1982) gives a figure of 2,400,000 in which he includes industrial workers, truck drivers, and wage earners in banks, offices and other agencies.[148] Milani (1994), by including even workers in manufacturing and health services, gives an estimate of 1,924,053 persons, or 22 percent of the labor force in 1976. Since manufacturing was the largest segment of the industrial 'working class', he believes that the 'working class' was the largest urban class in the 1970s. What is evident is that the industrial workers, played a relatively peripheral role in the Islamic Revolution. This is not only because of their size, but the lack of independent labor organizations and trade unions. Also, the interchange of the members of this group , and the rural origin of many of workers, played a crucial role in hindering them to create their own organizations. Milani (1994, p. 64), a student of the Islamic Revolution, points out: 'Despite its large size, the working class as a whole posed no serious threat to the Shah's regime'.

Traditional Sectors

Although the massive modernization programs influenced and changed many aspects of Iranian society, the traditional segment of Iranian society continued to exist, develop, and have socio-economic significance. These traditional groups can also be divided in three categories: a) upper, b) middle, and c) lower traditional groups.

The urban traditional upper and middle occupational groups. Iran's traditional upper and middle occupational groups mainly consisted of the bazaris and small shopkeepers situated within the bazaars or related to it. The core of these groups consisted of merchants, money lenders (*sarrafs*), shopkeepers within the bazaar organized by skills and specialties, their *senfs*, shop assistants, etc. The bazaris were highly influential in the small towns and rural areas that depended on the import of commodities from the cities. The bazaar, like many other traditional spheres of Iranian society, was influenced by the Shah's modernization programs. During the Shah's three first reform Plans (1949-1967), which were largely oriented to agriculture, the bazaar remained relatively untouched and its economic dominance in the urban areas was preserved. During this period, the bazaar's opposition to the Shah and its participation in political protest against the regime, such as the uprising of the June, 1963, had more socio-religious grounds than purely economic ones. But with the Shah's modernization plans, since the implementation of the Fourth Plan (1968-

72), through which the orientation of economic policy was focused on the industrial and service sectors, the role of the bazaar in the context of modern changes became vulnerable. The bazaar faced competing sectors of modern boutiques, shopping centers, and new entrepreneurs. Still, in spite of the appearance of new economic groups and sectors, the bazaar retained its important role in Iranian society – at least in the traditional sectors of urban life.

On the eve of the Islamic Revolution, the bazaris controlled half of the country's handicraft production, two-thirds of its retail trade, and three quarters of its wholesale trade (Abrahamian, 1982, p. 433). Altogether, the size of the retail and wholesale sectors, which included all the bazaars, grew from 481,026 persons in 1966 to 561,583 in 1976 (Milani, 1994, p. 63). If one adds to the bazaris the small shopkeepers whose economic activities depended on the bazaars, the figure would be much higher. The Shah's modernization programs and economic plans did not only fail to weaken the socio-economic position of the bazaars, but, on the contrary, led to economic prosperity and development of the bazaars. General economic expansion, in part due to oil revenues, accelerated the economic activities of the bazaars. The bazaars, however, kept their socio-economic importance among the large scale urban populations, especially through their control of food and major commodities of the small shopkeepers.

> The bazaar retained their independent craft and trade and craft guilds, whereas almost all other occupations had lost their unions and professional associations. Saved from the radical unions that had appeared in the 1940s, the guild elders were able to turn the clock back to the 1920s and reassert their power over the many thousand shop assistants, handicraftsmen, workshop employees, and small peddlers working in the urban bazaars (Abrahamian, 1982, p. 433).

Bazaars remained the major economic centers of the traditional spheres of the cities. A sphere, which as a result of the substantial migration of people with traditional patterns of life from rural areas, became the most expanding field of the urban life. Paradoxically, the Shah's modernization programs created new urban groups, migrants, who in their socio-economic position and cultural views were much closer to the bazaris than to the modern socio-economic groups and their cultural outlooks.

Although the bazaar indirectly enjoyed economic advantages from the Shah's modernization programs, and were an important group in civil society of Iran, they remained politically marginalized. The Shah pursued policies to reduce the influence of the bazaar and the ulama in Iran. They hindered the bazaris from receiving necessary credits that otherwise were available as a result of major expansion of income connected with increases in the price of oil in the 1970s. The policy resulted in a state-decision in 1972 intending to replace the traditional breadbaking businesses by modern automated ones. About 6,000 bakery workers lost their jobs (Arjomand, 1988, p. 107). The exclusion of the traditional sector of the urban societies continued with the establishment of *otaq-e asnaf* (the office of guilds) in 1975, for the purpose of controlling prices. Many students, mainly the sons of military sergeants and officers, were hired to inspect the shops. Some 8,000 merchants and retailers were imprisoned and a large number exiled and fined (Arjomand, 1988, p. 107). Implementation of the policy of 'destroying the traditional sectors' of the cities, resulted in intensified linkages between the bazaars and small shopkeepers–whose economic position was threatened by the establishment of modern shopping centers and restrictions put on them by the state–and the radical clergy.

The urban lower traditional groups. These groups mainly consisted of workers of bazaars and other traditional sectors related to the bazaars, such as porters, *shagerds*, cleaners, workers of public baths, slaughter houses, etc. There is no satisfactory statistics on these groups, but their close connection with and economic dependency on bazaars made them natural allies of bazaris.

The rural lower occupational groups. Although the peasants are not an urban occupational group, they played a role in contributing to the ranks of urban marginal groups. According to the 1976 National Census of Population and Housing, of a total labor force of 8,698,947 persons, there were 2,991,869 persons involved in agricultural activities.[149] Peasants were the largest part of the Iranian population. But the Shah's agricultural reforms and the system of loans provided to the peasants weakened their independence and led to a decrease in agricultural production. Many peasants, unable to pay back their loans to the banks, and attracted by job opportunities in the cities, sold their pieces of land and moved. The peasants of Iran have never been a revolutionary force and never participated in uprisings and revolutions against the central government. There are several explanations for their conservatism and 'passivism'.[150]

Peasants have not been active in Iranian socio-political movements, for instance those directed against shahs,[151] in part because the shahs have used their power against local landowners and have also provided improvements in village conditions. The shahs of the Pahlavi (1925-1979) commanded considerable respect among the peasant communities of Iran. They had introduced a number of socio-economic reforms such as construction of roads and dams, developed the health and educational systems in the villages, and brought about some land reform. The Islamic Revolution was an urban revolution, in large part without the involvement of the village peasantry (Arjomand, 1988, pp. 107, 194) (but, of course, involving those peasants who had migrated to the cities).[152]

Although the peasants did not participate collectively in the Islamic Revolution, some of them who moved to the cities became the core of the marginal groups of the cities. They constructed the basis of the power of radical clergy. Finding them as radical supporters, Khomeini and other radical clergy were in a position to force other oppositional groups to accept their unquestionable leadership.

Authoritative Modernization and the Creation of the 'Dispossessed'

The Shah used the income from oil mainly to push through five 'Seven-year Plans' to modernize Iran. The first Seven-year Plan (1949-55) was aimed largely at supporting agricultural, infrastructural, and social projects (Amuzegar & Fekrat, 1971, p. 40). But the nationalization of the oil industry and the boycott of the Western companies led to a drastic curtailment of oil revenues and the First Plan was crippled. The second Seven-year Plan (1956-62) had a budget of 1.12 million dollars, allocated as follows: agriculture and irrigation, 29.88 percent; transportation and communication, 40.48 percent; industry and services, 11.19 percent; and social services, 18.45 percent (Amuzegar & Fekrat, 1971, p. 42). During the period of the Second Plan three large dams, railways, highways, and several industries were built. Special attention was paid to the cities. The streets of some sixty-three towns were paved with asphalt and such basic utilities as power and piped water were supplied to a large number of cities and towns (Amuzegar & Fekrat, 1971, p. 45). During the third Seven-year Plan (1963-67), with a budget of 3,093 million dollars, the sectors receiving the greatest financing were transport and communication, agriculture, power and fuel, and industry.

During the three Seven-year Plans (1949-67) the state wanted to change and modernize both industry and agriculture. There were no significant differences between resources allocated to agriculture and to industry. But in the fourth Seven-year Plan, the general policy of the state concerning planned modernization favored industry. The fourth Five-year Plan (1968-72) was the most ambitious of all other plans. The fourth Plan began with a budget of 480 billion Rials, an amount that was increased during the plan period to 621 billion Rials as a result of the growing income from oil exports (Mehner, 1978, p. 184). During this time, agriculture and animal husbandry was to receive 65 billion Rials and the development of Industry and mines would receive 99 billion Rials. In addition to industry and mines, the other sector which received priority was transportation and communication, which would receive 100.3 billion Rials (Amuzegar & Fekrat, 1971, p. 54).

Implementation of the fourth Plan resulted in the rapid development of the industrial sector and a decrease in agricultural production. As a result of the stagnation of agriculture, the influx of rural population to urban areas increased. The movement of the rural people to the towns and cities was not a new phenomenon, but one that began after the Shah's land reform in 1962. The Shah, through a law dated 9 January 1962, initiated a reform program that came to be called the White Revolution. The first phase of this planned revolution began with a land reform program intending to destroy the traditional power of landlords and some clergy who owned the lands called *vaqf-e khass*, which were privately endowed. From 1962 to 1969 a total amount of 16,000 villages were purchased by the state, and 743,406 farm families received land (Amuzegar & Fekrat, 1971, p. 117). The main policy of land reform was to replace landowners with rural cooperatives. Between 1963 to 1969, 8,102 rural cooperatives were constructed with 1,339,762 members. The number of loans granted to these members were 3,685,799 (Amuzegar & Fekrat, 1971, p. 120). The increases in cheap agricultural imports and the high cost of loans did, however, make it difficult for many small farmers to remain in the rural areas.

In addition, because of established priorities, some low-ranking groups in the rural areas were excluded from receiving land. One of these groups were *khoshneshins*, people who had no land and worked for landowners in the summers and moved to the small towns and urban areas and worked there in the winter. Because they did not own land, groups such as *gavbands* and *khoshneshins* could not be members of agricultural cooperatives. In the further distributions of lands such as *khaleseh* villages and *nasaq*, membership in an agricultural cooperative was a condition for receiving land, and, as a result, the poorest rural people were excluded.

> At the distribution end of the operation, policy was directed to the dispersal of nasaq among those who in the law were eligible to receive it and in accordance with standard priorities. Patterns of privilege followed closely what we have already seen happening with the crown lands and khaleseh distribution: the *gavband* and the *khoshneshin* were excluded while the farmer worker, the man without customary rights in the nasaq, came last among the eligible recipients. Excluded also was anyone who at the time of distribution was not a member of the village rural cooperative society (Denman, 1978, p. 253).[153]

The land reform led to the rapid differentiation of the traditional setting of the rural areas. Many poor people lost their traditional bonds and found it harder to stay in such areas. By failing to give any or enough land to the majority of the peasants, the land reform accelerated the massive migration from the rural areas into the cities (Arjomand, 1988, p. 73).

The rapid development of the cities also created many job opportunities that attracted such marginal people to the urban areas. In the 1950s, 68.6 percent and 31.4 percent of the population lived in the rural and urban areas, respectively; by 1976, slightly more than 47 percent of the population lived in urban areas, an increase of 50 percent in two decades. The number of large cities also increased: in 1966, Tehran was the only city with a population over 500,000. By 1976, four cities had populations this large (Milani, 1994, p. 66). In general, the years after the land reform of 1963 was a period of rapid expansion of the urban population. For instance in 1966, only 38 percent of the entire population lived in towns with populations over 5,000; in 1976 nearly 48 percent lived in such towns. Cities with populations over 100,000 made up only 21 percent of the population in 1966, whereas in 1976 it had increased to 29 percent (Abrahamian, 1982, p. 431). Tehran, the capital and largest city, grew from 2 million (1961) to more than 10 million today.

The increase of urban population was largely due to movement of people from rural areas to the cities. In 1976, out of a total population of 33,709 million, 5,056 million, about 15 percent of Iranians were migrants (Arjomand, 1988, p. 217). The rural roots of the migrants can be confirmed by the statistical figures used by Arjomand (1988), which indicate that the labor forces of the predominantly peasant sector declined by 19 percent. Rapid changes and movement led to the development of a special type of modern city. The cities were divided among three different patterns of lifestyles. The modern upper and middle occupational groups usually lived in the modern areas of cities,[154] used the modern parks, cinemas, theaters, shopping centers, bought new cars, and visited foreign countries.[155] The second group, the traditional middle occupational groups and the industrial workers, lived in the traditional central and southern areas of the cities. These peoples were largely religious and had a more traditional lifestyle. The bazaar still made up the heart of the traditional areas of cities. The third group were the 'new-comers', the rural people who moved to the cities hoping to find jobs and a better life. According to Kazeroni and Golabi (1979), the social origin of about 80 percent of heads of households of marginals in the 'outer zone' areas of three major cities of Iran, Bandar Abbas, Boshehr, and Hamedan, is rural. The other 20 percent are born in the same cities.

The Shah's modernization Plans did not take into consideration the unintended consequences of the implementation of such ambitious programs. For instance, during the 1970s, instead of implementing housing projects in the southern areas where the migrants settled, the state spent the major part on constructing and developing the modern areas. Meanwhile, the industrial investment between 1963 to 1972 increased from 17.1 billion Rials to 99 billion Rials. The housing and construction increased during this time from 12.2 billion Rials to 23 billion Rials. As a result of a shortage of housing, rents rose and forced many of the 'new-comers' to settle in the areas out of the city zone called *kharej-e mahdodeh* (outer zone of the cities). The constant flow of people to the cities resulted in the construction of many shanty towns. As will be discussed, the settlement of these people in the 'outer zone' of the cities led to confrontations with municipal authorities.

The Shah's modern industries and bureaucratic system needed skilled and educated workers. Therefore, the migrants, who were largely illiterate and trained in agriculture, could not be absorbed into bureaucratic or industrial jobs, nor could they work in the modern service sector. They were forced to become street-sellers, porters, free-workers of the bazaars, square-workers,[156] vegetable sellers, construction workers, peddlers, and so forth. About 30 percent of heads of households of marginals with such *ad hoc* jobs had not worked during an entire year, according to one study conducted in six major cities (Kazeruni & Golabi, 1979, p. 55). The same study (1979, p. 56) reports that many marginals had to borrow money from banks and other private funds because of their low income levels. About 56 percent of all the marginals in the six cities were in debt to banks as a result of borrowing for purposes of consumption.

The lack of a place in the modern or traditional socio-economic spheres of cities made them a 'disembedded' mass. They could receive a place in the urban society of Iran only through a revolutionary change of its very structures. 'Khomeini has been especially associated with sympathy for the impoverished masses, whom he tirelessly described as *mazlum* (oppressed) and *bi gunah* (innocent). His solutions for improving their socio-economic conditions were not specific, but he did condemn what he viewed to be the government's over-commitment to urbanization, industrialization and over-reliance on foreign investment'. (Akhavi, 1980, p. 101).

The migrants–referred to by Khomeini and the radical clergy as the *Mostaz'afin* (dispossessed)–was a large group of people who as a result of the Shah's land reform and Westernizing policies migrated from rural areas and small cities to the large cities. Due to their rural background they had high birth rates and with the better medical care in the cities they had large families with many children. As a result of the unavailability of traditional, i.e. rural, occupations, and due to the economic pressure of life in the cities, many of their children became assistants of shopkeepers and craftsmen in order to support their families.

Some of my interviewees believed that many marginals worked within the modern industrial sector and should be counted among the industrial workers. To assure myself about the occupational characteristics of the marginals, after a long period of searching for evidence, I found a study which was conducted by 'The Social Research Institute of Tehran' in 1973. Table 8.2 indicates the occupational situation of the marginals in six major cities including Tehran.

As we see, the marginals who had regular work is about 33 percent of the entire population. But those are not necessarily industrial workers. About the occupational skill of the marginals in these six major cities, Kazeroni and Golabi (1978, p. 54), point out that more than 56 percent of the marginals are unskilled and about 21 percent are skilled and semi-skilled workers, but the skill of most of them is only proper to be assistants (*shagerds*) of workshops. About 14 percent of the employed marginals are self employed, such as shopkeepers and sellers. The rest are engaging in various activities, such as shepherd, farming, begging, and so forth.

The marginals were a new urban group, which as the authors of *Ketab-e jom'eh* put it, a poor (*mahrom*) social group: 'They are neither urban nor rural, namely the city did not integrate them or push them back. This situation not only concerns their housing or residential area, but also all aspects of their economic, cultural, and social life, forcing them to struggle with this 'not urban and not rural' condition' (*Ketab-e jom'eh*, 1979).

Table 8.2 Employment situation of the people residing in the 'outer zone'

Occupational situation	Tehran		Bandar Abbas		Ahvaz		Kermanshah		Boshehr		Hamedan		Total	
	No	Per.	No	Per.	No	Per.	No	Per.	No	Per.	No	Per.	No	Per.
Ad hoc work	350	41	163	27	173	26	80	34	50	29	52	44	868	33
Wage earner	281	33	97	16	130	20	55	23	39	23	41	35	643	24
Self-employed	46	5	38	6	28	4	19	8	7	4	7	6	145	6
Job-seeking unemployed	23	3	28	5	15	2	6	3	4	2	4	3	80	3
Passive unemployed	264	31	254	42	268	41	99	41	63	38	39	33	987	37
Housewife	146	17	123	20	145	22	49	20	42	25	23	20	528	20
Student	104	12	78	13	65	10	43	18	15	9	11	9	316	12
Incapacitated	2	2	22	4	19	3	7	3	6	4	5	4	71	
Other	-	2	31	5	39	6	-	-	-	-	-	-	72	
Children	238	28	193	31	218	33	59	25	56	33	28	23	792	30
Total	852	100	610	100	659	100	238	100	169	100	119	100	2647	100

Source: The Social Research Institute of Iran (1352/1973), and printed in Persian in Kazeroni & Golabi (1979) 'The statistical presentation of marginal people (*hashiyeh neshinan*), in *Ketabe jom'eh*, No. 12, October 1979.

The marginal migrant (eclectic urban-peasant) lifestyle was the pattern of life of the migrants from the countryside to the big cities. It was manifested in a mixture of urban patterns such as wearing modern (urban) clothes, visiting cinemas, and watching television, on the one hand, and keeping their traditional peasant patterns of behavior in terms of housing, religious activities, education of their children, and undisciplined patterns of economic and social activities on the other.

During the period after the uprising of June 1963, the Shah speeded up his reform policies. Considerable oil revenues were to be channeled, through the Third plan (1962-1968), Fourth plan (1968-1973), and Fifth plan (1973-), into economic activities. 'The two completed plans helped the Gross National Product grow at the annual rate of 8 percent in the period 1962-1970, 14 percent in 1972-1973, and 30 percent in 1973-1974'.[157] As a result of spending over 3.9 billion on infrastructure and producing over 500 miles of rail track and 13,000 miles of roadway, the inhabitants in many villages near the towns, could easily commute between the two. Though they resided in modern towns, they did not assimilate fully into modern urban culture. On the contrary, they created their own eclectic culture that was not peasant, traditional, or modern. It simply was a mixture of some aspects of urban cultural life such as watching television, driving cars, visiting the cinema, and participating marginally in urban commercial life, on the one hand, and traditional and religious patterns of life on the other. These people, at the outset of their immigration, settled out of the legal residential areas of cities. They were continually challenged and harassed by the city's authorities, and had difficulties gaining access to electricity and drinking water.

Mostaz'afin, the 'dispossessed', were not the only people living in the 'outer zone'. The people who originally came from rural areas or small towns and resided in the poor 'forgotten' areas of the cities without access to the resources of the middle occupational groups or rich areas were also a part of these urban groups. A short overview of the areas in which these urban groups of 'dispossessed' live will help shed some light on some corners of the social life in Iran that the Shah was unlikely to see or to consider as the consequence of his modernization programs. A report presented after the victory of the Islamic Revolution in one of the two main newspapers of Tehran, *Keyhan*, provides a glimpse of these residential areas. Under the title, *Govd neshinan ra daryabid* (Help the cavity-residents), *Keyhan* pointed out:

> At the entrance of *Shahid Harandi* avenue, we see small shops and large stinking *joys* (water channels) telling us about the dreadful situation at the avenue's end. After passing the third or the fourth alley, one sees the ugly sights as a waiting hungry dragon glimpses its prey /.../. Descending more than 20 dusty and damaged steps, we stop at the door of a house. I knocked

> on the door, and an old, tired, sun-burned man appears /.../. He is a municipal worker earning a salary of 1,300 *toman*, from which he must support six persons. From this he pays 280 *toman* in rent. Someone else told us that their wives and children must go to the area's only *feshari* (water-tap) to wash clothing /.../. We go to another *Govd*, Govde Salehi; its stairs are so steep that we must rest on the way up. At a distance we see a woman bearing two buckets filled with dirty water, which she pours down the middle of the alley. Other women do the same. I call out and ask her why she did that? She answers with surprise: 'where do you want me to pour it? In a house where we empty the toilet with a bucket, where else shall I pour the washing-water?' I ask, how do you handle the lack of running water [in the house]? She answers: 'we do nothing, we go to the *feshari* and carry back our drinking-water (*Keyhan*, 7 June 1979).

In the same article, *Keyhan* wrote that the number of people living in a house in that area could be 100 persons. To emphasize my point about the origins of these people, I present another excerpt from this article:

> I asked if the state provides you land and the condition of life in your village becomes better, are you ready to return to your village? He answered, I have been living here for 20 years, and my children graduated here from high school, in which village they can live? Another person said: Mister, we are used to here, where can we go? If the state paves the Govds (holes) and gives enough land to us, we would construct [our homes] and do not need the state's help.

Political Opposition to the Shah

At the beginning of the Revolution of 1979, the Shah's political opposition consisted largely of:

1. *The National Front and the Liberation Movement of Iran.*
2. *Fadaiyan-e khalq.*
3. *Mojahedin-e khalq.*
4. *The ulama, the clergy.*

The National Front had 'political capital' from the national struggle against foreign imperialism, mainly the nationalizing of the oil industry during the period of 1947-1953. The National Front's struggle was a political challenge and never had an 'anti-West' position. The struggle for nationalizing the oil industry under the leadership of its charismatic leader Muhammad Mosaddeq, and its modern political and socio-economic perspective, were its chief legitimizing factors. Mehdi Bazargan, one of the ministers in the Mosaddeq's cabinet from 1951-1953, when he was a member of the National Front, became as leader of the LMI the first prime minister of the Islamic Republic. Some within the modern middle occupational groups, such as lawyers, technocrats, teachers, professors, high school students and merchants supported these two liberal organizations. The Fadaiyan-e khalq was a Marxist organization, mainly supported by high school students and young educated people from the modern middle occupational groups. The Mojahedin-e khalq was a 'modern Islamic' organization which advocated a 'socialist Islam'. Some traditional middle occupational groups (youth, teachers, and high school students) constituted its support. Both the Fadaiyan and the Mojahedin were relatively small groups limited to intellectuals and students. They engaged in armed struggle against the Shah. The main anti-opposition activities of SAVAK, the Shah's vicious security forces, were concentrated on these two organizations. Consequently, on the eve of the Revolution, the Fadayian's and the Mojahedin's main leaders and ideologists were imprisoned and the organizations greatly weakened.

  The ulama did not constitute a homogeneous opposition group to the Shah. They largely formed three groups that differed according to their social positions and interpretations of Islam. These groups could be characterized from left to right: (1) Radical clergy such as Ayatollah Mahmoud Taleqani, Ayatollah Ruhollah Khomeini, and Ayatollah Montazeri, all of whom rejected any compromise with the Shah. (2) Moderate clergy such as Ayatollah Shariatmadari, who were ready to compromise with the Shah on the basis of the 1906 Constitution. (3) More traditional clergy such as Ayatollah Khorasani, Mar'ashi Najafi, and Golpayegani. Ayatollah Taleqani was a highly respected religious and political leader who cooperated with Mosaddeq and National Front under the 'movement for nationalizing the oil industry' and the national movement against foreign imperialism and the Shah (1944-1953). He was imprisoned several times and, as a high-ranking supporter of LMI, hardly a 'fundamentalist'. Taleqani was a link between Khomeini and the liberals of the NF and the LMI. Khomeini was one of the ulama who considered Islam not just a religion but a political ideology as well, and aimed toward political power.

Khomeini's teacher was one of the most prominent *marja'-e taqlid*, Ayatollah Borujerdi, who had an ambivalent attitude toward the issue of political power. Borujerdi, in a certain sense, accepted the theory of a non-religious, but Islamic, government of Iran.[158] In the 1920s, Borujerdi forbade (shortly after the Reza Shah was crowned) through a *fatva* the ulama from participating in political affairs. At that time he was *marja'-e taqlid* (the legitimized religious leader).[159] For almost 40 years, most of the clergy were outside the Iranian political arena. This meant that, in particular, Khomeini, whose father had been murdered by a governor, would not engage himself in active opposition to the Shah as long as Borujerdi was alive, due to Borujerdi's authority as *Marja'-e taqlid* (source of emulation). After Borujerdi's death (1961), the ulama began to intensify their critique of the regime of Muhammad Reza Shah, the son of Reza Shah, for his non-Islamic dealing with Muslims affairs. In particular, Khomeini severely criticized the Shah and his regime and launched a political movement in the main cities of Iran. This began Khomeini's political career. The Shah suppressed the revolt and Khomeini was arrested and deported to Turkey. After the movement of 1963 and Khomeini's deportation, some of the most influential ulama, Ayatollah Khoi' Najafi, Ayatollah Khurasani and Ayatollah Mar'ashi' Najafi, felt that the clergy should avoid the dirty business of politics and should devote themselves to purely religious studies. Consequently, the political arena, from 1964 to 1975, was dominated by new leftist and religious young groups who were influenced by the Cuban revolution and the theory of 'urban armed struggle', although some clergy continued to be politically active.

In the years 1973-76, the regime became more repressive and concentrated its attack on the two main leftist organizations, Fadaiyan-e khalq and Mojahedin-e khalq, which had launched an armed struggle against the Shah in the beginning of the 1970s. In the context of the regime's concentration on leftist groups, some religious groups had the opportunity to propagate radical ideas among the poor and traditional urban people who migrated to the cities and became slum-dwellers. This group would play a crucial role as the social base of the radical clergy in the Islamic Revolution.

As pointed out earlier, there was massive movement from the rural areas to the cities. The migrants tended to be strongly traditional and religious. They were not fully integrated and assimilated into the urban societies. For instance, in these 'outer zone' areas, there were frequent confrontations between these groups and municipal authorities regarding supplies of water and electricity, and over permission to build in the outer zones of the cities. This together with housing shortages and rent increases, became a critical problem for the authorities.[160] Eventually the confrontations between these people and local authorities deepened and spread especially, but not only, in Tehran. In autumn, 1976, the regime's arbitrary actions to regulate the construction of illegal houses outside of the city zone (*kharej-e mahdodeh*) of Tehran and many other cities improved. This construction was mainly a result of migration to the big cities from small towns and villages, which led to a shortage of housing and an enormous increase in rents in the large cities. To stop the uncontrolled construction of houses and shanty houses outside the legal zones of such cities, municipal authorities tried to destroy such places by force. In many cases bloody confrontations between municipal authorities and police on one side, and the 'dispossessed' migrants were unavoidable. The Shah was forced to replace Prime Minister Hoveida with a technocrat and former finance minister, Jamshid Amuzegar in mid-1977. The movement of the marginal 'dispossessed' against the municipal authority and the police continued until the beginning of the mass demonstrations of other urban groups–in particular the modern and the traditional middle occupational groups–in the winter of 1977.

Exploiting the confrontation between the migrants and local authorities, young religious groups propounded radical religious ideas among the marginals. As they increased in number, they became together with the traditional occupational groups the major groups of urban society (this is in terms of size, not in terms of political importance, at least not before 1975, since the clergy, the modern middle occupational groups, and the army were certainly more important). They became the most visibly active group in the movement of 1975-79, the main social basis of Khomeini's and the radical clergy's support, mobilized in the Islamic Revolution. The leftists were largely out of the picture–either because of arrest, exile, or their fragmentation.

The Islamic Revolution of Iran had its core social basis in the clergy together with the 'dispossessed' and the traditional middle occupational groups. The modern middle occupational groups and organizations such as the NF and the LMI[161] were important allies of this core. It is worth pointing out that the revolution did not begin with the protests initiated by the clergy in Qum in 1977, but by the mass protests and revolts of the marginal migrants in Tehran and Ray in 1976. They struggled against city officials and police who wanted to destroy their 'illegal houses'. Several people were killed and many were injured. Khomeini came to appear as the only noteworthy alternative to the Shah, since the traditional middle occupational groups and the marginal migrants sharing many traditional religious values with the clergy supported him. While the modern industrial and oil workers in Iran are rather substantial in number–estimated at 800,000 or more (Abrahamian, 1982) at the time of the Revolution–they played a relatively peripheral role in the revolution (Arjomand, 1988, p. 108).[162] They were fewer in number than the marginals, and they lacked the close alliances with the clergy, the traditional, and modern middle occupational groups.

The picture is one in which a new emergent groups (large in number, much larger than the industrial workers) awaits a 'voice', a role in modern society, through which to defend or advance their interests and address their problems and frustrations. *The clergy gave them an effective and visibly dramatic voice and role in an urbanized Iran.* The clergy were also important for the traditional middle occupational groups but less so for the bureaucrats or modern professionals, who were better represented by the NF and the LMI, or other organizations. Of course, the clergy also had access to the modern middle occupational groups through their alliances with the Liberals (as pointed out below).

In 1976, a new administration came to power in Washington and pressured the Shah to liberalize his regime. This encouraged liberal groups such as lawyers, human rights activists, poets, and editors to organize themselves and begin to openly criticize the regime. In the years 1977-78, the political arena was dominated by two opposition groups, namely liberals such as the National Front and the Liberal Movement of Iran on the one hand, and 'radical religious' on the other, in the fragmentation and weakness of the leftists, many were killed or imprisoned. Two parallel political processes went on against the Shah. The liberals intended to reestablish a democratic and constitutional political system. The religious radicals under the leadership of Khomeini, among others, rejected any compromise with the Shah and intended to bring down the monarchy. The liberals, such as those in the NF and the LMI had no mass support among the majority of the urban population. But they had, to a great extent, traditional political legitimacy (*heysiat-e siyasi*) among some of the modern middle occupational groups and the intellectuals. Khomeini and his radical clergy had cultural legitimacy (*heysiat*) among the traditional middle occupational groups (bazaris, among others), religious intellectuals and especially among the marginal/migrant groups in the urban areas. During the last year of the Revolution, many of the traditional religious institutions, such as mosques and Huseyniehs, became centers for organizing demonstrations. In the face of growing demonstrations and strikes, the clergy, the bazaris, small shopkeepers, and younger volunteers organized the distribution of food, provisions, and fuel to households. Bazaris and some small shopkeepers sold food to the poor at low prices. This set the stage for the revolutionary process, which resulted in the establishment of an Islamic Republic.

9 The Islamic Revolution

In this part of the work, the process of the Islamic Revolution, in particular the radicalization of the movement and the political alliances which led to the triumph of the Revolution and the seizure of political power by its religious leadership will be examined.

The process of the Islamic Revolution was a process of sociopolitical reconstruction of the leading position of the ulama in Iranian civil society. The ulama during more than fifty years of Pahlavis' authoritative modernization had been increasingly marginalized and reduced from their prominent position in civil society. They had lost much of their social influence. The radical clergy used the unique historical opportunity which the Revolution created to regain their leading position in civil society. But the radical clergy did not only want to become the leaders of civil society. They wanted also to seize political power and use the state machinery to reconstruct society according to the new ideas of an Islamic universal order. The Islamic Revolution was a revolution taking place in modern times and in a modern society. Therefore, the radical clergy, in order to gain legitimation and acceptance in the modern Iranian civil society, had to adapt their purely religious and traditional ideas to more modern concepts. The modern terms such as 'republic', 'parliament', and 'constitutional assembly' were among the slogans that the radical clergy used to gain political legitimation in Iranian civil society. Political compromises and exhibition of tolerance to rival political groups, such as the communists, were other political principles which the radical clergy skillfully exploited. Through the revolutionary process, they found a major social group in civil society which many other political groups in opposition and the state as well had ignored, namely the 'dispossessed'. Politicization of the 'dispossessed' provide them a very strategic means in regaining the leading position both in civil society and in the Revolution. The process of the Revolution, by which the radical clergy managed to regain their leading position in civil society and become the leaders of the Revolution, will be discussed in this chapter.

The Alliance Between the Ulama and the Middle Occupational Groups

The interdependency of bazaris and the clergy was a key factor in Iranian socio-political conditions and developments in both the Constitutional and Islamic Revolutions. In the Constitutional movement of 1905-9, the alliance between the clergy and bazari merchants was oriented to reducing the power of the monarchy and limiting the influence of foreigners in the economic life of society, which had historically been controlled by the bazaars. Neither the clergy nor bazaris–or modern liberals for that matter–were ideologically oriented or politically prepared to do away with the monarchy–and the bazaris as the main social group in the cities strove only for political reforms, not revolutionary changes. In the movement of the 1970s, the alliance was oriented to the removal of the Shah and the monarchy, with the radical clergy providing the charismatic voice and leadership. This clergy had a theory of an alternative state to the monarchy and spoke in a language understandable to the great masses of the urban areas. The liberals in the NF and the LMI could not offer an independent theory or realistic alternative for popular political power (at least with the military out of the picture, see discussion below).

The bazaris had traditional religious and economic reasons to back the clergy and to play a role in the revolutionary process. As pointed out earlier, from the outset of Islam, there were close connections and interdependencies between the bazaris and the ulama. At the onset of the Islamic Revolution, the bazaris were faced with a major powerful socio-economic group, i.e. the new capitalists who controlled more than 85 percent of the major private firms engaged in industry, banking, foreign trade, insurance and urban construction (that is, modern, large-scale capitalism). This group had the support of the Shah in his modernization and development plans. State policies were oriented to its interests and facilitated its development, with little or no concern about the conditions and future of the bazaris.

Among the traditional middle occupational groups (bazaris, among others), there were numerous sources of grievances and resentment against the policies of the Shah's government and the new industrial and entrepreneurial elite whose interests had been helped: they were being edged out of wholesale trade; threatened by the establishment of new retail networks and outlets; import licenses went to the modern entrepreneurs (Bakhash, 1990, p. 192). All of this entailed a potential loss of economic and social status, increased competition with the modern entrepreneurs and growing concentration of economic power in the hands of a few. In addition, the

Shah's clumsy efforts to control the economy, or to introduce new laws and regulations affecting the economy had negative effects on the bazaar. For instance, during the 1970s, when inflationary pressures became great, the Shah attempted to control prices in ways that hurt the smaller bazaris. The latter were jailed, fined, and banned from their home towns, as a result of the regime's oppressive action against them.[163]

In spite of the Shah's modernization program, the bazaar continued to dominate a large part of Iran's domestic economy. As mentioned earlier, the bazaris controlled half of the country's handicraft production, two-thirds of its retail trade, and three quarters of its wholesale trade (Abrahamian, 1982, p. 433). The bazaar continued to finance many religious activities, seminaries, and places of meeting such as hoseyniehs, mosques, religious schools, mourning ceremonies–the most important of all *moharram* ceremonies, and pilgrim journeys. People who make the ritual pilgrimage to Mecca become *haji*. A *haji* is normally more self-confident and respected by others than a non-*haji*. Bazari merchants, who made the pilgrimage to Mecca and became *hajis*, procured a certain 'religious capital' that helped them in their economic affairs in the Muslim community. To be a good merchant in the bazaar is not only a purely economic matter, but also–and sometimes more so–a religious matter. In the bazaar not only the commodity is judged, but also the merchant who supplies it. As pointed out earlier, the bazaris are dependent on the clergy to legitimate them and their economic activities, and the clergy depend on the economic power of the bazaris for support, in part to establish and maintain their schools and religious buildings as well as religious activities in general.

The traditional socio-economic interdependency between bazaris and clergy, which in times of turmoil and change manifests itself as a political alliance between them was greatly reinforced by the Shah's modernization/development policy. This policy, intentionally or unintentionally, marginalized them: it eroded the traditional power and prestige of the clergy through the secularization of schools, government, and public life; it fostered the development of large-scale capitalism with industry, banking, and foreign trade with minimum consideration for the traditional economic-and-religious linkages represented by the bazaar as an Islamic social institution.[164] The Iranian bazaar not only provided strategic economic support for the clergy during the revolutionary process, but also furnished it with meeting places and places to hide from the Shah's police.

The clergy also allied themselves with the modern middle occupational groups (professionals, middle managers, white collar workers etc.)

represented by the NF and the LMI. This alliance might appear obvious in the context of the general opposition to the Shah, especially since the clergy (or, at least, the radical clergy) were oriented to modern politics and parliamentary government (although initially the Constitutional parliament or congress was to determine the future form of the Republic).

The clergy's alliance with the NF and the LMI partly legitimized them and helped convince Western countries of their democratic intentions. It also played a role in the neutralization of the army (discussed below). On the basis of this alliance and strategy, the LMI's respected leader Mehdi Bazargan became the first prime minister of the Islamic Republic of Iran. A year later in connection with the occupation of the US embassy, he was removed and replaced by a clergy, Bahonar, and later by Raja'i (also a former member of the LMI and a deeply religious person).

The new middle occupational groups, although gaining in many ways from the Shah's modernization program, had only limited possibilities to advance or to protect their interests. They were denied a role in public life and the political processes that they felt their education and status in society warranted. Also, during the 1970s, their income levels and standard of living were threatened by inflation. In the face of an autocratic state, there was little they could do about this. They had a choice between accepting whatever fate that the Shah's (often arbitrary) policies led to, or attempting to change the Shah's policies. They protested in various ways, for example in written declarations, organized around professional groups and universities (Bakhash, 1990, p. 15). Later, many were to join the street rallies and demonstrations, as in the case of many students.

The various opposition groups accepted Khomeini before the Revolution. They went to Paris to visit him, acknowledging his political importance and his role as a political leader.[165] He was an opponent of the Shah, in part because he was perceived to be 'clean', uncontaminated (an important value as a basis for status and authority in Muslim societies)–for example, he never compromised with 'Satan'. Also, he developed a new political idea–linking the concept of 'religious government' with popular modern politics–which oriented and activated the radical clergy to participate in modern political arenas and processes, and to beat out other groups and potential competitors lacking compelling or revolutionary ideas in the Iranian context of the 1970s. This innovative, powerful idea eventually was exported to other Islamic countries (with observable effects in Algeria, Egypt, and Turkey, among others). The Islamic Revolution institutionalized and elaborated upon Khomeni's theory of 'The Reign of Islamic Jurists' (*Velayat-e faqih*).

The Effective Neutralization of the Army

As a consequence of the alliance between liberals and clergy (and the support of the USA in its opposition to communists and leftists and its support for liberals and clergy) the army announced its neutrality just during the last days of revolutionary struggle. This facilitated a peaceful shift of power from the Shah to the new government of Bazargan. This meant also that particular power resources were not readily available, and that certain games (and particular rules) of political mobilization and struggle were at stake and not others.

Four important factors explain why a very modern and powerful army was neutralized in the struggle for state power.

1. The very effective organ of security control within the army.
2. The loyalty of the army to the Shah as supreme commander.
3. The crisis of legitimacy.
4. Army professionalization.
5. Effective negotiation and compromise with the Council of the Revolution.

(1) After the Shah's *coup d'état* of 1953, the Shah with the assistance of the CIA constructed a very effective security organization, named *rokn-e do* (Section Two), within the army to eliminate any possibility of leftist infiltration. Fear of communism on the part of the Shah and the USA, generally oriented and shaped the policy of security control over army officers. Not only officers but also their families were controlled. Familiarity with leftist or political activists could cost an army officer his job, or at least, his career within the army. Effective control of personnel eliminated almost any possibility of a *coup d'état* from within the military.[166]

(2) The modern army of Iran had been organized and reinforced by the Pahlavi dynasty. The military forces, especially high-ranking officers, were treated royally by the Shah, and many of them received special economic and social benefits. Consequently, the military was particularly loyal to the Shah. In addition, ideological propaganda constructed a structural imagination of the Shah as the main pillar of social, economic, and political stability.

(3) The Royal Army was the proper name for the military forces of Iran. The military was a necessary component of the royalist order of Iran. *On the one hand it meant that without a strong and loyal army, the Shah would not have been able to establish or maintain himself in power. At the same time, the army could not have been such a powerful and prestigious factor in Iranian society without the Shah.* When on December 30, 1978, the Shah appointed Bakhtiyar prime minister and replaced the military government of Azhari by Bakhtiyar's civil and reformist government, the army's real crisis began. It became clear to the army leadership that the Shah was reaching a compromise with the opposition. In January 1979 the Shah left Iran for good to come to Cairo. The modern and powerful royal army was left without a supreme commander (a position held by the Shah). The question then became how the royal army of Iran would act without the Shah. In a certain sense, its leadership was uncertain and hesitant. Other factors, of course, entered in.

(4) Iran's modern army was founded by the first Pahlavi, Reza Shah, in part, as an instrument to overcome internal power centers (for instance, by subjugating many of the tribal leaders) in the country and to create a modern state with a centralized government to meet the threat from England and the Soviet Union. Reza Shah also had ambitions to win back the Iranian provinces taken by the Russian empire in the course of the Iran-Russian wars in the 19th century (cf. Wilber, 1981, pp. 131-32). After Reza Shah's abdication in 1941, his son Muhammad Reza Shah reconstituted the army (after its dissolution at the end of World War II, in connection with the Allies invasion of Iran) and professionalized it. With substantial oil revenue and military aid from the USA, the Shah expanded the armed forces from 120,000 in 1953 to 410,000 men with a budget of $7.3 billion in 1977 (Abrahamian, 1982, pp. 420-435). During the 1970s, many Iranian officers were either educated and trained in the USA or trained by American officers in Iran. On the eve of the Revolution, Iran had a well-trained and powerful army, one of the dozen best equipped armies in the world (Arjomand, 1988, p. 120). The army was educated in professionalism, and, in particular, oriented to defend the country against foreign enemies. It was not, however, prepared to confront the Iranian people. This explains, in part, why the army–notwithstanding its involvement in power struggles between the opposition and the Shah from summer 1978 to February 1979–remained largely unified and could accept the transition of state power as a way out of confronting civilians and as a way of maintaining its status as a professional organization dedicated to defend the country from foreign enemies.[167]

(5) In 1978, when the successes of the revolutionary movement set the stage for a shift in power, the role of the army became a crucial question. The opposition's contacts with the army aimed to neutralize it and to secure a peaceful transition of power. The NF and the LMI, representing non-clerical groups in the leadership of the opposition, had contact with the army in the autumn of 1978 (Chehabi, 1990). In January 1979 Bazargan, the leader of the LMI was appointed as prime minister by Khomeini. Ayatollah Musavi Ardebili, a high-ranking clergyman, intensified talks with the military leadership to reach a compromise and assure their neutrality. The LMI had sympathizers in the army (Sullivan, 1981), making it easier for them to influence the armed forces' leadership. The NF and the LMI advocated openly the centrality of the Iranian army, but referred to it as the Army of Iran rather than the Royal Army of Iran. They criticized leftists who demanded 'destruction of the Shah's army'. They became the representatives of the army in the Council of Revolution, even after the revolution. Negotiations succeeded in convincing the majority of the armed forces to remain neutral and allow the transition of power to the opposition.

US Policy and the Threat of Communism

Iran's geopolitically strategic position, oil resources, and the historical threat from Russia (later the USSR) not only preoccupied the Iranian governing elite but later the Western powers, particularly the USA, as well. In the period following World War II, the USA's role was direct and of great military and political importance, even in advising and influencing the Shah. This situation made for a certain potential for liberalization of the Iranian state, and the initial opening of the revolutionary process. In 1976 the Carter administration came to power and pressured the Shah to liberalize his regime. The liberalization encouraged some groups of liberals such as lawyers, human rights activists, poets and editors to organize themselves and to begin to openly criticize the regime. As indicated earlier, the political arena during the period 1977-78 was dominated by two opposition groups, namely the National Front and Liberal Movement of Iran, on the one hand, and the radical religious, on the other hand, who were able to mobilize mass support in opposition to the Shah.

Once the Iranian political situation became highly uncertain, and potentially revolutionary, important foreign powers not only articulated their policies toward the Iranian crisis but tried to influence it. The Soviet Union propagandized against the radical clergy and in favor of a constitutional monarchy; they feared the emergence of a powerful clergy and an Islamic Republic.[168] Turkey also preferred a secular government. On the other hand, the USA preferred the clergy to the communists or other leftists. *All, however, wanted the neutrality of the military and the emergence of a stable regime.* Thus, there emerged a form of international consensus on a socio-political equilibrium based on the neutrality of the military, the avoidance of civil war, and the establishment of a stable regime. This geopolitical consensus certainly played a strategic role in the military not splitting or intervening,[169] thus setting the stage for several of the defining features of the Islamic Revolution.

The Process of the Revolution

Modern revolution is a process of struggle involving, on one hand, new outsider elites together with popular masses, and, on the other, an exclusionary regime in control of the state. Particular elites led the struggle. The Revolution of 1979 was such a process that began with a revolt brought about by residents living outside of 'the legal areas' in Tehran. Gradually it became a statewide movement that brought Khomeini and other clergy to power. During the revolutionary process, two main elite groups from the opposition engaged in the struggle for taking state power, namely, the clergy and the NF as well as the LMI. Within the regime, there were at least three possible alternatives to power: the Shah, the army, and liberal loyalists.

The first year of the revolution, 1977, consisted of the Shah's efforts to suppress the revolt and to re-establish full control. During the second half of the revolution 1977-1978, the Shah was no longer an alternative. Competition for state power went on among liberal loyalists, the army, and a coalition of the NF, LMI, and the clergy lead by Khomeini.

As pointed out earlier, the military was unable to act independently during, as well as, after the revolution. Just a few months before the victory of the Revolution, the Shah tried the option of martial law with a military government led by General Azhari. This half-hearted military government, which was intended to be legally legitimized, was not able to cope with growing statewide opposition and protest. After General Azhari's fall, the army divided into two wings, those who formed a minority group within the army and wanted to suppress the opposition movement by military force, and those who were the majority and accepted an official compromise with the opposition (as the best option for the country). After Azhari's fall, liberal royalists, through Shahpoor Bakhtiyar (the last prime minister of the Shah), came to power. But they were merely a provisional government. As a result of a negotiated compromise with the opposition, the majority group in the army assumed a neutral stance.

The Shah's army, as a stabilizing factor in that unstable part of the world, was very important for the West and in particular for the USA.[170] Even the USSR was supportive of stability at the expense of revolutionary change.[171] A neutral position by the army gave the opposition the freedom to act decisively against Bakhtiyar's government and to crush the weak minority group in the army inclined to military action against the revolutionary opposition. In the absence of a competitive political party or secular leader, Khomeini, with the support of the NF and the LMI, became the sole alternative to the Shah's power. During the Revolution, the physical power of the opposition, namely the people demonstrating on the streets, was mainly divided into two categories: the modern middle occupational groups and the intellectuals, who saw the leader of the LMI, Mehdi Bazargan, as a guarantee of their desire for political reforms, on the one side; and the traditional and marginal urban groups, who wanted drastic and fundamental socio-economic and political change and saw Khomeini as their uncompromising leader, on the other. The latter group, and particularly the marginals, formed the majority of and the most radical of revolutionary forces. The marginals had a crucial role in the growing political power of clergy both during the revolutionary process and in institutionalizing their power after the Revolution.

To a great extent, the revolutionary process, in its final phase, took place as political discourse and political struggle, largely without the use of organized armed forces (civil war, etc.).[172] People were mobilized, discourses competed, negotiations took place, and there emerged a negotiated order, or *several negotiated orders in sequence but largely dominated by the clergy with the backing of the marginals*. The mobilization of the marginals was a crucial factor.

The story of the Islamic Revolution then is one of competition among elites for legitimacy and popular support in the context of a largely de-militarized situation, although not without violence. The radical clergy led by Khomeini won against other possible elites including the moderate clergy, nationalists, and liberals. Leftists were out of the picture: they were already weak, they were unacceptable to the military or to the USA, and they were not likely long-term allies of the radical clergy. The nationalists and liberals lacked the opportunity and inclination to mobilize popular political support among the urban populations. Nor was their vision of society able to gain significant support among the poor masses of Iran, as suggested above.

The revolutionary process is not only a process of destroying the old political order, but, it also involves a social and political construction of revolutionary leadership and its institutions. The last and most important year of the revolutionary process witnessed a growing collaboration between the traditional middle occupational groups and the migrants. The economic centers established to help the migrants, coupled with efforts to involve them in political demonstrations, gave them a vision of participating in the new social life and a sense of belonging to the urban society. It was a crucial counteraction to their alienation in the public life of cities, and was a decisive move to gain their support for the radical clergy. Contradictions between municipal authorities and migrants from the countryside to the big cities, especially Tehran (dwelt at the 'outer zone') helped to speed up the revolutionary process as early as 1976. These non-organized riots received much-needed help from the entrance of traditional middle occupational groups into the revolutionary scene on January 1977.

On January 7, Ettelaat one of the two main daily newspapers in Iran, published an article entitled 'Iran and the red and black reactionaries' (*Iran va erteja-e sorhk va siah*) which spoke out against certain anti-regime clergy.[173] In the article, the regime accused the clergy of being anti-modern, reactionary, wanting to pull back 'the vehicle of the development of Iran' and communists attempting to sell the country to foreigners. The article also charged that Khomeini was not a real Muslim, but a British spy who had written erotic Sufi poetry. The derisive article shocked the traditional community of Qum. The bazaar, shops, and religious schools, including the 'Seminary of Qum' (*hoze-ye elmiyeh-ye Qum*), closed down. About 5000 theology students rushed to the streets to demonstrate against 'the Yazidi[174] government' and demand the return of Ayatollah Khomeini. Demonstrators clashed with the police and many were killed or injured. This was the first step in the social construction of leadership in the Islamic Revolution. In the following days, Khomeini called for more demonstrations. Many prominent clergy including the moderate, Ayatollah

Shariatmadari, claimed that Dariush Homayon, the minister of information, officially apologize for the article and resign. Khomeini, who was in exile in Iraq, called the students of Qum 'heroes who stand against paganism' (*taghut*). He rejected any attempts at dialogue with 'the American regime of the Shah' and called for further demonstrations. Shariatmadari, who was one of the most important ayatollahs in the opposition still resident in Iran, together with many other clergy, bazari and other opposition leaders, called upon the country to observe the fortieth day of the Qum martyrs by staying away from work, gathering in the mosques and mourning the dead.[175] Applying this religious tradition as an institutional form for the struggle against the Shah was also to introduce and reinforce the clerical influence and leadership in the movement. On the fortieth day after the Qum demonstration, the major bazaars, religious schools, shops, and universities in most large towns closed down and the people gathered in the mosques where the clergy held memorial sessions for martyrs. In Tabriz, the hometown of Ayatollah Shariatmadari, the mourners rushed to the streets and clashed with the police. Many were killed and injured and about eight hundred people were arrested. It was the first time in Iran's modern history that the 'usual people', to such an extent, were arrested for *political activities* against the Shah.[176]

The traditional middle occupational groups, emigrants and intellectuals were participating together in this political revolt against the regime. Religious leaders and even secular leaders of the NF asked the whole country to honor the martyrs of what came to be known as the Tabriz Resurgence by gathering in the mosques on the fortieth day following the massacre. On that day, the memorial processions in many towns and cities turned violent, attacking banks, luxury hotels, restaurants, liquor stores, Resurgence Party offices, police cars and royal statues. Using the mosques as gathering places for the mourners and demonstrators, the radical clergy, who were directly participating in the organizing of the demonstrations, reinforced their leadership in the movement. Once primarily concerned mourning for Tabriz martyrs, the demonstrations came to be dominated by the purely political slogans such as 'Death to the Shah' and 'Greeting to Khomeini', showing the future tendency of the revolution and its leadership.

The 'Dispossessed' and Radicalization of the Movement

Confrontations between the people living at the 'outer zone' of the cities and municipal authorities were frequent in the 1970s. Between 1975-77 the confrontations intensified. In the summer of 1977, the municipal director of Tehran, Gholamreza Nikpey, was removed by the Prime Minister (Aqeli, 1993, p. 325). Aqeli points out that this removal was the result of his role to destroy dwellings in the 'outer zone' and confrontation with the people in these areas. The new director of the municipality, Javad Shahrestani, announced that: the houses of 'outer zone' which were constructed several years ago would not be destroyed (Aqeli, 1993, p. 326). The confrontations were spontaneous acts of the people living in the 'outer zone'. In the Spring and Summer, 1977, many confrontations took place in 'outer zone' areas such as Kazemabad, Javadiyeh-ye Tehran pars, Majidiyeh, Shemiran nov, and so forth.[177] Pakdaman (1986, pp. 75-77) presents examples of the confrontations of these people with municipal authorities:

> In October, 1977, several thousand people gathered at the front of Farahabad municipality to protest against the destruction of their houses. Silence of the authorities made them angry. They occupied the municipality, broke the doors and windows, and damaged everything they found.

Another center of resistance was in Seleymaniyeh, near Niroyeh havai[178] (center of the Air Forces) where the people resisted and confronted the municipal authorities, and burnt at least five municipal cars (Pakdaman, 1986, p. 78). In that confrontation, the people attacked the municipal authorities and soldiers, burned the cars and killed a bulldozer driver who drove on two persons killing them. In Nasiri street (in the 'outer zone' area), when the authorities came to destroy their houses, they stoned the authorities. (Pakdaman, 1986, p. 79). Pakdaman points out:

> Here [in 'outer zone'], confrontation of the people and the authorities turns very quickly to brutality, and the oppressive state, as a result of the offensive resistance of 'the people of the outer zone', retreats. This retreat, which in the logic of the Aryamehri order [the order created by the Shah] has not been seen, witnesses the beginning of the end (Pakdaman, 1986, p. 79).

The Tudeh Party (communist) also wrote about the confrontations between the people of the 'outer zone' and municipal authorities. In its organ *Navid* in the summer of 1978, it reported the confrontations in Shemiran nov, Majidiyeh, Shamsabad, Afsariyeh, Kazemabad, and Moshiriyeh. It also reported that in Kazemabad, municipal authorities were confronted with substantial resistance of the people, and that in the confrontation a person had been killed (*Navid*, August 1978).[179] The confrontations between the people of the 'outer zone' and municipal authorities intensified during the period of 1975-77. But it must be stressed that the 'dispossessed' politically, and as the eventual army of the radical clergy, began to participate in the wide movement only a few months before the victory of the Revolution. Just a few days before the return of Khomeini to Iran, when Prime Minister Bakhtiyar closed Tehran's airport intending to block Khomeini's entrance, the movement entered a critical phase. The bloody confrontations between demonstrating groups–who acted now more and more offensively–and military forces now became more frequent. These confrontations point up the role of the 'dispossessed' groups in the more frequent revolutionary struggle.

Many of those people, who confronted the military forces during the days prior to the Revolution, were the 'dispossessed'. The following events that took place a few days before the return of Khomeini point this up. One of the major confrontations took place in Eisenhower Street near Tehran University in the violent period January 27-29, 1979. Many of the demonstrators who were in Shahyad Square (close to Tehran airport) and the streets nearby it awaiting the arrival of Khomeini, were making their way back to the University of Tehran on January 29 when they were challenged by military forces.

> The people who intended to participate in reception of Imam Khomeini, when they heard that he was not allowed to come, demonstrated on their way back form Shahyad, in Eisenhower avenue. They were confronted with military forces in which tens of peoples were killed and many injured (*Keyhan*, 28 January, 1979).

One who participated in the demonstration put it this way:

> Before moving from Shahyad square, the people, who were very angry, began to talk about attacking the airport and to 'make the airport safe' for Khomeini's arrival. Other groups wanted the people to march toward the

university of Tehran–where the clerics were gathered in the University's mosque demanding Khomeini's return–to ask for radical measures (*eqdamat-e asasi*). It was apparent that the people who spontaneously wanted to attack the airport were 'illiterate poor people' from southern areas of city. It was not a normal demonstration but a revolutionary march.[180] When we arrived near 24 Esfand Square, suddenly military forces began to shoot. Many were killed and injured /.../. But I must say that many of those who actually made the barriers on the streets were the 'illiterate and poor people' from southern areas (interviewee, Hamid).[181]

Also, photographs printed in *Keyhan* newspaper, showing people making barriers, for example on Eisenhower street, suggest the origin of the 'dispossessed' participating in the revolutionary actions.

Reports about the demonstrations of 27-29 January in Tehran witnessed the radicalization of the movement and the major role of the 'dispossessed' in the radicalization. For example, *Keyhan*, January 29, reported that 'southern and eastern Tehran were drowned in smoke and flames'. Also, *Keyhan*, February 1, reported that: 'the majority of [bloody] events took place in Railway Square (*Meydan-e rah ahan*) (in southern Tehran), Simetri avenue and 24-e Esfand Square (in central Tehran)'. Some 'dispossessed' came from the residential and working places around the Railway Square of Tehran. It is noteworthy that even in the bloody confrontations which took place in the areas around Tehran University, such as Simetri and 24-e Esfand Square, the 'dispossessed' were highly visible.[182] One should not conclude that because these demonstrations took place in the modern areas of central Tehran, it was mainly the modern middle occupational groups who dominated these events. Without denying the significant participation of the modern middle occupational groups in these demonstrations, witnesses suggests that when the demonstrations became bloody and confrontational the 'dispossessed' were more active than other revolutionary groups.[183] *Firstly*, the bloody confrontations of 27-29 January and latter 1-3 February taking place around the University of Tehran, occurred because of the regime's refusal to allow Khomeini to return to Iran. *Secondly*, the radical clergy took refuge in the university's mosque demanding Khomeini's return. The radical clergy's supporters were gathering in the university and other places around the university. *Thirdly*, many 'dispossessed' groups of southern Tehran simultaneously, participated in radical confrontations in that area. For example, *Keyhan* (2 February, 1979) reporting on the major confrontations of 1 February under the title 'smoke and flame in Tehran' wrote: 'the demonstrations of yesterday mainly took place in southern areas of city'.

Growing participation of the 'dispossessed' in the final days prior to Khomeini's return, acknowledged the radical clergy, who had well organized communication channels through young religious groups, about the importance of these marginal groups. In order to increase their popularity and gain support of these groups, they began to establish 'Islamic stores' that distributed very cheap, and in some cases, free of charge foods and clothes to these peoples. During the last 15 days prior to the Revolution, hundreds of such stores were established.

> Najaf abd: Through establishment of 20 'Islamic Stores' the shortage of provisions, which occurred as a result of closure of business is disappeared (*Keyhan*, 19 January 1979).
> Hamedan: Upon the invitation of Ayatollah Madani, the 'Foundation of the Islamic Movement', in which many people participated, is now established (*Keyhan*, 19 January 1979).

The same newspaper reported that, in addition to Islamic stores, many 'Islamic Loan Foundations' (Islamic foundations that did not take interest for their loans) were established. Such foundations were also established in Tehran and many other cities. Other Islamic foundations were also established mainly by the bazaris. These foundations declared that they would make loans even to peasants. For example, in Shiraz the 'Foundation of Islamic Corporation' declared that peasants can receive loans in order to cultivate their lands from this Foundation, established on Zand Avenue and at the Aqa Qasem Mosque (*Keyhan*, 20 January 1979). Through paying loans, delivering free fuel (which was used for warming houses) to poor people, selling very cheap or free-of-charge foods and clothes, and providing the poor with free fruits, the radical clergy with help from bazaris, presented to the 'dispossessed' and others a 'human' alternative to the Shah's regime.

One of the major events of those days concerned a high ranking military officer. On Monday 31 January, 1979, a bloody confrontation between the demonstrators and the military forces located at the start of Simetri avenue took place. During the confrontation, General Latifi, passing the square of 24 Esfand in his car, was attacked by angry people and injured. According to *Keyhan's* rapport, the General stopped his car and shot at people.

> With his pistol in hand the General came out from his car and began to shoot and injured one person. When the people saw him shooting, they attacked him and through kicking and beating and the use of knives injured him /.../ some people brought him to the university. When the ulama became aware of the event, opposed the people's action and ordered them to take the General to the hospital (*Keyhan*, 1 February, 1979).

One eye witness tells the history of General Latifi in the following way:

> I did not see him shooting and tried to convince the people to stop beating him /.../, you know, it was impossible. They were not that kind of people to whom you could talk; you know people from *govdha-ye jonub-e Tehran*, Kazemabad, Javadiyeh, and I do not know where else (Majid).

I had been at the University of Tehran when the General was brought to the university. Many of the people following the group who took the General were poor people who had village or small town accents.

Another characteristic of the movement were the particular targets for attack. Many places which were considered as symbols of the Shah's destructive socio-cultural modernization and Westernization, such as cafes, cinemas, restaurants, liquor stores, and even brothels were attacked and destroyed by radical revolutionary groups. *Keyhan* (30 January, 1979) reports:

> The demonstrations of yesterday in Tehran in the tens of streets became very brutal and led to constructions of barricades, barriers and burning in the middle of streets. Meanwhile, the south of the city was drowned in smoke and flame, in Western Tehran, the area around Tehran University, Amir abad, Aisenhover, and Simetri avenues, demonstrators, through burning tires, wood, and other things, constructed barriers on streets /.../. In these events which led to confrontations between the military and demonstrators, one was killed and 8 injured. In the demonstrations of yesterday, 20 liquor stores, a cabaret, and a brewery were burned (*Keyhan*, 30 January, 1979).

On February 1, 1979, *Keyhan* reported:

> In the demonstrations of yesterday, during confrontations on Simetri avenue, four persons were injured, 3 cafes and one cinema were attacked

and all their facilities burned. During these demonstrations, the brewery of Tehran, cafe *Shekofeh nov* were burned/.../ Also, from 10 AM to 2 PM, several liquor stores in Rah ahan avenue and other streets around it were burned.

The targets of attacks indicate that the people who participated in these radical actions and destroyed or damaged cinemas, liquor stores, beer industries, and cabarets were strongly traditional or against such 'anti-religious' activities and their symbols. In general, it was not modern occupational groups who destroyed the cinemas or cabarets.

Radicalization of the movement increased during two days of bloody struggles in Tehran and other major cities. In the events of February 11-12 which brought about the Islamic Revolution of Iran, the 'dispossessed' were very active. Muhammad and Gholam, who actively participated in the Revolution, in particular attacks on military bases in Tehran, tell their stories about the final day of the Revolution:

> It was about 10.30-11 a.m., we succeeded, through making a hole in the wall of *Mosalsal sazi* (the machine gun factory), to go in and seize many weapons /.../. There were many people participating in the attack on *Mosalsal sazi*, but I think those who were most active in the attack were poor people from the southern areas /.../. You remember that it was very cold, but some of these people had little clothes, or had very old and torn clothes. Although, there were many young participating in the attack, you could see even old poor men among the revolutionaries[184] (Mohammad).

The other witness, Gholam, continues and tells about the events at the military base:

> When we arrived at a relatively large room in which you could find some military equipment and bullets, one of them [the poor people from southern Tehran] said: look! even this bloody cement room, in which they keep their rubbish, compared to my little *kharabeh* (damaged residential place) in which ten persons live, is a palace (Gholam).

Participation of the 'dispossessed' in the bloody confrontations does not mean that other groups, such as the youth from modern occupational groups, did not participate even in these confrontations, but were marginal and not in leadership positions. While the 'dispossessed' participated actively, they were also being drawn into an implicit alliance with the groups from the middle and lower urban traditional occupational groups.

Another history about the active role of the 'dispossessed' in the Islamic Revolution is told by *Keyhan* newspaper. *Keyhan* reported detailed events which resulted in seizing on of the most important military bases in Tehran, *Eshrat abad*:

> **An old man ordered the people: Seize *Eshrat abad***
> He was short and his face full of the trace of chicken-pox disease. He had a hard beard on his face that covered his face down to his neck which was black of smoke. A dirty hat hid his bald head. The hat was drawn down until his ears. But from the line over his eyebrow, his bald head could be seen. His clothes were dirty and torn which were colored by spots of oil and dirt. A pair of old nylon shoes covered his feet. The old man stayed a while, looked around; wrinkles of his face hid the lines on his skin created by his suffering. We were in the small square in the front of Esharat abad's military base. It was crowded around us. Sometimes we heard ambulances passing. Young people were moving around. In the front of us, soldiers were prepared behind the wall. The black mouths of machine-guns could be seen. The people were hesitating. Everybody said something. The old man raised his hands; he had two bottles in his hands. At the bottom of the bottles were soap and over that a dirty liquid of fuel, and in it a dirty string was moving. The old man put the bottles on the ground and set fire to the fuse. He took up the bottles, turned to the crowd and shouted: 'staying and waiting is not useful, attack ... attack'. Then he rushed toward the military wall. The bottles were burning in his hands. Soldiers started shooting; people fell down on the ground. The old man stopped and under the rain of bullets shouted, attack.... The square started moving. A few seconds later, the old man reached the wall and threw the bottles. The bottles reached the target and exploded; the old man shouted and fell down (*Keyhan*, February 14, 1979).

In the same newspaper, and newspapers published during February, photographs from the revolutionary armed struggles in Tehran indicate the social origin of many of armed revolutionary forces. For example, pictures of revolutionary forces who returned to the army bases to receive military training and to become 'the permanent defenders of the Revolution'. Also, photographs of the vehicles used during the armed struggles in Tehran. Many of the cars were old *vanet bars* (vans), which often were used by some of the 'dispossessed' to gain their livelihood.

Many of the 'dispossessed' knew that they played an important role in the Revolution. One of their representatives said: 'Since the victory of the Revolution, we have heard just empty talk, and have not seen any objective action for the people of this area; It was the people of this area who made the glorious and great victory of the Revolution possible, not the people of the northern area of the city' (*Keyhan*, 7 June, 1979). The 'dispossessed' claimed their share of the Revolution. For example, the inhabitants of *Shahrak-e masoudiyeh*, who had no water, electricity, or asphalt, wrote a letter to *Keyhan*, saying: 'We have played our particular role in this great Revolution and we hope that our children continue the way of Revolution; but we have expectations too, and because the commands of Imam Khomeini about helping *mustaz'afin* ['dispossessed'] are obligatory, we want the state to send a representative to our place to solve our problems so that we do not, as past years, remain in the worst condition of living, but instead after the Revolution feel the taste of a comfortable life' (*Keyhan*, 14 July, 1979).

Institutionalization of the Revolution

Political

Bazargan's provisional government was a liberal government, not a clerical one. In part, Khomeini chose liberals to head the government to show his democratic intentions and to legitimize his leadership for the whole people as well as to gain support from the West and to isolate the Shah and his supporters. In the final phase of the Revolution, the clergy isolated liberals and removed Bazargan's government. This process took some time. On March 1979, a referendum approved the establishment of the Islamic Republic of Iran. Khomeini rejected the formation of a Constitutional Assembly (*majlis-e Moassesan*) and proclaimed that the only legitimate assembly for writing the new constitution of the Islamic Republic of Iran was the Council of Religious Experts (*majlis-e khebregan*). This Council was elected, met and began to write the Islamic Constitution of the new state.

The seizure of the US Embassy on November 1979 brought about the fall of Bazargan's government and prepared the way for a more religious government. One month later, the constitutional referendum was held and the Islamic Constitution approved by an overwhelming majority (over 90 percent). To complete the institutionalization of the Islamic Republic, presidential elections were held in January, 1980, and Abul Hasan Banisadr became the first president of the Islamic Republic.[185] He wanted to cooperate with the Islamic-leftist party, Mojahedin-e khalq, and proposed Masoud Rajavi, the leader of the Mojahedin, as his prime minister. The clergy vetoed this. There was a political stalemate, since he refused to accept a number of radical clergymen as ministers.

In June, 1981, the clergy's armed forces, the Komitehs and *Pasdaran*, attacked the presidential offices in Teheran and other cities of Iran as well as those of the Mojahedin-e khalq. Banisadr together with Masoud Rajavi escaped by military aircraft to Paris. The clergy carried out substantial executions and eliminated political opposition groups, thus fully consolidating their power and their theocratic state. The first purely clerical government of modern Iran was formed in the summer of 1981. Shortly after Banisadr's fall, his prime minister Raja'i became president and Hojat al-Islam Bahonar became prime minister. They were assassinated in August 1981 and Ali Khamene'i–the present 'successor' to Khomeini –was elected president.

Economic

The bazaars remained important centers of re-distribution even after the revolution, and played a key role during the Iran-Iraq war as a rationing institution. Also, government policies favored or protected the bazaars. There was a certain shift from of influence from the *taghutis* (non-Muslim capitalists who were favored during the Shah's regime and had controlled the main import-export channels of the Iranian economy) to the bazari merchants.

Also, the characteristic interdependency between the bazaris and the clergy continued after the revolution. However, the clergy in taking state power and gaining access to state resources–not least Iran's oil revenues–became more independent of the bazaris, whereas the latter remained dependent on the clergy for political power to support their interests. Still, the bazaar, as an Islamic social institution, continues to play a central role in the socio-economic and cultural integration of the rural peasantry in the villages of Iran. Also, the clerical state of Iran depends on the bazaris' support to legitimize their socio-economic policies.

Post-revolution policies reinforced the commitment of the marginals. Many were given plots of land on the outer rims of the cities on which to build their homes. They also obtained business licenses and were given jobs as 'religious investigators' and in the Revolutionary Guards (which, after the Iran-Iraq war, were integrated into the armed forces[186]). As pointed out below, the availability of substantial state resources enabled an institutionalization of the revolution; while the Iran-Iraq war was important for mobilization and eliminating internal opponents, it also *in the long run*, threatened the institutionalization process (by draining off resources, killing many young people, increasing the authority and status of the military, etc.).

There have been many economic disruptions and distortions as a result of the Revolution, in part because in a number of instances the clergy blocked important economic policies which they felt were inconsistent with their interpretation of the Qur'an (see Bakhash, 1994). But it appears that the government and Parliament have over time become more and more rational in facilitating and supporting the economic performance of Iran, its international trade, and not least its oil sector. The latter is particularly strategic since the Iranian state–and the clerical leadership–depend on it for revenues to finance programs and developments that institutionalize the revolution. All in all, the war with Iraq probably caused more serious disruption than did the Revolution itself.

Revolutionary Organs

On the eve of the Revolution, when state power was disintegrating as a result of demonstrations and confrontations between the police and military and demonstrators from the slum areas, local power centers, known as Committees (Komitehs), gradually took shape. These were often headed by local radical clergymen who supported Khomeini and were an effective organ for excluding other groups (for example leftists), establishing the local power of the clergy, and acting as security guards of the Revolutionary Courts (*dadgaha-ye enqelab*). As Bazargan, the first prime minister of Islamic Republic of Iran, put it, 'the committees are everywhere, and no one knows how many exist, not even the Imam himself'.[187] The Komitehs continued to act as police forces until the middle of the 1980s, when they were integrated with the state police authority.

Another organization of force which was established and operated in parallel with the Komitehs and played a crucial role in the first decade after the Revolution was the Revolutionary Guards (*Pasdaran-e enqelab*). It consisted largely of young people from the slums and the traditional middle occupational groups who were organized by radical clergy and religious groups who did not trust the armed forces. The Guard, which began as a relatively small armed force for protecting the Islamic state against 'anti-revolutionary forces' (*zedde enqelab*), grew into a large military force during the Iran-Iraq war.[188] Gradually they became an important part of the army, and their leaders assumed key posts as high-ranking officers.

Religious/Symbolic

Besides the establishment of an Islamic state with religious leadership, there were many other symbolic changes that marked the beginning of a new order. Many examples can be given, but it is enough to point out that every Friday mass prayer sessions are held at the University soccer stadium. Also, the Imam jom'as (leaders of friday prayer) became influential representatives of the new state. They organized demonstrations in favor of Khomeini and other radical clergy. They controlled non-clergy officials, liberals, and others as well as worked to limit the influence of the more traditional ulama. They also in effect supervised all provincial governors (*ostandaran*).

In response to the demands of the key revolutionary social group, the 'dispossessed', the Islamic state founded *Bonyad-e mostaz'afin* (The Foundation of the Dispossessed) to initiate and organize assistance for these people. For example, *Bonyad-e mostaz'afin* built modern houses in the northern area of Tehran, Yosefabad, for 300 families of the martyrs of the Revolution (*Keyhan*, 16 July, 1979). The reporter, Mahmud Ekhtiyari, pointed out the origin of these families: 'Tens of families of the *shuhada* (martyrs)of the Revolution, who come from the southern area, and the miserable Govds of Tehran, by the office of housing, were moved to these flats. Some of these families have never been in the northern areas of Tehran' (*Keyhan*, 16 July, 1979). The leader of the Islamic Revolution, Khomeini, was also aware of the importance of the 'dispossessed', both for the victory of the Revolution and for its continuation. Accordingly, he declared a *fatva* in which the people who wanted to do 'un-obligatory pilgrimage'[189] to Mecca were obliged to pay the costs to 'dispossessed' (*Keyhan*, 16 July, 1979).

Although the reports concerning the 'dispossessed' are limited, one can find records of the origins of many of the martyrs of the Revolution. The pictures of the martyrs and bloody confrontations, printed in newspapers during the final days of the process of the Revolution, give a sense of their origins.[190] The cars, vans, and small tracks in which revolutionary forces moved in Tehran during the final day of the Revolution belonged mainly to the 'dispossessed'. These vehicles were normally the sources of their income. Those who participated in the Revolution and remember its process are familiar with the urban areas where the sermons of the martyrs were held.

In sum, the greatest impact of the revolution has certainly been political and institutional. Obvious here is the politicization (the participation of large masses of people, especially the marginals and urban poor, in political processes). This process continues, even without political parties. Political factions operate and play an important role today. Learning to participate and negotiate in political processes sets the stage for future changes. For the marginals, their local political conditions–recall the earlier problems with municipal authorities–and the opportunities to participate and be integrated to a greater extent into the economic, political, and symbolic life of Iran have entailed radical changes.

The Victory of the Modern and the Traditional Civil Societies

The victory of the Islamic Revolution of Iran depended on the revolutionary alliance between key groups in the traditional and modern civil societies. The Revolution could never have been a success if the consensus about the aims of a revolutionary transformation had not been reached between the representatives of the two civil societies. As mentioned earlier, modern, liberal groups were engaged in a struggle for liberalization of the regime during the long period of the dictatorship of the Shah. The two major representative of these groups, the National Front and the Liberation Movement of Iran, had consistently criticized the Shah for his dictatorship. However, they never advocated a revolutionary change of the regime. As they expressed in several pamphlet during the 1960s and 1970s, they wanted to reform the regime and to help create a democratic system of governance. 'Free election' was the main slogan of these groups. During the stormy process of the Islamic Revolution, they faced a unique situation in which they had two alternatives:

1. Staying out of the revolutionary process and compromising with the Shah in reforming the regime.
2. Participating in the Revolution and compromising with the ulama.

The extremely rapid development of the Revolution and the shah's obstinacy limited any possibilities for compromises between the regime and the opposition. There were very few who would risk their position and take contact with the regime for negotiating without taking in consideration Khomeini's social authority and power. It could have drastic consequences for those who negotiated any compromise with the Shah.[191] Besides, historical experiences of liberal groups had shown them that the Shah was not a reliable partner in political negotiations. They made the choice not to compromise with the Shah. The National Front, for instance, even excluded Shahpour Bakhtiar, the Shah's last prime minister, from their organization because of his close association with the Shah.

Accordingly, they participated in the revolution and cooperated with the religious leadership. They realized that there were not only religious and traditional groups who participated in the revolution, but also many modern groups, such as teachers, bureaucrats, students, leftists, and so forth. They provided them with a social force which could balance the power of the religious leadership of the Revolution. The democratic demands of the modern urban groups was one of their main claims during the modern history of Iran. Accordingly, they begin a process of negotiation with the religious leadership to reach an agreement with them.

Khomeini and other religious leaders also had reasons for cooperation with the liberals. The reasons can be summarized in the following points:

1. *Isolation of the Shah.*
2. *Support from the liberals.*
3. *Neutralization of the army.*

Khomeini and his religious group knew that they must isolate the Shah if they were to achieve a relatively rapid victory. Any negotiation and contact between the Shah and the liberals could weaken the religious opposition and prolong the life of the regime. Cooperation with the liberals, thus, became an important means to success of his religious leadership and ultimately the Revolution. Khomeini and the other religious leaders were fully aware of the democratic goals of the modern urban groups and the liberals. The importance of support of such groups for the victory of the Revolution forced the religious leadership to change their opposition to the liberals and to negotiate with them. One of the most important periods of negotiations took place during November and December 1978, just a few months before the overthrow of the old regime. Mehdi Bazargan, the leader of the LMI, led negotiations on the part of liberals. He was in direct contact with the religious leadership in Iran–Ayatollah Beheshti among others–and journeyed to Paris to meet Khomeini and discuss his conditions for cooperation with him.

Although at the very beginning of the revolutionary movements, in particular the riots of Tabriz in February 1978, Khomeini did not take the liberals seriously, the movement forced him to recognize their influence among the modern urban groups. For example, the mass demonstrations of November 1978 in Tehran organized by the National Front demonstrated the influence of the liberals among urban occupational groups. Karim Sanjabi, the leader of the Front, claimed democracy and freedom for Iran. The modern civil society made itself more and more visible in the revolutionary struggles against the dictatorship of the Shah. Mass participation of the modern middle classes in the peaceful demonstrations against the Shah and their slogans for democracy and freedom alarmed Khomeini, particularly their demands for democracy.

Besides, Khomeini had to isolate the Shah through attracting all groups in the opposition through various maneuvers and to hinder them from being influenced by the shah's promises. In the process of negotiations, Khomeini and the religious leaders changed their conceptualization of 'Islamic governance' as the only alternative to the monarchy and accepting the idea of a republic. They began to articulate the concept of an 'Islamic republic'. This was a result of negotiations and contacts between the liberals and the radical ulama. After the last journey of the LMI leader, Mehdi Bazargan, to Paris and his meeting with Khomeini, it became clear that a consensus had been reached between these two groups. It became more evident when the names of the members of the 'Revolutionary Council' were released to the press. Both Bazargan and Karim Sanjabi, the leader of NF, were among the members. The compromise between the ulama and the liberals became public and was reinforced by Khomeini's declaration that Bazargan is the legitimized prime minister of Iran. The first prime minister of the Islamic Republic would be a liberal who during a long period of his carrier had made clear his democratic intentions. As a result of the compromise, a few days before the victory of the Revolution, Khomeini declared Bazargan the 'lawful prime minister of Iran'. The clergy in Iran supported Bazargan and mass demonstrations legitimized Bazargan as the prime minister of the Islamic Republic of Iran soon to be established.

Although there was a compromise between the liberals and the ulama about 'republicanism' as Iran's new political order, the specific content of such a republic was controversial. During the struggle against the old regime and the negotiations about the content of the new one, the politicians from the both groups publicly advocated that liberty and freedom be established in Iran after the overthrown of the Shah. Khomeini tried to tone down the fear of a religious dictatorship. He said in an interview from Paris that even the communists would be free in the Islamic republic.[192] The efforts of the political leadership of the Revolution intensified in the second half of January, 1977. The Islamic government would be presented as a democrat, liberal one. The lack of a well-known center for the Revolution helped to moderate the modern middle classes' fear of a religious dictatorship. Many moderate collaborators of Khomeini and the ulama were given the opportunity to utter their own version of the Islamic Republic as if it was Khomeini's or the 'Revolutionary Council's' intentions that they do so. Abul Hasan Banisadr, the first president of the Islamic Republic, in his interview with *Keyhan* in Sunday 22 February declared the democratic routines of the new regime:

> The Islamic governance would be established by a referendum. /.../ Censorship either with the objective means or subjective ones is totally against Islam and Qur'an. In our opinion, everybody must be free to publish whatever they want.

Khomeini, in an interview with the Lebanese leftist newspaper *Al-safir*, declared that 'women are free to wear *chador*[193] or not'. He also talked about the establishment of a democratic chosen 'constitutional assembly' which would replace the old constitution with a new one (*Keyhan*, Sunday 22, 1977). The two most important newspapers, *Keyhan* and *Ettelaat*, did not hesitate in providing headlines for the democratic utterances of Khomeini and other leaders. All in all, such events together with the establishment of a liberal government, in which both the FN and the LMI members were participating, convinced many people of the democratic potentialities of the new regime. The alliance succeeded in neutralizing the army through giving it guarantees about its future existence and winning the Revolutionary struggle against the old regime. But the struggle was not over. The challenge to democratic governance began the day after the transformation of power to the new revolutionary regime.

Challenge Over the Name of the Republic

One of the first controversies between the ulama and the liberal government took place over the name of the new regime. The referendum would legitimize the future regime of Iran. In the revolutionary climate at the time and because of the charismatic power of Khomeini, the liberals realized that the referendum would put an end to the monarchy and establish a republic. The question was, then, which kind of republic was going to be legitimized by the referendum. Accordingly, the formulation of the referendum's question to which people would say 'yes' or 'no' was of great importance especially for liberals who wanted a democratic republic. The name of the republic became a burning matter for both groups. Eight days after the fall of the old regime, the prime minister Bazargan, without discussing the matter with Khomeini and other ulama, announced the referendum's question. He declared in a press announcement that the question to be answered by the people would be: 'Islamic Democratic Republic, yes or no'. In the same message, he also proposed other measures for the normalization of his governance, such as 'the dissolution of the Imam's Committees, and the transformation of the duties of the revolutionary courts to the government'.[194] The prime minister intensified his complaints over alternative or competing power centers. About the uncontrolled power of the revolutionary courts, he stated in an interview with a French news agency: 'I had no information about the executions of the army generals before I read about them in the newspaper. I was neither involved in the decision making about these executions nor in executing them'.[195] In the same newspaper, the 'office of Imam' announced that Khomeini was moving to Qum for permanent residence.[196] Four days later Khomeini moved to the religious city of Qum near Tehran, and it seemed that he intended to leave the political arena to other clergy and the liberal state.

Bazargan used the opportunity to sharply attack the armed forces of the 'Imam committees' and other extremists. He announced that 'if the intervention of such groups continues, the government is obliged to resign. The Committees and other extremist groups not only are barriers for the government, but also a great danger for the security and the existence of the country and the Revolution'.[197] The spokesman of the government Amir-entezam announced that the control of the Committees would be transformed to the government.[198] The measures of the liberal government to centralize power and 'normalize' the revolutionary situation alarmed the radical clergy, since it threatened their influence over the Revolution. The clergy had a great influence among the irregular armed forces gathered in the *Komiteh-haye enqelab-e eslami* (the Committees of the Islamic Revolution). They encouraged them in attacking other political organizations and democratic groups. The liberal government's attempt to limit the irregular power of the clergy and Committees alarmed them as well as Khomeini himself about the future of their role in a republican Iran. Khomeini began his direct attack on the government's and prime minister's attempt to 'normalize' the revolutionary situations and to establish and popularize a democratic basis of the republic. In a meeting in Qum, Khomeini criticized introducing of the word 'democratic' in the formulation of the question for referendum, through saying that the 'Democratic Republic is a Western form and we cannot accept that'. He said also that a new ministry called '*vezarat-e amr-e be ma'rof va nahye az monkar*' (the ministry of enjoin the good and forbid evil) independent of the government would be established. He added that 'we would make current Islamic laws'. To gain the social support for such drastic changes, he stated that 'we will construct houses for all 'dispossessed' and change the banking system in favor of the people'.[199]

The challenge over the form and content of the new republic continued. The liberals and democratic forces tried to counterbalance the gradual growth of the radical clergy. The 'Lawyers Association' through Matin Daftari, a prominent member, announced a call for creation of a 'Natinal Democratic Front'. A provisional group for organizing such a front was gathered and began to work. They announced their programs as follows:

> The immediate referendum for changing the monarchy. The immediate election of the revolutionary coordinating council. The immediate trials against traitors and homicides. Election of a group for preparing the new constitution. Guaranteeing the freedom of political parties, unions, and associations. Elimination of discrimination against women. Recognizing the autonomy of minority groups. The ultimate elimination of censorship.[200]

The newspapers were effectively used by both sides to mobilize support for their political issues. The huge demonstrations of March 6 in memory of the charismatic leader of the nationalization of the oil industry in the late 1940s and early 1950s, Muhammad Mossadeq, alarmed the clergy about the liberal's considerable social support.

One of the most specific characteristics of the Islamic Revolution was the participation of women. Iranian women, both those from the modern occupational groups as well as traditional ones, made up a very important part of the demonstrations and confrontations with the Shah's regime. After the political victory of the Revolution in February 1979, the challenge of gaining the support of women was one of the most crucial matters for both the liberals and the radical clergy. In an attempt to win women's support and reduce the modern urban women's fear of the introduction of religious laws against them, Khomeini declared that: 'women must participate in the major matters of the country. /.../ they have a legal right to divorce'.[201] But, Khomeini's attempt was not as successful as he hoped because of the daily attack of *hezballah*[202] groups under the leadership of Hadi Ghaffari, who personally participated in some attacks against the centers of Mojahedin-e khalq. Frightened of the democratic groups' attempt to legitimize and institutionalize democratic concepts and principles, Khomeini intensified his attack on liberals by attacking the liberal state. Khomeini and the radical clergy were aware that the government's democratic intentions could endanger the radical clergy's position in the emerging republic. In a meeting of the ulama and religious students in Qum, Khomeini sharply accused the state of being weak in changing the monarchical bureaucratic system. He criticized the state in its 'step by step' policy and said that 'if the Revolution only moved step by step, they would break its legs in the first steps'.[203] In his speech which was broadcast on TV, he challenged once more the idea of the 'Democratic Republic' and said:

> Now that we have to decide about the form of political system–even if the people have uttered their opinion through the demonstrations and the Revolution–to prevent the eventual problems in the future, now that is decided to have a referendum, you [the clergy] have to go to the villages and cities and inform people. Because the referendum is a very important phenomena which determine the future of the country, and if we want to have an Islamic country, a referendum must be done. It is important, thus, that you, who are able, go to the familiar or unfamiliar areas and cities and explain the political issues for the people and invite them to vote to the Islamic Republic, not one word more or less. /.../ I would vote to the Islamic Republic.[204]

He said that the departments and ministries are running in accordance with the same procedures as during the Shah's regime. The 'naked women' in Western clothes are working in such departments; 'no problem, they can work, but they must wear Islamic clothes'.[205] Khomeini showed his support for the establishment of a religiously legitimized regime in which the radical clergy and their values had a particular position.

The Revolutionary Alliance Splits

During his political career, Khomeini, as an experienced political leader, rejected any attempt of different groups to force him to take a particular position for or against other political groups. Before taking political power, he was a populist who was greatly interested in widening the bases of his political support.[206] Khomeini succeeded in mobilizing the support of almost all oppositional groups in carrying out the Islamic Revolution. But, after the overthrow of the Shah, confrontations began between the two major groups, the liberals and the radical clergy, and forced Khomeini to give up his traditional silence in favor of one group over the other. The break between Khomeini and the liberals was an unavoidable result of the revolutionary process. Few politicians and analysts questioned such a development. But many hoped that such a break would be in favor of the liberals. The latter together with other democratic forces in Iran's revolutionary society advocated a democratic form of government, increasing their popularity among the modern urban classes. Besides, they seemed to be in control of the state and had good connections with the army. Khomeini and the radical clergy, in order to establish an Islamic regime, were obliged to deny the liberals' state power and hinder the establishment of a Western-like democratic regime. The seizure of entire political power was a crucial means in reconstructing society according to the theory of *velayat-e faqih*. Besides, Khomeini and other radical clergy were aware that the Pahlavi's rapid modernization of Iranian society eliminated many of the traditional bases for their authority. The traditional civil society had been marginalized and lost its importance in countervailing both the state power and the new forces in the modern civil society. *Khomeini's intention was not, therefore, to regain the lost influence of the ulama in civil society, but rather to gain political power over civil society and the state, thus eliminating the traditional duality of power between state and civil society.*

The political alliances and events that began with the nationalist movement of the 1940s and 1950s and continued during the whole period of the reign of the Shah, had alarmed the ulama about the attraction of new political ideas which even influenced their traditional allies, the bazaris. Many bazaris had enjoyed the modern changes and had nothing against the liberals' reign. When Khomeini decided to attack the liberals and remove them from political power, he also attacked the bazaris. Receiving support from the 'dispossessed', he declared that the bazaris had failed to participate in the revolution:

> If you obtain the statistics for the martyrs of the revolution–everybody can obtain the statistics–you cannot find one person form the government [the new government]. You cannot find one merchant, one aristocrat, one army officer. /.../ The martyrs came only from the Muslim masses and the poor.[207]

The liberals, who came under Khomeini's direct attack, intensified their attempts to limit the power of the radical clergy and to counterbalance the impact of Khomeini's attack. To restrain the military power of the radical clergy, the government declared that the 'revolutionary committees', would be dismissed and their power transformed to the state.[208] On the same day, the celebration of international women's day in Tehran became a declaration against the coercive veil.[209] The leftists also intensified their actions for mobilizing urban support against the radical clergy. In the women's demonstrations on March 8, the *hezballah* groups attacked the demonstrators and injured some of them. At the same time the radical ulama intensified their efforts for confronting the liberal movement. Hashemi Rafsenjani, one of the most important actors in organizing the radical clergy in a party called *Hezb-e jomhuri-ye eslami*, warned the religious forces against any failure to organize against the liberal attacks.[210]

The conflicts could not yet end in favor of the radical clergy at a time when the leadership of the army had not been completely replaced–although the rapid executions of army officers were going on all during this time. The radical clergy did not have a grip over the army and the bureaucratic system. In other words, they still needed the alliance with the liberals. The newspapers reported secret negotiations between the state and Khomeini. In a meeting between prime minister Bazargan and Khomeini in Qum, a temporary agreement was reached. On the following day,

Khomeini declared his support for the state and asked everybody to support 'the temporary revolutionary government' in its effort to realize the referendum and to establish an Islamic Republic. Simultaneously he warned the people to be careful and not be fooled by the liberals. He said:

> You, wherever you are, be aware and defend your rights. Do not listen to the lies. Do not listen to the groups who do not know anything about Islam and are against Islam. They want to cheat the people. Your way is the way of Islam. Your way is to establish the Islamic Republic. I vote for the Islamic Republic and want you also to vote for the Islamic Republic, not a word more or less, Islamic Republic. Those who talk about 'republic' must know that 'republic' only means Islam, not a 'democratic republic' that others talk about. The 'democratic republic' is a Western form. They want to bring the same problems in new forms to us. Neither did they participate in this revolutionary movement. Those who want today to enjoy the fruits of the revolution have never participated in this movement. /.../ Do not accept those who have been abroad and came for picking fruits; do not accept those who passively looked at the events or helped the [Shah's] regime and have became revolutionary now. We do not accept those who have poisoned pens and writes against Islam and spread the notions of 'nationalism' and 'democratic' among the people; do not accept them.[211]

There were a few who did not know who were 'nationalists' and who were 'democrats'. The prime minister Bazargan was one of the most important persons in advocating the establishment of an 'Islamic Democratic Republic' instead of an 'Islamic Republic'. It seemed that according to the agreement between Khomeini and Bazargan, Khomeini agreed to declare his support for the state and Bazargan would accept the notion of an 'Islamic Republic' as the question of the referendum. In the referendum of February 12, 1979, the monarchy was abolished and the Islamic Republic legitimized as the new political system of Iran.

The referendum was one of the modern political means successfully used by the revolutionary forces to legitimize the new political order. Many were aware of the shortcomings of religious or sacred legitimacy in modern times. Using the electoral institution was not just a temporary means that depended on the alliance with the liberals, but a lasting political method for legitimizing the Islamic regime in accordance with modern political processes.[212]

The liberal state received other opportunities to counterattack the radical clergy's attempt to push them out of the state power. In April 1979, the two sons of one of the most prominent religious leaders of the Islamic Republic, Ayatollah Taleqani, were arrested by the Revolutionary Committees (Komitehs). Ayatollah Taleqani left Tehran in protest. Several oppositional groups used the opportunity and through demonstrations and gatherings protested against 'irresponsible armed groups'.[213] The prime minister Bazargan announced that he did not know anything about the event and put the blame on irregular armed forces. At the same time, struggles in Turkmanstan between Turkman groups and the army and Revolutionary Guards intensified. Khomeini and the radical clergy, referring to the events in Turkmanstan, warned the opposition not to use the protest of Ayatollah Taleqani to attack the revolutionary forces.[214] The mass demonstrations of April forced the radical clergy to try to solve the crisis between Taleqani and the Revolutionary Guards and Committees. Through the mediation of Khomeini's son, Seyed Ahmad, Taleqani and Khomeini met and through negotiations reached a compromise. Taleqani returned to Tehran and opened his offices again and one of the most important crises among the religious leaders of the Islamic Republic was solved.

The compromise was important for the opposition to re-establish their position and to continue their open activities. The liberal state, on the other side, exploited the retreat of the radical clergy and reinforced some reforms such as 'self governance' of Kurdistan and establishment of 'province councils'. Some incidents, however, such as the assassination of Ayatollah Mottahari, one of the prominent religious leaders and the member of Revolutionary Council limited the opportunity for the state to isolate the radical clergy. Such events provided the radical clergy suitable means of propaganda to continue their 'struggle against America'. The struggle against America had during the post-war period been a legitimate means of modern oppositional politics and, in many cases, paved the way for dictators to legitimize their reign as 'anti-imperialistic'. In the shadow of struggling against the 'big Satan' America, radical revolutionary guards and committees arrested, tortured, and killed many young individuals from the opposition. They violated almost daily the very weak freedoms of speech and publications which existed as a result of the Revolution. Using the assassination of Ayatollah Mottahari in May 1979, the radical clergy intensified their attacks on 'American agents' (*ommal-e amrika*) and put restrictions on the main newspapers. The first newspaper to be attacked was *Ayandegan* which published daily in Tehran. The radical clergy extended their control over the two other major newspapers, *Keyhan* and

Ettelaat. The characteristics of the main titles changed. Statements made by the radical clergy and revolutionary organs relating to 'revolutionary courts' and the 'revolutionary persecutor' Sadeq Khalkhali, came to occupy the first pages of the newspapers.

At the beginning of June, there arose a dispute over the establishment of the *majlis-e moassesan* (constitutional assembly) between the opposition, the state, and some religious leaders, on the one side, and the radical clergy on the other. The radical clergy rejected the promised establishment of the 'constitutional assembly'. They saw this as a step toward legalization of the modern civil society. They consequently rejected any attempt to legitimize the existence of influential social and political groups. As mentioned earlier, the clergy's main intention in trying to seize political power was to establish control over the state as well as civil society. The acceptance of the 'constitutional assembly' could endanger such an order and allow modern civil society to influence the very constitution of the republic. Therefore, the issues around establishing the assembly became one of the main sources of conflict between the modern civil society and the radical clergy. After several months of discussions and attacks against one another, Khomeini declared that: 'we want to constitute an Islamic country; we do not want a Western country and we do not want the constitution of Moscow or America'.[215] Instead of the establishment of the 'constitutional assembly', Khomeini suggested an assembly constituted of religious leaders who were well educated in Islamic law. The new assembly came to be called *majlis-e kehbragan* (the assembly of experts). The modern civil society lost one of its most important struggles to the radical clergy who thereby reinforced their position in power.

In establishing control over the civic sphere as well as the state, the radical clergy could not accept the power of the bazaar either. Khomeini several times after the political victory of the Revolution criticized the bazaris and accused them of selling overpriced commodities, exploiting Muslims needs, and being unjust Muslims.[216] At the beginning of July 1979 he said that: 'The bazaris are corrupted. They believe that when they turn the lights on and celebrate [the birthday of the Hidden Imam] they can satisfy the Hidden Imam'. In some cases, the bazaris were threatened by the death penalty 'if they do not reduce the prices and stop the hoarding of commodities which are important for peoples' daily life'.[217] In such circumstances several meetings between the prime minister Bazargan, the popular and moderate religious leader Ayatollah Taleqani, and Khomeini took place in order to manage the conflicts between the radical clergy and the state. Khomeini's understanding of an Islamic regime did not differ from the radical clergy's. They wanted to eliminate all social and political elements which could reinforce the separation between the Islamic regime and civil society. That is, *they aimed to create a theocratic state which would reign over a homogeneous mass called umma.* The independence of civil society which was one of the most important bases of the original power of the Shi'ite ulama would be a threat to the new regime. Both the new and the traditional civil societies were considered unnecessary for a theocratic regime. At the same time, in the short period after the revolution, the civil societies proved that they could create difficulties for a regime to be run in accordance with Islamic intentions. However, the elimination of the modern civil society, which had grown to a substantive power during the revolutionary period, was more urgent than repression of the traditional civil society.

The exclusion of civil society from any substantive influence on the political decision making and on the executive organs had to be institutionalized through the modern means of election and constitution. The shift from 'constitutional assembly' to an assembly constituted of religious experts was an important step in exclusion of the liberals and the opposition from the decision making organs and guaranteeing the power positions to the radical clergy. On the eve of the election for 'the assembly of experts', Khomeini declared that: 'if the constitution is not going to be Islamic, neither I nor the people would pass it'.[218] As a result of discussions and meetings between the prime minister Bazargan, Ayatollah Taleqani, and Khomeini a compromise was reached according to which the 'Revolutionary Council', which was dominated by the radical clergy, was amalgamated with the state. Such a compromise was celebrated by demonstrations and meetings. The liberal prime minister had aimed to include the 'Revolutionary Council' under state control, but, the unregulated organs and centers of power acted under the direct influence of the radical clergy. The amalgamation became the beginning of the end of the liberal state in revolutionary Iran. Many departments and ministries came under the control of the radical clergy. Some radical clergy, who came to play important roles in the future of the Islamic Republic, such as Bahonar, Rafsenjani, Khamenei and Mahdavi Kani, placed controls over the 'Ministry of Education', the 'Ministry of Defense', and the 'Ministry of Public Administration'.[219] The radical clergy began the invasion of the state apparatus and the exertion of legitimized coercion. The clerics' steady colonizing of the state power culminated in the fall of the liberal government and establishment of a clerical government. The prime minister Bazargan was surprised by the seizure of power by the radical clergy. Shortly before his fall in an interview with Oriana Fallaci he said:

> Something unforeseen and unforeseeable happened after the revolution. What happened was that the clergy supplanted us and succeeded in taking over the country.[220]

In September 1979, the democratic Ayatollah Taleqani who, because of the massive support for him among the people, was one of the most influential persons in balancing the power matrix of Khomeini's clergy, died. The radical clergy saw one of the greatest barriers to seizing political power and excluding the liberals eliminated. The hope of establishing a democratic governance was buried together with Taleqani.

In October and November 1979, the attacks on the liberal and oppositional newspapers, associations, and organizations intensified. The open attacks on the oppositional activities, such as demonstrations and those who were selling newspapers in the central Tehran and other major cities, witnessed that the life of the liberal 'provisional government' was over. In November 4, 1979, a student group connecting with the radical clergy occupied the American Embassy, declared the USA the 'main enemy of Islamic Iran' and demanded that all connections with the USA be terminated. They also accused the government of trying to establish a 'good relationship' with the 'enemy of the people', the USA, and 'to prepare the ground for its comeback in Iran'.[221] The leftists, who saw the anti-American content of the Revolution disappearing, celebrated the takeover. The most organized and powerful of all other leftist organizations, Fadaiyan-e khalq, marched to the Embassy to demonstrate their support for the anti-American students.[222] In a very short meeting with Khomeini, the prime minister Bazargan resigned and the liberal government fell.

The Revolution in which a major part of the urban groups had participated and helped to overthrow the Shah resulted in establishment of an Islamic regime in which the radical clergy colonized almost all organs of influence. Thus, they begin to eliminate distinctions between civil society and state.

Part III
DISCUSSION AND CONCLUSIONS

10 The Two Revolutions: Comparative Reflections

Overview

After the Arab conquest and Islamicization of Iran, Iranian socio-economic and cultural institutions went through crucial changes which led to reconstruction of the pre-Islamic society. The new Islamic society of Iran was reconstructed in part according to Islamic rules and norms. The reconstruction led to a historical division of power between state and the ulama. The relationship, coexistence, and conflicts between these two sources of influence and authority have played a crucial role in the shaping and reshaping of institutional and constitutional contradictions and changes in the Iranian society over a history of five hundred years. The sphere of the ulama's influence and the main source of their power have been the traditional civil society of Iran. Their traditional interconnections with the main socio-economic centers of cities, namely the bazaars, and their closeness to the urban poor, provided them with crucial means of influence in the urban life of Iran. In addition, the theory of *velayat* (vicegerent), which is the position of vicegerency of the Hidden Imam, provides a theological basis of legitimation for their prominent position in society. In the ideological sphere, the state, since the final decades of the reign of the Safavids (1501-1722), was not able to effectively challenge the theory of *velayat*. Even modernization efforts had to take into consideration the position of the ulama and the bazaris and to avoid direct confrontations with them.

Confrontations such as the Tobacco Movement and the Constitutional Revolution were consequences of state efforts to influence and change the traditional position of the bazaris and the ulama and change the balance of power in its favor. In the political arena the ulama, up to the first decades after the Constitutional Revolution, had a leading position and functioned as representatives of the people in challenge against and negotiations with the state. The institutionalized tradition of their leadership of the people provided them with a valid basis to act as revolutionary leaders in political movements and revolutions. Both the Tobacco Movement and the Constitutional Revolution bore witness to such a leadership. Although the ulama were the leaders of the movements, the outcomes and configurations of such movements were not completely shaped by their desires. The will of the bazaris and other urban groups which was incorporated in an unpredictable process of events limited the realization of the ulama's intentions and desires. The most interesting example of the influence of other groups and the process of movement is the Constitutional Revolution. The bazaris began the movement against the state's economic policy, the ulama joined the movement to support the bazaris, and intellectuals participated in order to establish a democratic regime. But the outcome of the Revolution was not in favor of one of these groups but a compromise. The ulama who wanted *adalatkhaneh* (the house of justice)–by which they aimed to establish their monopoly over the judicial system–accepted the intellectuals' idea of establishing a constitutional regime. The second main group in civil society, namely the bazaris, whose immediate demand was economic reform and the change of the Belgian chief of customs, became through the process of the Revolution constitutionalists. And the intellectuals who wanted the establishment of a constitutional regime according to the Western models had to accept the supremacy of the ulama over the Majlis (parliament).

After the victory of the Constitutional Revolution there was a period of instability and insecurity as a result of the weakness of the central government and the presence of foreign armies. Iran was at the edge of dissolution. The ulama and many other urban groups for the first time faced the danger of disruption of the country. The ulama of *'atabat*'s bitter experience of engagement in the revolutionary events of Iraq in 1918-20, and their return to Iran, was another reason for them to retain their connections with the Iranian bazaar and the ulama. This could be guaranteed only if Iran could exist as an independent country. Therefore, Reza Khan's *coup d'état* in 1922 not only was viewed negatively by many ulama, but in some cases was praised by some prominent ulama. Political neutralization of prominent ulama during the reign of Reza Shah, left the political arena to leftists and nationalists. Through political dictatorship, Reza Shah brought about basic changes in Iranian society. A powerful central state was constructed, communication systems were improved, military forces reformed, modern middle occupational groups were created, and so forth. After the abdication of Reza Shah and at the beginning of the reign of the next, and the last, Pahlavis, Muhammad Reza Shah, Iran witnessed a period of more than ten years of political democracy and freedom. During this period the political arena was dominated mainly by nationalists and leftists.[223] The *coup d'état* of 1953 put an end to this democratic period and became the beginning of the next period of authoritative modernization which was disrupted by the abdication of Reza Shah. The Shah's *coup d'état* not only put an end to the development of democratic institutions, but also weakened the domination of the nationalist and leftist ideologies. At the beginning of the 1960s a group of new radical clergy appeared in the political arena and challenged the Shah's authoritative modernization program. The developing influence of radical clergy depended partly on the internal change in the ranks of the ulama, namely the death of the apolitical *marja'-e taqlid*, Ayatollah Borujerdi. A new generation of young radical clergy under the leadership of Ayatollah Khomeini emerged in the political arena and exhibited its ability to mobilize parts of the urban people against the Shah.

But the modern changes of Iranian society which took place during the reign of Pahlavis had in many cases changed the urban society of Iran. Social differentiation, such as creation of a powerful bureaucratic state, new social groups, institutions, ideologies, and so forth, led to a challenge to the social authority of the ulama. The change of the balance of power between the state and the ulama, also led to further differentiation in the ranks of the ulama. These changes led also to ideological differentiation. Modern religious ideologies such as those of Ali Shari'ati and Mojahedin-e khalq provided a new and revolutionary interpretation of Islam. Radical clergy, who were a group influenced both by the new ideological and socio-economic changes in the Iranian society, found the new ideological framework against the Shah in Khomeini's book *Hukomat-e eslami, velayat-e faqih* (Islamic governance, vicegerency of *fuqaha*). In this book, Khomeini presented a new interpretation of the theory of *velayat* and suggested the seizing of political power by *fuqaha* (Islamic jurisprudents). For the first time after the Occultation of the Hidden Imam, he legitimized creation of an Islamic state without the presence of the Hidden Imam. Modern interpretations of Islam by new intellectuals and political groups provided a proper basis for religio-intellectual popularity of Khomeini's political theory of *velayat-e faqih* (vicegerency of the Islamic jurists).

Although Khomeini's book was published in 1971, its content, together with the radical clergy, remained marginal to civil society of Iran.[224] Khomeini who possessed a high level of political capital (*heysiat-e siyasi*), was much more important than his theory of *velayat-e faqih*.²²⁵ The Shah, under US pressure, initiated political openness intending to reform the political system. While the leftists and other intellectuals planned to use the new reforms for weakening the Shah and improving democratic reforms, the radical clergy under the leadership of Khomeini propagated the Shah's abdication and a change of regime. At the same time, in the lowest ranks of urban society, an 'apolitical' struggle was going on between the 'dispossessed' and municipal authorities. Political demonstrations of middle occupational groups and religious propaganda among the 'dispossessed' politicized their demonstrations. The 'dispossessed' became the main revolutionary army of radical clergy because of the traditional and religious views of these peoples, their socio-economic connections with the bazaris who were the natural allies of the ulama, and religious propaganda of young religious groups among them. Using the 'apolitical' and 'spontaneous' power of this group, the radical clergy and Khomeini succeeded in seizing the leadership of the Revolution and forcing other revolutionary groups, such as liberals to accept their hegemony. When the victory of the Islamic Revolution of Iran was completed in February, 1979, radical clergy had their own army of 'dispossessed' who were mainly organized in revolutionary committees (*komiteh ha-ye enqelab*). 'In Tehran alone, there were 1500 revolutionary committees'. As Bazargan [the first prime minister of Islamic Republic of Iran] put it, 'the committees are everywhere, and no one knows how many exist, not even the Imam himself'.²²⁶

Khomeini and the radical clergy succeeded in seizing political power and establishing an Islamic state, partly because of the existence of a revolutionary theory which was presented by a man with a high level of political capital (*heysiyat-e siyasi*), and partly because of the existence of new urban and marginalized groups which received a voice through the clergy's leadership of the Revolution and in turn supported the radical clergy.

Early Modernization, Foreign Penetration, and Political Revolution

The Shi'ite ulama were a very influential power center in the Iranian society during the reign of the Safavids. After the fall of the Safavids in 1722, the ulama transmitted their main sources of power from relationships with the state to those with civil society. Accordingly, in order to keep their religious authority, they were especially interested in securing a balance of power with the state. From the middle of the nineteenth century, the Qajars changed their traditional policy and began to reinforce their political authority through closer connection to the West. The impact of Western influence harmed mainly the ulama and the bazaris. Hence, the traditional conflict between the state and civil society of Iran was sharpened, and the ulama, in order to keep their custodianship of civil society, participated in a 'movement against the tyranny' which gradually developed into a movement for the establishment of a constitutional regime.

During the constitutional movement for the mobilization of the people, the ulama's use of the Shi'ite utopia concerning the 'appearance' of the Hidden Imam crystallizes the importance of that utopia in the continuation of Axial civilizations. The 'appearance of the Hidden Imam', as all other religious and ideological utopias, was not just a religious image of an ideal order. Utopian beliefs and the search for a perfect political and social order has been a major factor of civilization's history. Religious utopias, as Max Weber puts it, are the salvational religions' promises to overcome the imperfect reality of human existence and the establishment of a perfect transcendental order.[227] The tensions between the unfair and non-accepted reality and the legitimate expectation of a desirable social setting either in the past or future construct the cornerstone of all utopias. Eisenstadt characterizes the period of the Axial Age, during which the great religions appeared, as a period of restructuring and constitutionalization of the basic tension between the transcendental and the mundane order (Eisenstadt, 1982). As he points out:

> The development and institutionalization of such conceptions of a basic tension, chasm between the transcendental and the mundane order, gave rise in all these civilizations to attempts to reconstruct the mundane world- human personality and the socio-political and economic order according to the appropriate transcendental vision, to the principles of the higher ontological or ethical order (Eisenstadt, 1994, p. 5).

According to Shi'ite theology, bridging the chasm between the transcendental and the mundane order was the duty of the Prophet and his successor, the Twelve Imams descending from his *beyt* (home, family). The theory of *gheybat* (Occultation) creates a dilemma for Shi'ites in legitimating their conflicts with the political power in their societies.

Shi'ites had *de facto* accepted illegitimate political power in the Muslim community while awaiting the appearance of the Hidden Imam, who was the only legitimate leader in the community. The Occultation of the Imam, by no means meant the absence of the Imam from the community. He was occulted but existing among the people. Accordingly, the Great Occultation meant the lack of direct contact with the Imam. His religious leadership of the community, hence, was transferred to the Shi'ite ulama and Shi'ites' adherents were to follow them in their interpretations of the just patterns of life. Because of the persecution of Shi'ites during the first centuries after the Occultation of the Hidden Imam, and the minority position of Shi'ites, the theory of *taqiyya* was formulated which justified Shi'ites' hiding of their faiths from the tyrannical Sunnis. The institutionalization of *taqiyya* reinforced Shi'ites' ambiguity and ambivalence to political power. They were awaiting their real political leader, the Hidden Imam.

The seizure of political power by a Shi'ite dynasty, the Safavids, in 1501, faced the Shi'ites with a new dilemma. They reconstructed and constitutionalized the reign of Shi'ites on behalf of the Hidden Imam by formulating of the theologian term *niyabat-e Imam* (vicegerency of the Hidden Imam). Increasing the number of Shi'ites, by establishing the Shi'ite as Iran's state religion, led to increasing the sphere of influence of the Shi'ite ulama. The chasm between the pre-Safavids inferior and non-just mundane order and the complete and transcendental order of the Hidden Imam, was restructured and institutionalized by the theory of *niyabat-e Imam*. As mentioned earlier, in the last decades of the reign of Safavids a new restructuring of the contemporary strategy for bridging the mundane and the transcendental order was created. *The niyabat-e Imam* was transferred from the political leaders to the ulama and a division of the political and religious leadership took place. During the centuries following the fall of the Safavids, the ulama, as a result of the lack of direct connections with the state and threats from the state, institutionalized and reinforced their leading position in civil society. As Eisenstadt states:

> The political order as the central locus, or one of the central loci of the mundane order was usually conceived as lower than the transcendental one and accordingly had to be restructured according to the precepts of the later–above all according to the perception of the proper mode of overcoming the tension between the transcendental and the mundane order,

of 'salvation' or of the implementation of the appropriate transcendental vision (Eisenstadt, 1994, p. 6).

The ulama thus accepted the political order only as a temporary power whose duty was to protect the Shi'ite community against foreign invasion. The internal affairs of civil society was not a realm of political influence and intervention. The socio-economic (bazaar) and sociocultural institutions were the realm of the influence of ulama as the only way of 'salvation' while awaiting the appearance of the Hidden Imam. Such structures were naturally based on the mutual recognition of the state and the ulama. This traditional coexistence between the ulama and the state was violated by Western conceptions and the displacement of state power as protector of the Shi'ite society. The Western's economic impact harmed mainly bazaris who were the 'natural allies' of the ulama. Bazaris were the first group in Iranian society who in the last decades of the nineteenth century questioned in active protests the very basis of the legitimation of the state. Three main factors involved the ulama in the anti-state's social movements:

1. Their relations with the bazaris who actively participated in the movement.
2. The negation of their leading position in civil society.
3. A perceived need to counter the socio-cultural impact of the West.

The continuation of the movement and the emergence of demands for the establishment of a constitutional regime faced them with a new social and theological challenge. Mass demands for restructuring traditional settings of the society forced the ulama to create the theological justification for reconstruction of the mundane and inferior world. Although constitutionalism was a Western phenomena, it could be used in reconstruction of the mundane political order of Iranian society–adjusting it to the transcendental 'higher ontological or ethical order'. *Constitutionalism, according to the ulama, would limit the power of the state and eliminate or reduce the impact of the West.*

The social changes taking place during the constitutional movement changed also the role of the ulama in the Iranian society. The constitutional movement violated the traditional theological homogeneity of the Shi'ite ulama and divided them sharply into two groups, namely constitutionalists and anti-constitutionalists. As Burns points out, social changes are not logical constructions, but products of historical processes (Burns, 1994, pp. 161-92), during which social organizing principles and rules became the object of reflection, reform efforts, cooperation as well as social struggle (Burns, 1994). Accordingly, the constitutional movement was not simply a result of the ulama's desire and intentions for limitation of state power, rather a result of historical changes which took place during the second half of the nineteenth century. The constitutionalist ulama realized the difficulties of keeping their prominent position in civil society on the traditional basis of 'peaceful' coexistence with the state. The theoretical basis of mutual coexistence of the ulama and the state was to be restructured and adjusted according to religious codes. Constitutionalism was the only possible means by which the ulama believed that they could both retain their prominent position in the society and limit the power of the state.

Although the ulama were the leaders of the Constitutional Revolution, they did not have any intention to seize the entire political power. The constitutionalist ulama's main intention was to limit the state power and exert control over it. They wanted to extend and widen the realm of civil society, i.e. ulama's sphere of influence. By establishing a Majlis, the state's *u'rf* jurisdiction, which was a limited legislative right for constituting some customary laws, controlled and used by the state earlier, could be transformed into civil society. Of course, as mentioned earlier, it was not the primary aim of the ulama, but a result of the dialectical process of the movement during which the constitutionalist ulama adopted the idea of constitutionalism and adjusted it to the structural setting of Iranian society and Shi'ite theology.

One of the most interesting characteristics of the process of Constitutional Revolution was the special forms of the peoples' protest. The main means used by the ulama and other urban groups in 'demonstrating' their protests was not demonstration, but taking *bast* (refuge) and closing the affairs and shops of the bazaars. To protect themselves from the execution of a judicial or customary verdict of guilty, the *bast* was used by the Iranian people almost over the entire Islamic history of Iran. Closing the bazaars was also a traditional way of showing participation in religious mournings by the bazaris. But during the Constitutional movement, these two institutionalized form of protest were widely used for political purposes. These means of protest received new religio-political symbolism. To take the *bast* in the holy shrines all over the country was a symbolic action of asking for support from Muhammad's *ahl-e beyt*, and the Hidden Imam as the only true and just leader of the Muslim community. They also wanted to reinforce the position of the ulama and their monopoly upon leadership in the movement. Simultaneously, the religious institution of *bast* was used mainly by bazaris and other urban people even to take refuge in the foreign embassies and companies. For instance, while the ulama went to Qum and resided in the holy shrines, the bazaris closed their affairs to support them, asking for their return to Tehran, and took refuge in the embassy of England in Tehran.

Closing the bazaars changed its religious character and received a political symbolism. Many attempts were made by the state to open the bazaars by force.[228] The economic importance of the bazaars and the socio-religious importance of the ulama, made it almost impossible for the state to reign without these two groups. Although the institution of *bast*, as a result of the modernization and differentiating of Iranian society declined and even died, closing the bazaars and other affairs was used also during the process of the Islamic Revolution as a symbolic action of protest against the Shah.

Autocratic Societal Transformation and the Islamic Social Revolution

The story consists of several stories and sub-plots. The Shah did bring about a revolution, although not the one he intended.[229] We should recognize, however, that he also modernized Iran to a great extent: he introduced and developed new institutional arrangements in the areas of economy, education, science, and professional life. But, in the social environment of his government and the network of actors around him, there were other important groups who had different conceptions and a different story to act out. They did this dramatically and successfully, partly reversing, partly transforming the revolution that the Shah initiated.

I. The Islamic revolution of Iran can be characterized as a revolution of marginal groups–or groups threatened with marginalization–mobilized and allied against a modernizing elite that exercised its power within a centralized, autocratic power structure–a power structure that allowed little room for expression of dissatisfaction or for (re-)negotiation of state policies and programs. In a word, the society was characterized by a regime that combined an autocratic, and in many ways, traditional political/administrative structure with a commitment to rapid economic and social modernization (not democratization, however).[230] The modernizing Shah attempted to do away with the previous dualistic system of authority–with the clergy and state leadership–with one exclusively dominated by a centralized bureaucratic state. The development process–and consideration of its various impacts, including unintended consequences–excluded key societal groups, in particular the clergy. In a Muslim society, this is a critical exclusion, but nevertheless understandable, given the Shah's particular development model. Other groups, such as the middle occupational groups, the bazaris as well as the modern groups, which might have played a role in developing public discourses and negotiating a more balanced, integrated development path, were also largely excluded. Any modernization process–as a restructuring and ultimately transformation of society–generates winners and losers. This is particularly the case when carried out in autocratic, often arbitrary manner (or at least, there is a greater sense of having been made to suffer losses). Given that the Shah's modernization initiative was so centralized and concentrated, it identified him as the symbolic source and the agent responsible for the disasters and evils plaguing Iran ('Satan', in the discourse of the Ayatollahs). In this way, his regime–indeed, the entire modernization project–became highly vulnerable to systematic criticism, illegitimating, and potential mobilization of opposition to stop the project.[231]

The Shah saw himself as establishing a strong central government to modernize and Westernize Iran. The religious groups were considered barriers to the achievement of these goals. The institution of the bazaar seemed old-fashioned, certainly not the basis on which to build a modern industrialized Iran. His initiatives were in part to realize a vision–to deal with a complex of 'problem situations', economic, political, or military (e.g., Iran's geopolitical context). These projects were then justified in part by arguments and calculations to make a better, more powerful Iran ('a great civilization'). They would also contribute to the glory and prestige of the Monarchy, and its State.

The Shah's modernization was as rapid and comprehensive and disruptive as it was, in part, because of the vast resources, economic as well as political/administrative, which he had at his command. He established steel and petrochemical industries; he helped the private sector develop a range of consumer industries; he built roads, dams, railroads, and ports. Power was used often absolutely (and from the perspective of many of those affected, arbitrarily) to transform cities and villages: bulldozers demolished private homes and working class districts; the government forced villagers to sell their farmlands and often razed entire villages in order to create agroindustries (Bakhash, 1990, p. 11).[232]

The Shah's modernization and secularization had a profound, and in many cases negative, impact on key societal groups. His command over economic resources as well as political power easily led to what appeared to many to be arbitrary and reprehensible actions. Given the centralized way that changes were initiated–and responsibility taken for launching projects and programs–the Shah readily became the center of the world. Literally and symbolically he became responsible for all Iranian development. Many of the social changes associated with modernization appeared 'foreign', or Western. Indeed, they were often Western copies or derivatives having contributed to the development of other countries. In some instances, they came with foreign advisors: Western law codes, educational systems, consumer goods, new cultural forms such as extending freedoms to women, and new freedoms for young people attending colleges and universities. These made both the Shah's government and his entire undertaking more vulnerable to critique and effective opposition–once all of those negatively affected or opposed began to organize themselves and to express and to coordinate their opposition. There was not only dissatisfaction, but organized groups able and willing to play a leading role in opposing the Shah.

The Shah and his government had access to and utilized considerable economic resources (oil revenues) as well as political power and authority to set in motion modernization projects: economic, infrastructure developments, education, legal and administrative systems etc. Modernization entailed, in part, remaking the country, and, in view of the modernization model or ideology to which the Shah adhered, this also entailed systematic secularization. In part, this meant replacing religious schools with secular, public schools and expanding modern university education. It meant establishing new markets, changing market conditions, making banking policies and foreign trade policies that had fateful consequences for various groups, such as the bazaris. All in all, the Shah's modernization program radically disturbed societal relationships, the status, authority, wealth, sense of place, etc. of previously important groups such as the clergy and bazaris as well as new, more socially undefined groups such as the new middle occupational groups.

II. The various projects had diverse consequences. They not only entailed obvious positive developments such as economic growth and material development–development of infrastructure, wealth, economic and military power. There were many negative impacts: economic losses (or losses relative to comparative groups), loss of status and authority, social dislocation and disorientation, normative violation, even violation of sacred principles–which set the stage for the readiness or openness of some societal groups to try to do something about them.

III. In this study have been identified four major groups for which modernization/ secularization developments had negative effects: clergy, the traditional middle occupational groups (bazaris, among others), the urban marginals, and the new middle occupational groups. The clergy and the bazaris were traditional groups, with established places in the society, as well as, in the religious discourses of the Qur'an and *hadith*). The new middle occupational groups and urban marginals emerged as a direct result of the Shah's modernization program. Of course, what has been of major interest is how these groups were coordinated or brought into collaboration in their opposition to the Shah. This entailed not only organizing–constructing or activating social linkages–but cultural construction: the formulation of political concepts, slogans, myths, and, eventually, an ideology.

IV. The negative impacts of modernization took place in a society with very limited institutional arrangements for criticizing, negotiating, and correcting misdirected projects. Those negatively affected had few or no institutional means to express their dissatisfaction and to negotiate changes, or reformulating policies and programs (Lipset, 1960). If there was to be any redress, any redirection of societal arrangements, programs, projects, and plans, they had to shape these on the spot, in the course of the struggle. Reactions against the Shah, his policies, the effects of his programs were often immediate, localized, uncoordinated and undirected. Of course, the clergy and the middle occupational groups were able to express themselves in writing and public discourse more effectively. Some opponents had direct or indirect contacts to key people in the government. The marginal migrants did not, of course, have these possibilities.

The interaction between opposition and regime partly generates new problems and opportunities, new 'rules of the game' and relationships. The Shah's regime, by refusing to negotiate with any of the opposition, threw the various groups together–and effectively gave over leadership of the 'opposition' to those with the greatest charisma and capacity to mobilize and organize. *This also made the future of the oppositional process and protests more radical.* Thus, the Shah and his government might have negotiated a constitutional monarchy, giving over power to parliament and political parties in a more or less peaceful transition. By resisting this, by excluding the possibility of systematic negotiation and institutional restructuring, he set the stage for a radical-led 'religious' revolution and the establishment of an Islamic state.

V. A key process in any major societal transformation is that of building up a coalition (alliance) and mobilizing behind a vision of a new order. In this case the radical clergy provided part of this vision.[233] But more was needed: in particular, the various groups in opposition had to overcome their fragmentation and to deal with problems of coordination.

As stressed earlier, there was already strong network ties to build upon, such as the historical linkages between the clergy and bazaris. At the same time, the clergy commanded status and authority in a Muslim society that could be activated or mobilized in the setting in motion of a socio-political movement against what they defined as evil. The clergy also discovered that they could 'move the urban masses', and also organize them. In addition, the situation itself provided incentives to collaboration between the different opposition groups, in part because of the Shah's rejection of negotiation and compromise until it was too late. This gave them a common goal: *removal of the Shah and the establishment of a new regime*. Also, they aimed to establish a new order, but, as long as this was an abstract vision, they could interpret this in substantially different ways (for instance, the meaning of 'Islamic republic', 'equality', 'justice', 'freedom').[234]

The opposition groups and interests activated existing organizations and networks as well as organizing new ones. This process of social buildup went together with the development of politically effective ideas (concepts, slogans, myths, etc.), organizing principles, and strategies. This process always entails social learning, innovation, reformulations and restructurings in the course of the confrontations and struggles with the *ancien regime*.

One important part of the learning and innovation had to do with coalition formation and collective mobilization. This also concerns the question of places and times to meet–and here the clergy had the advantages of socially defined protected places and times, which other groups, like the leftists and nationalists, lacked. The clergy could make use of Islamic religious culture, in which certain times and places are sacred, honored and protected within the culture: for example mosques, shrines, and religious events. The clergy, with its robust networks, could mobilize urban masses (cf. Bakhash, 1990, p. 15).

VI. In the interplay between socio-political movements and state authority (Andersen and Burns, 1992; Flam, 1993), the 'rules of the game' are continually being tested, redefined, transformed. Under conditions that the opposition gains in strength, they escalate their demands. Groups or organizations that were hesitant or opposed to joining earlier, find that in *the new circumstances*, they want to, ought to, must join in–the incentive structure changes.

VII. The shift in power entails, not only the circulation of similar elites, but a coalition of elites coming to power with a new perspective, new values and norms, new bases of authority and power as well as status, new institutional arrangements, and programs. This is what makes the shift revolutionary. In these processes, where authority is not only being weakened but transformed–the old order is collapsing and a new order is being established–the way is opened to innovations and the expansion of creativity.[235]

This study suggests that the Shah's social constructionism was strictly bounded by the social environment. He and his supporters were not the only social agents able to affect developments. Construction–in part through selection processes–of social rules and institutional arrangements *was also exercised by other agents and social groups, namely those participating in the Islamic Revolution. The revolutionary movement not only opposed but actually reversed some of the innovations in institutional arrangements established by the Shah. New arrangements–a new order of social rules– were established and are now being tested and elaborated in post- revolutionary processes.*[236]

Comparisons of the Two Modern Revolutions

In the twentieth century Iran has gone through two modern revolutions: the Constitutional and the Islamic. In the Constitutional Revolution Iranian society was in a state of relatively low social differentiation and political diversity. The state structure was based on the traditional Perso-Shi'ite monarchy. This relatively stable ruling system was disturbed by foreign influence and modernization/centralization of state power at the end of nineteenth and beginning of twentieth centuries. The state's attempts to change the traditional power balance between the state and two powerful groups in civil society, the ulama and the bazaris, resulted in a broad movement against the state and foreign influence which developed into the demand for Constitutionalism. Accordingly, the Constitutionalist Revolution of Iran was an outcome of the process of this movement and socio- political alliances between groups participating in the movement.

Iran under the Pahlavis had gone through major socio-economic changes that resulted in the creation of new social groups and modern institutions. The Pahlavis' modernization programs not only modernized and differentiated the social structures, but also, as a result of reforms, the political opposition to their reign. New political parties and groups were constituted by new social groups demanding a place and a voice in the socio-political arena of society. The modern civil society of Iran not only consisted of the two main social groups, i.e. the ulama and the bazaris, but also of new groups, such as the modern middle occupational groups and industrial workers, and major urban marginal groups, the 'dispossessed'. The Shah's centralization of state and elimination of all political influence of civil society on the state resulted in a revolution which put end to 2,500 years of monarchy in Iran. The Islamic Revolution of Iran was, thus, a type of collective action of civil society against an isolated state.

However, a comparison of these two modern Revolutions of twentieth century Iran shows the similarities and differences of the Constitutional and the Islamic Revolutions based on social continuity and change of social groups and socio-political institutions. Table 10.1 is an attempt at such a comparison.

The leadership of both revolutions, as the *first* dimension of comparison, was a religious leadership. The ulama exercised such leadership during the Constitutional and the Islamic Revolutions and established their control over the leadership of the Revolutions. Although in both Revolutions the ulama had the leadership, they did not make up the same group in the Islamic Revolution as in the Constitutional Revolution. Pahlavis' modernization programs had also influenced the ulama and divided them politically into three main groups:

1. *The traditionalists.*
2. *The constitutionalists.*
3. *The radicals.*

Some of the ulama, such as Ayatollah Golpayegani and Ayatollah Mar'ashi-ye Najafi, in the line of the tradition of Ayatollah Borujerdi, remained apolitical. They were almost totally engaged in purely religious activities. The constitutionalist ulama were those who believed in the Constitution created by the Constitutional Revolution, according to which the ulama should supervise over the legislative organ, the Majlis. They were not against the Shah's reign and had chosen mostly a position of quiescence. One of the most important ulama of this group was Ayatollah Shariatmadari. His political participation was limited to periodic advice for re-establishment of the constitution of 1907. He was a prominent *marj'a-e taqlid* and known as a moderate and reformist religious leader.

Table 10.1 The comparison of the Constitutional and the Islamic Revolutions

	The Constitutional Revolution 1905-1909	The Islamic Revolution 1977-1979
Leadership	Constitutionalist ulama	'Fundamentalist' ulama
Revolutionary alliance	The ulama, the bazaris (merchants), intellectuals	The ulama, the bazaris, liberals
Revolutionary forces	Clergy, bazaris, Bakhtiyari tribe	Middle occupational groups, the 'dispossessed'
Ideological framework	Constitutionalism, Shi'ite traditional theory of state	*Velayat-e faqih*, republicanism
State	Monarchical dictatorship	Monarchical dictatorship combined with modern institutions, such as parliament
Army	Weak army, depended on foreign support, participated	Strong national army, became neutralized

The radical ulama consisted mainly of Ayatollah Khomeini and his students. The beginning of these groups' activities went back to the revolt of 1963 in which Khomeini was arrested and exiled. This group had initially no clear alternative to the reign of the Shah. Their opposition to the Shah was mainly based on some of his modernization programs which they considered un-Islamic. The political ideology of this group was developed after the uprising of 1963, and especially through Khomeini's lectures in Najaf. In accordance with socio-economic changes, their political profiles changed and modified. One of the most interesting changes in their traditional (o)position towards the modern institutional changes was the question of women's participation in the political arena of the country. In the religious agitation which led to the uprising of June 1963, the ulama criticized the Shah for giving franchise to women, but in the Islamic constitution of Iran the franchise of women is guaranteed.

The radical ulama, known as fundamentalists, received their main political manifesto in 1970, through the publication of Khomeini's book 'Islamic governance'. As mentioned earlier, Khomeini presented a new revolutionary theory of political leadership in Muslim community, which changed the very basis of the relationship between the political realm and civil society. In a political situation where leftists were marginalized, and almost out of the game for making alliances, and liberals, as a result of the lack of liberal institutions, were very weak, in the critical years of 1977-79, the radical ulama established their monopoly over the leadership of the movement and led the triumph of the Islamic Revolution of 1979.

The *second* dimension of comparison are the characteristics of revolutionary alliances in the Constitutional and Islamic Revolutions respectively. The revolutionary alliances were made against counter-revolutionary alliances and their target was to defeat the counter-revolutionary alliances and overthrow the old regime. The alliances between revolutionaries on the one side, and counter-revolutionary groups on the other, however, depends on the social structure and institutional settings of the revolutionary societies. How the social institutions are related to each other are of great importance in making alliances and in the outcomes of their collective actions. As already discussed, the religious and economic institutions were closely interconnected and constituted a historical matrix for the urban life in Iran. The modernization and centralization of the state led to disruption and violation of the institutionalized channels used by civil society to influence the state authority and decision making. The bazaris and the ulama harmed by the new politics of the state–and the lack of channels of influence–strengthened their traditional alliance. Of course intellectuals from different social groups, and even bureaucrats and state officials participated in the revolutionary alliance, but the core group of alliance consisted of the ulama and the bazaris. In one of the first secret meetings held by revolutionaries in the beginning of 1906, for discussing the tactics of the protest, the core alliance of the revolution, the ulama and the bazaris, were in a leading position. Among 57 participants from different social groups, such as bureaucrats, state officials, Zoroastrians, journalists, and the Bakhtiyari tribe chief Sardar As'ad, the administration and leadership of the meeting was dominated by bazaris and the ulama, such as Malek al-Motakallemin, Seyyed Jamal al-Din Va'ez, and Haj Shaykh Mehdi Sharif (Malekzadeh, 1950, pp. 6-17). The intellectuals, through influencing the bazaris and the ulama, played an important role in ideological mobilization of revolutionary forces. It must be noted that the bazaris participating in the revolutionary alliance were led by the merchants whose interest was affected directly by the 'concession policy' of the Qajars and the impact of the state.

In the Islamic Revolution of 1977-79, the core alliance of the revolution consisted of the radical ulama, the bazaris, and the liberals (mainly represented by the LMI). A more marginal role was played by other liberal groups in the revolutionary alliance such as the National Front. In the Constitutional Revolution the intellectual group consisted of almost all groups in opposition to the Shah other than the ulama and the bazaris. But in the Islamic Revolution the intellectual group, as a result of more than seventy years of modernization, was differentiated and divided. From such a heterogeneous group it was only liberals who were accepted by the religious leadership of the Revolution as allies. Many other groups, such as leftists, were excluded from the revolutionary alliance. The LMI and the NF had connections with the bazaar and the army. During the last months before the victory of the Islamic Revolution, both the LMI and the National Front tried to guarantee the prominent position of the army but also to neutralize it in the Revolution. Of course, the army would accept the guarantees more readily from liberals than from the radical clergy. Because of the army's standing, the participation of the LMI and National Front in the revolutionary alliance could guarantee the peaceful transformation of power to the revolutionaries.[237] The leaders of the LMI and the NF, Mehdi Bazargan and Karim Sanjabi, were included in the 'Revolutionary Council' chosen by Khomeini to lead the revolution. Bazargan even became the first prime minister of the Islamic Republic of Iran.

One arena of confrontation between the religious revolutionary leadership, radical clergy, and the Shah was the competition for liberal support. Khomeini, aware of the Shah's attempt to attract some of the liberals of the LMI and the NF, accelerated his cooperation with the liberals, intending to isolate the Shah. The Shah's willingness to cooperate with the liberals came very late and mainly those from the National Front, such as the Shah's last prime minister, Shahpoor Bakhtiyar, shared his tragic destiny.

But in the Iranian Revolution as in other revolutions, such as the French (1789), Russian (1917), and Chinese (1949), political alliances, which were constituted with the target of overthrowing the old political system, could not be continued by the groups participating in the alliance after reaching their primary target. Post-revolutionary periods are always characterized by power conflicts between formerly allied groups in the establishment of the new regime.

The *third* dimension of comparison consists of the revolutionary forces that, in cooperation, brought about the two modern Revolutions of Iran. The main social groups participating in the Constitutional Revolution were the clergy, the bazaris, the intellectuals, the urban poor, and the limited-but-significant Bakhtiyari tribesmen. As an urban revolution, the Constitutional Revolution engaged the urban groups of civil society in the revolutionary process. A process which began with the demand for some change in state politics and ended with the change of the very characteristics of the political system. In the process of revolutionary confrontation with the regime middle-ranking bazaris, poor urban people, and low-ranking clergy, *mullahs* and *tullabs*, actively participated. During the civil war of June 1908 to July 1909, revolutionary forces were dominated by the bazaris, who were influenced by the modern ideas of constitutionalism.

On the eve of the Islamic Revolution, which was also an urban revolution, the major changes in the structures of the population resulted in the creation of new social groups. The emergence of these new groups, the modern middle occupational groups, the industrial workers, and the 'dispossessed', created new grounds for revolutionary participation. Although the participation of the modern middle occupational groups in the Revolution strengthened the position of liberals, the LMI, and the National Front and helped make the revolutionary coalition of the liberals and the ulama possible, the main radical force of the Revolution, which was crucial in overthrowing the Shah, was the 'dispossessed'. These new social groups which, as a result of the land reform and other modernization programs of the Shah, left their traditional socio-cultural milieu and moved to the cities, in coalition with the traditional middle occupational groups, became the base of the 'revolutionary army'. This 'army' was used by Khomeini and other radical ulama to reinforce their position of leadership during the Revolution and to establish their monopoly over state organs after it.

The *fourth* dimension of comparison between the two Revolutions is the ideological framework of the Constitutional and the Islamic Revolutions. At the beginning of the Constitutional movement of Iran, neither the leaders nor the participants were aware of the targets of their collective actions. Three main streams of targets for different groups participating in the Revolution can be isolated:

1. The bazaris' goal was to change the customs regulations.
2. The ulama mainly wanted to limit state power.
3. The intellectuals wanted to liberalize the political system.

The bazaris, who were actually the first group to react against the economic impact of foreign companies, began the protests against the concession policy of the state. The Tobacco Movement was the first example of the bazaris' wide participation in the movement against the state by demanding the abolishment of the concession. As Gurr pointed out, the second phase of the process of revolution is the politicization of discontent (Gurr, 1970). During the movement, the bazaris' discontent became politicized and presented as a demand for constitutionalism. But, in the case of the ulama, every social action created a demand for their participation as the civil counterpart to the state and the leaders of civil society. This was the case in both the Tobacco Movement and the Constitutional Revolution. The prominent position of the ulama in society was threatened by the impact of the West and by state attempts to centralize and establish its power according to modern models.

Accordingly, the ulama's immediate cause for participation in the Revolution was not to gain economic or professional advantages, but to defend and reinforce their position in civil society and to limit the power of state. As such, in contrast to Gurr's theory, their movement from the very beginning was a political one. But they, like the bazaris, adopted the political idea of constitutionalism in order to adjust their position to a new society undergoing modern changes. The third group, the intellectuals, were mainly educated in Europe and influenced by liberal ideas generated by Western social movements, in particular the French Revolution. This was a small group who, from the very beginning of the Movement, had political intentions and would influence a liberal change of the political system.

The Constitutional Revolution of Iran did not began with a script or blueprint for action. The constitutionalism of the revolutionaries was constructed during the long period of events and challenges which, in 1909, made the victory of the Revolution possible. In other words, the Constitutional Revolution was an outcome of a social movement against foreign intervention and the tyrannical rulers of the Qajars. Brecher pointed out 'revolutionary movements rarely begin with a revolutionary intention; this only develops in the course of the struggle itself' (Brecher, 1972, p. 240). Also in the case of the Constitutional Revolution, the process of revolution led to the adoption of Constitutionalism just a few months before the first victory of the Revolution in August 1906. The main intellectual challenge by which a new model of constitution–under the supervision of the ulama–occurred during the second phase of the revolutionary process in 1906-1909. The leaders of the movement, the ulama, adopted the modern idea of constitutionalism as the only possible alternative to tyrannical monarchy because they lacked an alternative. During the first and second Majlis, they tried to modify the liberal constitution and establish control over it. For them, constitutionalism and the establishment of Majlis would be an appropriate means through which to limit state power. But because the constitution of new laws entailed introducing secular laws that could weaken the position of the ulama as interpreters of Shari'a, the ulama established their supremacy over the constitutive Majlis.

Meanwhile, the ideological framework of the Constitutional Revolution was, more or less, dominated by Constitutionalism as the main conviction of all the revolutionary groups. The ideological convictions of different groups participating in the Islamic Revolution were differentiated and heterogeneous. The ideological arena consisted of a mosaic of different ideologies and political convictions. Only the ideological differences among the socialist/communist groups extended from armed forces of Marxist Leninist Fadaiyan-e khalq, through Maoist groups, such as Peykar-e khalq, to the Russophile and 'parliamentarian' Tudeh Party. In between the communists and the radical ulama, there were different political ideologies and organizations. One of the most important ones was Mojahedin-e khalq, who had a different religio-Marxist blueprint for revolution. There were also other groups, as already mentioned, such as Liberals and nationalists, who had other scripts for the revolution.

The most important vision presented by the radical clergy was Khomeini's theory of *velayat-e faqih*. He presented a new model of state consisting of *fuqaha* (Islamic jurisprudents). He called it *Hukomat-e Islami* (Islamic governance). *Hukomat-e Islami* was not originally compatible with the modern forms of political systems, such as republicanism. But, through the process of the Revolution and as a result of negotiations and coalitions, this model became compatible with the modern institutions of political rulership, such as parliament, election, constitution, and so forth. Accordingly, if there is something that can be called the blueprint of the Islamic revolution, it is crystallized in the famous slogan of the demonstrations: *Esteqlal, Azadi, Jomhuri-ye eslami* (Independence, Freedom, The Islamic Republic).

The *fifth* dimension of comparison is the state. In the time of the Constitutional Revolution, the state was a monarchical dictatorship. Mozaffaredin Shah, who was forced to sign the decree of constitutionalism in August 1906, and his son and successor, Muhammad Ali Shah, were absolutist kings who based their reign on the 'concentrated means of coercion' in their hands. Muhammad Ali Shah used all the means of coercion he could mobilize in order to defeat the revolutionaries. In addition to the military forces of Cossacks led by the Russians, he made alliances with several tribes against revolutionaries.

The structural characteristics of the reign of Muhammad Reza Shah were also based on monarchical dictatorship. A major difference was the use of modern institutions for 'concentration of the means of coercion' by the last Shah. Although structurally the Shah's state had a facade of modern political institutions, such as parliament, constitution, election, and political party(ies), it was far from democratic. The Shah based his power on the three main coercive groups: the army, the police, and the security police, SAVAK. The regime began to strengthen its grip on all kinds of political activity in the period following the 1973 rise in oil prices. The Shah dissolved the system of governmental parties, the *Iran novin* party and the *Mardom* party, and created a one party system, based on a new party *Rastakhiz* (resurrection). The Shah's regime began registering people in the new party. Registration was, in many cases, a comic exhibition. Mass registration took place in factories, schools, trade unions, public sector, and many other working places. Many of these registrations were considered by the people as 'an insurance against unexpected accidents'.

The 'unexpected accidents' were the problems that could be created by SAVAK for those who were not members of the new party.

In 1974, SAVAK began a hard attack against political organizations, such as *Fadaiyan* and Mojahedin. Many of their members were killed during confrontations with SAVAK and others were tortured to death in SAVAK centers. Some of their imprisoned members who were already sentenced were simply executed by SAVAK. The regime's offensive was not limited to the opposition, but extended against all deviation from the state's policy and plans. As mentioned earlier, through the establishment of *otaq-e asnaf*, the regime attacked small shopkeepers for the rise of prices. A major attack of the regime was concentrated on the 'dispossessed'. Their houses in the 'outer zone' of the major cities were attacked by municipal authorities with heavy machines. The Shah's attempt to strengthen his grip on the political arena continued until political changes in the USA that led to American government's pressure on the Shah for the democratization of the political atmosphere of Iran.[238]

The *sixth* dimension of comparison is the situation of the army in the Constitutional and Islamic Revolutions. As mentioned earlier, the military power of the Qajars were mainly tribal. Their attempts to create a regular army, such as Nezam-e jadid of Abbas Mirza, were unsuccessful. At the time of the Constitutional Revolution, the regular army was very weak and based mainly on the Cossack divisions led by Russian officers. During its first phase, the Revolution did not defeat the limited military power when the decree of the constitution was issued by Muzaffar al-Din Shah in 1906. But, during the civil war of June 1908 to July 1909 military forces were faced by armed revolutionaries and as a result of a long and bloody confrontation, they were defeated. In many cases, the state used tribesmen as its counter-revolutionary military forces.

On the eve of the Islamic Revolution, the Iranian army was the world's sixth largest army and a major stabilizing factor not only within Iran, but also in the entire region. As mentioned earlier, the modern Iranian army was not designed for confrontation with the urban people. It was equipped with modern weapons to defend the country against foreign enemies. The position of the army was very important for the outcome of the Revolution. Although some desertion occurred among the conscripts at the end of 1978, the army remained largely intact, a fact of which the opposition was well aware, as was Khomeini (Arjomand, 1988, p. 121). Accordingly, the aim of the leaders of the Revolution was not to defeat the well equipped and strong army, but to win over several key generals of the army and make an agreement with them. They wanted to neutralize the army not to confront or defeat it.

11 Conceptual Reflections: Islamic Civil Society, Modernization, Revolution

Civil Society and the Notion of *Umma*

Ernest Gellner (1994) claims that civil society cannot occur in Muslim communities because the unique and exclusive sacralization of one faith makes pluralism impossible (1994, p. 195).There are certain problems with this proposition. He mixes the religious notion of *umma*, which is the concept of a religious community in relation to its Messenger, namely the Prophet, with the peoples residing in different Muslim countries. For him the citizens of Egypt, Iran, and Iraq are just different bits and pieces of the *umma*. Using the notion of *umma* as a homogeneous phenomena existing all over the 'Muslim world' is to neglect the reality of different cultural and institutional arrangements in the various 'Muslim' societies. He does not take into account in his discussion the socio-cultural and even economic diversities in different Muslim countries. The notion of *umma* was used by Muhammad to unify Arab tribes. But over the centuries after Muhammad's death, this notion became subject to re-interpretation and change. Even shortly after Muhammad's death and in the context of the military success of Muslim Arabs, the Muslims of other occupied countries, such as Iran, were not treated equally with Arabs and were 'second class' Muslims. Iranian society after the establishment of the Safavids (1501) and Shi'itization of Iran left the Arabic and Turkish *umma*–if such an expression can be used. Secondly, Gellner's definition of the whole Muslim community as the same *umma* leads him to misunderstand contemporary social movements. He reduces social movements in Muslim countries, such as 'fundamentalism', to merely 'nationalistic' movements without any concern about social forces and power balances in these countries. Here again the territorial and particular differences in

Muslim countries are neglected. He reduces the notion of culture to an abstract religious belief that determines socio-political structure of the 'Muslim world'. In his argument, the Muslim world is a simple sum of *Muslim men* and *similar* entities of *umma*. The social adoption of Islam and the particular social development and historical events that led to the appearance of a mosaic of institutional and organizational arrangements in different countries is missing in his abstract generalizations.

Civil society, according to Gellner, is a result of the historical appearance of 'modular man' who is engaged in free economic and political activities. His historical analysis exhibits a 'timeless' tableau on which all economic and political developments exist simultaneously. He claims that: 'the modularity of modern man was probably a pre-condition of the industrial miracle, and it is certainly a pre-condition of Civil Society'. (Gellner, 1994, p. 103). The modularity of man, which he translates also as individualism, was a pre-condition of the modern society. According to him, industrialism and the market economy are the result of the existence of 'modular man'. Politically, the 'modular man' 'who can freely choose a political party' is a pre-condition for democracy. Gellner's interpretation of civil society is decontextualized and leads him to ignore, among other things, the chronological order of the appearance of market economy and political democracy. The European modern history confirms the non-asymmetrical development of the market economy and political democracy. The system of market economy was developed long before the change in political institutions and structures. Long before the appearance of enfranchised citizens, the West European economy was characterized by developed markets. It is noteworthy that, as late as 1927, England did not have equal franchise which included the whole people. 'In fact, it was not until the Fourth Reform Act of 1918 that all adult males were given the vote, and universal suffrage had to wait until 1928'. (Ball, 1981, p. 17). Apparently, the economic 'modular man' preceded the political 'modular man'. This suggests that the 'modular man' is a theoretical construction detached from a socio-cultural and historical context. The 'modular man', however, was not an abstract entity prior to the establishment of new economic and political institutions. It was actually a dialectical relationship between individuals and groups engaged in historical events which led to creation of both modern institutions and modern man. Hence, existing of 'modular man' is not a pre-condition for democracy but a component of its many-sided reality. For example, one cannot say that in Germany, during the 1920s and 1930s, the 'modular man' disappeared and was replaced in the form of collectivistic nazism.

Gellner defines civil society not in terms of its countervailing social institutions, but through the extent of state power. He writes: '[Civil Society] refers to a total society within which the non-political institutions are not dominated by the political ones, and do not stifle individuals either'. (Gellner, 1994, p. 193). His definition of civil society is based on individualism, neglecting the dialectical relationship between state and political and non-political institutions which balance their field of influence and authority. Institutionalization of the relationship between the bazaar and the ulama in Iran, which established the leading position of the ulama in civil society, created a strong civil center of authority which, during a long period of Iranian history, influenced and balanced state authority.

In contrast to the views of some scholars, the notion of civil society is not a solely Western term. It actually appeared at the very beginning of the establishment of the Islamic political order. 'It is interesting to note that the first Islamic community was referred to as *al-mujtama' al-madani* (civil society), with 'civil' here indicating the establishment of the city that was composed of Muslim segments allied on tribal and geographic lines, as well as Jews and others who were allied on similar lines. The social structure reflected the diverse power of the society that were accepted by the Prophet'. (Moussalli, 1995, p. 83). This points up that the term civil society was not exclusively Western, although the definitions and meanings certainly varied. Islamic civil society was based on diversity. Pluralism in terms of religion and lifestyles was accepted. Moussalli (1995, p. 83) goes even further and mentions Islamic constitutions where each tribes or religious segment was given the right constitutionally to conduct its affairs.

Gellner's argument against the concept of an Islamic civil society is dubious in the face of historical facts of Iranian society, but also the Arab world's. Neither in the Arab world nor in Iran was there ever a society consisting of a unified body called *umma*. The Islamic societies consisted of different ethnic, religious, and tribal groups who created a mosaic of diversity and pluralism. The ulama was a distinct and important group of civil society not only in Shi'ite Iran but also in the Arab world. Moussalli emphasizes the role of the ulama in civil society of Arab world and points out:

> Producing legal opinions to resolve new or controversial issues was not the prerogative of the state, but that of the private scholars who themselves were forming a tremendously powerful body in civil society and were organized into legal schools and doctrinal trends. Because their legitimacy was grounded in civil society and not in formal governmental institutions, the influence of the ulama was moral and therefore beyond the coercive power of the state (Moussalli, 1995, p. 84).

As we see, the aspect of power of the Sunni ulama in the Arab world stressed by Moussalli and other scholars is largely based on the ulama's religious position and not much on their social relationship with other segments of civil society, and the most important, not on the institutionalization of such relationships. In the Sunni world, because of the closer connections between the Sunni ulama and the state, they were apparently not able to establish the same leadership role in civil society as the ulama of Iran. As Ibrahim (1995, p. 31) puts it, the ulama were one of the influential groups in Islamic civil society. Other leaders, elders, and notables of the traditional formation also performed several functions in the overall governance of pre-modern Arab society. In Shi'ite Iran, the ulama through their historical interconnections with communities and social institutions beyond the influence of state, created a substantial civil authority countervailing state power. In Shi'ite Iran, the ulama could not, however–or did not want to–develop a structure comparable to that of the church in the West, but they succeeded in developing closer connections to the civil institutions and to gain a prominent position in civil society. They succeeded, through their functions as *marja'*, Mujtahid, vicegerents of the Hidden Imam, Islamic jurists, marriage managers, tax collectors, collectors of *sahm-e Imam* (the share of Imam), living among peoples, and so forth, to became a central urban group in civil society. Moreover, the ulama, both in the Sunni and Shi'ite communities, were the leaders of social uprisings against the state. As Mardin (1995, p. 287) points out concerning the characteristics of Sunni communities:

> It is true that the ulama were often leaders of populist outbreaks against the unjust ruler. In that sense they constituted a structural counterpoise to the political hegemony. Elsewhere I have described this role of the ulama as a possible equivalent, equilibrating forces similar to those created by Western civil society.

In sum, neither the concept nor the function of civil society as a complex of social institutions and communities countervailing the state is alien to the Muslim world.

One important group in Iranian traditional civil society were tribes (Arjomand, 1988). They have, until modern times (until the 1920s), always participated in political struggles. As mentioned earlier, the historical role of the tribes in Iranian society–especially their significance for political changes–cannot be ignored. The tribes played a particularly prominent role in the Constitutional Revolution. Some tribes, such as Bakhtiyaris of the central, and Turkish tribes of north eastern Iran, were engaged in the revolutionary and counter-revolutionary struggles of 1906-1909. There is, however, not much data about the connections of the tribes with other parts of Iranian civil society, in particular with the bazaris and the ulama. In some cases, the ulama of Isfahan had significant connections with some tribes of that area, such as Bakhtiyaris, who played a significant role in the Constitutional Revolution on the side of the revolution. But some other tribes, such as some Kurdish and Turkish tribes, supported the counter-revolutionary state in that revolution.[239] Because this work focuses largely on the Iranian urban community and institutions, the tribes have not been a focus of analysis.[240]

As a result of state modernization programs, the institutions and boundaries of the traditional civil society of Iran successively changed and lost some significance as a countervailing power to the state. New institutions and groups, which were created as a consequence of the Constitutional Revolution and Reza Shah's authoritative modernization, new boundaries and alliances were established which came to be the cornerstone of the emerging modern civil society of Iran. It flourished in the democratic period of 1941-1953, and showed its significance in the uprising of June, 1963, and the Islamic Revolution of 1977-79. Many groups, both traditional occupational groups, modern middle ones, and the marginals, participated in the Islamic Revolution of Iran. They had apparently different intentions and desires for participating in a change process. While the modern middle occupational groups participated to restore and reinforce the modern civil society through eliminating dictatorship, the middle traditional occupational groups wanted to eliminate a socio-economic and cultural process by which the Shah threatened their whole existence. Finally, the radical clergy aimed to establish a new order, not simply to restore a previous one.

Modernization of Traditional Politics

Among the structural properties that influence revolutionary processes and outcomes are the pre-revolutionary traditions of political challenge. The history of political challenge in a society initially determines those means that the leaders of a revolution use in a struggle against the old regime. The mobilization of people for collective action is more effective when the leaders use traditional means that are already familiar in civil society. In the Constitutional Revolution of 1905-1909, for instance, the leaders used three traditional means of influencing and challenging the state authority, namely closing bazaars; using *manbars* (pulpit) and taking *bast* (taking refuge in holly shrines or home of Mujtahids). But, during the Revolution, some of these institutions were transformed to new forms with new characteristics. For example, when the ulama, in demonstrating their objections to state politics, left Tehran and moved to Qum, many bazaris took refuge in the English Embassy. Taking refuge in foreign embassies and companies then became a new means of struggling for state power.

After the Constitutional Revolution of Iran, the country had experienced crucial socio-economic and political changes that created new conditions for political challenge. As a result of social differentiation and political changes, new political groups appeared in the political arena of Iran. The constitutionalism and parliamentarism that was created by the Constitutional Revolution led to the institutionalization of a new political culture in which the new middle occupational groups played a crucial role. The political groups of the new middle occupational groups, i.e. leftists and liberals, dominated the democratic period of 1940s. One of the main political groups of that time was the National Front under the leadership of its charismatic leader, Muhammad Mosaddeq. This group's demands for the nationalization of the oil industries resulted in the premiership of Mosaddeq in May 1951. From 1944 to 1953, after the withdrawal of the prominent ulama from the political arena, the liberals, through the leadership of Mosaddeq, became the champions of nationalism in Iran. They gained broad support in Iranian civil society, and even from the traditional supporters of the ulama, the bazaris. The democratic and social challenge of the liberals during the 1940s created a tradition of legal challenge for seizing power. Although the dictatorship of the Shah left no room for democratic challenge, the liberals remained loyal to legal means of political challenge. Furthermore, the *coup d'état* of 1953 convinced them of their constitutional right to rule. The NF and later the LMI, as well, considered themselves the legal government of Iran which was confined to civil society.

Accordingly, constitutionalism created modern political methods and processes. Even the extra-parliamentary methods that had been used to support Mosaddeq in 1952, when he was forced to resign as a way of confrontation with the Shah, suggest the crucial change and decline of the traditional means of political struggle. The institution of *bast* completely disappeared, and, in the absence of the ulama, the *manbars* were apoliticized. Two new institutions of struggle, demonstrations and strikes were born. Even elections were used to support the national camp of National Front against the Shah and his candidates. The political sphere of Iranian society was changed dramatically through the appearance of new political groups and institutions.

After the death of Ayatollah Borujerdi and the appearance of Ayatollah Khomeini and other radical clergy in the political arena, political opposition to the Shah took on a new character. In the first collective action of the radical clergy after the Constitutional Revolution, they used their traditional means, the *manbars*, against the Shah. The religious uprising of 1963 not only exhibited the revitalization of clerical opposition to the state, but also the shortcomings of the merely religious illegitimation of the Shah. The ideological changes in position by the radical clergy after the events of 1963 make it evident that they could not continue to challenge the modern state of the Shah with only traditional means and justifications. For example, Khomeini, who opposed the women's franchise in 1963, encouraged them to participate in the Islamic Revolution, and declared the necessity of their participation in the elections of the Islamic Republic. At the opening stage of the Islamic Revolution, the radical clergy not only used modern means of mobilizing the people, such as demonstrations, strikes, and mass media, but also advocated the establishment of a Constitutive Assembly, free elections, republicanism, establishment of a modern state, public franchise, and political associations.

The modern changes in the traditional ideologies and orientations of the ulama began with the Constitutional Revolution, during which the ulama adopted constitutionalism as a means to retain leadership of civil society. In the early 1960s, after the defeat of the nationalist movement of 1940s and early 1950s, the clergy reappeared in the political arena and tried to regain their formerly prominent position as leaders of civil society. But, in a much more differentiated society than that of 1905, modern changes, such as the appearance of new social groups, modern ideologies, and new political traditions and groups, made them unable to mobilize civil society against the Shah. Furthermore, the traditional standing of Ayatollah Khomeini, the leader of the uprising of 1963,[241] not only indicated the impropriety of such ideas in the modern civil society of Iran, but also made the radical clergy aware of the need for ideological changes. The revolutionary ideological changes could not be brought about by other groups of clergy who were apolitical and did not participate in the struggles against the Shah. The histories of great revolutions suggest that the revolutionary elites who formulate revolutionary ideologies and demand replacement of the old regimes are those who have been denied access to power and influence. As Goldstone points out:

> In the English Revolution, it was lay preachers–disdained by the king and the Arminian leaders of the Anglican Church, but believing themselves educationally equal and morally superior to the regular clergy–who articulated the vision of a Puritan commonwealth. In the French Revolution, as Darnton has shown, the fiercest attack on the status of nobles came not from the leaders of the high Enlightenment (who were largely royalists) but rather from the lower ranks of journalists and provincial lawyers, men whose status as commoners and modest incomes limited them to secondary roles in the ancient regime (Goldstone, 1991, p. 415).

But not every political group that is excluded from or has limited access to power and influence can formulate revolutionary ideologies against the state. The elites who formulate revolutionary ideologies are those who already have legitimacy in civil society. Furthermore, they must be able to convince the people that the new ideology is the only reasonable alternative to the existence of the old regime and that it will create a better society. These two factors are necessary for an ideology to become revolutionary and dominant. But it does not mean that a revolutionary ideology is already understood by those who begin a revolutionary movement. The ideologies of revolutions become modified and changed through the process of revolution during which its leaders are forced to make alliances and adjust themselves to contingent events. Khomeini's *velayat-e faqih*, as the ideological framework for the Islamic Revolution, was changed in this way. The claim of the radical clergy for abolishing the monarchy was initially combined with creating an 'Islamic Governance', state in which the *fuqaha* (Islamic jurisprudents) were the only legitimate rulers. But the revolutionary process forced the radical clergy to share with the liberals the concept and institutional arrangements of the Islamic state.

The Shah wanted to restructure Iranian society according to his own blueprint. In 1963, he implemented a reform program, called the White revolution, intending to transform traditional Iran into a modern society in accordance with Western patterns. He succeeded in changing the traditional society of Iran, but not according to his plan. He created new social groups, but not the ones he wanted to create. He created modern cities, but not the ones he wanted to create. Instead, he created cities entailing shanty towns, shortage of water and electricity, traffic, and unemployment. He created modern universities intending to produce a skilled labor force for industries and service sectors, but he simultaneously created a center of political opposition and challenge. The unintended consequences of the Shah's 'revolutionary' blueprint were far too complicated to be 'planned' away. The reform programs reinforced many aspects of civil society of Iran. The powerful new urban groups, the 'dispossessed', appeared, and other modern groups, such as the modern middle occupational groups and industrial workers, grew in size and significance. The new groups were denied channels of influence on state decision-making. If the modern middle occupational groups and the industrial workers were at least accepted socially, the very existence of the 'dispossessed' was subjectively denied and objectively challenged. The beginning of the Islamic Revolution changed the very basis of their confrontation with the state. Their defensive struggle for permission to stay in the 'outer zones' of the cities and shanty towns transformed into an offensive revolutionary action for gaining acceptance. Through the Islamic Revolution they became a significant part of Iranian urban society.

At the same time, the modern middle occupational groups, which the regime continually excluded from the political arena, had exhibited their desire for political participation through the events of the 1940s and early 1960s. In the Islamic Revolution, they also participated in demonstrations against the Shah to bring about democratic changes which could influence the state and its decision-making. They did not initially support the radical clergy's *Hukomat-e eslami* (Islamic governance) as an alternative to the old regime. Their mass participation in the demonstrations and protests appeared after the compromise between Khomeini and the liberals that led to appointment of Mehdi Bazargan, the leader of the LMI, as the 'lawful prime minister of Iran'.

Thus, the Islamic Revolution of Iran (1977-79) was an uprising of civil society against an autocratic state implementing crucial and rapid changes. It was not a Revolution of one 'class' against another, but a social Revolution of several social and political groups who were denied access to the state, against social groups who had access to state power. In contrast to the 'breakdown' theories, such as that of Goldstone (1991), the Revolution did not began with state breakdown. State breakdown was the result of the revolutionary process of 1977-79.

Religion and Revolution

Historically, many of the Shi'ite ulama were oriented to play a key role in political power. Therefore, not surprisingly, Iran's history provides many examples of religious revolt against governments. But the Shi'ites failed earlier for three main reasons:

1. They had never been the only accepted or legitimate alternative to state power.
2. Modern Iran was a heterogeneous and fragmented society, which made it difficult for the clergy to mobilize substantial support, thus reinforcing their relative marginality and political weakness.
3. Earlier Shi'ite revolts lacked a vision of an alternative socio-political order. In contrast to earlier engagements, the Islamic Revolution had one person, Khomeini, who provided this new vision. Moreover, the vision involved the mobilization of masses of people at a time when conditions for such mobilization were right.

Nevertheless, in the history of modern Iran, both nationalism and Marxism failed over time as strong competitors against radical religious ideologies. Many leftist political groups and parties, such as the Tudeh Party, disqualified themselves as an alternative to the regime through their pro-Soviet policies and anti-religious orientation. Although the nationalists were weakened in Iran under the Shah's reign, they were active in the revolution and served as leaders for some intellectual and the modern middle occupational groups. During the revolutionary process, the ulama and, particularly, Khomeini took upon themselves the role of representing the *mostaz'afin* (dispossessed). Since the notion of *mostaz'afin* had no particular definition, it was crystallized in heterogeneous social groups of urban poor, namely the marginals or 'dispossessed'. Khomeini's radical will to power, which he formulated as 'No compromises, the Shah must go', was the most relevant and understandable slogan for the marginals and their hope for a better future.

Consequently, the clergy's success in taking political power in Iran depended on a very large and non-integrated group whose existence was a direct result of the uneven development of Iran's economy and society (cf. Arjomand, 1988, pp. 197-202). This group struggled with the Shah's army in the streets during the early phase of the revolutionary process. Later, they came to form the body of Revolutionary Committees and Guards (*Komiteh ha va Pasdaran-e enqelab*). Thus, paradoxically, the Shah's *uneven modernization set the stage for the clerical seizure of state power, a success that had eluded them in earlier periods* (and, in particular, the revolutionary process at the turn of the century). They failed earlier in part because they lacked sufficiently powerful social support and the conditions for popular politics. In the 1977-1979 Revolution of Iran, they mobilized sufficient social support to gain power and to institutionalize a new regime, in the context of a neutralized armed forces. They succeeded, therefore, in making a religious revolution in a century characterized by increasing secularization of societies (at least in a certain sense; see Burns (1994), Bellah (1980), and others on secular religion). There are several key defining features of the Islamic Revolution, namely:

(1) The clergy had a history of involvement in politics. Earlier, for example in the Tobacco Movement of 1892 and the Constitutional Revolution of 1905-09, politics was largely elite politics. What was particularly noteworthy about the clergy in the Islamic Revolution (especially the radical clergy with Khomeini) was their orientation to and involvement in popular politics–their readiness and capability to mobilize masses and to lead the process of attempting to reconstruct society through political means (Eisenstadt, 1994). This was a result of Khomeini's theory of *velayat-e faqih* by which seizing the entire political power by the Shi'ite ulama was legitimated.

(2) The clergy, particularly the radicals, provided *an original vision of a new society* at a time when the old order (and old visions) were collapsing. Their vision entailed a major successful innovation in our century, namely the linking of a religious view of society–society led by men of God and guided by the word of God–with a modern principle of popular based government and the reconstruction of society through political processes. In the context of the Islamic Revolutionary process,

there were few compelling alternative visions. For example, the nationalists and Western-oriented intellectuals, business leaders, and bureaucrats had a vision of a modern, largely secular Western society. This was, however, opposed by most of the clergy and was not a particularly attractive vision to large segments of the population who played an important role in the Islamic Revolution. The competition that the radical clergy faced was largely from the moderate clergy and liberal movements such as the NF and the LMI. Among other things, these groups aimed for one or another type of reform, and, at most, a constitutional monarchy. The secular movements, in particular the National Front, had some support in the military and bureaucratic groups. With the neutralization of the military, the game became one of popular politics, competition among groups for popular support, the mobilization of masses, especially in the revolutionary phase before the establishment and institutionalization of a set of political institutions.

Here, the radical clergy had an advantage–new social groups, the urban marginals, who were bearers of rural traditionalism and religiosity, but who had no voice, and were not organized, were not represented in political processes. They were genuinely outsiders to Iran's modernization and modern transformations. Leftist groups ignored them, concentrating on the 'working class' who were very limited in size and significance in the Iranian context (except for the oil workers). The nationalists and liberals also ignored them, in large part because their ideology and social interests oriented them elsewhere. In the end, *the clergy mobilized them–men as well as women*[242] *–and gave them a voice, a central, visible role in the politics of Iranian society. In turn, they became the key socio-political base of the radical clergy. Together, the radical clergy and the marginals/ migrants, along with the support of the middle occupational groups, constituted a force that won against other forces in the Islamic Revolution and carried through a particular (among several possible alternative futures) Islamic Revolution.*

(3) The military, in large part, stayed out, setting the stage for a more purely discursive and political process.[243] This opened the way for the clergy to play a key role. Violence was relatively limited,[244] especially in view of what could be envisioned to have happened if the military had split or had continued to be used by the Shah to further resist or block the revolutionary process. However, the radical clergy were prepared to use their revolutionary guards and violence to threaten or dominate opponents and to take full control. This was a part of the post-revolutionary process.

(4) Seizure of all political power had never been the aim of the ulama in traditional Iran. At the end of nineteenth, and in the beginning of twentieth centuries, the Shi'ite ulama participated in political movements against the state in order to reinforce their social position in the society. The ulama's participation in the Constitutional Revolution depended mainly on their social position in the traditional civil society of Iran, where the traditional Shi'ite theory of state was still applicable to the new changes. The modern notion of constitutionalism could be used by the ulama in order to reinforce their position in civil society and to limit state power.

In the Islamic Revolution, the radical clergy led by Khomeini envisioned the construction of a new social order by political means: mobilizing people, engaging in demonstrations and other political acts, and, ultimately, taking and using state power to realize their visions. This movement not only had a totalistic vision but operated with the principle that society can and should be reconstructed through political mobilization and state politics, and thus it demonstrates a characteristically modern orientation (Eisenstadt, 1994). By the 1970s, the clergy especially the 'radical clergy' with Khomeini, among others, were not only playing a key role in the opposition, but even propagated the modern idea of popular politics. This gave them the orientation, the conceptual frame, and strategic dispositions to develop political skills at mobilization and engagement in power politics. This also was a basis for them to pragmatically form alliances with liberal forces, grounded in part on their common acceptance of modern political discourse and political institutions, such as Parliament. But the radical modern idea of reconstituting society by political means– and a particular not fully modern order at that, a new Islamic society– would have remained purely a vision, a dream of a holy man in modern times, if it had not been for the religious army the 'dispossessed': available to be mobilized and led by clergy speaking a new discourse and exercising a revitalized authority.

Revolution as Process

Revolutions involve a rapid transformation of socio-political structures, institutions, and values according to a new ideological framework. Revolutions usually result from and through the social actions and interactions of major groups of a particular society. Although there are formal similarities between different revolutions, each revolution is bounded by the social context in which it occurs and has its own unique characteristics. The historical development of social structures, institutions, and values, create constraints and possibilities for collective acts and the occurrence of revolution.

Revolution as a Medium for Structural Transformation

Skocpol, in her book *States and Social Revolutions*, explores structural causes of revolutions. She defines revolution as 'rapid, basic transformations of a society's state and class structures /.../ accompanied and in part carried through by class-based revolts from below'. (Skocpol, 1979, p. 4). Skocpol develops a notion of revolution related to the Marxian concept of revolution, namely social revolution: 'revolts from below' which lead to 'basic transformations of a society's state and class structures'. She uses the French, Russian, and Chinese revolutions as case studies.

Skocpol (1979) considers revolutions a medium for the transformation of one structural order into another. What is missing in such an analysis are agents and the revolutionary process. Revolutions as social actions of several groups with different intentions–as well as its sociocultural context–becomes a highly deliberate and conscious activity through which people destroy the old order and create *a new one*. Hence, it seems that the new order is already known by revolutionaries prior to and at the beginning of the revolution. In such an analysis the creative process of revolutions is lost. As Sewell (1995) points out, some sociologists of revolution tend to miss the revolutionary quality of revolutions. What makes revolutions revolutionary is that they transform both antecedent conditions and the way that consequences follow from these conditions.

Skocpol's structuralist theory of revolution as a 'basic transformation of a society's state and class structure' provides a deterministic framework of structural change with revolution as its medium. She tends to ignore the fact that revolution is a creative process which not only changes the old structures, but also creates new ones. It is not only that pre-existing structural ruptures affect the change and generation of new structures, *but the process of revolution itself is a creative force that alters the pre-revolutionary conditions of change*. Skocpol's interpretation of revolution as a medium for transforming class structure seems to capture some aspects of Marxian structural determinism. Since the very basis of revolutions are revolts and pressure 'from below'–in the case of the modern revolutions, peasants and workers–revolutions must lead to change in the structure of social classes. According to this tradition, some Marxist scholars considered the Shah's land reform in 1963 a result of the Constitutional Revolution (1905-1909).[245] Even Skocpol's later argument about the Islamic Revolution of Iran exhibits the same neglect of the dynamics of the revolutionary process. She recognizes the uniqueness of the Islamic Revolution and emphasizes the role of ideas and culture in shaping political action (Skocpol, 1982, p. 268). She mentions some structural properties of pre-revolutionary Iranian society, such as the interconnection of the traditional centers of urban communal life, the bazaris, and the clergy, who were the leaders of the bazaars (Skocpol, 1982, p. 271). The Shah's efforts to destroy the traditional spheres of society, such as the bazaars and the authority of the clergy, revitalized the connections between these two groups. The clergy, according to Skocpol could claim, 'as well or better than the monarch, to represent authentically the will of the Hidden Imam' and provided leadership, social networks, and religious symbols that could be used in the mobilization against the Shah (Skocpol, 1982, p. 273).

Here Skocpol appears to be open to a process approach with active, creative agents. However, she stresses (1979, p. 18) and stresses again (1994, p. 9) her commitment to a structural and non-voluntarist approach and her opposition to voluntarist, or purposive, approaches:

> The great heroes and villains of other accounts–the bourgeoisie and the proletariat, the Jacobins, Bolsheviks, and Maoists–fond themselves in my accounts downplayed or thoroughly 'situated' in institutional and conflictual circumstances. Encompassing cultures and ideologies–such as the Enlightenment, Marxism-Leninism, or Confucianism–that bore so much explanatory weight for other scholars, became much less important for me. I treated revolutionary leaderships not as the master planners of revolutionary crises or outcomes, but as 'marginal elites' /.../. My structuralism thoroughly deromanticized–and to some degree devillainized– revolutions. Perhaps in part for this reason, that structuralism was the most disturbing part of my theoretical advocacy for a very wide range of scholars, people otherwise holding many different views and values about revolutions /.../.
>
> /.../ While disagreeing sharply with each other, both rational-choice and culturalist scholars believe that they have more voluntarist approaches than I do to explaining social revolutions. It remains to be seen, however,

whether the kind of structuralism I advocated in 1979 needs to be abandoned, modified, or supplemented to achieve theoretical advances in our explanations of revolutions, past and present (Skocpol, 1994, pp. 9-10).

Again, what Skocpol neglects is the process of revolution as a dialectical and creative action involving interaction between people, one that has *unintended consequences*. During the Islamic Revolution, for instance, the vicegerency of the Hidden Imam by the clergy was not explicitly political propaganda. Khomeini's theory of *velayat-e faqih* was a vision of a group of clergy, not whole groups participating in the Revolution.

According to Khomeini's theory, the proper form of governance in the Muslim community is *hukomat-e eslami* (Islamic governance). Although the radical clergy tried to introduce this concept as the slogan of the Revolution, they were forced to change the word *hukomat* (governance based on religious decrees) to *jumhori* (republic), as a result of the process of challenge and alliance-making. The contingencies of the events of the Islamic Revolution induced the ulama to accept and propound republicanism, which they had rejected fifty years earlier as un-Islamic. *Hukomat* was not the only claim of the clergy that was changed by the transformative revolutionary dynamic. Acceptance of the *majlis-e moassesan* (consultative assembly) as the supreme executive organ for deciding the nature and form of the new regime after the victory of the Revolution was another important change made in response to the events of the revolutionary process. Other groups participating in the Revolution, such as the LMI and the NF, also changed their initial claim and strategies of participation in the Revolution.

The Revolutionary process had its own logic. Radicalization of the movement by the entrance of 'dispossessed' in the arena of political challenge changed the moderate opposition of the NF and the LMI against the Shah and forced them to accept a rapid and more radical revolutionary change. As the leader of the LMI and the first prime minister of the Islamic Republic of Iran, Mehdi Bazargan, said in a TV interview shortly after the Revolution: 'We wanted rain but received inundation'.

Revolutions as a Creative Process

Revolution is not then a simple medium for transforming one social order to another irrespective of the interaction of revolutionary and counter-revolutionary forces, negotiations, and unintended consequences of mass actions. But criticizing an overemphasis on structure does not mean that structure is not important in revolutionary transformations. As Parsa mentions: 'the target of collective action, and consequently the nature of social conflict, is largely conditioned by social structure and /.../ the capacity of disadvantaged groups and classes for collective action' (Parsa, 1989, p. 14). But this does not mean that the people choose the target of revolution at the beginning of the movement. *The target of revolution is developed and reconstructed during the revolutionary process*. Revolution, as I see it, is not the 'collective choice' of people who decide to change a certain socio-political system into another, as Michael Taylor (1988) proposes from a rational choice perspective. It is a result of a number of more or less independent events or contingencies that begin long before the occurrence of the revolution. The revolutionary events compose a process of interaction between different revolutionary groups, and partly between these groups and counter-revolutionary forces. Therefore, no group that begins a revolution has a defining or determining idea about its ultimate outcome. The process of revolution involves different social agents whose interaction–together with the reaction of counter-revolutionary forces– determine its outcome. *It is not a 'choice', but rather a development that occurs among different social groups that polarizes the whole society and forces other groups to take part in it*. Yet, the revolutionary process is often a complex of events by which one group, alliance, or charismatic leader, may, over time, establish its hegemony over the revolutionary forces. Which group succeeds in establishing its hegemony over the revolutionary forces depends on the extent of social support it gains during the process of the revolution. The revolutionary support that the radical clergy received from the 'dispossessed' in the Islamic Revolution of 1977-79 was of great importance for establishing their hegemony over other political groups.

Accordingly, many of the initial attitudes and plans change through the contingent events of revolutionary process. Even early changes that resulted from compromises based on initial power balances between different revolutionary groups are modified. In both the Constitutional and the Islamic Revolution of Iran, the ideological frameworks that became the dominant guidelines of the Revolutions were constructed through the revolutionary processes. The events that came to be called the Constitutional Revolution began as a claim for a new chief of customs. Constitutionalism developed through the dialectical process of the Revolution. Cobban

(1968) points out the mythical aspects of the French Revolution and questioned the very bourgeois basis of that Revolution. The Constitutional Revolution of Iran was not a bourgeois revolution fitting an evolutionist understanding of history.[246] There are different ways to see and understand the historical events. 'History, said Napoleon, is a myth men agree to believe' (Cobban 1968, p. 93). The historians of the Constitutional Revolution of Iran, such as Kasravi (1951) Malekzadeh (1949), Kermani, 1951), and Adamiyyat (1976), provided their own interpretations of the Revolution. Kasravi and Kermani, for instance, believed that the religious leaders of the Revolution were, from the beginning of the movement, constitutionalists who concealed their intentions (Kasravi, 1951, p. 49). But later, Kasravi mentions that the leaders of the Revolution 'did not know the meaning of constitutionalism, as they came to know later, and did not want the constitutionalism, as it was in Europe'. (Kasravi, 1951, p. 259). The Constitutional Revolution of Iran was a result of a movement that began with the demand to change the chief of customs, turned into a demand for establishing *adalatkhana* (house of justice), and developed into a demand for establishing the parliament and constitutionalism.

The Islamic Revolution was also a revolution that began with different groups making claims that went through crucial changes through a series of challenges and alliances. The social revolution of Iran started with the 'dispossessed' seriously confronting municipal authorities in the shanty towns. Politically, it was started by two different groups, the intellectuals and the clergy. The intellectuals, who gathered in *shab-e she'r* (poem nights) meetings in the institute Goteh for instance and who, in 1977, claimed democratic reforms, began a *process* of illegitimizing of the Western political ties of the monarchy at the same time that it was under pressure from the American president, Carter, to introduce democratic changes. The clergy began the political revolt against the regime by demanding the return of Ayatollah Khomeini to Iran.

The intellectuals began their challenge against the dictatorship of the Shah with conventional means. Responding to signals from Carter's administration for democratic change, the intellectuals began an organized political struggle against some of the tyrannical functions of the regime, such as censorship and torture. In June 1977 'The Writers Association' was revived; in July, a 'group for Free Books and Free Thought' formed. To exert pressure on the Shah's regime and to articulate the process of *ijad-e faza-ye baz-e siyasi* (establishment of the open political sphere), the intellectuals continued to establish other associations. In the fall of 1977,

'The Iranian Committee for the Defense of Freedom and Human Rights', the 'Association of Iranian Lawyers', and the 'National Association of University Teachers' were formed. The political tactic of the intellectuals from the modern middle occupational groups was to 'challenge the Shah on his field'. Through the establishment of conventional democratic associations and organizations, the intellectuals wanted to make use of democratic means to struggle against the Shah. This group accepted the traditional rules of challenge against the Shah, which was a heritage from the political events of 1940s. The trend of accepting the 'democratic' rules for political challenge was even accepted within the jails and among the political prisoners. For example, the political prisoners of Tabriz who wrote letters to *komision-e shahanshahi* (Royal Commission) complaining about their trials and conditions reflected the attitudes of many leftists at that time.

Of course, the turn in the position of the leftists–both the modern Marxist groups and Mojahedin-e khalq–was a result of the process of their armed struggle against the Shah. Marxist Fadaiyan-e khalq, for instance, changed their tactic of armed struggle, which was influenced by the theory of the founders of the Organization of Fadaiyan-e khalq, Masoud Ahmadzadeh and Amir Parviz Poyan, who advocated 'armed struggle as both strategy and tactic' of the struggle, to a more moderate position espoused by Bijan Jazani. Further, as a result of the catastrophic attack of SAVAK on the Organization in 1976-77, in which many of the members were arrested or killed in armed confrontations, the very legitimacy of the strategy of the Organization was questioned by the jailed members. Mojahedin-e khalq did not have a better situation. The Organization was divided and the majority of members turned to adopt a Marxist ideology in 1977. This event is also called *coup d'état* of the Marxists individuals, led by Taqi Shahram, within the organization. Accordingly, Mojahedin as an organization was very weak and realistically out of the game.[247]

At the same time, the religious opposition to the Shah began its challenge by bloody demonstrations in Qum demanding the return of Khomeini from exile. From the very beginning of the unrest of the movement, they rejected the conventional, democratic means of political challenge against the Shah. Meanwhile, the representatives of the modern middle occupational groups attacked the government, and not the Shah. At the beginning of the movement, the radical clergy concentrated their attack on the Shah and monarchy. Both tactics–demonstrations and direct attack on the objective symbols of the Shah's regime, such as cinemas and liquor stores, and the simple formulation of the target of the movement, 'down with the Shah' and 'long live Khomeini'–were more easily understood by the poor people, in particular the 'dispossessed', than was the complicated and abstract political language of the intellectuals. Using the traditional link between the clergy and the bazaris, accompanied by skillful use of religious discourses, such as the events of martyrdom of the Third Imam in Karbala, the radical clergy established the early leadership over the movement. Seizing the leadership of the mass demonstrations of 1978, the radical clergy wrote and read declarations of such demonstrations. They, in a sense, appropriated the revolution from the secular intellectuals. Meanwhile the leftists were discussing the role of the 'working class', who were one of the last social groups to participate in the Revolution. The liberals discussed the establishment of a democratic political system, while the radical clergy tightened their grip over revolutionary events and developments.

The Role of the 'Dispossessed'

One of the most extraordinary events during Iran's revolutionary movement was the entrance of a radical mass, the 'dispossessed', who came to support the religious leadership of the movement. Neither the leftists nor the radical clergy anticipated this event. The 'dispossessed', as discussed earlier, had daily confrontations with municipal authorities. But, through joining political demonstrations, they found a means of pressuring the police and municipal authorities. During the process of the revolution, their 'illegal' houses were safe from attacks. They also found a sphere in which they could play a social role in a society that did not accept them as members. The participation of this group in the demonstrations, combined with the reinforcement of the position of the radical clergy, forced other social groups to accept the leadership of the radical clergy and to participate in the revolutionary events. The radicalization of the revolutionary movement by events such as the massacre of Black Friday in September 1978, changed the plans of many intellectuals who, through constituting democratic groups, were awaiting popular support of the main social groups such as the modern middle occupational groups and the industrial workers. Hence, the democratic process, together with the regime of the Shah, were at the point of collapse. For most advocates of democracy and liberalism, the choice was between standing against the Revolution or participating in it and trying to influence its development.

In addition to the entrance of the 'dispossessed' in the movement, many other contingent actions and developments generated events that made up the process of the Revolution and its outcome. Actually, at the initial phase of the movement, no person or group intended to establish a republic in Iran. Furthermore, no person or group wanted to compromise or share leadership with others. The outcome of the Revolution was a result of a chain of events that forced different groups to cooperate and make alliances. The Islamic Republic was one consequence of such compromises. The radical clergy, who, in many of their declarations of the demonstrations, formulated the claim for an Islamic government, were also forced to accept a Republican form of government. The role of the powerful army in political negotiations with both radical clergy and the liberal LMI was important for changing the position of radical clergy.

The participation of the 'dispossessed' in the Islamic Revolution has been the subject of some controversy. The doubts about their role played in the events between 1978 and 1979 take two forms, one theoretical and the other social. Some analyses of the Islamic Revolution, such as that of Misagh Parsa (1989), reject the role of the urban migrants. Using Tilly's theory of revolutions, he discusses the theoretical problem presented by the participation of the 'dispossessed' in the Revolution. Parsa argues:

> The theoretical problem with this analysis is that uprooted individuals rarely possess the necessary resources, solidarities, and organizations for mobilization and collective action. The very experience of being uprooted is likely to reduce their capacity for collective action by dissolving preexisting solidarity structures (Parsa, 1989, p.5).

For both Parsa and Tilly, the problem of the participation of the urban migrants in the Revolution does not center around the objective question of their participation, but rather a theoretical concern. To label the urban migrants as uprooted individuals is to impose a deterministic and functionalistic understanding of social change. The urban migrants who left their traditional social context and moved to the cities did not exist in a vacuum and outside of all social contexts. Individuals are 'knowledgeable' agents in Giddens' (1984) sense of the term. Through their knowledge of rules, individuals act in a given social context.[248] But, the knowledge of rules, if it is to be useful, must be generalizable and applicable under different social conditions. It makes up a schema to which individuals have access and can be applied across a wide range of circumstances.[249] The transposability of schemas is to say in other words, that they can be applied to a wide and not fully predictable range of cases outside the context in which they are initially learned (Sewell, 1992, p. 17). The 'uprooted' urban migrants do not remain uncontextual individuals and groups, but rather they use their already learned schema to 're-establish' in the new social context.[250] The word 'uprooted' seems unsuitable since it refers to a natural process of life and death of plants. 'The social context that compose the objective milieu of social group is not the same as physical space' (Bourdieu, 1977, p. 84). People can be separated from their original physical space, but, thanks to their original schema, re-create their new social space in another physical part of society. That is what Bourdieu calls the transposability of schemas. In the case of the 'dispossessed', it is a process of transformation of their schema and remobilization of resources in becoming an urban group.

Parsa's point about the incapacity of the 'dispossessed' for collective action because of the dissolution of 'preexisting solidarity structures' is unconvincing for two reasons. First, the solidaristic bonds with a social group *can* provide them means for collective action, but they can also function as barriers to collective action. During the history of collective action in Iran, we see no collective action by peasants, although they possessed 'preexisting solidarity structures'. But just the transformation– not the loss–of the traditional schema of this group, and their collision with new urban structural settings led to the development of a *mixed schema*, as a result of the reproduction of their new socio-economic context. Second, the history of revolutions reveals mass mobilization of the urban poor, who normally are outside much of the official economic system of the cities. The participation of the urban poor in revolutions has always entailed radicalization of the movement. This was the case in both the Russian and the French Revolutions. Cobban, for instance, discusses the role of the French 'urban poor' and points out that there was 'a period of intense rural over-population and under-employment, coupled with complaints of the flight of labor to the towns' prior to that country's Revolution (Cobban, 1964, p. 140). He also mentions the increase of begging among the urban poor. He notes some circumstances that did not differ much from the situation of the 'dispossessed' prior to the Islamic Revolution. He cites, 'that spirit of disorder, of independence, of roguery, of raping and theft, which infects the lowest class of the people. Parents /.../ train their children as beggars, the children become insensibly accustomed to idleness, and from that it is only one step to debauchery and crime' (Cobban, 1964, p. 136). In the revolutionary context the deviants give up their petty crimes and became agents of history.

But, participation of the urban poor in the revolutionary process does not mean that their collective action entails a conscious action to reach a well-defined goal. Here, the term 'mass mobilization' may be preferable to that of collective action because of the creative and transformative nature of a the revolutionary process, which modifies and, in some cases, changes the aim of the action. The word *mass* implies that people participate in the revolution, irrespective of their immediate membership in particular social groups. Different social groups, and leaders, participate in a revolution with different ideal targets. But during the revolutionary process, a particular group, party, leader, or alliance seizes leadership of the movement. Of course, some degree of concordance must exist between the revolutionary leadership and social groups participating in the revolution.

Accordingly, the 'dispossessed' did not initially need to have a collective target and make a collective decision to participate in the Islamic Revolution and support its radical leadership. Parsa says that 'even if the uprooted populations were to engage in collective action, they would be more likely to attack other social groups such as landlords or merchants through rent strikes or food riots rather than the state' (Parsa, 1989, p. 5). Again, by generally assuming that the urban migrants are 'uprooted' people, he makes the same mistake, which is to decontextualize the 'dispossessed'. The 'dispossessed' are *new urban groups* of Iranian society on the eve of the Islamic Revolution. And, as such, they had to fight for their own existence, which was denied by the Shah's regime. Their daily confrontations with municipal authorities forced them to confront the state. Furthermore, through revolutionary action, they found a place, a voice, and a role in urban life, which they kept even after the victory of the Revolution.

One of the most important phenomena of the Islamic Revolution is that masses of people, in particular the 'dispossessed', overtook and went beyond many of the leaders in the Revolution's final days. The targets of the Revolution were established among the people, making a compromise with the Shah's regime absolutely impossible. On the last day of the Revolution, 12 February, 1979 (22 Bahman, 1357), the army declared its neutrality, and Khomeini declared that he still had not ordered *jihad* (*Keyhan*, 12 February, 1979). But simultaneously, the 'dispossessed' and leftist groups, independent of each other and without any common leadership, had begun the final attack on the regime. A bloody war went on in the streets and revolutionary forces defeated and occupied police stations, centers of security police, jails, the Royal Special Guards and several headquarters of armed forces. Many places such as police stations, army headquarters, and state organs were occupied by irregular armed forces of 'dispossessed'.[251] The 'dispossessed' not only contributed to making the victory of the Revolution possible, but they also gained a key role in the new revolutionary Iran: they became the armed forces and police of the radical clergy.

Ideological Compromises During the Process of Revolution

The importance of ideology as a factor that serves to unify the opposition against the Old Regime has been discussed by Arjomand (1988, 1993) and Skocpol (1982) among others. The ideology that dominates during a revolutionary process has its roots in the socio-cultural structures of the pre-revolutionary period. Accordingly, it indicates the socio-cultural basis of ideological arrangements. As mentioned above, the leaders' ideological interpretations of the revolutionary process and its targets must express the frustration and demands of the social groups participating in the Revolution.[252] Accordingly, Khomeini's incessant addressing of the *mostaz'afin* ('dispossessed'), whose welfare was the major social target of the Revolution, combined with his simple formulations and interpretations, was understood and accepted by the 'dispossessed'.

Abstract ideologies cannot be readily understood by revolutionary masses in the streets and squares. Therefore, the leaders of revolutions must reduce ideological abstraction by establishing concrete public discourses. Slogans constitute the most important means of accomplishing this. While 'peace, land, bread' was the slogan of the Russian Revolution of 1917, and 'liberty, equality, fraternity' was the slogan of the French Revolution of 1789, the Iranian Revolution's slogan was 'independence, freedom, Islamic Republic'. These slogans partly reflect the pre-revolutionary socio-economic situation of the social groups participating in these revolutions, and partly the changes and compromises resulting from the process of revolution. In France, for instance, the leadership of the Revolution was in the hands of urban groups gathered in the Constituent Assembly. Many of the members of the Assembly were themselves propertied men who would not normally accept the egalitarian claims of peasants and the urban poor. The Assembly tried, for instance, to channel the revolutionary will of the peasants, who demanded the reduction of all dues paid by them. The Assembly attempted 'to apply the decrees of August 4th-11th, 1789, by which the Constituent Assembly proposed to abolish those dues that were feudal in origin, while at the same time maintaining those payments or services that were of the nature of economic rent' (Cobban, 1968, p. 96). But the course of events and the will of the peasants who objectified them through revolutionary participation led to the abolishment of all dues that qualified ownership. *The disappearance of those dues was an unforeseen and unwanted by-product of the Revolution* (Cobban, 1968, p. 97). The peasants revolted and simply ceased to pay their dues. As Lefebvre pointed out, 'they liberated themselves, and the successive Assemblies only sanctioned what they had accomplished'.[253] The events of the Revolution, in particular pressure from the peasants and urban poor, resulted in the appearance of representatives of several new groups, such as *petit bourgeois*–who were the main group participating in the urban uprising–and ordinary soldiers, in the next revolutionary Assembly, the *convention*. The more radical politics of the *convention* was influenced by the course of revolutionary events. Accordingly, the slogan 'liberty, equality, fraternity' reflected the wills of social groups participating in the Revolution.

In the Iranian Revolution of 1976-79, the core revolutionary slogan, 'independence, freedom, Islamic Republic' was a reflection of revolutionary forces and alliances. Of course, the core slogans of revolutions are not an already established product provided by leaders of the movement. Core slogans emerge from the compromises and alliances among the leaders of revolutions and their followers. In addition, the alliances and compromises themselves do not exist on the eve of revolutions. They result from a dialectical process of revolutionary events that crystallize in confrontations with the old regime. The characteristics of the revolutionary alliances depend on two main factors:

1. *The degree of representation.*
2. *The main radical revolutionary groups.*

(1) In a popular movement, there are always different groups, parties, and political figures, who vie for the leadership of the movement. But the verification of their claims depends on social groups who

participate in the real confrontations with the old regime in the streets and squares. The movement shows whether or not the groups who, at the very beginning of the revolution, claim representation, actually have popular support among the revolutionary forces. In the Iranian Revolution, different political leaders, parties, associations and religious groups claimed to represent the Revolution. But the revolutionary process of 1977-79 ratified the leadership of the movement in favor of two main groups, namely the radical clergy and the liberals. The alliances between these two groups was influenced by the settings of the revolutionary forces. As mentioned earlier, industrial workers and the bureaucrats were among the last groups to join the Revolution in the winter of 1978. Accordingly, even the revolutionary forces were not the same in this last period of the Revolution. The main revolutionary forces at the beginning of the uprising were the traditional occupational groups, small shopkeepers, some poor urban groups, intellectuals, and, of course, the radical clergy. The dynamics of the revolution provided the two key groups of contemporary civil society of Iran, i.e. the clergy and liberals, a suitable context in which to formulate their own demands for political change as the target of the movement. The radical clergy declared the overthrow of the Shah and the establishment of an Islamic government as the aims of the movement. At the same time, the liberals (the NF and the LMI) declared radical democratic change as their aims. But several factors forced these two groups not only to move closer to each other, but also to modify their preliminary aims for the Revolution:

1. The entrance of the modern middle occupational groups and the 'dispossessed'.
2. The position of the army.
3. The position of the USA and other Western countries.

The course of events, in particular the entrance of the modern middle occupational groups, forced the radical clergy to take into consideration the liberal standing of the new groups, to take a more moderate stand in their claims for establishment of an Islamic government, and to show willingness to cooperate with the liberals. The rapid radicalization of events as a result of the entrance of the 'dispossessed' compelled the liberals to try to reinforce their connections with radical clergy. The process of alliance-making was reinforced by two other factors. The powerful army of the Shah, despite mass demonstrations and revolts, showed no sign of disintegration and remained the primary means of defending the old regime.[254]

The position of the army was of great importance in the transfer of power to the revolutionary government. The USA was forced to chose between two alternatives: support the Shah and push Iran into a long civil war–which certainly would alter the stability of the Gulf area–or accept a peaceful transformation of power to a new government, even an undesirable one, which could lessen the threat to American interests. The strong American-style army of Iran was, in this respect, a good guarantee for the USA. The liberals played a role in the revolutionary alliance that made this transformation possible. The radical clergy, whose immediate aim was to seize political power, reinforced their alliance with the liberals through choosing the leader of the LMI as the prime minister of the provisional government. Accordingly, the radical clergy, who did not want anything less than the establishment of an Islamic government, for their main slogan was '*nezam-e shahanshahi nabod bayad gardad, hukomat-e estami ijad bayad gardad*' (the monarchy must be abolished, the Islamic governance must be established), were forced to change the notion of *hukomat-e estami* (Islamic governance) to *jumhuri-ye eslami* (Islamic Republic). Gradually, the compromise between the liberals and the radical clergy was crystallized in the core slogan of the Iranian Revolution, 'independence, freedom, Islamic Republic', and reflected in the organization of mass demonstrations.

(2) The critical moment of confrontations between the revolutionary forces and the army of the old regime is of great importance in the balance of revolutionary powers and representations. Whether a political group ends up in either a hegemonic or lower position in the political leadership of a revolution depends on the degree of *radical support* it receives from revolutionary forces. In other words, the political group, party, or leader who has the support of the most radical group or groups participating in the revolution, determines to a significant extent their place and influence in the leadership strata. In the Iranian Revolution, Khomeini and other radical clergy received their main support from the bazaris, small shopkeepers, and the 'dispossessed'. The 'dispossessed', who were the most militant social groups supporting the radical clergy, played a crucial role, not only for the victory of the Revolution, but also for reinforcing the position of radical clergy in the revolutionary alliance. The bravery of the 'dispossessed' in confrontations with the military forces gave those who could influence them a prominent position, not only in the revolutionary process,

but also in the power competition for the revolutionary leadership in the period after the victory of the Revolution. Thus, the radical support of revolutionary social groups highly influenced the characteristics of revolutionary leaderships, alliances, and further developments.

Revolutionary Islam

Murtaza Mutahhari, one of the most known ideologists of the revolutionary clergy in Iran, in his survey of the 'Islamic movements of the last hundred years' states that Islam by its nature is a revolutionary movement and a Muslim is a reformer, a warrior of changes (Mutahhari, 1985, p. 10). Through such a presentation of modern Islamic movements in Iran, radical clergy and their supporters minimize the social basis of such movements and reduce them to an abstract religious essence that has existed throughout Iran's Islamic history. Many other religious ideologists of the Islamic Revolution of Iran, including some religious opponents such as Shari'ati and Mojahedin-e khalq, included such abstract factors in their interpretations of the revolutionary movements of the modern Iran.

The Islamic Revolution of Iran, for reasons discussed in this work, could not take place in any time before the 1970s. The outcomes of the Constitutional Revolution, the political movements of the 1940s and early 1950s, and the religious riots of spring 1963 arguably lend support to this claim. Although, the clergy played a leading role in each of those events, many parallel and interactive socio-economic and political events had throughout the process of authoritative modernization of Iran by the Pahlavi shahs made possible the Islamic Revolution of Iran. The radical clergy's participation in modern political events in Iran provided them experience in playing modern politics, using modern political concepts and discourses, and negotiating and forming coalitions. Their prominent position in civil society of Iran, their capacity to mobilize people, and, perhaps most important of all, the appearance of a large urban group, the marginal migrants, which provided them with their own army, put them into a leading position in the opposition to the Shah. Utilizing modern political strategies and their own army, they led a major revolution of this century. This revolution became a model for many other radical Islamic movements in the Muslim world. But, it is important to stress that the Iranian Revolution is rooted in Iranian society and its social institutions. It can never be copied, although the Revolution has encouraged many in

Islamic countries to engage in revolutionary movements. Socio-economic and demographic changes are major factors providing conditions for the emergence of revolutionary social movements in many Muslim countries. The rapid migration from rural areas into the major cities, as a result of authoritative and selective modernization, and the inability of the urban economy and infrastructure to integrate these peoples into urban life are critical factors in providing conditions for the emergence of radical Islamic movements as in Egypt and Algeria.

The modern Islamic movements throughout the Muslim world have to be sociologically and comparatively explored to generate a general theory about them. My work on the Islamic Revolution of Iran provides some of the theoretical tools with which to study such Islamic movements.

Notes

1. The term clergy, used in this work, is addressing both the ulama and other low-ranking religious groups. The term ulama refers to those prominent and highly educated and trained clergy.
2. The place of shopping; the main socioeconomic center in the traditional part of cities.
3. One of the most interesting examples of the social reality of common Islamic cultural forms in a Muslim community is their language games. In his research about Arabic language, M. Piamenta has shown that Islam, as a culture of everyday life, influences the language games between the members of Islamic communities wherever they are.
4. The differences between Sunnis and Shi'ites have shaped and colored the political mosaic of the Middle East–and still does, as the analysis in this paper implies. For instance, the regime of Hafez Asad in Syria is a Shi'ite regime, notwithstanding that a majority of the Muslims in the country are Sunni; the regime of Iraq is Sunni in a country with a majority of Shi'ite. Thus, both regimes are 'minority' regimes in religious terms, although, since they are dictatorships, this characterization only has potential significance for some time in the future when political transformations take place. The current Shi'ite regime of Iran has a good relationship with Syria and supports Hafiz Asad by exporting free oil to Syria, and has had war and continuing tension with the Sunni regime of Saddam in Iraq. But this is not to say that the complexity of the socio-political arenas of the Middle East can be explained only or mainly in terms of religious differentiation.
5. Eisenstadt, S.N. (1995) 'Reconceiving Modernity', Uppsala: SCASSS.
6. For such interpretation of modernity, see for example, Eckstein, Harry (1983).
7. Arjomand, Said (1995) Revolution in World History, vol. I: Ancient and Medieval Revolutions, Ms.
8. Among these labels, 'fundamentalist' seems to be the most accepted political and journalistic term, by which one tries to relate the Islamic Revolution to American Protestantism in the early twentieth-century. But what is politically, ideologically, and journalistically accepted does not automatically mean that it is identical with social reality. 'American fundamentalists, reacting against contemporary social gospel preachers, argued that the goal of true religion was not to change society but to save souls by preserving the literal interpretation of the Bible-especially on such

doctrinal issues as Creation, Judgment Day, and the Virgin Birth'. (Abrahamian, 1993, p. 16). But Iranian radical clergy (fundamentalists?) from the very beginning of their appearance, were a political group strongly concerned about socio-political issues. The other aspects of American fundamentalism were a return directly to original religious texts– particularly the Bible–for understanding the true meaning.

9   Muslim religious leaders who possessed a great degree of religious knowledge; the most prominent group in the rank of clergy. In this work, sometimes the word 'the ulama' and sometimes 'the Shi'ite ulama' and in some cases 'the ulama of Iran' are used. In all cases, however, the meaning is the same, namely the overwhelming majority of Iranian ulama who are not Sunnis but Shi'ites.

10 A revolutionary armed organization mainly constructed during the war against Iraq.

11 Revolutionary armed forces constructed during the first days after the victory of the Islamic Revolution that functioned as the main armed force of radical ulama.

12 In this work, the term 'class' is used largely in the sense of occupational groups.

13 Cited in Arjomand (1995), 'Revolution in World History'.

14 Ideological crises was already apparent among the leftists. SAVAK's successful attacks on the largest leftist organization, Fadaiyan-e khalq, and the common belief among many prisoners that the armed struggle has not been as successful as they assumed to be, had led to ideological differences among Marxists. This led to the creation of new political groups.

15 For example, I had to take away many comments that had to do with why the leftists or the liberals failed in seizing political power in Iran.

16 Economic activities, for instance in the bazaar, were influenced and changed by Islamic systems of taxation and law. Traditional activities such as the ancient ceremony of new year (*novrouz*), had been changed and adjusted to Islamic norms and moral codes.

17 Even in the Arab language, we hardly find a word that can mean 'the nation' in that way we are used to understanding it. The words such as *umma*, meaning the community of believers, *sha'b* or *qawm*, meaning 'people' or 'kinsfolk'; *jins*, meaning 'species' or 'race', and even watan, meaning home land, do not properly mean the world nation (Hjärpe, 1990). In the modern era, Arab politicians and intellectuals used to use the word *mella(t)* as translation of nation; but even *mella(t)* means a group of people residing in some area. *Mella(t)* has more associations with religious people than citizens of a country. Ayatollah Khomeini and Ayatollah Montazeri, for instance, used the world *mellat* in association with religious believers,

such as *mellat-e Islam* or *mellat-e Masih* (Christians). For further discussion see B. Lewis, *The Political Language of Islam*, 1988.

18   The Verses used here are from Richard Bell's English translation of Qur'an, 1939.

19   The reign of the Prophet in Medina has been used by many ulama and intellectuals in Muslim communities to legitimate their opposition to any attempt to separate state from religious authority.

20   The best illustration of the Shi'ite theory of the legitimate state can be found in some statements in their *adan* (calling to pray) and in their prayer. They say: *Ashhada anna la elaha ellallah, va ashhad anna Muhammad al-rasul Allah, va ashhada anna Ali-yan vali allah* that means 'I witness that there is no god but God, and I witness that Muhammad is His messenger, and I witness that Ali is God's deputy'.

21   According to religious sources, there are some Shi'ite branches other than the Twelver Shi'ites, but I will only present and discuss the Twelver one, which is the belief of the Iranian people and as so is the largest Shi'ite branch.

22   Arjomand (1988) stresses that the Revolution did away with a key principle of Shi'ite tradition (and also modern political thought), namely the separation of religious and political authority. Also, see Bakhash (1994) about the continuing problems and tensions relating to the tight coupling of religious and political authority since the Revolution.

23   See Ibish Yusuf, 'The Political Doctrine of al-Baqillani', Islamic Studies, IV 1965.

24   H. Laoust, 1936, in Ann. K. Lambton, *State and Government in Medieval Islam*, 1981, p. 108.

25   Also, other theologians, such as Ibn Jama'a and Ibn Taymiyya, had contributed to final separation of political and religious authority in the Sunni community. But the work's main theoretical aim does not let us discuss further the Sunni theory of state.

26   Sir John Malcolm, in his book, *History of Persia*, discusses the power of the Safavid Shahs and especially explains the Shah's role as 'the just ruler' and the last judge who protected the people against bureaucratic oppression by officials. There are also many stories about Shah Abbas' secret participation in the every day life of the people to examine their loyalty to the Shah and his government.

27   The place for ritual ceremonies of Sufis. Sufism was initially used by the Safavids to challenge the legitimacy of the Sunnis and take political power. Lambton says that 'Sufism was a dominant faith among Shi'ites until the time of the reign of the last Safavid, shah Sultan Husayn. In that time Shi'ite ulama such as the most famous one, Mulla Moh'ammad Baqir Majlisi (d 1699), violently opposed against Sufism'. (Lambton, 1981, p.

268). Although Sufism has some influence on Shi'ism, because of the locality of Sufism, which mainly was spread in the northern provinces, and the existence of great and decisive differences between Shi'ism and Sufism, there is some doubt about the impact of Sufism on Shi'ite faith.

28 A place for performance of religious dramas.
29 Mosques used for Friday prayer, where Shi'ite's prayer ceremony was held and the *Khutbah* (a special duty of the imam of Friday prayer to mention the ruler of state's name at the beginning of the prayer) was read at the name of Safavids.
30 Some of Shi'ite ulama, such as al-Karaki, constructed a proper religious framework for the legitimacy of the Safavid shahs. Al-Karaki formulated the theory of *nayeb-e 'amm* (general vicegerency of the Hidden Imam), and *nayeb-e khas* (particular vicegerency of the Hidden Imam). With these two notions, he solved the problem of vicegerency for the Hidden Imam. According to al-Karaki, *nayeb-e 'amm* was associated with the ulama's symbolic right to conduct some religious ceremonies such as the Friday prayer, and by *nayeb-e khas* he meant the unquestionable vicegerency of shah to the Hidden Imam. Cf. Savory 1980, Lambton 1981, and Arjomand 1984.
31 See Amanat Abbas, 'In Between the madrasah and the Marketplace: The Designation of Clerical Leadership in Modern Shi'ism', in Arjomand (ed.), *Authority and Political Culture in Shi'ism*.
32 One exception is, however, the short reign of the Afshars who were Sunnids and challenged the authority of Shi'ite ulama.
33 Administrator of religious foundations based on land.
34 Independent interpreters of religious law, Shari'a.
35 'The share of Imam'; religious tax collected by the ulama to be used for their own costs or other religious purposes.
36 Even in modern times, the main sources of bazaris' income was based on foreign trade. They were against customs duties which could limit their economic connections with foreign countries. Even Khomeini in his book *Kashef al-asrar* criticized export-import duties and advocated free trade. (For more discussion see Abrahamian, 1993, pp. 39-42.)
37 Mujtahids who had dignitary presiding over *shar'* courts in the major cities.
38 See even Kheirabadi Masoud, 1991, and Savory Roger, 1980.
39 Cf. Lukes Steven (1985).
40 For more discussion, see A. Seligman (1992), *The Idea of Civil Society*.
41 Alexander Jeffrey (1995) 'Collective Action and Democratic Discourse: Social Movement as 'Translations' of Civil Society', Paper prepared for two occasions: SCASSS June Seminar of Revolutions and a festschrift for Alain Touraine.

42 For a more detailed discussion about this issue, see for example, A. Seligman (1992); Z. A. Pelczynski (1984), and Hall, (1995).
43 The main discussion is about Iran and not other Muslim countries and therefore I am not intending to handle the question of civil society of such countries. But it is worthy to say that there are several similarities in the main socio-political structures between Iran and other Muslim societies during the Islamic period of Iran.
44 Eisenstadt presented his view on civil society during seminars in Uppsala at 'The Uppsala Theory Circle and SCASS, Spring 1995. See also, Eisenstadt 'Civil Society and Democracy in Latin America: some comparative observations' in *Estudios Interdisciplinarios de America Latina v El Caribe*, 1993, No. 4, pp. 27-37.
45 See Arjomand (1988, pp. 192-197).
46 For a detailed discussion of this issue, see Said Arjomand, *The Shadow of God and the Hidden Imam*, 1984.
47 Ibn-e Sina is known in the West as Aveccina and is compared with Aquinas (Lambton, 1988).
48 Akhbari was a Shi'ite school that firmly rejected the power of Mujtahids in the society. They advocated inner-worldly salvation through the hermeneutic comprehension of the *Qur'an* and believed that the role of Mujtahids is incompatible with the clear holy texts and interpretation of such text by Mujtahids leads to *zann* (probability, uncertain knowledge) which is opposed to the truth of holy texts. They, consequently, opposed the role of Mujtahids as marja i-taqlid. For them taqlid (following a Mujtahid's decrees), was against the authority of Imams and was forbidden.
49 Some analyses about the state power in Iran attempt to present Safavids reconstruction of a sovereign Iranian state purely as Iranian 'nationalism' against the Ottoman empire. But even if Safavids immediate intention was to create a sovereign state, their socio-political project in using Shi'ism as state religion and adopting of the role of vicegerency of the Hidden Imam, gave them the monopoly over the leadership of the Muslim community. Safavids wars against Sunni Ottomans–particularly by Ismail I–were legitimized by rejecting Sultanate's claim on Islamic leadership of the Muslims. Not before the catastrophe of the battle of Chaldran, Ismail's last battle against the Ottomans, Safavids' undertone of claiming leadership of the whole Muslim community was moderated.
50 Ahl al-kitab are the people who are recognized by *Qur'an* as the religious groups who have holy books, such as Christians and Jewish.
51 For example, between Shi'ites, Sunnis, Kharijis and Mu'tazillis.
52 For further discussion see Lambton (1981) *State and Government in Medieval Islam*.

53   This is obviously not the Enlightenment's idea of the individual which Hegel formulated at the end of part I of the Jena lectures, 'The will of the individual is the universal will–and the universal will is the individual'. The individual, according to Hegel and the Scottish Enlightenment, is a particular individual who together with other individuals constructs the universal framework of existence, namely society. Individualism is a unifying project of universalism and particularism. The western individual is an independent person who is only dependent on other independent individuals. As Hegel puts it:
        'The concrete person who is himself the object of his particular aims, is, as a totality of wants and a mixture of caprice and physical necessity, one principle of civil society. But the particular person is essentially so related to other particular persons that each establishes himself and finds satisfaction by means of the others, and at the same time purely and simply by means of the form of universality, the second principle here' (Seligman, 1992, p. 46). Muslim individuals, on the contrary, are not as Hegel says, 'the object of his particular aims'; he is a mukallaf, who is to practice his own religious identity and to try to influence others to do so. If a person commits sin, it is other individuals' duty to influence him to desist from his sinful activity. But it is not only through verbal action that an individual is allowed to 'enjoin the good and to forbid evil', but also through physical force (Lambton, 1981, p. 311). Thus, the Muslim individual is the last chain in a transcendental hierarchy beginning with God. He is not 'an object of his aims', but a person who has to, through enjoining the good and forbidding evil, guarantee the existence of society and continuation of the divine order.

54   Jalal al-Din Movlavi, *Mathnavi Ma'navi*, Amir Kabir Press, Tehran 1366/1978, p. 1.

55   Although the validity of the theory of *taqlid* has been challenged by some Shi'ite scholars, such as Mulla Ahmad Ardabili (d. 1585/993), and *Akhbaris*, the triumph of *Usuli* school in nineteenth century reinforced the position of the ulama as *marja'-e taqlid*. For Ardabili's argument against *taqlid*, see Arjomand (1988), *Authority and Political Culture in Shi'ism*, pp. 263-266.

56   A name for the Hidden Imam who, according to Shi'ism, reappears to establish the reign of justice on earth.

57   The Shi'ite doctrine of *gheybat* (Occultation) and *de facto* acceptance of a Sunni state, on the other side, can be compared with the theoretical development in Christian theology from very early times that Christ would not come back in the lifetime of the Apostles and that the faithful would have to live on in a world led by non-faithful states. Primary acceptance of secular states by the Fathers of the Church led to appearance of other theories concerning the relationship between state and church. One of the Christian theories closest to the Shi'ite theory of state is that of St.

Augustine's. Augustine (d. 430 AD) in his great work *On the City of God* describes the relationship between state and society, and formulates two estates of worldly organizations for human existence. He argues that, by separating two kinds of social organization, i.e. state and the church from each other, one creates coexistence between them. By the very notion of the City of God, he means the Christian power center on the Earth, the Church. Hence, God's empire is the realm of the Church and as such separated from the secular realm of human society which is ruled by the state. But it by no mean refers to non-religious boundaries of the state. He means that the secular state, as a body of men, has to maintain *peace* so as to allow people to practise their religion, and to survey good order and prevent a sinful life (Strömholm, 1985, p. 92). As we see, the similarity of Shi'ites' attitudes towards the role of state as an organ whose task is to prepare the proper conditions for the faithful to realize their religious commitments. Further, Augustinus' separation between the tasks of state and those of the Church led to theological legitimation of two sources of laws, *positive secular law*, which is the State's domain, and the *moral law of the Church* (Strömholm, 1985, p. 92). Again, according to Shi'ite *fiqh* (jurisprudence) *u'rf* is secular jurisdiction and the task of state, and *Shar'* is religious jurisdiction and the task of the ulama. The similarity becomes more apparent when we consider Augustine's and other church fathers' interpretations of secular law. In the writings of Augustine saeculum meant 'existence', that is, the sum total of transitory human existence, past, present, and future, from the fall of Adam to the Last Judgment. (Berman, 1983, p. 109). Also, 'the church fathers in the second, third, and fourth centuries used saeculum [secular] to refer to the world of time-the 'temporal' world-as contrasted with the eternal kingdom of God' (Ibid.). This separation of tasks and claims creates the possibility for both the Empire and the Church in the Middle Ages Europe, and the shahs and the ulama in Shi'ite Iran to coexist and exert their respective authorities.

58   *Khoms* is a fifth of all profit earned in economic activity, to be paid to ulama for using in charitable aims. *Zakat* is the 'purifying tax' levied on the property of Muslims for purposes enumerated in *Qur'an*, chap. IX v. 60.

59   Pilgrimage to Mecca is supposed to be done by all Muslims before they die. After the pilgrimage to Mecca one becomes *haji* and have to not commit sin in his life. That is why bazaris who are haji, have a respectable and dominant position in the bazaar.

60   A system of inalienable endowment used for religious or charitable purposes.

61   Even through the system of *auqaf* many of *vaqf*-giving persons intended to secure the ownership of their property within their families. For instance, in 1607, Shah Abbas I constituted all his private estates and personal property

into a *vaqf* for the Fourteen Immaculate Ones (the Twelve Imams, Muhammad and Fatima), and vested the *tawliyat*, the office of *mutavalli*, or administrator of these *auqaf*, in himself, and thereafter in his successors. (Banani Amin, 1967, p. 18).
62. See also Bryan S. Turner, *Weber and Islam*.
63. Cf. Weber, (1968, p. 1160).
64. Weber (1968, p. 1164) considers 'office charisma' of the church as a result of construction of its sovereignty based on: 1) the rise of a professional priesthood ; 2) claims to universal domination; 3) rationalization of dogma and rites (kultus); and 4) all of these features must occur in some kind of compulsory organization. The fourth feature, organization as a bureaucratic body, is lost in the case of Islamic priesthood and therefore we cannot call that hierocracy.
65. *Atabat* is the name for holy Shi'ite shrines situated in the eastern area of the former Ottoman Empire. After the foundation of Iraq, they were situated in the main Shi'ite cities of Iraq: Najaf, Karbala, and Kazemayn.
66. Ability to interpret and exert the preliminary sources of Islamic law which are: *Qur'an*, *hadith* (the saying of the Prophet), and *Sunna* (the deeds of the Prophet).
67. A Mujtahids who is the most learned alem and his decrees are guidance and binding example for *muqalleds* (other Muslims who are unable to exert independent judgment in religious laws).
68. One example of the individual charisma of Shi'ite ulama is the role of Muhammad Ansari (d. 1864) the leader of Iranian Muslim community and the vacuum arising for almost a decade after his death.
69. Cf. Hamid Algar (1969) *Religion and State in Iran 1785-1906*; Said Amir Arjomand (1988) *Authority and Political Culture in Shi'ism*; Abbas Amanat (1988) 'In Between the Madrasah and the Marketplace'.
70. For conflicts that occurred between some Mujtahids because of religious endowments, see Ahmad Kasravi (1330/1951) *Tarikh-e enqelab-e mashrotiyyat-e Iran* (The History of Constitutional Revolution of Iran), and Kermani, Nazem al-Islam (1362/1983) *Tarikh-e bidari- ye Iranian* (The History of Iranians' Uprising).
71. For example, see Abbas Amanat 'In Between the Madrasah and the Marketplace', in Arjomand *Authority and Political Culture in Shi'ism*, 1988.
72. Arjomand, in his article in 'European Journal of Sociology', 1979, expresses some doubt about the aim of that letter. He says that that letter was not addressed to Shah Abbas.
73. For example, Safavids were supported by Turkman tribes, Qezelbash inhabiting eastern Anatolia, northern Syria and the Armenian highlands,

Afshars by Afshar tribe inhabiting north eastern Iran, and Qajars by Qajar tribe inhabiting northwestern Iran.
74 *Khutba* was a socio-political declaration reading by Imam jom'a prior to the Friday prayers in the congregational mosques. In the *khotba* Imam jom'a used to read the accepted political leader's name.
75 Two Perso-Russian wars of eighteenth century are examples of the ulama's role in mobilization of people in an army by declaration of jihad (holy war) against Russia.
76 Ann K. S. Lambton (1988) in her book *Continuity and Change in Medieval Persia* presents examples of the state's economic dependency on the bazaar.
77 In 1747, the great shah of Afshars, Nader shah was assassinated. After him a few of the Nader's descendants tried to rule the country but they never succeeded, and therefore it is more significant to use the death of the Nader Shah as the end of the Afshar dynasty. Even the death of the great *vakil* (regent) of the Zands, Karim Khan, in 1779 must be regarded as the end of the Zands dynasty, even if in 1789 a grandson of Karim Khan came to power. His power was limited to the southern areas. He was defeated by Agha Muhammad Khan, the first shah and founder of the Qajars, who established the center of his reign in Tehran and ruled Iran from 1779.
78 Oliver, 1802, in Algar, 1969, p. 44.
79 Imam Husayn is the Third Shi'ite Imam who was killed in Karbala in the month of Muharram. In this month the Shi'ites used to hold mourning ceremonies commemorating this tragedy.
80 Cf. Algar, *Religion and State in Iran 1785-1906*, p. 53.
81 *Nezam-e jadid* is translated both the 'New Army' (Algar), and the 'New Order' (Abrahamian). Although both translations are linguistically correct, the former is more accurate in the Iranian context.
82 Adamiyyat, *Amir Kabir va Iran*, in Charles Issawi (1971), *The Economic History of Iran 1800-1914*, p 294.
83 For further information about the opposition of Russia and England to Amir, see Fereydon Adamiyyat, *Amir Kabir va Iran*.
84 See, for example, Adamiyyat (1971) *Amir Kabir va Iran* (Amir Kabir and Iran); A. Eqbal (1951) *Tarikh-e mofassal-e Iran* (The Detailed History of Iran); Algar (1969) *State and Religion in Iran*.
85 Mulkara, 'On tactless behavior by the agents of the Régie', cited in Algar 1969 p. 209
86 Two traditional instruments for smoking tobacco in Iran.
87 Mulkara, cited in Algar, 1969 p. 215.
88 Also a letter printed in A. Kasravi (1951, pp. 17-18) which shows the characteristic and line of propaganda of the ulama in the movement.
89 It should be mentioned that Shaykh Fazl Allah Nori, because of his connections with some groups of guilds and merchants of the bazaar of

Tehran, was among the constitutionalist ulama. But, because of the question about the constitutive function of parliament, which he considered inconsistent with the Shari'a, he joined the opposition to the constitutionalism and defended the monarchy.

90 Z. Z. Abdullaev, in Charles Issawi (1971, pp. 42-52) *The Economic History of Iran 1800-1914*.

91 After the assassination of Naser al-Din Shah, his son Mozaffar al-Din Shah was crowned Shah in June 1896.

92 From 'Further Correspondence, July-September 1903', cited in Algar, 1969 p. 233.

93 Some analyses of the event, such as that of Kasravi and Algar, are in doubt with the originality of the *fatva*. Kasravi, for example, writes that it was said that the *fatva* was written by Sayyed Muhammad Ali, the brother of the publisher of Habl al-Matin who lived in Najaf (See Kasravi, 1951 p. 32).

94 See, for example, A. Kasravi, 1951; Malekzadeh, 1949; and Algar, 1969.

95 Muharram is the black month in which the Third Shi'ite Imam, Imam Husayn, was killed in Karbala.

96 Malekzadeh, pp. 47-48; Kasravi, p. 64.

97 Haj Mirza Muhammad Reza was one of the ulama of Kerman who led the revolt of Kerman against the governor and was deported to Rafsenjan.

98 Because of the participation of Haj Shaykh Murteza in the bast, Ayn al-Daula, as punishment of the Shaykh, gave the management of the Marvi *madrasah* to the Imam jom'a of Tehran.

99 For a comparison of the events and the attitude of the ulama, see, for example, Kasravi, 1969 pp. 81-86.

100 Printed in Kasravi, 1951, pp. 81-82.

101 See Nazem al-Islam Kermani (1362/1983) *Tarikh-e bidari-ye Iranian*, Tehran, pp. 444-53.

102 Denis Wright, *The Persian Amongst the English*, translated into Persian by Karim Imami, Iranian dar mian-e engelisiha, Zamineh Publishing, 1365/1986, p. 378.

103 See Malekzadeh, 1949, pp. 172-73; and Kasravi, 1951, pp.112-13.

104 Nazem al-Islam Kermani and Kasravi both discussed the importance of the ulama at that time for the social life of the people. Kasravi, tells a history which shows the reaction of the people to the emigration of the ulama to Qum. He writes: 'Forsat Shirazi says: I saw a woman having her veil on a peg was screaming that from now over your daughters' marriage ceremony must be done by the Belgian monsieur Nuaz, because we do not have any ulama (Kasravi, 1951, p. 107).

105 See, for example, Malekzadeh, *Tarikh-e enqelab*, 1949; Kasravi, *Enqelab-e mashrutiyyat*, 1951, Momeni, *Din va dovlat*, 1990; and Abrahamian, *Iran Between Two Revolutions*, 1982.

106 See, for example, Abdol Karim Lahidji, Constitutionalism and Clerical Authority, in Arjomand (ed.) *Authority and Political Culture in Shi'ism*, 1988.
107 Memoirs of a constitutionalist in Kasravi, 1951, p. 632.
108 See, for example, Malekzadeh (1949); Hairi (1977); Momeni (1993); Lahidji (1988).
109 See, among others, Malekzadeh (1949); Kasravi (1951); Momeni (1990).
110 Z. Abdullaev, in Charles Issawi, 1971, p. 46.
111 See for example, Kasravi, 1951 p. 266.
112 Nazem al-Islam Kermani, *Tarikh-e bidari*, 1953, p. 377.
113 See Shaykh Fazl Allah's letter to another Mujtahid, Aqa Najafi, residing in Isfahan, in Kasravi. *Tarikh-e mashruteh*, 1951, pp. 287-88.
114 For a more detailed presentation of this action of the anti-constitutionalist ulama, see Kasravi, ibid. 1951, pp. 224-26.
115 Shaykh Muhammad Isma'il Gharavi Mahallati, Al-La'ali al-Marbutah fi Wujub al-Mahrutah Bushehr, 1909), pp. 2-3, cited in Hairi, 1977 p. 100.
116 See, for example, Abdullah Mustaufi, 1942, p. 250.
117 The decrees of the ulama of atabat (holly Shi'ite places in contemporary Iraq) were important issues for legitimizing the movement in Iran.
118 Ahmad Kasravi (1951) and Malekzadeh (1949) cited many times the leaders of the Constitutional Revolution, such as Bihbahani, Tabatabi, Malek al-Mottokalemin, and Va'ez, who presented the Constitutionalism as the only way of establishing an independent state which could lead Iran out of foreign influence and dictatorship.
119 Makki, Twenty Years' History, vol. 1, p. 255, cited in Iran In the Twentieth Century, Reza Ghods, 1989, p. 94.
120 See R. Ghods, 1982, pp. 93-100.
121 At that time, republicans seized political power in Turkey and declared that country Republic.
122 Cf. Makki (1945); Ghods (1989); Milani (1994); and Malek al-Sho'ara Bahar (1944).
123 Cf. Issawi, Charles, 'The Iranian Economy 1925-1975: Fifty Years of Economic Development', in G. Lenczowski, *Iran Under the Pahlavis*, 1978, pp. 130-166.
124 Shahrough Akhavi, *Religion and Politics in Contemporary Iran*, 1980 pp. 32-59.
125 Makki, Twenty Years' History, vol. 6, pp. 250-273, in R. Ghods, ibid., p. 110.
126 Cited in Roger Savory, 'Social Development in Iran During the Pahlavi Era', in G. Lenczowski, 1978, pp. 85-127.
127 Some writers such as Makki (1945), Ghods (1989), and Milani (1994), pointed out that Reza Khan's participation in religious ceremonies was

intended to gain popular support. Bahar (1944, p. 184) meant that the religious ceremonies were of crucial importance for Reza Khan. Other writer such as L. P. Elwell-Sutton (1978) stated that 'he was himself a Moslem of average piety'.

128 Cited in Hairi, ibid., p. 143.
129 Na'ini, *Tanbih*, pp. 6-7, cited in Hairi, ibid., p. 166.
130 Two-hundred fifty-six merchants and guildsmen of Tehran bazaar (1922 open letter), cited in Ghods, 1989 p. 93.
131 It is noteworthy to mention that Katouzian's translation of the Persian phrase *Hukomat-i Melli* as democracy may cause some uncertainty about the main intentions of the National Front. The phrase's more proper translation is 'national government' or 'national reign'.
132 As discussed ealier, the Safavids established Shi'ism as the official religion of Iran in the sixteenth century and endowed the religious institutions with great wealth. By a system of *auqaf* from seventeenth century, the ulama were secured economic sovereignty. *Auqaf* was the ulama's source of income. Thus, the Shi'ite's ulama were less dependent on the state than were the Sunni ulama. Even after the Safavids' fall in 1722, the two traditional centers of authority, the Shah and the ulama, functioned independently of each other. For a few decades during Afshar dynasty's reign (1725-1749), the ulama were confined to the mosques and *madrasahs* (religious schools). But the Qajars (1778-1921) increased the administrative influence of the ulama over both private and public life.
133 The government also took away from the clerics the authority to notarize and register documents, thus denying them both important functions and important sources of revenue (Bakhash, 1990, p. 21).
134 The Shah's policy was highly successful. During the period from 1966-76, the number of persons with higher education quadrupled (to about 300,000) and the enrollment in universities and professional schools in Iran tripled (to about 150,000) (Arjomand, 1988, p. 74). The government also sent teachers (young men conscripted into the army and placed in the Literacy Corps) into rural areas to teach village children to read and write, laudatory in many ways, but perceived by the ulama as a Trojan horse to spread the seeds of secularism from the cities to the villages and to challenge the role of the clerics, or mullahs, as village teachers (Bakhash, 1990, p. 25).
135 Ghods (1989, p. 194) also points out Khomeini's difference with other mullahs, and his ability to use popular issues.
136 Cf. Chehabi, 1990, pp. 170-172. Chehabi pointed out that Taleqani's first lecture given on 27 October 1961, formed the basis of his later book, *Islam and Ownership*. This book influenced religious intellectuals in their discussions with leftists and nationalists.

137 Khomeini was influenced by radical Islamic ideas from Sunni religious theorists, Mawdudi and Qutb (from Pakistan and Egypt, respectively).
138 See, for example, Ha'iri (1977); Lambton (1988).
139 Anti-religious deeds or sayings that reject the unity of God, his righteous, Prophet, and Imams.
140 Extremely despotic ruler who claims divinity for himself and competes with God, such as the pharaohs of Egypt.
141 *Faqih* is a clerk who is educated in Islamic *fiqh*, i.e., laws and jurisprudence.
142 There was an interesting evolution in Khomeini's ideas. In his first book, *Kashef al-asrar* (1943) he advocated the necessity of the state but not necessarily a religious one. The 1971 book, *Hukumat-e eslami, velayat-e faqih*, argues for an Islamic or theocratic state as the only legitimate form of government, a state legitimized by the word of God, with the clergy as spokesmen and interpreters. Later (in exile in Paris) he articulated the idea of an 'Islamic Republic', which legitimates the modern state in the people. Ultimately, his real innovation is to combine these–the traditional, religious idea with a modern idea of the popular basis of political legitimacy. This becomes a truly powerful idea that spreads to other Muslim societies with highly archaic regimes, or regimes that are modern, secular at least in a certain sense, but not based on religious or supernatural legitimation.
143 The Khomeini network was based not only on his authority as an Ayatollah but on his extensive activities as a teacher and preacher. Khomeini was then not only an important intellectual but a religious activist, active in teaching as well as preaching. He put a great deal of emphasis on preaching. He also instructed a large number of preachers who were to spread his message among the common people in Iran (Arjomand, 1988, p. 98). Arjomand (1988, p. 98) points out the irony of the Shah's policy of internal banishment of dissident clerics, allowing them to spread their teaching further afield). Arjomand refers to Khomeini having trained 500 Mujtahids throughout his long teaching career; 12,000 students having attending his lectures in the years immediately preceding his exile in 1964. The leading radical ulama who have occupied the highest positions of power since the revolution have been, with rare exceptions, drawn from the large group of former Khomeini students.
144 Mehdi Bazargan was a founding member and the leader of LMI and head of the first provisional government following the Revolution.
145 The ulama, who became one of the most important group in the Islamic Revolution and dominated its leadership, can be classified as a status group. They fit properly Weber's definition of status group. 'Status' (ständische Lage) shall mean an effective claim to social esteem in terms of positive or negative privileges. The ulama's status is highly dependent on claiming a 'special social esteem', as vicegerents of the Hidden Imam, and 'hereditary

charisma', descendants to the Prophet. Hence, it is more proper to use the term 'status group' for the ulama than occupational group. Weber uses the term 'hierocratic status group' for religious leaders (See, for example *Economy and society*, 1968, pp. 305-7).

146 Assistants of workshops.

147 He was obsessed by a fear of political opposition. In an interview with foreign reporters in 1975, he said: 'The communists have no place in Iran, and we can never accept those who drank to the health of Pishevary'. By the latter group he meant the politicians of the National Front, who according to him, welcomed the establishment of the sovereign republic of Azarbayjan by Pishevary.

148 Such a mixture of people from such different sectors implies a misreading of the socio-political arrangement of the revolutionary forces. For example, the majority of truck drivers in Iran own their own trucks, and in many cases they enjoyed economic advantages from increasing imports, exports, and high internal transport. The lack of a developed network of railways increased the importance of trucks for transportation.

149 Printed in Milani (1994 p. 61).

150 In pre-modern Iran, because of the shortage of water, a strong state that could manage the system of irrigation was necessary. This may explain the lack of peasant upheavals in pre-modern Iran. In modern Iran, two other reasons for the lack of peasant revolutions are presented: the lack of 'a discontented middle peasantry', and the absence of 'a stable market - economy' (Kazemi & Abrahamian, 1978, pp. 259-93). Accordingly, both the Constitutional and the Islamic revolutions were urban revolutions.

151 A further factor explaining the quiescence of peasants is the geography of Iran, which leaves villages relatively isolated from one another, but linked to cities. Also, in the absence of rivers and sufficient rain, peasants cultivate by drawing upon underground water and irrigating. To bring up the underground waters–often at a great distance from the agricultural areas–required a technical system, qanat, of water distribution. These systems required collaboration among many villages. Local antagonism among landowners was an obstacle to collaboration. The Iranian state dealt with the conflicts among landowners and used soldiers to build new *qanat* and to repair old ones. When the Iranian central state was strong, agriculture flourished and contributed to the strength of the state. Peasants tended to support the Shahs who were a symbol of stability and safety.

152 The Constitutional Revolution was also an urban revolution.

153 Denman (1978) 'Land Reforms of Shah and People', in *Iran Under the Pahlavi*, Hoover Institution Publication, 1978.

154 Examples of such cities are Tehran and Shiraz. In such cities, in the modern northern areas, the upper and middle classes lived and were known as the

people from '*shomal-e shahr*' (these who lived in the northern areas). This term was usually used to categorize the rich and modern urban groups.
155 The Iranians visiting foreign countries, increased from 311,492 in 1971 to 1,377,325 in 1977 (Milani, 1994, p. 67).
156 Workers who gather in certain places of the cities waiting to be picked up by those who need workers. These workers usually received only short-term jobs.
157 See Ervand Abrahamian, *Iran Between the Two Revolutions*, 1982, p. 428.
158 Burojerdi accepted any government as long as it was constituted of Muslims and not non-Muslims.
159 The most high-ranking religious leader is accepted by the religious community and acts on behalf of the 'Hidden Imam'.
160 New laws were introduced under Amuzegar with the intention of protecting tenants against landlords, for instance the 'New Law of Landlords and Tenants'.
161 This is a liberal religious organization.
162 There are no official statistics about the size of the Iranian 'working class' before the Islamic Revolution, although there are various estimates, with considerable disparity among them. Abrahamian (1982) gives a figure of 2,400,000 in which he includes industrial workers, truck drivers, wage earners in banks, offices and other agencies, rank-and-file in the military, and the urban marginals. Arjomand (1988, p. 218), drawing on Halliday (1979) estimates 3.5 million in the working class. The largest part of these were employed in handicraft and small workshops. Only 7 percent were industrial workers.
163 Bakhash (1990) claims that 250,000 were fined during this period, 25,000 banned from home towns, and 8000 jailed. He gives no sources. Arjomand (1988) questions the figures, particularly the fines.
164 Many of the military, administrative and new capitalist families such as Yazdani, Khayyami, Namazi, Sabeti, and Elghanian, were accused by the clergy and bazaris of being non-Muslims and even anti-Muslims such as Bahai' and Jewish. These accusations were an important ideological weapon in the bazaris struggles against the new capitalists.
165 It is very difficult to estimate what proportion of the demonstrators and participants in the revolutionary movement came from each group. This makes a difference in our hypothesis about the role of the marginal migrants in the revolution. Arjomand (1988, p. 236) points out, 'The extent of participation of the recent migrants in the revolutionary movement is not clear /.../. there is evidence that the squatters, as distinct from the better-established and better-housed recent migrants did not play any significant role in the demonstrations of 1978-79'. Whether, as Bakhash (1990, p. 185) suggests, many of those who marched against the Shah were drawn from the badly

housed populations of the great urban centers, or as in our hypothesis, that the marginal migrants played a key role and the new middle classes played a lesser role, is difficult to determine on the basis of currently available data, but is a challenge to our own and others' research. More clear, in our view, is the fact that after 1978, the marginals were recruited into the dual government of revolutionary committees, police, army, etc. They became the clerics' officials, police, and army. And the modern middle occupational groups–including leftists as well as conservatives–were marginalized.

166 According to Arjomand (1988, p. 124), the Shah feared a *coup de grace*, even as he was leaving the country.

167 The Iranian army was, of course, deeply engaged in the war between Iran and Iraq and managed to regain its legitimacy (after losing it in the confron-tations with revolutionary forces) as an institution to defend Iranian territory against foreign enemies.

168 Recall that a number of Soviet states in the south and southeast of the USSR were Islamic.

169 Foreign agents such as the USA might have pushed for an all-out military effort to stop the revolution, or to initiate a military coup, or to split the military, etc., setting the stage for other potential scenarios.

170 The compromise between the army and the opposition was a result of an agreement between the USA's deputy general Huyser and the opposition. This agreement is known as the Huyser plan.

171 The Soviet Radio's Persian program presented the developments in Iran as a movement for political reform, not revolution.

172 'Notwithstanding wild rumors on the number of martyrs, being echoed by the media, the number of persons killed between October 1, 1978, and January 15, 1979, was between two and three thousand' (Arjomand, 1988, p. 120).

173 It must be mentioned that the regime controlled the newspapers and articles published in them were usually considered as regime's official declarations.

174 Yazid was an Omayyid caliph who ordered to kill Imam Husayn, the Third Shi'ite Imam.

175 Observing the fortieth day of a dead individual is an Islamic tradition in Iran.

176 Noteworthy is the fact that the former conflicts between the emigrants and municipal authorities had not been purely political.

177 All these areas were situated outside of the 'legal zone' of Tehran. During the days prior to the Revolution, in some of these areas, such as Javadiyeh-ye Tehran pars and Shemiran nov, people in these areas participated actively in local revolutionary actions against the military forces.

178 *Niroyeh havai* is the place where in the last two days of the Islamic Revolution several bloody struggles took place. The people of those areas participated actively in defeating the attack of Guard forces.
179 Navid, the underground-organ of the Tudeh Party of Iran, August 1978.
180 *Keyhan* newspaper also confirmed that 'yesterday's demonstration of Tehran exhibit offensive characteristics', and that ' millions of people, both in Tehran and other cities, did not demonstrate, but marched' (28 January, 1979).
181 The names given of interviewees are not their real names.
182 This is according to my own observations.
183 This is suggested by two interviewees, Mahshid and Karim, who participated in the final demonstrations in Tehran, and Isfahan.
184 The picture published in *Keyhan* newspaper of February 12, 1979, confirms Muhammad's witness. On the first page of *Keyhan*, a picture of two armed men, a young and an old man with old clothes and hat is printed.
185 Bani Sadr was a liberal but with strong religious commitments. He had led the organization of Islamic students abroad and had organized Khomeini's stay in Paris.
186 The war activated commitments and sacrifices, but also drained off important resources that could otherwise be used for institutionalizing the revolution. This situation–and also concern about the heavy human losses of Iranian forces–undoubtedly played a role in Khomeini's decision to accept a truce with the 'devil' Huseyn.
187 Arjomand, 1988, p. 135.
188 The Revolutionary Guards also reinforced the continued neutralization of the army–its disengagement from the internal political processes of Iran.
189 Generally, a Muslim individual must do one obligatory pilgrimage to Mecca before he/she dies: but those who want can do several pilgrimages. The pilgrimages that a person does after his/her first one–which is obligatory–are called 'non-obligatory pilgrimages'.
190 See, for example, the pictures in two newspapers, *Keyhan* and *Ettelaat*, between 1-12 February, the last ten days of the Revolution. One of these pictures is printed on the first page of *Keyhan*, 8 February, 1979. This picture shows many of the 'dispossessed' participating in a main demonstration in Tehran.
191 The destiny of Shahpour Bakhtiar, who accepted the Shah's invitation for being prime minister shortly before the victory of the Revolution is an example of such consequences.
192 *Keyhan*, January 1979.
193 *Chador* is a kind of cloth used by religious and traditional women to cover themselves in public places.

194 At the same time the armed forces from the poor areas supported the poor in occupation of apartments in different areas of Tehran. They were led by clergy who were against 'normalization' of revolutionary situation. Many of those saw the normalization as reproduction of the former regime's economic and social order. See, for example, *Keyhan* and *Ettelaat* of February and March 1979.
195 *Keyhan*, February 26, 1979.
196 Ibid.
197 *Keyhan*, March 1, 1979.
198 Ibid.
199 *Keyhan*, March 3, 1979.
200 *Keyhan*, March 6, 1979.
201 Ibid.
202 *Hezballah* means the party of God. It was a name for many groups led and used by clergy to attack the democratic and modern groups aiming to limit and eliminate their oppositional activities against the radical clergy.
203 *Keyhan*, March 8, 1979.
204 Ibid.
205 Ibid.
206 Cf. Abrahamian, *Khomeinism*, 1993. There are examples about his intentions of not creating enemies against him among the opposition against the Shah. For example, Ayatollah Mottahari attempted to banish the intellectual religious leader, Shari'ati, from the modern religious institution of Huseyniyeh Ershad by asking Khomeini to declare a *fatva* or to say 'something against him', but Khomeini did nothing and took a quiet position to not damage his positive image among the religious intellectuals. Also, when the political organization Mojahedin-e Khalq, which was constructed of modern religious revolutionary intellectuals, asked Khomeini for recognition of their armed struggle against the Shah, Khomeini took a quiet position to not lose the support of other religious groups.
207 *Keyhan*, March 8, 1979.
208 Ibid.
209 *Ettelaat*, *Keyhan*, March 8, 1979.
210 *Keyhan*, March 10, 1979.
211 *Keyhan*, March 11, 1979.
212 Of course, the Islamic Republic of Iran is not a democratic regime based on participation of various political parties and free elections. The main point I would like to mention here is the radical clergy's systematic use of the institution of election as a means of legitimization of the political order.
213 *Keyhan* and *Ettelaat*, April 10-13, 1979.
214 *Keyhan*, April 11, 1979.
215 *Keyhan*, May 16, 1979.

216 See *Keyhan* and *Ettelaat*, April-August 1979.
217 Since the beginning of the war between Iran and Iraq and rationing of the food and some other basic commodities, the Islamic regime, through giving the right of distribution of such commodities to some bazaris and small shopkeepers who supported the regime, tried to isolate some of the bazaris who were critical of the regime or had connections with the liberal state or the opposition.
218 *Keyhan*, June 21, 1979.
219 See, for instance, *Keyhan*, June 15-18, 1979.
220 Arjomand, 1988, p. 137.
221 The second speech by the students who occupied the American Embassy.
222 But, the revolutionary committees stopped them in the Takht-e jamshid avenue before reaching the Embassy. The radical clergy did not want the support of the leftists, because their intention was to seize the entire political power and exclude the liberals and the leftists from the political arena.
223 Some radical religious groups such as Fadaiyan-e Islam were also active at the end of this period. Even if it committed political assassinations, but it was a very marginal group in the political arena.
224 In the intellectual arena both Shari'ati's and Mojahedin-e khalq's religio-political ideas were much more dominating than Khomeini's.
225 This was also the case for the members of the LMI, in particular Bazargan.
226 Arjomand, 1988, p. 135.
227 M. Weber, The Sociology of Religion, Beacon Press, 1964 pp. 138-150.
228 Cf. with the closing of the bazaars and other business in Algeria during the liberation movement of the 1960s and closing of business in the occupied territories of Palestine.
229 The theory from which the discussion in this section derives is based on modern evolutionary theory (Burns and Dietz, 1992; Burns, 1995). Such a theory combines *environmental constraint and selectivity* (physical as well as social) and *bounded constructionism* (through human agency). Selectivity entails resource allocation as a function of the practices of groups utilizing a particular rule or rule system, that is, some practices lead to greater resource gains, support and legitimation, and, in general, reproductive robustness than others. Bounded constructionism refers both to the agential powers of actors, but also the constraints on agency and the limited capacities of actors in any given context to adapt, reform or transform social rule systems because of: (1) environmental constraints on the agents' actions. This includes geographic and physical as well as technological constraints and possibilities; (2) institutional and cultural constraints in the sense of the building blocks and possible problem-solving processes available, given an already existing institutional and cultural frame within which actors act and interact: values,

norms, relationships, and institutional arrangements, in short the established social order; (3) finally, the particular knowledge, skills, motivations, self-conception and -confidence of the social actors involved. A modern evolutionary approach stresses that there was no 'necessity' that made the particular revolution–and its outcome–inevitable. The actors involved could have done a number of things differently. Neither does the revolution need to end in greater societal 'integration' which refers to the 'need' of dislocated groups and individuals to be reintegrated into the societal community. The political movements that brought about the revolution were not especially oriented or dedicated to re-integration. The most radical of them wanted to reconstruct society, to create a new order–a social order where they saw themselves as playing a central role.

230 One might be tempted to see the revolution as a struggle between modernity/cosmopolitanism and traditionalism, but one should bear in mind that the new middle classes who participated in the revolution were very modern in their orientation. Also, as I have stressed elsewhere in this work, the radical clergy were not merely 'traditional', they made use of the modern myth of renewal through politics and political participation, the very idea of revolution.

231 See, for example, Andersen and Burns (1992), and Burns (1995) for studies of less dramatic struggles between the state and societal groups.

232 Bakhash (1990, p. 11) refers to a government law that permitted the government to transfer the population of whole villages from one district to another in order to concentrate rural populations and to provide for more efficient delivery of agricultural services.

233 See the discussion on the creative, dialectical process of formulating a vision or blueprint in chapter eleven.

234 For example, in the case of the notion of 'Islamic Republic', the radical clergy understood that the 'holy word' would serve as a type of constitution and that the clergy would be a key group in the governance of society. The new middle classes had a more vague and open conception, with 'Islamic values and norms' playing an inspirational but not determining role and that the formal constitution and government would be central in the governance of society. While the clergy interpreted 'justice' as religious justice, the middle classes were inclined to interpret it as 'justice before the law', applied equally to all and characterized by due process, in a word, the rule of law. Similarly, equality was interpreted in different ways: the clergy saw it as equality before Allah, while the middle classes tended to view it as equality before the law. 'Freedom' for the radical clergy was freedom from secularization and the Shah's repressive policy against the clergy and constraint on Islamic values, while the middle classes saw it more as freedom from arbitrary rule, from traditionalism and parochialism.

235 The most creative opening in former communist countries was precisely after the collapse of regimes. Then, the selection and institutionalization processes began to result in much greater restrictions on variety–both in terms of proposals and real possibilities. The free spaces are no long available.

236 In the period of consolidation and institutionalization there is often a process of radicalization. More moderate 'ideas' and 'arrangements' are selected out or driven out. The process can be viewed as a dynamic set of games, where as the process goes on the games are restructured, and new rules and selective environments operate (Burns et al, 1995). There are several interconnected games at any given time where one may dominate–in the sense that it determines, in part, the parameters and rules of the other games. Thus, the competition and conflicts between the clergy and the secular groups, or among the different clergy groups, or between the 'dispossessed' and the working class and the middle classes were submerged during the pre-revolution processes. Once power was taken by the revolutionary forces, conflicts and arenas that were latent or subordinate came into greater prominence, and set the stage for the post-revolutionary struggles.

237 For example, in its meetings, the National Front called for the neutralization of the army in the conflict and proclaimed: 'The national Islamic movement respect the army' and that 'the military forces are our brothers' (*Keyhan*, January 16, 1978).

238 The democratization initiated by the Shah. The pressure of the USA and its democrat president Jimmy Carter was so well known among the intellectuals that the new changes were called 'Jimmycracy', instead of democracy.

239 For example, Turkman tribes helped the anti-constitutionalist Shah, Muhammad Ali Shah, in his successful attempt to return to Iran in 1911.

240 There are also studies of the traditional function of tribes which point out the Iranian tribes' destructive action against settled areas. Torabi (1974), presents a detailed discussion about the strategy of people of villages and small towns of Azarbayjan for preventing the tribe's periodic attacks and plundering. Torabi points out that the tribe's plundering and attacks influenced the architecture of the villages and small towns. This is also evident for other parts of Iran, such as Fars and Boyr Ahmad and Kohkiloyeh, where the tribes were moving near rural or urban areas.

241 An example is Khomeini's opposition to women's voting.

242 The mobilization of women in these processes of political transformation is particularly noteworthy, as stressed by Eisenstadt (1994).

243 The process, as is well-known, involved the organized use of force and violence against people and property. But the armed forces were lightly armed force organized by the religious, and did not involve the established state forces of violence.

298 Notes

244 Estimates of the number killed during the revolutionary process (between October 1, 1978 and January 15, 1979) are two to three thousand (Arjomand, 1988).
245 In Spring 1963, the Marxist Tudeh Party said the reform was completing the changes that began with the Constitutional Revolution. Also, to legitimize violence as the only means of true revolutions, another Marxist organization, Fadaiyan-e khalq, like Tudeh Party, conceived of the reform as result of the Constitutional Revolution.
246 For a discussion of the difference between an evolutionist or developmental conception of history and one that is genuinely evolutionary, see Burns and Diets (1992,1995), also Sztompka (1993).
247 The jailed members of the organization, after their release from the prison, reorganized Mojahedin and, once more, became a very important political organization during and after the Islamic Revolution.
248 Also see Burns et al (1985), Burns and Flam (1987), concerning the role of rules in human action, social organization, and evolutionary action.
249 Bourdieu calls this schema *habitus*, by which he means 'a system of lasting, transposable dispositions which integrating past experiences, functions at every moment as a matrix of perceptions, appreciations, and actions and makes possible the achievement of infinitely diversified tasks, thanks to analogical transfers of schemes permitting the solution of similarly shaped problems' (Bourdieu, 1977, pp. 82-3).
250 The condition of the urban migrants was not worse than the immigrants who left their country and moved to modern industrial countries of Europe and North America. If there are barriers to their integration in the host societies, they create their own socio-cultural milieu. Of course, this creates problems for the traditional institutions of the host societies and challenges their very existence through acts of deviance that sometimes take a form of collective action, such the revolts of Latino immigrants of the USA, or the Indo-Pakistanian immigrants of England.
251 See, for example, *Keyhan*, 14 January, 1979.
252 As Bourdieu puts it: 'undertakings of collective mobilization cannot succeed without a minimum of concordance between the habitus of the mobilizing agents (e.g. prophet, party leader, etc.) and the dispositions of those whose aspirations and world-view they express' (Bourdieu, 1977, p. 81).
253 Cobban 1968, p. 97.
254 See the discussion in the part, *neutralization of army*, in chapter nine.

Glossary

Except for few Arabic terms, the majority of the 'Islamic terms' are in Persian.

beyt home, family
ahl-e beyt the members of the Prophet's family
a'lem pl. ulama; Muslim religious leaders who possessed religious knowledge
amir commander, leader
amir al-mo'menin the legitimate leader of believers
anjoman association
ashura the 10th of the Islamic month, *muharram*; the day of martyrdom of the Third Imam, Husayn, who was killed by Ummayyids in Karbala in the year 680; a day of anniversary and mourning
atashkadeh the place of fire; Zoroastrians' religious place
auqaf pl. of *vaqf*, pious foundations, religious endowments
basij-e pasdaran an armed organization which mainly consisted of the 'dispossessed' and people from rural areas during the war with Iraq
bast the act of taking refuge in the holy shrines or the home of prominent Mujtahids
bid'at Innovation against the ultimate and unchangeable Islamic law, Shari'a
dar al-harb the home of war; the home of infidels; the community of infidels; opposite to dar al-Islam
dar al-Islam the home of Islam; the Islamic nation, the community of Muslims
dawlat or *dawla*, state; according to the old Persian Empire, religion (din) was the base and dawlat (temporal power) its guardian
Fadaiyan-e khalq those who sacrifice themselves for the people; a Marxist political organization which used mainly the armed strategy against the regime of Shah
Fadaiyan-e Islam those who sacrifice themselves for Islam; a radical Islamic organization which was active during the political turmoil in late 1940s and early 1950s

faqih Islamic jurisprudent
fasad demoralization of Muslim community
fatva a declaration of a prominent *mujtahid* concerning religious laws or other matters of religion
feqahat Islamic jurisprudence
fitna disorder, civil war
gheybat Occultation of the Hidden Imam
gheybat-e kubra the Great Occultation of the Hidden Imam which began after the death of the last *vakil* (deputy of the Imam who had direct contact with Him) in 940, and continues until now
gheybat-e soghra the Lesser Occultation of the Hidden Imam which was about seventy years after His Occultaion; during his Lesser Occultation, He had contact with the Muslim community through His deputies (*vakils*)
hadith the sayings of the Prophet which are used as a source of Islamic law, Shari'a
halal religiously permitted
heysiat-e siyasi traditional political legitimacy
hozeh the place of religious education sometimes used as synonymous to madrasah
huseynieh the place for studying and analyzing the heroic deed of the Third Imam, Husayn, in Karbala in the year 680
Imam leader of the Shi'i community
Imamat the Shi'i theory of succession to the Prophet which means the protection of the right of the Prophet's family to leadership in the Muslim community
imara' the divine authority of Caliphs as compensation for the loss of their political authority
ilm religious knowledge
ithna ashari Twelver imami; Shi'is who believe in Twelve righthood Imams as the successor of the Prophet
ijtihad the competence for interpretation of the Islamic law and giving guidance in the matter of religion
ismat infallibility which is one of properties of the Shi'i Imam
jihad holy war; also, other actions of Muslim individual for radical changes of economic, social, and cultural conditions, according to a *fatva* of one or several Mujtahids
khaleseh royal domains

khanqah the place for sufis ritual ceremonies
kharej-e mahdodeh the areas outside of the legal zones of the cities
kholafa-ye rashedin rightly guided Caliphs; the four Great Caliphs who were the leaders of the Muslim community after the death of the Prophet
khoms a charitable tax which is a fifth of all the profit a Muslim gains in trade or other economic activities
khoshneshin people from rural areas who had no land and worked for landowners during the summer and moved to the cities and worked there during the winter
khutba the traditional religio-political declaration which the leader of the Friday prayer, *Imam jom'a*, used to read prior to the prayer and in which he addressed the legitimated political leader
kufr anti-religious actions or sayings that reject the unity of God, his Prophets, and Imams
madrasah religious school
Majlis-e moassessan the Constitutional Assembly
Majlis-e khebregan the Council of Religious Experts
manbar pulpit
Marja'-e taqlid the source of emulation;
Mojtahid who possessed a great degree of religious knowledge and can exert independent interpretation of Islamic jurisprudence
Mojahedin-e khalq a religio-modern political organization which used armed struggle against the Shah's regime
mashru-e-ye mashruteh constitutionalism according to Islamic laws
masjid mosque
mazlum oppressed
mostaz'afin 'dispossessed'
mulk kingdom
mukallaf Muslim individual who is to practice the duty of 'enjoin the good and to forbid evil'
muqalled believer who follow a Mujtahid or *Marja'-e taqlid*
mutavalli-ye auqf the manager and chief of religious endowments
nayeb-e Imam vicegerent of the Hidden Imam
nehzat movement
nezam order
Nezam-e jadid the new order
Otaq-e asnaf the center of guilds

Pasdaran-e enqelab-e eslami   the Guards of the Islamic Revolution; Revolutionary Guards

pishnamazi   the leading of the prayers

qadi   religious judge

raudakhani   the public recitation of the tragic story of martyrdom of the Third Imam, Husayn

sahm-e Imam   'the share of Imam'; religious tax collected by the ulama to be used for their own costs or other religious purposes

Shari'a   Islamic law

sherk   usurpation to God; assumption of companionship to God

shi'i-ye Ali   believer in Ali, the First Shi'i Imam, and his eleven successors

shura   consolidation

Sufism   monistic ideology of a sect who believe in the unity of God and man

Sunna   tradition; the deeds of the Prophet

taghut   despotic ruler who claims divinity for himself and competes with God, such as the Pharaohs of Egypt

takyeh   a place for performance of religious dramas

taqiyya   dissemulation of belief in time of danger

taqlid   emulation

tauhid   the unity of God; 'there is no god but God'

ta'ziya   dramatic theatrical exhibition of the martyrdom of the Third Imam, Husayn

tojjar   traders; the most prominent group among the bazaris

tullab   religious students

umma   the Islamic nation; the Islamic community

ulama   pl. of a'lem

vakil   deputy; message bearer of the Hidden Imam

vaqf   sing. of auqf, religious endowment

vazir   minister

va'z   the act of preaching in *manbars* (pulpits)

velayat   vicegerency of the Hidden Imam

velayat-e faqih   the reign of Islamic jurisprudents; Ayatollah Khomeini's theory for the construction of an Islamic state by which the *fuqaha* rule on behalf of the Hidden Imam

Wizara   the divine authority of office which was developed as a result of the decline of caliphs' authority

zakat   'purifying tax' on the property of the Muslims

Bibliography

Abdullaev, Z. Z. (1963) Promyshlennost i Zarozhdenie rabochego klassa Irana v kontse XIX nachale X X vv., Baku, In Issawi (1971) The Economic History of Iran 1800-1914.

Abrahamian, Ervand (1983) *Iran Between Two Revolutions*, Princeton: Princeton University Press.

―――― (1993) *Khomeinism*, Berkeley: University of California Press.

Adamiyyat, Fereydun (1323/1944) *Amir Kabir va Iran*, Tehran: Kharazmi Publication.

―――― (1355/1976) *Ideologi-ye nehzat-e mashrutiyyat-e Iran*, (The Ideology of the Constitutional Movement of Iran), Tehran: Payman.

Akhavi Shahrough (1980) *Religion and Politics in Contemporary Iran*, New York: State University of New York Press.

Al-Baghdadi (1928) *Usul al-Din*, Istanbul.

Al-Kulayni, Muhammad Y. (1960) '*al-kafi fi Ilm ad-din*', Tehran.

Alexander, Jeffery (1995) 'Collective Action and Democratic Discourse: Social Movements as 'Translations' of Civil Society', Paper presented in Uppsala: SCASSS June Seminar on Revolutions.

Algar, Hamid (1969) *Religion and State in Iran 1785-1906*, Berkeley: University of California Press.

Amanat Abbas (1988) 'In Between the madrasah and the Marketplace: The Designation of Clerical Leadership in Modern Shi'ism', in S. Arjomand, ed., *Authority and Political Culture in Shi'ism*, New York: State University of New York Press.

Amuzegar, J. and M. A. Fekrat (1971) *Iran: Economic Development under Dualistic Conditions*, Chicago: University of Chicago.

Andersen, S. and Tom R. Burns (1992) *Societal Decisionmaking: Democratic Challenge to State Technocracy*, London: Dartmouth.

Ansari, Shaykh Jaberi (1321/1942) *Tarikh-e Isfahan va Rey*, (The History of Isfahan and Rey), Tehran: *Roznameh va majaleh ye Kherad* Publishing.

Aqeli, Baqer (1372/1993) *Roz shomar-e tarikh-e Iran* (the Chronology of Iranian History), Tehran: Goftar.

Arjomand, Said A. (1988) *The Turban for the Crown*, New York: Oxford University Press.

―――― (1984) *The Shadow of God and the Hidden Imam*, Chicago: University of Chicago Press.

—— ed. (1984) *From Nationalism to Revolutionary Islam*, London: Macmillan Press LTD.
—— ed. (1988) *Authority and Political Culture in Shi'ism*, New York: State University of New York Press.
—— ed. (1993) *The Political Dimensions of Religion*, New York: State University of New York Press.
—— 'Revolution in World History, vol.1: Ancient and Medieval Revolutions' (1995), Ms. paper presented in Uppsala, SCASSS.
Azimi, Fakhreddin (1989) *Iran, the Crisis of Democracy*, London: Tauris and Co. Ltd.
Baer, Gabriel (1973) 'Basic Factors Affecting Social Structure, Tensions, and Change in Modern Egyptian Society', in Milson Manehem, ed. (1973) *Society and Political Structure in the Arab World*.
Bahar, Malek al-Sho'ara (1323/1944) *Tarikh-e ahzab-e siyasi-ye Iran* (The history of political parties in Iran), Tehran: Sherkat-e sahami-ye chap-e rangin.
Bakhash, Shaul (1994) 'Iran: The Crises of Legitimacy' working paper, ms.
—— (1990) *The Reign of the Ayatollahs*, New York: Basic Books.
Ball, Alan R. (1981) *British Political Parties: The Emergence of a Modern Party System*, London: Macmillan.
Banani, Amin (1967) 'The social and Economic Structure of the Persian Empire in its Heyday', paper submitted to the Harvard colloquium in the Tradition and Change in the Middle East, December, 1967.
Banani, A. & S. Vryonis (1977) *Individualism and Conformity in Classical Islam*, Wiesbaden: Otto Harrassowitz.
Bazargan, Mehdi (1983) *Enqelab-e Iran dar du harkat* (The Iranian Revolution in Two Stages), Tehran: Entesharat-e nehzat-e azadi-ye Iran.
Bell, Richard (1937) *The Qur'an, Translated with a critical re-arrangement of the Surahs*, Edinburgh.
Bellah, Robert (1980) *Varieties of Civil Religion*, San Francisco: San Francisco cop.
Berman, Harold J. (1983) *Law and Revolution: The Formation of the Western Legal Tradition*, Cambridge, Massachusetts: Harvard University Press.
Binder, Leonard (1964) *Iran, Political Development in a Changing Society*, Berkeley: University of California Press.
Bourdieu, Pierre (1977) *Outline of a Theory of Practice*, London: Cambridge University Press.
Brecher, Jeremy (1972) *Strike*, Straight: Arrow Books.
Burns, Tom R. (1995) 'Revolutions: Evolutionary Processes, Human agency, and the Transformation of Social Orders', Uppsala Theory Circle, Department of Sociology, Uppsala University.
—— (1994) 'Post-Parliamentary Democracy, Sacralities Contradictions, and Transitions of Modernity', In *Religio*, by Bulzoni editore, Roma, pp. 161-92.

―――― & Thomas Dietz, 'Social Action, Institutional Arrangements, and Evolutionary Processes' in R. Hollingsword ed., *Social Actors and the Embeddedness of Institutions*, M. E. Sharpe, New York, 1995.

―――― & Thomas Baumgartner, and Philippe Deville (1985) *Man, Decisions, Society*, New York: Gordon and Breach Publishers.

―――― and H. Flam (1987) *The Shaping of Social Organization*, London: Sage.

―――― and T. Dietz (1992) 'Cultural Evolution: Social Rule Systems, Selection, and Human Agency', in *International Sociology*, Vol. 7:259-83.

Calhoun Craig (1993) 'Nationalism and Civil society: Democracy, Diversity and Self-determination', in *International Sociology*, vol. 8, No. 4.

Chehabi, Houchang E. (1990) *Iranian Politics and Religious Modernism*, London: I.B. Tauris & Co.

Cobban, Alfred (1964) *The Social Interpretation of the French Revolution*, Great Britain: Cambridge University Press.

―――― (1968) *Aspects of French Revolution*, London: Jonathan Cape Ltd.

Dabashi, Hamid (1988) 'Two Clerical Tracts on Constitutionalism', in Arjomand, *Authority and Political Culture in Shi'ism*.

Durkheim, Emil (1984) *The Division of Labour in Society*, London:Macmillan Press Ltd.

Eisenstadt, S. N. (1982) 'The Axial Age', in *European journal of sociology*, nr. 23, pp. 294-314.

―――― (1985) 'Comparative Liminality', in *Religion*:15, pp. 315-338.

―――― (1993) 'Civil Society and Democracy in Latin America: Some comparative observations' in *Estudios Interdisciplinarios de America Latina v El Caribe*, 1993, Vol. 4, No. 4, pp. 27-37.

―――― (1994) 'Fundamentalism, Phenomenology and Comparative Dimensions', Jerusalem: Hebrew University of Jerusalem.

―――― (1995) 'Reconceiving Modernity', paper presented in Uppsala: SCASSS.

Eckstein, Harry (1983) 'The Idea of Political Development: From Dignity to Efficiency', in *World Politics*, No. 34.

Eqbal, Abbas, (1340/1961) *Mirza Taqi Khan Amir Kabir*, Tehran.

―――― (1330/1951) *Tarihk-e Mofassal-e Iran*, az zuhor-e eslam ta asr-e hazer, (The Complete History of Iran, from the appearance of Islam to the modern time), Tehran: Sherkat-e matbo'at Press.

Esposito, John (1980) *Islam and Development*, New York: Syracuse University Press.

Falamaki, Mansour (1977) *Baz-zendeh sazi-ye banaha va shahrhaye tarikhi* (Restoration of the Ancient Building and Cities), Tehran: University of Tehran.

Fathi, Asghar (1993) 'Seyyed Jamal al-Din Va'ez and the Significance of the Pulpit', in *Iran Nameh* Vol. XI, No. 2.

Fazel, Mohammed & Ray Jan-Ole (1979) *Business culture in the middle east*, Scandinavia: Scandinavian Institute for Administrative Research.

Gellner, Ernest (1994) *Conditions of Liberty: Civil Society and its Rivals*, London: Hamish Hamilton.
Ghods, M. Reza (1989) *Iran in the Twentieth Century: A Political History*, Boulder, Colorado: Lynne Rienner Publishers.
Giddens, Anthony (1984) *The Constitution of Society*, Cambridge: Polity Press.
────── ed. (1986) *Durkheim on Politics and the State*, Cambridge: Polity Press.
Goldstone, Jack A. (1991) 'Ideology, cultural framework, and the process of revolution', in *Theory and Society*, No. 20:405-453.
Gurr, Ted Robert (1970) *Why men Rebel*, Princeton: Princeton University Press.
Habermas, Jurgen (1984) *Borgerlig offentlighet*, Lund: Arkiv förlag.
────── (1990) *Moral Consciousness and Communicative Action*, Cambridge, Massachusetts: MIT Press.
Hairi, Abdul-Hadi, (1977) *Shi'ism and Constitutionalism in Iran*,: Leiden: E. J. Brill.
Hall, John A., ed. (1995) *Civil Society, Theory, History, Comparison*, Cambridge, UK: Polity Press.
Hazhir, Abdul Husayn (1935) 'Dar rah-e valiahdi-ye Abbase Mirza', Tehran: Mihr No. I.
Hjärpe, Jan (1983) *Politisk Islam,* Stockholm: Gohtia.
────── (1993) 'Islam, Nationalism, and Ethnicity', in H. Lindhelm, ed. *Ethnicity and Nationalism*, Nordnes.
Hourani, Albert (1991) *A History of the Arab Peoples*, Cambridge, Massachusetts: The Belknap Press of Harvard University Press.
Huntington, Samuel P. (1968) *Political Order in Changing Societies*, New Haven: Yale University Press.
Ibish, Yusuf (1965) 'The Political Doctrine of al-Baqillani', Islamic Studies, No. IV.
Ibrahim, Saad Eddin (1995) 'Civil society and Prospects of Democratization in the Arab World', in Norton Augustus Richard, *Civil Society in the Middle East*, Köln: Brill.
Issawi, Charles (1978) 'The Iranian Economy 1925-1975: Fifty Years of Economic Development', in G. Lenczowski, *Iran Under the Pahlavis*, Hoover Institution Publication, pp. 130-166.
────── (1971) *The Economic History of Iran*, Chicago: University of Chicago Press.
Kamali, Masoud & Tom R. Burns (1994) 'Why did the clergy succeed in taking state power only in modern Iran?', paper presented at the XIII World Congress of Sociology, July 18-23, Bielefeld, Germany.
Kasravi, Ahmad (1942) *Dar bare-ye Reza Shah Pahlavi*, (Concerning Reza Shah Pahlavi), Tehran: *Parcham* Magazin.
────── (1942) *Emruz cheh bayad kard?* (what must be done today?), Tehran: *Parcham* Magazin.

―――― (1330/1951) *Tarikh-e enqelab-e mashrotiyyat-e Iran*, Tehran: Amir Kabir Publication.
―――― (1942) 'Concerning Reza Shah Pahlavi', Tehran: Parcham Magazin.
―――― (1991) *Zendegani-ye man*, Dahsal dar Adliyyeh, (My Life, Ten Years in the House of Justice), Sweden, Uppsala: Resultat Media V AB.
Katouzian, Homa (1988) *Musaddeq's Memories*, England: LR Printing Services Limited.
Kazemi, F. and Abrahamian E. (1978) 'The Nonrevolutionary Peasantry of Modern Iran', in *Iranian Studies*, Vol. XI 1978.
Kazeroni & Golabi (1979) 'The statistical presentation of marginal people' in *Ketabe Jom'eh*, No. 12.
Keddie, R. Nikki and Hooglund Eric, ed. (1986) *The Iranian Revolution & The Islamic Republic*, New York: Syracuse University Press.
―――― (1981) *The Roots of Revolution*, An Interpretive History of Modern Iran, New Haven: Yale University Press.
―――― (1966) *Religion and Rebellion in Iran*, The Tobacco Protest of 1891-1892, London: Frank Cass & Co. Ltd.
Kermani, Nazem al-Islam (1362/1983) *Tarikh-e bidari- ye Iranian* (The History of Iranians' Uprising), Tehran: Agah Publishing.
Kheirabadi, Masoud (1991) *Iranian Cities, Formation and Development,* Austin: University of Texas Press.
Khomeini, Ruhullah Mosavi (1322/1943) *Kashf al-asrar*, Tehran.
―――― (1981) *Islam and Revolution,* Writing and Declarations of Imam Khomeini, Translated and Annotated by Hamid Algar, Berkeley: Mizan Press.
―――― (1979) *Hukomat-e eslami*, Tehran: Amir kabir.
Lahidji, Abdol Karim, (1988) 'Constitutionalism and Clerical Authority', in Said Arjomand, ed. *Authority and Political Culture in Shi'ism*, New York: State University of New York Press.
Lambton, Ann K. S. (1981) *State and Government in Medieval Islam*, London: Oxford.
―――― (1988) *Continuity and Change in Medieval Persia*, London: I.B. Tauris & Co. Ltd.
Lenczowski, George, ed. (1978) *Iran under the Pahlavis*, Stanford: Hoover Institution Press.
Lewis, Bernard (1993) *Islam and the West*, New York: Oxford University Press.
―――― (1988) *The political Language of Islam*, Chicago: University of Chicago Press.
Limbert, John W. *(*1987) *Iran: At War with History*, Boulder, Colorado: Westview Press.
Lijphart A., 'The Comparable-Case Strategy in Comparative Research', in Cantori L. & Ziegler Jr, ed., *Comparative Politics in the Post-Behavioral Era*, Lynne Rienner Publishers.

Lipset, S. M. (1963) Political Man: The Social Basis of Politics, Garden City, N.Y.:Doubleday.
Lukes, Steven (1985) *Emil Durkheim, His Life and Work*, California: Stanford University Press.
Makki, Hosayn (1324/1945) *Tarikh-e bist sale-ye Iran*, (Twenty Years History of Iran), Vol. II, Tehran: Chapkhane-ye Majlis (Majlis Publishing).
Malekzadeh Mehdi, (1949-1951) *Tarikh-e enqelab-e mashrotiyyat-e Iran*, (The History of the Constitutional Revolution of Iran), Tehran:
- Vol I (1328/1949) *Ketabkhaneh-ye Shoqrat* Publishing;
- Vol I (1329/1950) *Ketabkhaneh ye Shoqrat* Publishing;
- Vol. III (1330/1951) *Ketab forushi ye Ebn-e Sina* Publishing,.
Mardin, Serif, 'Civil Society and Islam', in Hall, John A. (1995) *Civil Society, Theory, History, Comparison*, Cambridge: Polity Press.
Mehner, Harald (1978) 'Development and Planning in Iran after World War II', in *Iran Under the Pahlavis*, Stanford: Hoover Institution Press.
Milani, Mohsen M. (1994) *The Making of Iran's Islamic Revolution*, Colorado: Westview Press.
Milson, Manehem, ed. (1973) *Society and Political Structure in the Arab World*, New York: Humanities Press.
Moaddel, Mansoor (1993) *Class, Politics, and Ideology in the Iranian Revolution*, New York: Columbia University Press.
Momeni, Bagher (1993) *Din va dovlat* (Religion and State), Spånga, Sweden: Baran Förlag.
Moussalli, Ahmad S., 'Modern Islamic Fundamentalist Discourses on Civil Society, Pluralism and Democracy', in Norton Augustus Richard (1995) *Civil Society in the Middle East*.
Movlavi, Jalal al-Din (1366/1978) *Mathnavi-ye Ma'navi*, Tehran: Amir Kabir Press.
Mustaufi, Abdullah (1321/1942) S*harh-e zendegani-ye man, ya tarikh-e ijtema'i va edari-ye daura-ye Qajariyeh,* (The Narration of My Life or The Bureaucratic and Social History of Qajars), Tehran: Entesharat-e zavvar.
Mutahhari, Murtaza (1985) *Islamiska rörelser på 1900- talet* (The Islamic Movements during Twentieth century), Lidingö: Islamicka kulturcentret i Norden, Sweden.
Nateq H.and Adamiyat F. (1989) *Afkar-e ejtema'i va siyasi va eqtesadi dar asar-e montasher nashode-ye dovran-e qajar* (The Socioeconomic and Political ideas in un-published documents of the Qajar period), Germany, Saarbruken: Navid.
Na'ini, Mirza Muhammad Husayn (1334/1955) *Tanbih al-ummah va tanzih al-mellah* (The admonition and refinement of the people), Tehran.
Norton, Augustus Richard, ed. (1995) *Civil Society in the Middle East*, Köln: E.J. Brill.

Nuri, Shaykh Fazl Allah (1993) 'Ketab-e tazkarat al-ghafel va ershad al-jahel', printed in *Iran Nameh*, Vol. XI pp.532-536.
Pakdaman, Naser (1365/1986) 'Ta Tabriz, Nazari be roydadha-ye enqelab-e Iran ta 29 Bahman 1356' (Until Tabriz, an overview on the Iranian revolution until February 19, 1978), in *Chashm andaz*, 1986, No. I, Paris.
Parsa, Misagh (1989) *Social Origin of the Iranian Revolution*, New Brunswick: Rutgers University Press.
Petczynski, Z. A., ed. (1984) *The State and Civil Society, Studies in Hegel's Political Philosophy*, New York: Cambridge University Press.
Piamenta, Moshe (1979) *Islam in Everyday Arabic Speech*, Leiden:Brill.
Rosenthal, Frantz (1977) 'I Am You', Individual Piety and Society in Islam, in Banani & Vryonis (eds) *Individualism and Conformity in Classical Islam*.
Sabine, George (1950) *A History of Political Thought*, New York: Rinehart & Winston.
Savory, R. M. (1970) 'Safavid Persia', in *Cambridge History of Islam*, London: Cambridge University Press.
────── (1978) 'Social Development in Iran During the Pahlavi Era', in G. Lenczowski, pp. 85-127.
────── (1980) *Iran Under the Safavids*, New York: Press Syndicate of the University of Cambridge.
Seligman, Adam B. (1992) *The Idea of Civil Society*, New York: The Free Press.
────── ed. (1989) *Order and Transcendence, The Role of Utopias and the Dynamics of Civilizations*, Leiden: E. J. Brill.
Sewell, William (1995) 'The History of the French Revolution and the Comparative Sociology of Revolution: Disjunctions and Complementarities', Paper presented in the workshop: Revolutions and Social Theory, Uppsala, June 27-July 1.
────── (1992) 'A Theory of Structure: Duality, Agency, and Transformation', in *American Journal of Sociology*, vol.98 number 1.
Shari'ati, Ali (1980) *Marxism and Other Western Fallacies*, Translated by R. Campbell, Berkeley: Mizan Press.
Sheikholeslami, A. Reza (1978) 'The Patrimonial Structure of Iranian Bureaucracy in the Late Nineteenth Century', in *Iranian Studies*, Journal of The Society for Iranian Studies, Volume XI.
Skocpol, Theda (1979) *State and Social Revolutions*, New York: Cambridge University Press.
────── (1994) *Social Revolutions in The Modern World*, New York: Cambridge University Press.
Strömholm, Stig (1985) *A Short History of Legal Thinking in the West*, Lund: Norstedts Publishing.
Sullivan, W. H. (1981) *Mission to Iran*, New York: W. W. Norton.
Sztompka, P. (1993) *The Sociology of Social Change*, Oxford: Blackwell.

Taylor, Michael (1988) *Rationality and Revolution*, New York: Cambridge University Press.
Teymuri, Ibrahim (1949) *Tahrim-e tanbaku ya avvalin muqavemat-e manfi dar Iran*, (The Boycott of Tobacco or the First Negative Resistance in Iran), Tehran.
Tilly, Charles (1993) *European Revolutions* 1492-1992, Oxford: Blackwell Publishing.
―――― (1978) *From mobilization to Revolution*, London: Addison-Wesley.
―――― (1975) 'Revolution and Collective Violence', in Fred I. Greenstein & Nelson W. Polsby, *Handbook of Political science*, vol. 3.
―――― (1984) *Big Structures, Large Processes, Huge Comparisons*, London: Russell SAGE.
Torabi, Ali Akbar (1353/1974) *Jame'-e shenasi-ye rostai-ye Iran* (The Rural Sociology of Iran), Tabriz: Entesharat-e nobel (Nobel Publishing).
Turner, Bryan S. (1974) *Weber and Islam*, London: Routledge & Kegan Paul.
Vatikiotis, P.J. (1987) *Islam and the State*, London: Croom Helm Press.
Weber, Max, (1968) *Economy and Society*, New York: Bedminster Press.
―――― (1964) *The Sociology of Religion*, Boston: Beacon Press.
Willer, Donald N. (1981) *Iran, Past and Present*, Princeton: Princeton University Press.
Wright, Denis (1365/1986) The Persians Amongst the English, translated into Persian by Karim Imami, *Iranian dar mian-e engelisian*, Tehran: Zamineh Publishing.
Yaghmai, Iqbal (2537/1978) *Shahid-e rah-e azadi, Seyyed Jamal-e Va'ez-e Isfahani*, (The martyr of freedom, Seyyed Jamal-e Va'ez-e Isfahani), Tehean: Entesharat-e Tus.
Zarinkub, Abdul Husayn (1337/1958) 'Yaddashti dar bare-ye Ta'ziye-ye Mah-e Muharram', Tehran: *Sukhan Magazin*, No. IX.
Zeldich, Morris Jr. (1969) 'Some Methodological Problems of Field Studies', in G. McCall and J. Simmons ed., *Issues in Participant Observation*, Mass.: Addison-Wesley Publishing.

Newspapers and Magazines

Chashm Andaz No. 1, summer 1986
Ettelaat: From 21 January 1979 to 25 February 1979
Iran nameh Persian Journal of Iranian Studies:
-Vol. XI, No. 2, Spring 1993: A Special Issue on the Modernization of Iran.
-Vol. XI, No. 3, Summer 1993, A Special Issue on the Constitutional Revolution.

Iranian Studies Journal of The Society for Iranian Studies, Vol. XI, 1978
Islamic studies Vol. IV, 1965
Ketabe jom'eh: No. 12, 25 October 1979
Keyhan: First period: from 16 January 1979 to 20 March 1979
Second period: from 21 April 1979 to 22 July 1979
Navid The Organ of the Tudeh Party
Parcham 1321/1942
Sokhan Vol. IX

Index

'Atabat, 28; 50; 54; 78; 79; 89; 91; 93; 101; 107; 108; 113; 114; 123; 149
Abbas Mirza, 38; 67; 68; 69; 70; 93; 245
Abbasids, 20; 23; 24; 25
Abdul Azim, 93; 94; 109; 112
Adalatkhana, 264
Agha Muhammad Khan, 39; 64
Ahmad Shah Qajar, 128; 129
Ahmadzadeh, Masoud, 265
Akhbari, 40
Akhbaris, 30; 51; 53; 58; 146
Ala al-Daula, 94; 95
Alam, Asadullah, 144
Al-Baghdadi, 24; 41
Al-Baqillani, 24
Alexander, J., 24
Al-Ghazali, 24; 41
Ali ibn-e Abu Taleb, 21
Al-Mawardi, 24; 41
Amin al-Sultan, 77; 90; 91; 93
Amini, Ali, 144
Amuzegar, Jamshid, 182
Anjoman-e sa'adat-e Iran, 101
Anti-constitutionalism, 111
Aqasi, Haj Mirza, 69
Ardebili, Ayatollah Musavi, 191
Arsenjani, Hasan, 144
Aryamehri, 196
Ashura, 134
Assembly of experts, 218; 219
Association of Iranian Lawyers, 265
Atashkadeh, 56
Auqaf, 27; 28; 29; 30; 33; 46; 50; 53; 54; 60; 74; 118; 120; 146; 147; 148
Ayn al-Daula, 92; 93; 95; 96; 97; 98; 108
Azhari, General Gholam Reza, 190; 192

Babiyeh, 70
Bahaism, 76
Bahonar, Hojjatoleslam Javad, 154; 160; 188; 204; 219
Bakhtiyar, Shahpour, 190; 193; 197; 241
Bakhtiyari, tribe, 102; 238; 240; 241
Baluchis, 85
Banisadr, Abul Hasan, 204; 210
Bank-e Melli, 131
Basij-e pasdaran, 9
Bast, 74; 77; 93; 94; 97; 109; 112; 230; 231; 252; 253
Bazargan, Mehdi, 3; 151; 164; 180; 188; 189; 191; 193; 205; 209; 211; 215; 216; 217; 219; 220; 226; 240; 256; 262
Bazarganan. See Merchants
Behbahani, Ayatollah, 82; 147; 150
Beheshti, Ayatollah, 160
Bonyad-e mostaz'afin, 206
Borujerdi, Ayatollah, 141; 147; 150; 181; 225; 237; 253

Calhoun, Craig, 26; 24; 36
Carter, Jimmy, 191; 264
Catholic church, 47
Charismatic individuals, 50; 51; 55;

313

59
Chinese Revolution, 241
Church, Catholic, 29; 42; 43; 47; 48; 49; 50; 55; 59; 76; 250
CIA, Central Intelligence Agency, 189
Civil Code, 146
Clergy, 252
Collective action, 10
Concession policy, 89; 107; 242
Confrontation of the 'dispossessed' with municipal authorities, 175; 182; 194; 196; 197; 207; 226; 245; 264; 266; 269
Confucianism, 261
Constitutional Revolution, 1; 2; 8; 12; 37; 62; 39; 76; 79; 80; 82; 84; 85; 66; 92; 98; 100; 89; 106; 107; 109; 110; 112; 113; 116; 117; 120; 121; 122; 123; 24; 128; 135; 136; 137; 141; 148; 168; 128; 224; 230; 236; 237; 238; 240; 241; 242; 243; 244; 245; 251; 252; 253; 257; 259; 261; 264; 274
Cossacks, Brigade, 244
Counterrevolutionary, 85; 100; 101; 102; 239; 245; 251; 263

Dadgaha-ye enqelab. See Revolutionary Courts
Dar al-Islam, 41
Dawlat (state), 25; 26
Democratic governance, 210
Dispossessed, 3; 8; 141; 166; 172; 176; 178; 182; 159; 196; 197; 198; 199; 201; 202; 203; 206; 212; 215; 226; 237; 238; 241; 245; 255; 257; 259; 262; 263; 264; 266; 267; 268; 269; 270; 272; 273

Divankhaneh (U'rf courts during the reign of Amir Kabir), 71; 72

Eisenstadt, S. N., 5; 6; 8; 24; 36; 37; 227; 228; 229; 257; 259
Elites, 4; 10; 192; 193; 236; 254
Enlightenment, 254; 261
Eshrat abad, 202
Ettelaat, 194; 210; 218

Fadaiyan-e Islam, 139; 141
Fadaiyan-e khalq, 179; 220; 243; 265
Fanon, Frantz, 152
Fath Ali Shah Qajar, 38; 58; 64; 65; 66; 67; 68
Fatva, 79; 80; 91; 101; 181; 206
Fitna (civil war), 25
Foreign powers, 24; 129; 140; 191
Fundamental Law, 113; 114; 115

Gheybat (Occultation of the Hidden Imam), 22; 23; 24; 44; 49; 55; 60; 61; 153; 227
Govd neshinan, 178

Haji, 187
Hasan Rushdiya, Haj Mirza, 89
Heysiyat-e siyasi, 226
Hezballah, 213; 215
Hezb-e jomhuri-ye eslami. See Islamic Republican Party
Hidden Imam, 6; 22; 23; 24; 25; 27; 29; 31; 39; 40; 42; 43; 48; 49; 53; 54; 55; 58; 61; 66; 79; 66; 101; 89; 115; 116; 117; 120; 137; 148; 155; 157; 162; 218; 128; 225; 227; 228; 229; 231; 250; 261; 262
Hierocracy, 40; 47; 49; 59; 67; 148
Hobbes, 24
Hoveida, Amir Abbas, 182

Hukomat-e eslami, 225; 255
Huseynieh Ershad, 154; 155; 165

Ibn Taymiyya, 41
Ikhvan al-Muslemin. *See* Islamic Brotherhood
Imam jom'a, 51; 71; 74; 75; 82; 94
Imamat, 23; 24; 60
Imara, 24
Imperial Tobacco Corporation, 77
Independence, Freedom, Islamic Republic, 270; 273
Industrial Revolution, 7
Iran novin (party), 244
Islamic Brotherhood, 139
Islamic consultative assembly, 114
Islamic Democratic Republic, 211
Islamic government, 24; 157; 158; 159; 160; 210; 267; 272; 273
Islamic Republic, 160; 209; 210; 235
Islamic Republican party, 154
Islamic Revolution, 1; 2; 3; 4; 5; 6; 7; 8; 12; 13; 14; 1; 24; 134; 152; 154; 156; 141; 168; 170; 172; 178; 181; 182; 159; 186; 188; 192; 193; 194; 201; 202; 206; 207; 212; 213; 214; 226; 231; 236; 237; 238; 239; 240; 241; 243; 245; 251; 253; 254; 255; 256; 257; 258; 259; 261; 262; 263; 264; 267; 269; 274; 275
Islamicization, 56; 128

Ja'far al-Sadiq, 22
Jihad, 58; 61; 68; 78; 270

Kamran Mirza, 121
Karavansarays, 31
Karbala, 43; 54; 55; 65; 134; 135; 147; 154; 266
Karim Khan Zand, 39

Kashani, Ayatollah, 75; 94; 139; 140; 141; 162
Kashef al-asrar, 6
Khaleseh (Royal domain), 173; 174
Khamenei, 160; 219
Kharej-e mahdodeh. *See* outer zone
Kharijis, 24
Khomeini, Ayatollah Ruholla, 6; 7; 13; 42; 144; 145; 150; 152; 153; 154; 155; 156; 157; 158; 159; 160; 141; 163; 172; 176; 180; 181; 183; 188; 191; 192; 193; 194; 195; 197; 198; 203; 204; 205; 206; 208; 209; 210; 211; 212; 213; 214; 215; 216; 217; 218; 219; 220; 225; 226; 238; 239; 240; 241; 242; 245; 253; 254; 255; 256; 257; 259; 264; 265; 270; 273
Khoms (religious tax), 30; 31; 46
Khurasan, 129
Khuzestan, 129
Komision-e shahanshahi. *See* Royal Commission
Komitehs, 9; 204; 205; 212; 217; 257
Kuchik Khan, 24
Kurds, 85

Land Reform, 144
Liberation Movement of Iran (LMI), 151; 154; 165; 168; 180; 182; 183; 186; 188; 191; 192; 193; 209; 210; 240; 241; 253; 256; 258; 262; 267; 272; 273
Lors, 85
Lutis, 37; 149

Madrasahs, 11; 62; 82; 88; 132; 133; 146; 147; 148; 150; 164
Madrasah-ye Faydiya, 64
Majlesi, Mulla Muhammad Baqer, 40

316   *Index*

Majlis (consultative assembly), 96; 97; 98; 100; 101; 108; 110; 111; 112; 113; 114; 115; 116; 120; 121; 122; 123; 24; 129; 135; 136; 139; 140; 141; 147; 224; 230; 237; 243
Majlis-e khebregan. See Assembly of experts
Majlis-e mashvarat, 96
Majlis-e moassesan. See Islamic Constitutional Assembly
Malek al-Motokalemin, 99
Mamluks, 25
Manbars, 11; 37; 62; 80; 99; 122; 252; 253
Marja'-e taqlid, 28; 30; 31; 42; 44; 50; 51; 53; 79; 113; 141; 181
Marxism, 152; 153; 256; 261
Mashruteh, 96; 108; 110; 111; 112; 113
Mashruteh-ye mashru'a, 111; 112; 113
Merchants (of bazaar), 32; 45; 56; 57; 67; 72; 73; 74; 75; 77; 78; 83; 84; 89; 90; 91; 93; 94; 98; 133; 140; 148; 154; 167; 169; 171; 180; 186; 187; 204; 238; 240; 269
Migration (internal), 170; 174; 182; 275
Military forces, 70; 100; 128; 189; 190; 197; 198; 199; 224; 244; 245; 274
    Mirza Taqi Khan 'Amir Kabir', 69
Modarres, 129; 135
Modarresin, 45
Modern civil society, 8; 12; 121; 123; 163; 164; 166; 209; 214; 218; 219; 237; 251; 254
Modernization programs, 12
Modular man, 248; 249

Mojahedin-e khalq, 213; 225
Montazeri, Ayatollah Husayn, 160; 180
Mosaddeq, Muhammad, 139; 140; 141; 150; 151; 163; 180; 252; 253
Mottahari, Ayatollah, 217
Mu'tazilis, 24
Muhammad al-Baqer, 24
Muhammad Ali Shah Qajar, 101; 106; 108; 111; 114; 115; 121; 244
Muhammad Reza Shah, 12; 24; 167; 181; 190; 225; 244
Muhammad Reza Shah Pahlavi, 12
Muharram, 93; 134; 144
Mujtahids, 23; 24; 27; 28; 30; 33; 37; 39; 40; 42; 44; 45; 50; 51; 54; 59; 93; 94; 102; 107; 119; 120; 141; 146; 147; 148; 150; 252
Mullahs, 45; 110; 165; 241
Muqalleds, 28; 30; 31; 45

Nader Shah, 50; 39; 64; 146
Nahj al-balaghah, 24
Naser al-Din Shah, 82
National Association of University Teachers, 265
Nationalization of the oil, 133; 172; 212; 252
Nauz, Monsieur, 90; 92; 93; 95
Navid, the organ of Tudeh Party, 197
Neutralization of the army, 188; 208
National Front (NF), 133; 145; 151; 163; 165; 168; 180; 182; 183; 186; 188; 191; 192; 193; 195; 209; 240; 241; 253; 258; 262; 272
Niyabat. See Vicegerency of the Hidden Imam

Nuri, Sheykh Fazl Allah, 82; 89; 111; 112; 113; 114; 115; 116; 119; 123

Occupation of the American Embassy, 220
Office of *sadr*, 49
Ottoman Empire, 26; 67; 72
Ottoman Sultans, 25
Outer zone, 175; 177; 178; 182; 194; 196; 197; 245

Parliamentarism, 7; 106; 110; 252
Pasdaran-e enqelab. See Revolutionary Guards
Perso-Russian wars, 39; 58; 67; 68; 69
Pesian, Colonel, 129
Pishevaran, 163
Pishnamazi, 43
Plan, developmental, 169; 172; 173
political order, 6; 9; 10; 38; 39; 40; 121; 158; 194; 210; 216; 228; 229; 249; 256
Political parties, 128; 140; 145; 163; 207; 212; 234; 237
Political prisoners, 265

Qezelbash, 20
Qum, 28; 54; 64; 72; 73; 95; 98; 135; 136; 148; 182; 194; 211; 212; 213; 216; 231; 252; 265

Radical clergy, 1; 6; 7; 8; 9; 13; 14; 144; 150; 160; 141; 163; 165; 171; 172; 176; 181; 183; 159; 186; 188; 192; 193; 194; 195; 197; 198; 199; 206; 212; 213; 214; 215; 217; 218; 219; 220; 225; 226; 235; 240; 241; 244; 252; 253; 254; 255; 257; 258; 259; 262; 263; 266; 267; 270; 272; 273; 274
Rafsenjani, Hashemi Hojjatoleslam, 160; 215; 219
Raja'i, Muhammad Ali, 188; 204
Rastakhiz Party, 244
Raudakhani, 43; 74
Razmara, General Ali, 139
Referendum, 1; 7; 144; 203; 210; 211; 212; 213; 216
Religious taxes, 28; 29; 31; 46; 55; 58; 83; 148
Revolutionary Committees (Komitehs), 215; 226
Revolutionary Council, 217; 219
Revolutionary Courts, 205
Revolutionary forces, 123; 193; 202; 207; 216; 217; 240; 241; 263; 270; 272; 273
Revolutionary guards, 9; 205; 217; 259
Royal Commission, 265
Ruqabat-e Naderi (religious endowments confiscated by Nader Shah), 51
Russian Brigades, 114

Sadr-e Azam, Prime Minister, 89; 90; 91; 92; 93; 94; 96; 109
Safavids, 11; 25; 26; 27; 28; 29; 30; 31; 32; 39; 40; 42; 44; 48; 49; 50; 51; 52; 56; 57; 61; 39; 64; 65; 66; 81; 85; 146; 128; 226; 228; 221
Sahifat al-Sajjadiah, 24
Sanjabi, Karim,, 139; 209; 240
Sardar As'ad Bakhtiyari, 103; 240
Sarrafs (bazari money lenders), 84; 167; 169
SAVAK (the Shah's security police), 144; 156; 180; 244; 245; 265
Sayyed Jamal al-Din Afghani, 106; 108

318 *Index*

Sayyed Jamal al-Din Va'ez, 99
Seyyed Jamal-e Va'ez, 38
Shah Sultan Husayn, 28; 43; 49
Shari'ati, Ali, 152; 153; 154; 155; 156; 164; 165; 225; 274
Shariatmadari, Ayatollah, 180; 194; 195; 237
Shaykh Ja'far Najafi, 54; 149
Shaykh Murtaza Ansari (charismatic Marj'a-e taqlid), 51
Sheykh Khaz'al, 129; 134
Shi'ism, 1; 4; 6; 11; 12; 1; 21; 22; 23; 24; 25; 26; 27; 28; 29; 30; 31; 32; 36; 37; 39; 40; 41; 42; 43; 44; 48; 49; 50; 51; 52; 53; 54; 55; 56; 57; 58; 59; 60; 61; 39; 64; 65; 66; 68; 74; 76; 81; 85; 66; 89; 106; 107; 114; 117; 119; 120; 134; 135; 137; 146; 154; 157; 159; 141; 162; 165; 226; 227; 228; 229; 236; 244; 249; 250; 256; 257; 259; 275
Shi'ites, 21; 22; 23; 24; 25; 27; 28; 39; 42; 44; 48; 39; 93; 114; 141; 227; 228; 256; 275
Shi'itization, 32; 49; 57; 221
Sufism, 44; 76
Sunnis, 21; 23; 27; 56; 57; 39; 228; 275

Ta'ziyah, 11; 62; 77
Tabriz, 13; 27; 31; 67; 68; 69; 70; 71; 78; 89; 90; 91; 100; 101; 102; 111; 113; 123; 195; 209; 265
Taghut (paganism), 158; 195
Takyehs, 38; 55; 65
Taqi Shahram, 265
Tasu'a, 134
Tobacco Concession, 77

Tobacco Movement, 39; 77; 78; 79; 80; 66; 88; 106; 107; 128; 224; 242; 257
Traditional Civil Society, 11; 12; 37; 38; 62; 120; 122; 123; 141; 162; 163; 166; 214; 219; 128; 251; 259
Tudeh Party, 133; 138; 140; 150; 162; 163; 168; 197; 243; 256
Tullab, 45; 91; 95; 97; 98; 112; 144; 148; 150; 164
Turkmanstan, 217

Umayyads, 20; 22; 24; 25; 44
Umma, 12; 21; 41; 48; 219; 221; 248; 249
United States, 140; 188; 191; 203; 226
University of Tehran, 197; 198; 200
Usulis, 30; 40; 51; 53; 146

Vaqayeh-e etefaqiyye, 73
Vaqf, 36; 50; 39; 81; 82; 94; 146; 147; 148; 149; 164; 166; 173
Vazir, 26; 56; 89
Velayat-e faqih, 6; 8; 152; 156; 159; 160; 165; 214; 225; 226; 244; 254; 257; 262
Vicegerency of the Hidden Imam, 25; 27; 39; 40; 42; 43; 53; 58; 61; 66; 128; 225; 228; 262

White Revolution, 144; 173
Wizara, 24
Working class, 169; 232; 266
Writers Association, 264

Yazid, ibn-e Ma'aviyah, 101; 154

Zakat, 30; 31; 46
Zoroastrianism, 26